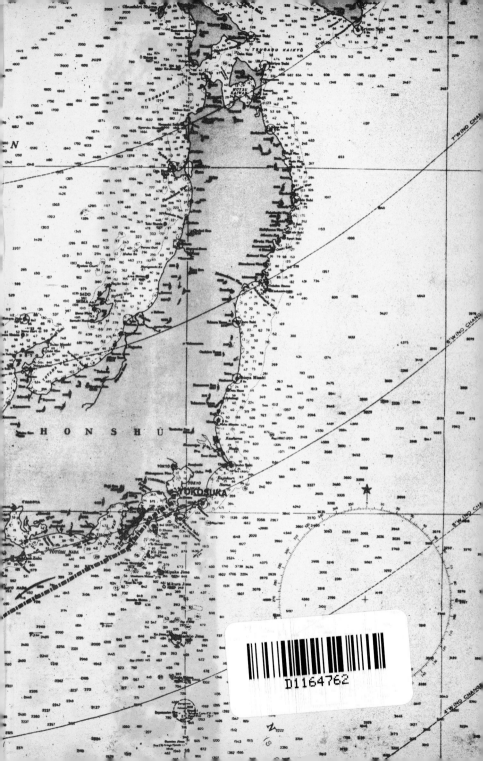

BUCHER:
MY STORY

BY COMMANDER LLOYD M. BUCHER,
USN,

CAPTAIN USS *PUEBLO*,

WITH MARK RASCOVICH

DOUBLEDAY & COMPANY, INC.
GARDEN CITY, NEW YORK
1970

Library of Congress Catalog Card Number 77–119919
Copyright © 1970 by Lloyd M. Bucher

Printed in the United States of America
First Edition

For Rose, my devoted Navy wife, with love, and

To my shipmates who served with me in *Pueblo* and in captivity, with highest praise for them

To all people who have helped Father Flanagan and Father Wegner make Boys Town a true home for the homeless boy

To all the officers and men of the Navy with whom it has been my privilege to be a shipmate

To my countrymen and my country, with unswerving loyalty.

ACKNOWLEDGMENT

I hereby acknowledge my deep debt to the chief scribe of this book, Mark Rascovich whose talents, including knowledge and love of the sea, have made the telling of my story possible. He has throughout the writing of this book shown the kindest possible disposition to myself and my family. Since this is so, it goes without saying that his own family have suffered during his absence. To them I owe another great debt, and I do thank them. I contend that no person, kindly disposed can become acquainted with Mark Rascovich and fail to place him in high esteem.

Further I acknowledge the thousands and thousands of Americans who kept the Men of *Pueblo* in their minds and hearts during our captivity. And to those who in addition remembered us in their prayers, it is my privilege to send you the profound thanks and gratitude of all of us.

To the memory of our departed shipmate Duane Hodges, I will always be faithful and I acknowledge our great debt to him; he sacrificed his life to destroy many highly classified documents which might otherwise have fallen into the hands of the Communist North Koreans.

PHOTOGRAPH CREDITS

CHAPTER I

". . . REPORT TO COMMANDER, SERVICE FORCE,
U. S. PACIFIC FLEET, FOR TEMPORARY DUTY AS
PROSPECTIVE COMMANDING OFFICER IN CONNEC-
TION WITH REACTIVATION USS PUEBLO (AKL 44)
AT PUGET SOUND NAVAL SHIPYARD AND DUTY
ABOARD THAT VESSEL WHEN PLACED ON COMMIS-
SION AS COMMANDING OFFICER."—(*Extract of
orders to LCDR Lloyd M. Bucher, dated De-
cember 9, 1966.*)

As I look back now on the great crisis of my life, the illegal
seizure on the high seas of my ship, USS *Pueblo*, by North Korean
warships on January 23, 1968, I cannot help wondering exactly
when and where events took the first capricious turn toward disaster. I am not a man who has avoided adventure and excitement;
to the contrary, I have sought them out, but always within the
framework of careful planning and discipline. Yet, I ask myself
why it happened that I, Lloyd Mark Bucher, a man of humble
origin who had made himself a dedicated but otherwise anonymous naval officer, was singled out by fate to play a notorious
key role in an incident that drastically affected the lives of hundreds of other people and shook to its foundations the defense
policy of my country. A high government official outranking the
five admirals of the Court of Inquiry had reversed their harsh
recommendations for courts-martial and letters of censure, sum-
ming up his action with a well-meaning but calculated largess:
"They have suffered enough!" The matter was therewith supposed
to be officially closed. But with the exception of a few with

reasons to fear further disclosures, or who did not want their preconceived notions about old naval traditions disturbed by matching them against brutal realities of the world conflict to-day, and to all thoughtful people in or outside the U. S. Navy, the matter remained far from closed. There were too many un-answered questions to ease the minds of either uncompromising traditionalists or objective skeptics. The officers and crew of my ship remain uncertain as to whether they are the heroes pro-claimed by some, or feckless parties to a humiliating surrender, as accused by others. For me, the captain of their ship, the case of the *Pueblo* will never be entirely closed and I must forever carry part of the burdens of doubt weighing each man who was with me during the climactic confrontation and the subsequent sufferings in North Korean prisons. And I carry my own too, of the kind which are difficult to share because of the lonely qual-ity of the responsibilities of command.

Pueblo first touched my life on a December morning of 1966 at a U. S. Seventh Fleet base of Yokosuka, Japan, where I was serving as Assistant Operations Officer of Submarine Flotilla 7. A yeoman came into my office and handed me a message which contained orders detaching me from my present duty, directing my return to the USA as prospective Commanding Officer of AKL 44, to travel via Hawaii for briefings on a highly secret Op-eration Clickbeetle at fleet headquarters there; then on to Washington, D.C., for more of the same from Naval Security Group; and finally reporting to the 13th Naval District HQ and Puget Sound Naval Shipyard of Bremerton to take command of AKL 44. Operation Clickbeetle was then the code name for a program of electronic and radio intelligence gathering by small unarmed naval auxiliaries operating independently in areas close to potential enemies. The AKL 44 was to become the USS *Pueblo* after being refitted and recommissioned for that special purpose.

The orders had conflicting emotional impact upon me. One was the bitter realization that they meant I had been "surfaced" out of the submarine service, a polite term for submariners who are transferred to other duties because they have reached the limits of usefulness and no longer have good prospects to command a boat of their own. The orders came as a painful turning point in my career. For eleven years my life had been dedicated to seagoing experience aboard submarines, and my goal had been to command one. I had long known that the lack of an advanced degree in mathematics would prevent me from becoming captain of a nuclear submarine. I still hoped to merit one of the diesel snorkel boats that continue to prove their usefulness in a variety of special missions. Indeed, I had been officially recommended by my past five COs for such command, and with my basically optimistic outlook, I fully expected it to come about, even though I knew I was competing with sixty-nine qualified captains for fourteen available boats. However, the new orders dashed the last of my hopes to remain in the submarine service. I would no longer be part of an elite group whose tightknit organization and unmatched esprit de corps had been for years a great source of pride for me. Instead I was to become involved with a mysterious operation about which I had some knowledge through my work at SUBFLOT SEVEN, but without having developed any particular admiration for the way it was being handled. It seemed in no way a happy exchange.

Yet, on the other hand, here was also the fulfillment of every professional naval officer's ambition—a command at sea. This does not come by any means to all of us, even when qualified, for the simple reason that there are less than a thousand ships for over seventy thousand officers. So, swallowing my deep underlying disappointment and accentuating this positive aspect, I picked up the telephone and called my wife who was quartered with me on the Yokosuka base together with our two sons:

"Hey, Rose! Guess what? . . . I've got my own ship at last!"

There was a squeal of delight. "Yee-ey! Wonderful! Which one?"

In spite of my efforts to sound exuberant, I could not help a slight hesitation in my answer. Rose knew the names and numbers of all our submarines as well as I did. "She's the USS *Pueblo*."

"The *Pueblo*? . . . What's that?"

"An AKL . . . that means Auxiliary, Cargo, Light."

Her "Oh" had a distinctive descending note of dismay.

"You can disregard the 'Cargo' part of her designation in this case," I reassured her (and myself.) "I'm not going to become the skipper of a freighter. It's part of a classified operation and all I can tell you is that I have to return to the United States, go to Washington for special briefings, then to Puget Sound Naval Shipyards to put *Pueblo* in commission."

"Does that mean that we all get to go home?" Rose asked.

I avoided that subject which was a complicated one in itself. "I'll tell you all about that over dinner tonight, Rose. In the meanwhile, I've got a lot of things to get busy with here. Bye." I hung up on her a little too abruptly and then proceeded to accomplish very little that day of the many details necessary to detach myself from SUBFLOT SEVEN. Instead I made the rounds of other offices to acquaint my friends with developments, an activity that ended in a lengthy luncheon which was meant to be a celebration. My fellow officers offered their congratulations and toasts to the success of my first command, but there was a tinge of commiseration for a submariner who was leaving the boats, and as the conversation gradually switched from speculations about the *Pueblo* and her mission to submarine talk, my feelings remained those of loss rather than triumph. Very soon I would be separated from these good friends and colleagues and regardless of mutual assurances to the contrary, we were bound to become estranged by widely divergent activities.

After luncheon, I left my companions and drove alone to the naval docks of Yokosuka Harbor to take a good look at a facsimile of the ship I was to command—the USS *Banner*, another AKL converted to accomplish her devious purposes and the prototype vessel of an evidently expanding Operation Clickbeetle.

If *Banner* had been painted black and buff instead of Navy-gray and carried the standard cargo-handling booms rather than masts festooned with complex systems of antenna, she could have passed for any one of thousands of small coastal and interisland tramps who scrounge a living along peripheries of the major oceanic trade routes of the world. She looked puny and un-navylike in the company of the sleek destroyers and frigates tied up to neighboring piers. As Assistant Operations Officer for SUB-FLOT SEVEN, I have been aware of *Banner*'s secret operations and knew that her unimpressive appearance was a very deceptive one.

Banner's captain was a Lieutenant Robert Bishop. He showed me around his ship with an enthusiasm and pride that made me suspect he would have liked to keep command of her through several more missions off Soviet Russian and Chinese coasts. The cramped quarters providing for three times the normal complement of an AKL would not give an old submariner claustrophobia, but might well seem terribly confining to officers and crew used to more spacious accommodations of the surface navy. The once open welldeck forward now held a boxlike superstructure which was crammed with electronics communications and monitoring equipment; the thirty-odd specialists assigned to this department were known as CTs and their mysterious lair as the SOD-Hut (Special Operations Department). The former cargo holds had been converted into storerooms, freezer compartments, and additional crews' sleeping quarters containing triple-tier bunks. The bridge had fairly good visibility, but there again, every inch of space was used and the arrangement made it impossible to move from the port to starboard wing without taking wide detours around conning and navigation equipment. The engines were a pair of General Motors diesels driving twin screws that could produce 13.1 knots when hard pressed. An auxiliary engineroom generated the additional electrical power required by the SOD-Hut. The whole ship registered 960 tons and measured 176 feet over-all length (as against 2200 tons and 320 feet for the average destroyer). Indeed, she was smaller than many tugboats.

In the captain's stateroom, a cubicle just large enough for two of us to sit down and talk over the problems of this kind of ship and Operation Clickbeetle, Lieutenant Bishop gave me much food for thought. He told me about being harassed by Communist-bloc ships, including Red Chinese trawlers who surrounded him on one mission in the Yellow Sea and acted so threateningly that assistance from the Seventh Fleet destroyers and Fifth Air Force planes were alerted before he was able to extricate himself. On another occasion, a Russian patrol vessel played her game of "chicken" a little too close and actually collided with *Banner*, luckily without holing her lightly built hull.

He spoke about personnel difficulties with his detachment of electronic and radio intelligence specialists, the highly trained and temperamental CTs who considered themselves above usual shipboard chores and privileged to ride along as passengers when not occupied with their black arts in the SOD-Hut. As few of them were experienced sailors, they found themselves thoroughly sickened and bruised aboard their storm-tossed cockleshell. Keeping up harmonious cooperation between his regular ship's company and his complement of CTs was further complicated by the fact that *their* Detachment Commander was senior in naval rank to the captain, a lieutenant commander versus a lieutenant. And then there were problems with the ship herself, an obsolete design built for entirely different logistic functions in a crash program of World War II, she showed her advanced age of twenty years through a repetitive variety of petty ailments culminating in at least one total breakdown of both her engines.

Lieutenant Bishop also hastened to impress upon me that regardless of all these difficulties, his missions off distant hostile shores had been remarkably successful in gathering useful intelligence information. The prima donnas of the SOD-Hut had earned their keep by tuning in their instruments on Communist radar and communications networks, developing sophisticated new methods of monitoring the activities and intentions of military forces avowedly hostile to the USA. The cranky little ship had taken them across distant unfriendly seas, survived insults of man and nature, and returned battered but undaunted to her home port of Yokosuka. No wonder that the higher echelons of command in the far-away Pentagon were impressed enough to want more. Insulated as they were by remoteness of rank and distance from any common operational travails, Bob Bishop and his *Banner* were providing them with a perfect opportunity to implement Defense Secretary Robert S. McNamara's theories of cost-effectiveness.

I was impressed myself, but more from the point of view of the challenge I was being presented and which had the effect of dispelling much of the depression I had felt before this visit. Challenge has always been a tonic to my spirits and while talking to *Banner's* captain, it dawned on me that my departure from

SUBFLOAT SEVEN might have some fascinating compensations after all. When I left late that afternoon, I was in a better mood to inform my family of some of the problems they must face on very short notice. These included leaving the comfortable housing provided the families of naval officers stationed in Japan, and giving up the low rents and living expenses that went with it. I was now hopeful that my intriguing new assignment would make up for any temporary inconveniences.

Rose greeted me with a warm hug and exuberant "Hi, skipper!"—but for all her valiant effort to be jolly, she could not hide the familiar tension of Navy wives on the verge of a move. She was also concerned about our two sons, Mark and Mike, fourteen and twelve years old, respectively. Orders involving change of billet came on an average of once every two years and although they were supposed to mark the ascending rungs on the ladder of a Navy career, they were also the cause of severe disruptions. Entire households had to be packed and shipped, sometimes with indefinite information about the new location; good friends separated by long distances; children yanked out of school, often in mid-term, to be briefly exhilarated by an exciting period of travel, followed by the disturbing confusion of strange new classrooms, teachers, and classmates. While I was fortunate in having a family with a strong sense of responsibility toward one another, as well as toward the Navy, I was never unaware of the pressures that the capricious uncertainties of my life subjected them to.

That evening, our talk over dinner was deliberately kept on a cheerful level of excitement about the prospects of an intriguing new job that had, at least, brought me the command of a ship. Mark and Mike had already guessed that they would be leaving their school on the Yokosuka naval base before the end of their fall term, but this disruption was countered by an eager anticipation of a trip back to the USA.

Rose was also ready to go home after a tour of over two years in Japan, although she did speak of her suspicions that my orders might result in a long separation. We deferred such talk and managed completely to avoid the subject of submarines. I was asked a lot of questions about the *Pueblo* which I had some difficulty answering fully because security regulations exclude an officer's family, as well as unauthorized outsiders, from classified details of a ship's operations. I got around that by describing the *Pueblo* as a sister ship of the *Banner* and her mission as important special "research"—the euphemism used by the Navy itself. Rose and Mark exchanged puzzled glances, but they knew better than to press me about it. It was not until after the boys had gone to bed that she asked the question uppermost in her mind:

"Isn't the deal that you will bring the *Pueblo* back to Japan without us?"

"It looks that way. I don't see much chance of getting around the rules." I explained that they were based on a treaty with Japan which stipulated that only families of officers serving aboard ships homeported in Japan, or on duty at shoreside installations, could live there in Navy housing with all the benefits of trading at the commissary exchange. As my ship was not yet commissioned in the United States and was likely to have a long period of conversion work in the Bremerton Shipyard, plus the usual shakedown and training cruises, I would be away from Japan for at least four months during which period my family would either have to return home, or move off the base, obtain regular passports and visas, and live like tourists within the Japanese economy. The Navy would provide them transportation back to the United States, but since my new command would be officially homeported in Yokosuka, this would not include a round-trip ticket. Since a lieutenant commander's pay made trans-Pacific passages for three out of the question, and because I couldn't support them on the already inflated Japanese economy for four months or longer, the logical solution was to let the Navy send all the Buchers to the states where we could at least be together for a while until the *Pueblo* took me back to the Far East. Nevertheless, I am the sort of man who often questions the obvious and sets himself against inflexible bureaucratic rules. So, instead of telling Rose to submit to the inevitable, I said, "Maybe I can find a way to get around the rules somehow."

"It is a ridiculous situation," she said, making a statement rather than a complaint. "But we'll make the best of it."

Any more serious discussion of our predicament was interrupted by the arrival of several neighboring couples who dropped in to help us celebrate my accession to the envied status of the captain of my own ship. They were submarine people, of course.

The next eight days were hectic. Besides breaking in my replacement on the staff of SUBFLOT SEVEN, I fought a fruitless battle with the housing authorities to find some means of allowing my family to remain in Japan during the four months I anticipated it would take me to return to Yokosuka with my *Pueblo*. Because of the special treaty between our respective governments regarding the stationing of armed forces personnel in Japan (a locally sensitive political issue), I received sympathy, but no satisfaction. The only result was that poor Rose lost time and had to pack everything in a mad rush for shipment to Jefferson City, Missouri, her own family's home town, where she decided to take refuge during the coming period of uncertainty. There was little I could do to help her because any time I had left over from SUBFLOT SEVEN, I spent aboard *Banner*, familiarizing myself with all her physical details, talking to her officers and crew, minutely examining her logbooks, and studying all of her operational reports. During this period, Bob Bishop was relieved of her command by LCDR Charles R. Clark, an old acquaintance from the submarine service who had also been "surfaced" into Operation Clickbeetle. His arrival reassured me because it confirmed that submariners were being made commanding officers of these intelligence ships, not as a graveyard assignment, but because we were considered experienced in the kind of long-range independent missions the operation required. Our elite status with all its special responsibilities remained reasonably intact. This was good for our morale.

On the evening of December 22, our friends threw a farewell party attended by many old shipmates and the staff of SUBFLOT SEVEN. Some of our Japanese friends joined us and graciously brought farewell gifts. In the last hour of the 23rd, the Buchers made Tokyo Airport with all their baggage and dragged themselves aboard a jet transport. Japan, which had been so much a part of our lives during the past two and one-half years, was suddenly vanishing in the darkness beneath us, its bright lights dimming like fading memories. A few hours later we met the dawn over the Pacific Ocean and, as we crossed the International Dateline, I held an impromptu classroom lecture at 35,000 feet altitude, explaining to Mark and Mike why we had to live through December 23 all over again, most of it in Hawaii.

We spent Christmas in a Honolulu hotel. This broke our trip, captured some holiday spirit, and allowed the boys happy "sleighrides" in the white surf. At this time I got my initial briefings for my new assignment at CINCPAC.

On New Year's Day 1967, we were in the Los Angeles area where we had arrived just in time to attend the Rose Bowl football game—the first real football we had seen since leaving the USA. We also saw, and were less impressed with, the new breed of militant hippies whose peculiar antics we had only read about in old magazines. After a week in California, we flew on to Jefferson City, Missouri. This was the end of the line for Rose, Mark, and Mike.

There followed another hectic week in the town where we had been married seventeen years ago. There was little time for reunions with Rose's relatives, as we had to rent a house, buy a car, and enroll the boys in a school.

January 20 was a day of parting, something a Navy family should get used to to the point of taking it for granted, but which somehow never loses its pain. Jefferson City's airport was bleak and cold with snow flurries dusting the runways. Mark and Mike armed themselves with a stoicism that had the effect of indifference, which I both resented and understood. Rose's naturally cheerful beauty, of which I have remained acutely conscious throughout our marriage, contained lines of sadness that brave smiles did not eradicate. Final hugs for my boys with stern admonitions to take care of their mother and do well in school. Final exchanges of kisses with my wife that both hurt and soothed.

Then I trudged through the gate and up the long steps of the ramp, a last wave with a forced grin before acknowledging the company-prescribed cordiality of a pert stewardess who directed me to a lonely seat in the half-empty cabin. Fasten seat belts and try to relax as the Boeing waddled and whined toward its take-off position, then launched itself with a roar into the winter sky.

Missouri, Jefferson City, Rose, Mark, Mike were obliterated by veils of gray vapors rushing past my tiny window as we hurtled along an invisible airway toward Washington. It seemed to me that lately I had been doing nothing but flying *away* from everything I knew and loved.

CHAPTER II

"... AT TIMES, WHEN DEALING WITH SHIP'S
SUPERINTENDENT ASSIGNED TO PUEBLO, HE BE-
CAME OVERZEALOUS IN REQUESTS FOR CERTAIN
WORK HE WANTS ACCOMPLISHED ON PUEBLO AND
OVERTAXED THE PATIENCE OF SHIPYARD WORKERS.
HOWEVER, HE APPEARS MOTIVATED SOLELY BY A
KEEN SENSE OF LOYALTY TO HIS UNIT WITH THE
BEST INTERESTS OF THE NAVY UPPERMOST IN HIS
MIND."—(*Extract from Fitness Report for
LCDR Lloyd M. Bucher, period February–
June, 1967.*)

I found Washington, D.C., in the grips of its usual raw January weather that cast a chilling gloom over its drab slums and
magnificent edifices alike. I was met at the airport by an old friend
and shipmate, from the submarines, Lieutenant Commander
John P. "Woody" Wood, who put me up in his apartment for
the ten-day period of my special briefings. Woody, a cheerful and
considerate extrovert of my own kind, was stationed in Washington and became a welcome relief from the sedentary intelligence
types inhabiting the various security organizations which I found
to be involved with Operation Clickbeetle in a bewildering
number.

Many Americans in or outside the military profession believe
all of our strategic intelligence services have been drawn in under
the mighty black cloak of the Central Intelligence Agency (CIA).
I know otherwise, but was surprised to find how many others
operate quite independently without over-all coordination and

plagued by petty interagency jealousies and rivalries. As I was much later to personally discover, our Communist adversaries have been unable to unravel this system and often become quite hysterical about the CIA, to whom they attribute omnipotent power over all American life (like the NKVD types do over their own). But, to my knowledge, I never dealt with a single member of that organization. The National Security Agency (NSA), yes —after being passed through a formidable series of security checks that admitted me to a minor inner sanctum of their head-quarters in Maryland. There I met with some pipe-smoking characters who affected the dress and manner of the faculty of an Ivy League college. As they talked, they either scrutinized me with X-ray eyes or stared through the ceiling toward some intellectual heaven from which they had momentarily descended for my benefit. I listened to them as attentively as I could, said little myself, and took notes which I checked for accuracy and solemnly stamped TOP SECRET. As I departed (again through multifarious security checks, this time in reverse order), I found myself wondering if these men had ever enjoyed a wild Saturday night drunk, got into a good fight over a poker game, abandoned themselves to a hot extramarital affair or, for that matter, brazenly run a stop light before the eyes of a traffic cop. I doubted it. They lived in a world apart, twentieth-century monks secluded in modern monastic cells where they plotted campaigns against a Red rather than a black Archangel.

With other intelligence groups closer to the Navy, I felt more at home; however, never entirely comfortable in their presence. There were representatives of the Naval Security Station (NAVSECSTA), through whom I was introduced to Lieutenant Stephen R. Harris who was scheduled to join *Pueblo* at a later date as Officer in Charge of the CTs that would form the heart of our operations. He was a different type of officer than any I was accustomed to working closely with. A Harvard graduate who had majored in languages, then specialized in electronic intelligence after joining the Navy, he had an erect bearing that was neither athletic nor military, a distinctive beaked nose that somehow failed to harden the fixed studious expression of his face, a mild, softspoken manner that was nevertheless direct. I quickly discovered a penetrating awareness and brittle sense of humor behind Steve's pedantic façade. While he looked like he had spent much of his life ashore behind desks, I found out to my relief that he had served two tours of duty afloat on destroyers—notorious for making or breaking real sailors. While we were almost totally opposite types, I liked and trusted him at once and felt we would be able to get along well on a basis of mutual respect.

This became more evident as our briefings proceeded. Steve Harris made himself very helpful in conducting me through the rigidly compartmented intelligence community with which he had long since become familiar, and constructively participating in arguments involving such things as the necessity to expand *Pueblo*'s personnel and equipment allowances beyond what was authorized for standard AKL-type ships assigned to routine supply missions (in which category many still insisted upon regarding her in spite of *Banner*'s experiences). He even kept an open analytical mind in the matter of his thirty-odd CTs who were scheduled to be treated as separate entities with their own privileged chain of command, rather than a ship's department under full control of her captain.

The former problem was solved by a deft bureaucratic flip-flop that changed our ship's designation from AKL to AGER (Auxiliary, General, Environmental Research)—creating by a few strokes of pen and paintbrush a brand-new type of naval vessel whose crew and equipment allowances automatically became unencumbered by precedent, thus presumably giving their captains a wider latitude in recommendations and requisitions.

One of the most serious problems in Bob Bishop's eyes and one that he elaborated on during our talks in Yokosuka was associated with the dual command within the *Banner*. Specifically, the problem revolved around the undefined relationship between the ship's Commanding Officer and the Officer in Charge of the Detachment. Bob Bishop told me that questions of who was responsible for what were continually coming up and were often resolved only after bitter controversy between himself and *Banner*'s OIC. Bob explained to me that the question had been raised to the ostensible command chain (those responsible for the planning of AGER operations), where

Banner was concerned, namely Commander, Naval Security Group
Pacific who was at the time Captain Gladding of CINCPACFLT
Staff. I made up my mind to pursue this question relentlessly
while in Washington for my initial briefings. I could see many
possible areas where the loosely defined responsibilities within
the command framework could and already had in *Banner*
caused much consternation and serious morale difficulties.
I initiated correspondence with others who had experience in
the relationship of Commanding Officer and OIC in the AGER
field (*Liberty, Oxford,* etc.). In the AGER the problem had been
partially solved by making the special detachment of personnel
a ship's department and their Officer in Charge—a Department
Head. This simple expedience eliminated most of the inherent
problems relating to "who's in charge here." However, even they
still had many problems, but I figured that if we could at least
get the Navy to make the OIC and his detachment a regular
ship's department we would have a much better handle on the
resolution of the many problems now extant in *Banner*. At least
the relationship would then be covered explicitly in Naval Regulations. It was really inconceivable to me that this was not now
the case. And that these small ships had in reality been left outside normal rules for ships afloat.

During my briefings at Naval Security Group Pacific Headquarters in Hawaii, I became aware that the problem was already known
and thought was being given to its solution. There were some who
thought that the detachment should be a department and others
who thought that making the detachment a department would
actually hurt the program in that much of the direct control exercised by the Security Group would be lost. This applied to fiscal,
personnel material and actual operations. Nevertheless, I was
certain that the answer was only to be found in Naval Regulations
and that meant the detachment had to be made a department.
This so that no question could ever arise over who was to give the
order and whose word was final. In my mind, the only person that
could possibly be invested with this responsibility was the captain of the ship and no one else. On to Washington and the Headquarters for the entire Naval Security Group. There I was told
that the problem would indeed soon be resolved by making the

detachment a department. This information came to me from several briefers and finally from the commanding officer, Captain (now Rear Admiral) Cook. Needless to say I was satisfied with the solution. However the order was never issued to effect the changeover. The reason as I understand it was because of the many objections made within those at NAVSEGRUPAC at CINCPACFLT Headquarters in Hawaii. So the problem was unresolved and caused me no end of problems throughout the brief life of *Pueblo*.

To this day, the details of my briefings involving Operation Clickbeetle cannot be fully revealed as even long after it became defunct, many of the records are still classified TOP SECRET. The Soviet Russians had been conducting similar activities around our coasts and areas of naval and rocketry operations for many years, using long-distance trawlers whose normal fishing gear was supplemented by sophisticated electronic and radio monitoring equipment. They carried a crew of fishermen who fished, but also their own detachments of CTs who could eavesdrop on our communications networks and analyze our various detection and control radar systems. Our Navy had been aware of what they were doing for a long time and so was the general public through press reports about spyships lurking among the Soviet fishing fleets operating thousands of miles away from their own coasts. However, spyship is a misnomer since spying is a covert activity, usually breaking the law of the country against whom the spying is directed and often the accepted codes of international law under which the community of civilized nations live. Electronic intelligence gathering in international waters does not fall into that category, whether the ships involved choose to be disguised or not, the only purpose of such disguise being to keep the opponent from knowing where his secrets are being pried into, and it will likely remain henceforth an accepted military technique conducted under the universally accepted principle of the freedom of the high seas. But the ground rules are strict. One does not purposely invade territorial waters, which is not only technically unnecessary, but likely to cause an international incident. One does not act or look provocative, which is why conspicuous armed warships such as destroyers or cruisers are seldom used (they are also very expensive to operate). One does not compromise one's rights under the freedom of the seas by breaking the rules of the road, or any other illegal action. The Russians had been entirely scrupulous in these respects and when our Navy was inspired by their success to counter them with a program of their own, the captains of our intelligence gathering ships were very carefully instructed to play the game strictly within the rules. Do not intrude. Do not provoke. Do not interfere illegally. Do not intimidate or allow yourself to be intimidated. Maintain your rights to the high sea. Along with briefings about the secret technical methods we were to use, these ground rules were constantly drummed into me until I thoroughly understood them and accepted them.

I had many meetings with people of many intelligence departments, like with staff representatives of DCA (Defense Communications Agency), ACNONAVCOM (Assistant Chief of Naval Operations for Naval Communications), and JCS-6 COM (Communications for Joint Chief of Staff). Some took the form of dry lectures, others the kind of give-and-take sessions that left one with a feeling of having absorbed considerable amounts of useful knowledge. Both my brain and briefcase became burdened by what seemed to be heavy state secrets far out of proportion to the very modest ship I was to command. But the most positive result was to restore the self-esteem of a "surfaced" submariner through the realization of being made a key participant in a very important, hush-hush project. It made it much easier for me to soothe Rose over the long-distance telephone about petty family problems bedeviling her in Jefferson City (the boys were, of course, miserably behind their classmates in curricular booklearning while posturing as sophisticated world travelers). And I did not turn green with envy when Woody received orders to take command of the submarine *Archerfish*. I actually found myself enthusiastic over Operation Clickbeetle and looking forward to taking over my own ship.

Then my ten days of briefings in Washington were suddenly over and I found myself in a high state of anticipation as I boarded another jetliner, this one bound nonstop across the country for the Pacific Northwest. My spirits were not dampened by the freezing drizzly morning when I staggered under the load of three suitcases off the Seattle-Bremerton ferry. Perhaps there came a trace of foreboding when I spotted in the rain-splattered basin of the naval shipyard, the unmistakable ugly shape of a pair of AKLs, made even uglier by their molding green blotches of anticorrosion paint with running sores of bleeding rust. One of them had to be the USS *Pueblo*. Which one did not matter as they both looked like abandoned derelicts when compared with the great warships being serviced in the yard, or even with *Banner* as I remembered her from Yokosuka. But I hurriedly trudged up on the hill to the Bachelor Officers' Quarters (looking as old and decrepit as my ship), checked in, dumped my gear in my assigned room, then rushed down to Base Personnel Section and announced my arrival and readiness to get to work. A somewhat bored Duty Officer accepted my papers and after officially registering my presence, remarked that as far as work was concerned, this was Sunday, and nobody was working on anything but a high priority nuclear submarine and a couple of destroyers being urgently refitted for the Vietnam war.

Indeed it was Sunday—January 29, 1967—exactly forty days since I had left Japan and traveled better than ten thousand miles to take command of my first ship. I now had to accept another long day's wait in which I could only relieve my impatience by walking through the rain to the docks and sloshing back and forth alongside a silent and deserted *Pueblo*—twice, thrice, and six times —until thoroughly soaked and impregnated with the resolve to turn this ugly duckling into the finest, most efficient intelligence ship of Operation Clickbeetle. I was going to put my plans into effect first thing Monday morning, but in the meanwhile there was nothing better to do than repair to the Officers' Club bar where I was bound to find the company of some congenial submariners.

When a new commanding officer steps aboard his ship for the first time, he usually expects to find her ready for sea and to be ceremonially received by his Executive Officer who has mustered all hands in parade formation to mark the occasion. I was accorded no such formality on Monday morning of January 30. No Exec had as yet been assigned to *Pueblo*, only two junior officers and a dozen enlisted men who were struggling to coordinate their activities with shipyard personnel and bring some order out of chaos. So all ceremony was dispensed with as ridiculously inappropriate. As for being ready for sea, my ship showed few signs of the progress that might have been expected after being under refit at Bremerton since last July. She still had the musty smell and disarrayed appearance of one recently resurrected out of the mothball fleet. Her decks were cluttered with tools and scaffoldings of half-finished projects. Her interior spaces were unworkable and unlivable; her main and auxiliary engines torn down for repairs; the complicated electronic installations of her all-important SOD-Hut barely begun, and, most discouraging, much of the modification work that should have been included was not, while such that had, had been done inadequately. My tour of inspection brought me one shock after another, culminating with the realization that *Pueblo* could never meet her scheduled commissioning date in March, nor, therefore, reach Japan in time to begin operations that spring. When I rushed over to the office of the work superintendent to discuss the situation, I discovered that both *Pueblo* and her sister ship, *Palm Beach*, were the objects of a fantastic tangle of tragi-comic confusions. The principal reason for this was that virtually nobody at the shipyard knew exactly what they were being refitted *for*. It occurred to me that this bleak blue Monday was the beginning of a long period of frustrating tribulations that might stretch into weeks, perhaps months, of delays.

Even if LCDR Leo Sweeney, our ship's superintendent, had possessed the necessary security clearance to be given complete information as to *Pueblo*'s forthcoming mission, it is doubtful that he could have better expedited the work of fully preparing her for it. Neither a shipyard official nor a ship's captain can arbitrarily change the position of even a mooring cleat aboard a United States ship, let alone do anything that remotely approaches a major design modification, without written authorization from the Type Commander of the Fleet to which the particular ship is attached, and who in turn can only act with approval of the Naval Ships System Command. Regardless of the worth of recommendations submitted by naval construction specialists or seagoing captains, they always have to be measured against available time and money. Shipyards must allocate priorities to keep the most urgently needed units of the Navy afloat and operational. Their work of construction, modification and maintenance must be accomplished within budgets that require the virtually impossible feat of tightly squeezing every last penny while at the same time deftly juggling it. Strangely enough, the system works in its cumbersome way by virtue of being accepted by all concerned as a necessary evil, but only as long as it involves the standard type of vessels like destroyers, submarines, cruisers, carriers, attack transports and admirals' barges—whose specifications, tables of allowances and personnel organizations are firmly tabulated in NAVSHIPSYSTCOM's vast banks of filing cabinets. When a lowly AKL suddenly shows up assigned to a newly invented program and is supposed to be converted to accomplish some mysterious purpose about which nobody is allowed to hold open discussion, then the system tends to crack and fall apart.

The case of *Pueblo* was a classical one. Not only did LCDR Sweeney lack the necessary security clearance to be given a thorough grasp of her problems, but the same thing applied to his superiors, including the admiral commanding Puget Sound Naval Shipyard. It soon transpired that a number of officers occupying various niches in assorted other headquarters ostensibly concerned with *Pueblo* were likewise committed to a status of ignorance about her. To top it all off, the two officers and fifteen men of my own deck and engineering department who had so far reported aboard, could be told nothing beyond that their ship had to be prepared to take to sea fifty more men than she was originally designed for over periods of thirty to forty days "on special research missions."

None of the information making up my elaborate briefings in Washington had filtered through to executive personnel of the shipyard—not even the change of designation from AKL to AGER, which I thought had been firmly decided upon. As a consequence, they were proceeding with her recommissioning according to the old rule books and their standard specifications for a cargo-carrying AKL—this in spite of the fact that they had just finished converting her holds and foredeck for an obviously different purpose. When I told them she was henceforth to become an AGER, I received a blank "what-the-hell-is-that" look and then had all my explanations wind up in a cul-de-sac of classified information they were not cleared to know. And regardless of this, LCDR Sweeney, a stubborn Irishman with a disarming sense of humor, could do nothing without written approval passed down the blocks of his own ignorant pyramid of higher authorities.

While this very intelligent man was personally sympathetic, he could initiate no official action to build into *Pueblo* better berthing and messing space, obviously because my detachment of thirty CTs and the six additional electricians and engineers to man the auxiliary engineroom powering their SOD-Hut had all been secreted out of the plans. LCDR Raper's and my efforts to put this to rights by writing carefully composed letters to ranking individuals of higher commands who might be in a position to *know* what it was all about, at first brought hopeful stirrings of action, then were promptly compromised by another harsh reality of naval shipyard work: *the budget cut!* A cool one million dollars was suddenly withdrawn from *Pueblo's* recommissioning and conversion account.

To her captain who had to support himself and his family on $900 per month, this seemed an astronomical sum of money, far more than could possibly be spent on his small secondhand ship. But I was learning naval economies the hard way, including such outrageous figures as $5000 just to bead in the AKL designation on her bow which I knew would eventually have to be removed and rebeaded as AGER. This hardened me to keep fighting for better berth and messing spaces, more expensive, yet more important, because they affected my crew's morale and, therefore, their efficiency.

January passed into February, then dragged on into March with the only really impressive volume of activity being paperwork and conferences. Actual progress on *Pueblo* was hardly visible and she seemed no closer to commissioning than when I had arrived six weeks ago. I became aware that I was making myself very unpopular in the yard and getting the reputation of being an unreasonable chronic complainer. But then the requirements of secrecy robbed me of the use of reasonable logic in many of my arguments, so a bullheaded persistence without compensating explanations had to remain my principal weapon. It was as galling to me as to the shipyard authorities. But I could not relent because of my fundamental responsibility to my ship and her mission in Operation Clickbeetle, and a concern intensified by several letters from Captain Clark of *Banner*—who had by then completed three rough intelligence-gathering cruises off Siberia.

Chuck Clark made good his promise to keep me informed by personal letters, rather than let me wait for information copies of his official reports which might have taken weeks to pass through tortuous channels and reach me inhibited by formal navalese prose. As it was, he mailed me graphic descriptions of his crowded little AKL being tossed about in winter storms in the Sea of Japan, making the marginal conditions aboard almost intolerable. Of ice forming topsides in the wild freezing weather, threatening stability and requiring all hands to turn to with picks and mallets to save the ship from capsizing. Of the audacity of Soviet Russian patrol vessels who came out of Vladivostok to perform harassing maneuvers that came within a few yards of collision, and intimidations that included signals of HEAVE TO OR I WILL FIRE, accompanied by threats with manned cannons. Of difficulties in communicating with home-base because of capricious radio propagation conditions in the area, or even communicating internally within the ship because her system was the rudimental one of a World War II auxiliary supply vessel. He gave me a sobering preview of what I was soon to face with my ship; however, also emphasizing the success intelligence-wise of the missions and that all that was really needed was iron nerve and stomach, plus *fortitude*. The implication that I had the opportunity to improve on the many physical and organizational deficiencies of *Banner* during my outfitting of *Pueblo*, were not lost on me. Yet, I could not even disclose the gist of Chuck's letters to the people working on my ship (or to her few officers and crew, for that matter), and the net effect was only expressed by more unreasonable proddings on my part.

Chuck Clark made me feel sorry for myself as I climbed over the tangles of welders' hoses that cluttered my decks, or crawled through interior spaces obstructed by shipfitters' tools and their owners who alternated long periods of inertia with noisy bursts of activity. I envied him the clean sea air sweeping his bridge—even the bitterly cold one of the Siberian coast—as I sat in the stuffy office of the World War I admi..istration building of the shipyard, trying to cope with reams of standard paperwork that seemed to have little relationship with a most unstandard situation.

I would have gladly exchanged for his small stateroom aboard *Banner* my cell in the BOQ where I lived in the depressing atmosphere of World War II barracks' décor and tossed through sleepless nights of brooding over my problems. But the fact that Chuck was out there conducting successful intelligence sweeps for Operation Clickbeetle bolstered my resolve to join him as soon as possible with a ship better prepared for the job than his.

For all the irritating setbacks, I had on the whole plenty of support to keep my spirits reasonably buoyant. Those of my officers and men who had reported for precommissioning duty impressed me with their cooperative attitudes and generally high level of intelligence. Long sessions of yard work with its confused mixture of activity and lassitude, orders followed by counterorders, civilian workmen trailing grease and debris above and below decks, deafening rackets turning to the oppressive silence of an unexplained halt in the work, all tend to seriously affect the morale and discipline of a ship's company. Even the strong are tempted to do as little as they can get away with and escape as soon as possible to the nearest canteen or liberty in the nearby towns. The fact that they must often sit around during duty hours with nothing to do but wait makes it all the more trying. But my first contingent of officers and men gave me few troubles of this kind.

Among the enlisted men was Quartermaster 1st Class Charles Law, a muscular steady veteran of the Regular Navy at the age of twenty-seven, who was one of the few among us with seagoing experience aboard AKL-type vessels. Seaman Edward "Stu" Russell, who was not too long out of boot camp but came to the ship with a bachelor's degree from USC and a cheerful eagerness to tackle any job assigned him. Chief Engineman Monroe Goldman, an engineer who had a way with men as well as machinery and later became my Chief Master-at-Arms. Armando Canales, Yeoman 1st Class, who came highly recommended, but with no experience on small ships, but with his willingness to learn was able to plow through the blizzard of paperwork.

Out of the six officers to be assigned to *Pueblo*, only two had reported when I took command and they had to take on a lot of extra work until the others dribbled in over two-months intervals. There was Lieutenant (jg) David Behr, a graduate of California Maritime Academy, who was just completing his obligation to the Navy and would not accompany us to Japan, but nevertheless devoted himself to the ship's outfitting with a will that was somehow enhanced by a gritty personality. Dave planned a career in the Merchant Marine and had already made himself a competent seaman of the kind *Pueblo* sorely needed, but he was very young and beneath his muscular aggressiveness were some self-doubts and I found that he frequently needed reassurance as well as occasional doses of restraint from me, but I liked his spirit very much.

My Chief Engineer was completely different from Dave Behr. A professional career man of thirty-seven, Chief Warrant Officer Gene Lacy had served aboard a variety of ships, including Navy icebreakers in both arctic and antarctic seas. He had been awarded battlestars in the naval campaigns of the Korean War. A tall handsome man of evenly pleasant disposition, Gene inspired confidence and cheerfully tackled his job of putting *Pueblo*'s antiquated diesel engines into reliable condition after their long lay-up, supervised the installation of a brand-new auxiliary engineroom (which did not necessarily mean *new* machinery), then took on additional duties as temporary Supply Officer, plus those that would normally have fallen to the Executive Officer who had yet to report aboard. Gene managed all this without missing a watch while commuting back and forth to his home in Seattle, which meant getting up at five in the morning to make the hour-long ferry ride to Bremerton, then reversing that trek in the evenings, as often as not in abominable weather that did not seem to bother him. He was my most experienced and reliable officer who also became my best friend on the ship.

These were some of my men with whom I was trying to recommission *Pueblo* and make functional her deck, engineering and ship's service departments. But then, there was also her basic reason for being so rudely awakened out of her hibernation in the mothball fleet, her electronic intelligence gathering capability manned by thirty-odd CTs. The spaces which the shipyard had created out of her former cargo hold and built over her old well-deck, were being filled from bulkhead to bulkhead with racks and consoles of communication, detection and ECM instruments, which were actually outnumbered by the testing equipment necessary to check out their accuracy, the whole complexity being wired together by literally thousands of yards of conduits and electrical ganglions. This installation work was being done by a subcontractor with the assistance of a dozen of the CTs who were subsequently to sail with *Pueblo* and operate the system. In keeping with the security classification of these spaces, the first thing they made operative was the heavy steel door that was stenciled *AUTHORIZED PERSONNEL ONLY* and always kept closed and locked. Men working in there were also part of my crew, yet a breed apart. While I had full clearance to pass through their steel door any time I wanted to, I did not have the specialized technical knowledge to be able to judge what was going on and so decided to stay out of the details and merely hope for accurate reports from the two 1st Class enlisted men, James Layton and Mike Barret. In the absence of their officer in charge, Lieutenant Stephen Harris, whose arrival on the scene was being continually delayed by extended briefings in Washington, I had little alternative but to rely on these men who impressed me with their serious dedication and superior intelligence. I did not suspect at the time that virtually all of the "secret" equipment they were installing behind their steel door could have been purchased in any commercial radio equipment store in Seattle—and that because of faulty plans, it was being installed upside down!

A close companion in misery was the captain of *Pueblo*'s sistership, the USS *Palm Beach*. The two ships had been picked out of the mothball fleet as identical with the commendable idea of executing all their precommissioning and conversion work according to one master plan. But something went wrong as the "twins" turned out to have many interior and exterior differences. They had been towed to Bremerton without any careful comparisons above or below decks. As a result, the joint plans had to be changed to different individual ones, causing delays to both ships and additional irritations to their impatient skippers. LCDR Doug Raper was, like myself, a "surfaced" submariner and although scheduled to operate his *Palm Beach* in the Atlantic version of Operation Clickbeetle, we became closely allied in our constant skirmishes against the forces of procrastination, confusion, and bungling. During the working day we visited each other's ships, which were tied up at the same dock, to compare progress (or lack thereof). We exchanged information copies of our voluminous paperwork and often composed joint recommendations, supplications and protests with which we bombarded both the minor and major entrenchments of Navy bureaucracy. In the evenings we met at the Officers' Club bar where we either cried in each other's beer or toasted our few victories with something stronger. Our respective crews had much the same relationship, opposite numbers exchanging information, acting in concert when possible and relieving tensions with informal bull sessions after work at the service clubs. It was a good relationship in which we were drawn closer by our mutual "problem child" status in the yard and our joint tactics of obtaining results by sheer abrasiveness.

Gradually, in singles and pairs, more of my crew and CTs reported aboard to adjust themselves to a situation and circumstances they had hardly been led to expect. Steve Harris finally arrived during the third week of March to take charge of his intelligence detachment and barely managed to hide his dismay over the rough accommodations and the disappointing state of completion of his operational platform. [Steve was a Harvard man and in many respects typified the kind of officer who would naturally gravitate toward the intelligence community of his service. Yet he had previously been sent to sea on special missions that might be described as hazardous.] His methodical intellect made him better suited to occupy the "think-tank" of a shoreside headquarters, rather than our floating bedlam. But this did not prevent him from trying to adjust himself and roughen his nails with hard work, nor inhibit his sympathetic personality from being helpful in departments beyond his own. I recall very well how, upon finding myself, Lacy and Behr in our usual overwrought state, he promptly offered to assume the job of temporary Executive Officer in order to relieve us of a lot of petty administrative details. It was a nice gesture and well meant—but I thanked him, refused his offer, and promptly sent him below to find out what was really going on behind that steel door of the SOD-Hut. During the next week he gradually acquired the haunted look of tense frustration like my own, suggesting that he too was finding things at variance with our extensive high-level briefings.

This was a time of virtually all work and no play. Even the many periods of sitting around and sweating out delays were quite exhausting, mentally if not physically. Bremerton is a small town with few diversions and strangely isolated from the large city of Seattle, whose lights illuminate the night horizon on the other side of Puget Sound, close, yet far away. The wilderness of the Olympic Peninsula with its snowcapped peaks and brooding deep rain forest seemed much closer, exerting a call of the wild in summer, but forbidding in winter. All activity was concentrated in the Navy Yard which reverberated with the yowl of grinding wheels and sparkled with the searing torches of welders all day and all night as work progressed around the clock on every kind of ship—except ours! I would look toward the glow of Seattle in the evenings and resist her temptations in favor of a few drinks and a short friendly game of poker at the Officers' Club. The ferry ride was too long to reach greater excitement and the hours of rest too short before meeting the next day's problems.

Once a week I would telephone Rose in Jefferson City and for a few minutes we would exchange discouraging reports about our lives apart. By now it was obvious to both of us that the separation had not been necessary as the precommissioning work was keeping me in Bremerton for long enough to have made it worthwhile to move my family there. But who could have anticipated that? Who could guess how much longer it would stretch out? Rose was lonely and Mark and Mike needed a father to help them over the rough spots of an already disrupted school year. Now I could not afford to move them at my own expense (*Pueblo* was still officially homeported at Yokosuka, Japan, although showing every sign of becoming a permanent resident of Bremerton), nor could my boys afford another change of schools. There was nothing else to do than sweat the situation out and exchange caustic jokes about it to keep up each other's spirits. About my personal travails, Rose made the most succinct comment:

"Poor Pete. You've been made Captain of the Navy's most fouled up Top Secret!"

April rolled around, the month when *Pueblo* had been originally scheduled to steam out to Japan ready to assume her duties in Operation Clickbeetle. But she remained at her dock of Bremerton Naval Shipyard, a sort of shabby cantankerous orphan among the more respectable missile frigates, carriers, and atomic submarines. Her cluttered decks were still mottled by ugly blotches of chromate paint streaming with the spring rains that swept daily over Puget Sound. Her insides, both open and secret compartments, were still a crowded disarray of incompleted work projects, difficult to move through and disheartening to behold. Gene Lacy's enginerooms were in better shape than any other department, but he fretted and puttered just the same, irked over the fact that if he had known we would still be at dockside rather than at sea, he could have taken the time for a more exacting job. The same hindsight plagued me, of course, but involving the entire ship.

The complete lack of destruct system had been worrying me for some time, inspired by the knowledge that we were intended to operate close to hostile shores patrolled by Communist navies, and intensified by the reports I received from Chuck Clark's *Banner* and her experiences of harassment. This did not mean that I expected to be attacked or seized on the high seas (all of my briefings about the sanctity of freedom of the seas had succeeded in driving such unpleasant thoughts out of my own mind). But what if my twenty-five-year-old ship suffered a total engine or steering breakdown when close to the Soviet twelve-mile limit off the Siberian coast? What, if in the same location, I became overwhelmed by violent storm conditions that might founder a small vessel like the *Pueblo?* In either case, our Communist adversaries could be in position to quite legally recover considerable intelligence data from the resulting wreck.

I took up this disturbing matter with Steve Harris shortly after his arrival, and also with the only others at Bremerton who had security clearance for such discussions, our opposite numbers aboard our sistership, *Palm Beach*. We all agreed that we should have more sophisticated destruct systems than the usual fire axes and weighted sacks and that there might still be enough time to have them installed while most of our classified instrumentation was yet to be completed.

    While none of us had the specialized knowledge to make specific recommendations, we knew that the Navy had explosives and demolition experts who would know what should be done. I fired off letters accordingly, short-circuiting intermediate commands to shoot directly at the top authorities, then sat back to await results, and waited through six endorsements.

    This letter requesting various improvements and recommending their accomplishment in the strongest possible language included recommendations for improvement to our watertight integrity (which was minimal), a proper Navy sound powered phone system that would permit reasonable damage control facilities and ship control, and an emergency destruct system for use in the event it might possibly be required. This letter went via the chain of command to CNO where it was passed to the Bureau of Matériel who passed it to the Army for consideration of the destruct recommendation. The upshot of the reply that was received many weeks later was that the system was too costly. As was the phone system etc. I was deeply concerned as well with the faulty anchor windlass system on the ship. I was aware that *Banner* on one patrol near China had lost power because of a bad load of fuel they had received and had almost drifted out of control into claimed Chinese territorial waters. One method that could save such a situation provided the water depth was sufficient was to drop the anchor. Our windlass/wildcat was demonstrably unreliable. I kept pressure on the shipyard and my Type Commander to alleviate these problems.

    Work continued in fits and starts of frantic activity alternating with maddening breaks of inactivity, the physical progress nowhere commensurate with the flood of paperwork containing suggestions, protests, explanations, and routine reports to assorted headquarters that I had to pump out of my small ship's office.

This was a particular time of trial for me because I was trying to cope with a situation entirely foreign to my temperament. Unlike many officers who take pride and delight in jousting windmill battles against the entrenched forces of shoreside bureaucracy, I am of the kind who regards such as drudgery and a bore—who derives his greatest challenge and inspiration from shipboard operations at sea—or under it. Even as a small boy of seven, when overwhelmed by those problems that could mar that magic age, I had tried to run away to sea with enough determination to make at least thirty of the four hundred miles necessary to reach it before apprehension by a truant officer. I subsequently learned that to make one's way through life and the Navy, one must accept responsibility for many dull routine chores that must be done. But I remained at heart a working seaman, a sailor's sailor, dedicated to his ship and his crew. I knew how to take advantage of shore leaves, either for recreation with my family or, if they weren't present, in lusty bouts of relaxation with my shipmates. However, prolonged confinement to the beach, such as I was enduring in Bremerton, left me restless and impatient to get back to sea. Time seemed to drag in spite of my efforts to keep busy with the hundreds of details involved in recommissioning. Progress seemed slow to the point of being imperceptible.

But progress there was and when Washington itself became impatient, it finally reached that tangible point where we could set a commissioning date that we had a reasonable chance of keeping—May 13, 1967. It would not mark the day of our release from the yard as there was bound to be work to finish up even before sea trials. But at least I would be in command of a fully commissioned ship of the U. S. Navy with Sail Orders beckoning in the foreseeable future. I celebrated by telephoning Jefferson City where I knew Rose had been waiting as fretfully as I, and announced my decision to dig into our savings to pay for round-trip tickets to Seattle so that my family could witness an important event in the "old man's career"—the commissioning ceremony of his first command. Her reaction was one of delight and relief with a slight undertone of cynical reserve which she only expressed by exclaiming: "Well! Maybe things are looking up a bit! I'll make the reservations and hope for the best about getting to use them."

"You will, honey!" I told her, trying to sound more convincing than my experiences really warranted. Without telling her so, I had also determined in my own mind that even if the *Pueblo* suffered another postponement, I was going to bring my family out for a long holiday weekend in May—and damn the expenses! I became so enthusiastic over the prospect that I managed to convince myself everything was going to go much better from then on. And as soon as I hung up the phone after a cheerful goodbye to Rose, I sat down at Canales' typewriter and personally wrote out another invitation to attend the commissioning of my ship. This one may have been more rash under the uncertain circumstances, but it was unthinkable that I exclude from the ceremony the only family I had really been close to before acquiring my own upon marrying Rose: Father Flanagan's Boys Town of Nebraska. The invitation had, of course, to be issued to just one individual of that great organization, its director, Monsignor Nicholas H. Wegner.

After finishing my letter to Father Wegner and mailing it off, I felt in such an optimistic mood that I turned my back on whatever troubles were left of that day, changed into civilian clothes, and set forth to hunt up some of my favorite stag relaxation. The company was congenial, good beer flowed freshly brewed from the tap, and the cards were honestly shuffled for stakes just high enough to make the game interesting. I love poker for the sake of playing it, not for profit; winning money is incidental to the excitement of matching luck and wits against an opponent. But on this occasion the several pots that I won came in especially handy. The police honored our inconspicuous gang of amateur gamblers with a raid and although there were other naval officers in mufti who were caught in the dragnet, I managed to get myself singled out for booking and a substantial fine. With my name appearing on the Bremerton police blotter, I had no alternative but to report my predicament to the Chief-of-Staff of 13th Naval District. Sailor's luck!

April with its fickle mixture of blustery showers and warming sunshine passed into May. For those who cared to notice such things, the fragrance of apple blossoms, wild dogwood, and sprouting pine forests could be detected faintly mingling with the shipyard's fumes of acetylene, paint, and oil. If one listened carefully, one could hear beneath the metallic percussion of men pounding out armor and boilerplate, the soft fluting song of robins and thrushes who had returned with another spring to the trees and shrubbery on the hill behind the workshops and lofts. Flights of ducks winged back and forth along Bremerton's deep arm of Puget Sound, whistling past the noisy docks and basins in their search for more peaceful nesting grounds. The Seattle ferry, which had during the long winter months run half empty for the benefit of sailors coming or going on liberty from ships under refit, was suddenly disgorging carloads of anglers and nature lovers heading for the rejuvenating exhilaration of the Olympic wilderness as it emerged out of its winter gloom. New life seemed to even stir the USS *Pueblo* who was at last looking smart with a fresh coat of paint, a cosmetic that could not recapture the old girl's youth, but at least gave the impression she was well cared for.

Almost all of my complement of ship's crew and detachment of intelligence specialists had reported aboard, the latter relieving my concern over their exclusive status by eagerly tackling the many less exotic chores necessary to make *Pueblo* livable and operational. I discovered many of these men to have an exceptionally high intelligence for enlisted rates in the Navy, and generally without the finicky temperaments reputed to go with it. While both they and their Detachment Commander, Steve Harris, grumbled about the smallness of our ship and cramped quarters that no amount of conversion could improve to perfection, they were all smart enough to cooperate with my efforts to make the best of it. My greatest worry about them I did not mention, but I had become aware after checking through their service records, that hardly any of these CTs had ever been to sea before! Breaking in new sailors on a cockleshell like *Pueblo*, destined to steam halfway around the world to reach her operational area was bound to be a hard process of acquiring their sea legs. But that was a problem we could only tackle when it presented itself; in the meanwhile the main one was to get away from this damned shipyard!

I was much concerned over the effects of continual delays on the morale of my crew who had little to do in the line of shipboard

duties except to clean up after the workmen and otherwise stay
out of their way. There was no "make-work" I could think up for
them that would not interfere with the conversion. Idle hands
are prone to mischief, or at best to become listless with boredom.
One answer would have been to send them to precommissioning
school, a normal procedure under the circumstances and valuable
to the many inexperienced men, but to my vexation this was not
allowed the *Pueblo* crew. Morale was particularly low among the
idle CTs of our incompleted SOD-Hut whose high intelligence
and intellectual levels made them restless and distraught with so
much time on their hands. There was no place on the base that
was cleared for them to study their classified courses for advancement in rates and they could only relieve the monotony with
endless games of Monopoly or bridge. I went to Admiral W. F.
Petrovic with the problem and although he was sympathetic to it,
there was not much that could be done. But we did receive a
small budget for schools and so I was able to send the CTs to
Firefighting School where they surprised everybody except me
with their performance. They set a near record for dewatering a
compartment after fighting a fire, only a team from a Pacific Fleet
aircraft carrier turning a faster time. Our CTs showed great spirit
of the kind I wanted aboard *Pueblo* and I was intensely proud of
them.

Gene Lacy worked like a Trojan in his own engineering department, kept track of the thousands of items of supply, and acted
as a steadying influence in the many small crises of the day. Dave
Behr had spring fever like a young buck in rut, bounding from
one project to the other and locking horns with workmen and
strawbosses, leaving a trail of bruised feelings along with frantic
speeded-up action or what sometimes amounted to sit-down strikes.
My intervention was frequently required, but on the whole his
bullying tactics got results. It now appeared less likely than usual
that we would have to postpone the current commissioning date
of May 13.

Our long-suffering superintendent Sweeney and I were still
clashing during working hours over what should or could be done
for my ship, promptly patching up our differences after 1700 hours

over a drink at the Officers' Club. Our daily battles and reconciliations were gradually cementing a firm friendship. Dockside kibitzers still looked over *Pueblo* with perplexed expressions and asked "What is it?"—but by now I had not only developed a thick skin, but also a degree of pride and enjoyment over my mysterious little vessel, and so was able to answer them without flinching:

"An environmental research ship."

While they pondered what that meant, I would slip away with an appropriate expression of being preoccupied with Top Secret business, but without letting on that it was well enough under control to allow me to devote some attention to organizing the reception to be given at the Officers' Club for a hundred-odd guests invited to attend our commissioning ceremony. It may seem a frivolous problem, but the Navy insists that such functions go off without a hitch, and woe to the commanding officer who drags his bottom over official social shoals! It will reflect as badly in his fitness report as a grounding of his ship. In this area, as well as the many other administrative and technical ones involved in running a ship, the skipper must rely heavily on the assistance of his Executive Officer. Through no particular fault of his own, mine did not show up until the afternoon of May 5.

I was in the fo'c'sle, at the time, trying to cope with another important petty detail of our ship's service equipment, the washing machine that had to keep us in clean underwear through many long weeks at sea. Quartermaster Law squeezed his greasy dungareed bulk into the compartment cluttered with disconnected pipes and hoses, and announced that a Lieutenant Edward Murphy was waiting on the welldeck to report to me. When I clambered back into the sunshine, I found myself facing a tall young officer immaculately uniformed in dress blues who was staring about the ship through horn-rimmed spectacles with a slightly appalled look on his face. That look intensified for a fraction of a moment when he became aware of my presence and took in the shabby work-a-day khakis and the eccentric straw hat that it was my habit to wear when inspecting work progress. If my appearance shocked him, he recovered quickly, formally saluted, and introduced himself.

I should have explained then and there that this was not a ship where quarterdeck formalities were either desirable or possible. But all I did was flip back his salute, offer him my hand and say: "Damned glad to have you aboard, Ed! How can I help you settle in?"

He had obviously never in his life imagined himself assigned to anything like *Pueblo*, but was not about to admit it. He answered that he expected no troubles and felt fully prepared to assume his responsibilities as Executive Officer. Politely refusing the cigarette I offered, he then relaxed enough to lean against a bulwark and launch into a casually articulate dissertation about his wife's moving problems and the more complicated ones of his widowed mother's drygoods business in their California home town. After an hour of this, I conducted him to my cabin where I told him some of *my* problems and formally accepted his orders and records. I noticed that he had qualified as an OOD (Officer of the Deck) and had attended Navigation School and served with destroyers as assistant navigator, but that his most recent assignment had been in charge of a motor pool of an inland naval installation. I also noted his religion to be Christian Scientist and that he was a graduate of Principia College which is run by that generally pacifist and anti-medical religious denomination. To my consternation, I also found out that my second-in-command was not cleared by Security to be fully briefed with the details of our intelligence mission. I could only assign him the standard duties of his billet, but that would at least relieve some of the workload on the rest of us, and he listened to my instructions with an earnest, owlish concentration that made me hopeful he was grasping them. I showed him the tiny stateroom which he would have to share with another officer, then our modest wardroom where I introduced him to Gene Lacy and Steve Harris. He refused a cup of coffee from our partially activated galley, this time flatly stating, "I never use it, thank you."

After spending the rest of the day acquainting himself with every part of *Pueblo* except her classified SOD-Hut, Lieutenant Murphy was invited to join our customary unwinding bull session at the Officers' Club bar. When he declined our usual drink of beer, I suggested that we should celebrate the arrival of our new Exec with something stronger, like martinis. An icily disapproving glint flashed through his spectacles, followed by a stiffly expressed, "Never use liquor, thank you. But I'll have a ginger ale." He nursed that soft drink for ten minutes, listening in studious silence to our chatter that was designed to relieve the day's tensions and perhaps explore solutions for the problems of the next. When his glass was down to a few melting pebbles of ice, he rattled it impatiently and excused himself, saying, "I must telephone Mother and take care of some family problems. Will be on deck at reveille tomorrow morning."

"Okay, Ed, but we don't actually stand formal reveille on *Pueblo*," I told him. "No room to muster all hands without shoving somebody over the side."

"Yes, Captain, I understand," Murphy answered with a thin smile. "But I'll be there at zero six hundred sharp, just the same. Thank you, sir, and good night."

After he had left, there came one of those prolonged doubtful silences while everybody waited for somebody else to express an opinion. I thought that Steve or Gene might damn Ed Murphy with the faint praise of "Seems like a nice guy," but they kept thoughtfully sipping their drinks. I sensed Dave Behr formulating a crack, like "Must have been Chaplain's Assistant on USS *Bluenose!*" and was ready to cut him off in mid-sentence; but he threw me with a deeply felt non sequitur: "Christ! My love life is going to hell on this job!" After the laughter subsided, silence resumed as our little wardroom group kept wondering how a stiffly proper officer who neither smoked tobacco, drank beer or liquor, or even indulged in the stimulant of strong Navy coffee, could ever fit into our freewheeling informal ways of work and play. On such a small ship as *Pueblo* with many different personalities and talents forced to live close together, compatibility was as important as competence, pristine perfection as unwelcome as sloppy dereliction. It was totally inappropriate for me to express any real uneasiness, but I had to break the depressing hiatus with a seriously meant quip:

"So I've got myself an Exec! From the looks of him, you guys had better mend your wicked ways and shape up."

There was a desultory chorus of chuckles. Then our beloved old archenemy from the yard's front office, LCDR Sweeney, breezed in, shed his official cares of the day and abandoned himself to a "happy hour" of high Irish spirits that quickly restored our own.

CHAPTER III

"AN ESTIMATED 22,547 MAN-DAYS HAVE BEEN
USED IN MAKING PUEBLO READY TO EMBARK UPON
A NEW CAREER . . . PUEBLO JOINS THE FLEET
PROUDLY IN THE KNOWLEDGE THAT THE RESEARCH
OPERATIONS SHE WILL CONDUCT WILL BE AN AID
TO THE NAVY AND MANKIND TOWARD COMPLETE
UNDERSTANDING OF THE OCEAN AND IMPROVE-
MENT OF NAVAL COMMUNICATIONS SYSTEM."—
(*Extract from commemorative pamphlet pub-
lished by U. S. Navy on the occasion of USS
Pueblo's commissioning, May 13, 1967.*)

To the few of us in Bremerton who were fully informed about
Pueblo and *Palm Beach*'s true backgrounds and purposes, there
was a note of irony in the wording of the beautifully printed commemorative booklet which the Navy issued to its complement and
guests at the dual commissioning ceremony. Their estimate of man-
days expended in the shipyard to reactivate and convert these
tugboat-sized auxiliaries was conservative, and, of course, failed
to break down those wasted in unraveling the tangled directives
of various conflicting commands concerned with the work. The
implications that we were about to benefit mankind through
oceanographic and communication *research* tickled smiles out
of our cynics and pangs of conscience out of our idealists. As for
myself, I briefly wondered why we could not honestly state that
these innocent-looking little unarmed ships were in fact intended
as potent weapons in the electronic cold war already initiated by
avowedly hostile forces. But I did not brood about any of this.

I was proud of my ship and certainly opposed to washing in public any dirty laundry left over from bringing her into being. I firmly believed in her mission, primarily because it was endorsed by our highest levels of command, but also because eleven years of cold-war operations in submarines had convinced me that counter-measures against Russian and Asiatic Communist naval actions were essential to our country's security. In this deadly serious intel-ligence game, compromises with truth and petty obfuscations seemed justified when measured against the stakes involved. And then, being a man with a normal infusion of vanity, I also took pride in having been chosen commanding officer of a United States ship and was determined to show off both to best advantage. My officers and crew became aware of this a few days before our commissioning when I turned into a spit-and-polish martinet who pulled an uncompromising inspection from *Pueblo's* stem to stern, leaving them with bruised feelings and laboring up to the last minute to cover all incompleted works with a perfection of cleanliness.

Saturday, May 13, burst upon us as a sparkling spring day whose warm sunshine dispelled any fears that our many scores of guests might be drenched by the frequent Washington rains. *Pueblo* and *Palm Beach* had been moved to Pier 5, decorated with bright gar-lands of red-white-and-blue bunting, and moored parallel to each other with a stage erected between them to accommodate two admirals and their aides, a professor who was to cover our posture as research vessels with a speech about oceanography, a couple dozen city fathers from the towns after which our ships had been named, and a pair of clergymen to invoke the blessings of the Almighty upon the occasion. The Navy band formed up with practiced precision to serenade the two-hundred-plus guests and families of the ships' complements and those of Puget Sound Naval Shipyard personnel who had labored to bring us to this stage of completion. They squeezed themselves into tipsy folding chairs placed row upon row across the crane tracks of the dock. Among them, I had admiring eyes for my Rose, pert and pretty in a brand-new yellow knit suit, with a fidgety but neatly dapper Mike seated alongside of her (poor Mark had been left behind in Jefferson City because of delinquent schoolwork). Vying for my special attention was my crew, looking startlingly different from its usual piratical appearance as they stood formally lined up on *Pueblo*'s spotless decks like recruiting poster models in their immaculately pressed uniforms.

All of us rose to our feet and bowed our heads as Chaplain Hayes gave the invocation, then sat down while Rear Admiral W. F. Petrovic welcomed the attending dignitaries and introduced the principal speaker. Professor Crutchfield, M.A., Ph.D., spoke about the importance of developing the vast resources of the seas and lauded the Navy's interest in keeping abreast with all phases of marine science. Rear Admiral William E. Ferrall, Commandant, 13th Naval District, read the Navy Department Orders to commission USS *Pueblo* (AKL 44) and, as the band played the National Anthem, the Union Jack and Commission Pennant were hoisted. Then I stepped before the assembly, read into the microphones my orders to assume command, and directed my Executive Officer, Lieutenant Edward Murphy, to set the first watch aboard my ship. The same part of the program concerning USS *Palm Beach* (AKL 45) was repeated, Admiral Ferrall reading her orders, the band playing again the National Anthem as her flags were hoisted, Doug Draper assuming command and directing his Exec to set the watch. Then the dignitaries representing the namesake towns of our ships offered gifts and expressions of good wishes . . . and the more than twenty civic-minded citizens of Pueblo, Colorado, who had made the long trip to Bremerton, presented us with our most up-to-date electronic equipment: a ship's entertainment center for piping music to wardroom and mess deck—a very generous gift! The formal part of the ceremony ended with a benediction spoken by my old spiritual father and mentor, Monsignor Wegner, who had honored me by traveling all the way from his post at Boys Town in Nebraska to take part in this function.

I had attended many commissionings before and knew their ritual by heart; they were the same whether performed for little AKLs or mighty warships, only the scale of attendance and publicity varying according to the size. But in spite of undertones of irony and the tragi-comical confusions which had gone on behind the scenes of *Pueblo*'s reactivation into the fleet, I found myself deeply moved by this occasion. It was not only because I was officially assuming command of my first ship, although there was plenty of emotion involved in this aspect too. While I might have preferred to have had her be one of my beloved submarines, the fact that she was such a strange problem-child somehow brought her closer to my heart and made me vow to make her something the Navy would take notice of (the irony of *this* would only become apparent much later). But I was mostly moved by the presence of Father Wegner and aware that many among this assembly were wondering why the director of an institution dedicated to salvaging waifs and delinquent boys was taking part in this naval ceremony. Of all those present, only my wife and son knew that I was the first alumnus of Boys Town of Nebraska to achieve command of a U. S. Navy ship. During my naval career I had spoken about being an orphan raised through a series of charitable institutions only to a few of my closest shipmates; not because of shame, but because I did not want to take advantage of our American predeliction for giving special consideration to our underprivileged. It has always seemed to me unfitting to draw attention to the privations and struggles of my early youth as it would be for an officer of a wealthy, secure background to brag about his—both categories must prove themselves entirely upon their own merits. My feelings about this had not changed, but with advancing maturity and rank I became increasingly conscious of owing a deep debt of gratitude to Father Flanagan's Boys Town, who had given me my best chance to make good in life, and was therefore entitled to share in my success. As much so as any proud parent attending this commissioning who had raised their son to honorably serve his country. To me, Father Wegner represented the only family that had given some stability to my turbulent boyhood and as I listened to him ask God to bless and keep safe my ship, I could not help thinking back on those years of very different circumstances.

I was born on September 1, 1927, in Pocatello, Idaho, but it was not until I reached the age of twenty-one years that I found out the true circumstances of my birth, having been satisfied to live with the knowledge that I had been adopted as an infant by a couple upon whom fortune did not smile. My very earliest recollections are of a few incidents involving my adoptive parents, Austin and Mary Bucher, and Austin's parents, all of whom lived in or near Pocatello. There are very dim memories of my mother, Mary, lying on her deathbed through a long illness. I was permitted to visit her every day for a little while when she would hug and kiss me, and give me pieces of candy she kept by her bedside. These visits are the only memories I have of her as I was barely three years old at the time. Sometime during my third year of life, she died of cancer, but while she still lived, I recall a few incidents involving my father who operated a small restaurant called the Mayflower in downtown Pocatello, where he presided as owner-chef. I remember him perching me on top of the meat-chopping block in the kitchen where his waitresses would stuff me with tidbits from the restaurant's dessert menu. My favorite treat was maraschino cherries.

I was not aware of the day when my mother died, only that the event was shortly followed by my being moved in with my grandparents who worked a small farm outside of Pocatello. That farm became my home until I was five and much more registered upon my conscious memory from that period, including my first bouts with nature and her sometimes harsh ways. Like that fine summer day when I was sitting on a narrow footbridge crossing an irrigation ditch running through our fields and spotted a bee floating by on the verge of drowning. I jumped down on the bank and rescued the struggling insect—which rewarded me with an agonizing sting before buzzing off and leaving me bawling for my grandmother. She gave me solace and treatment and perhaps advice about the perils of giving unasked help, but this innocuous experience had a lasting effect on my subconscious in that I dreamed about it on several occasions after growing up. Yet, I was perhaps slow to learn, because I also vividly remember the farm's only unproductive pet, a cantankerous parrot, who gave me another severe bite when I tried to untangle its foot caught in the wire of its cage. I still carry the scars from that attempt at being a good Samaritan. For a while I kept my association with animals on an imaginary level, like stalking, then taming a wild lion who lived on the edge of the woods bordering our farm and who Grandma insisted to be nothing more than an odd-shaped pile of junk. (Well, it was a magic lion who could talk to boys, play games and then turn himself into something quite ordinary just to frustrate non-believers.)

I remember my fourth birthday since it was the occasion of a rare celebration put on especially for my benefit—and as I long after came to realize—one my grandparents could ill afford. I was treated to both a birthday cake and my first remembered presents: a rubber ball that could bounce up into the sky, and a beautiful Teddy bear who promptly displaced the friendly lion of my imagination. It was certainly the most exciting day I had lived up to then among many that were happy and secure. But they were in fact terrible ones for Gramps and Grandma who were at the time desperately trying to keep themselves from being swept under by the upheavals of the Great Depression that followed the financial crash of 1929.

In the spring of 1933 we left the farm, piling our belongings into a creaky automobile in which Gramps intended to drive us toward a new life in the Promised Land of California—where, unbeknown to him, tens of thousands of bankrupt farmers were converging at the time. To me it was all a wildly exciting adventure, being totally oblivious of the agony of the mortgage foreclosure that suddenly yanked away the very soil my grandparents had worked throughout their middle-age to provide the family basic security. Nor do I recall saying goodbye to my father who was left behind demolished by the combination of my mother's death, the hard times, lingering effects of wounds he had suffered with the American Expeditionary Forces in World War I, and unfulfilled hopes of recovering his restaurant which he had lost through many gambling debts and unscrupulous partners. Those details were only related to me many years later after I thought I would never be able to piece together the fragments of my childhood. I can only personally recollect fleeting impressions, some delightful, some painful, of traveling over a vast rugged country of mountains, forest and desert in a 1929 Star sedan in which I was squeezed in with Grandma, Gramps, Uncle Howard, Aunt Florence, and all their jostling grips and bundles that shifted with every bump and turn of the long, long road to California. But I do remember the end of that road which brought me my first glimpse of what was to become a lifelong mistress and love affair—the Pacific Ocean.

I believe we settled on 9th Street in Long Beach where my grandparents took a job of managing some sort of apartment and old farmer-Gramps sold vacuum cleaners door-to-door to supplement our meager income. We may have been miserably poor with few real prospects to improve our lot, but I remained happy as long as I could cajole Grandma into taking me down to the beach each day from where I would expectantly look toward another Promised Land lying somewhere far out there beyond the horizon. Perhaps I buoyed her spirits with my own five-year-old enthusiasm, but I remember best that day when she gave me eight pennies to buy from the corner store a quart of milk and as I was bringing it home, the street suddenly began heaving beneath my feet in a weird undulating motion that continued to increase to a terrifying degree. I threw the bottle of milk away and rushed home as fast as I could run, but where I expected to find safety, I only found empty rooms with pictures slipping crazily askew and Gramps' rocker swaying all by itself in the middle of the buckling floor. A few moments later, my grandmother appeared from a neighboring apartment and shouted at me to stand under the hallway doorjamb where bits of falling plaster could not hurt me. After what seemed an eternity, the weird swaying and rumbling ceased and was replaced by hundreds of excited voices of people pouring out of hiding. I had just experienced the most severe earthquake ever recorded in the Southern California area and when several days later Gramps took me on a tour of the devastated areas, I was most impressed again by the beach—where thousands of Crackerjack boxes had been spewed out of the wrecked amusement pier and were scattered about, ruined by sand and salt water. This forcefully brought home to me the magnitude of the disaster.

Complaints from the tenants about a raucous little monster living with his grandparents in an otherwise sedate apartment house brought about my next move. This time I was taken in by Uncle Hap and Aunt Ann who lived in Glendale, a suburban community on the landward side of Los Angeles and far from my beloved sea. Uncle Hap was a wonderfully talented woodcarver of animal figures and ship models, but he earned a living selling tickets for the Southern Pacific Railroad. Aunt Ann was my adoptive mother's sister and made a genuine effort to make me feel welcome in her home and take the best care of me she could. They had a boy of their own, several years older than I, and an aviation buff who had inherited his father's creative skills which he used to build and fly beautiful little balsa and tissue paper airplanes; our relationship became severely strained when I wrecked some of these during unauthorized flights. There were also clashes with Uncle Hap who could not understand why I had good grades in school for everything except deportment. Aunt Ann's solution was the razor strop, but I kept getting into mischief. Within the year I was sent back to my grandparents, probably less because of being difficult to manage than for financial reasons (the depression was still lying heavily over the land).

My grandparents had in the meanwhile moved to Riverside (another landbound suburb of Los Angeles) and there I attended second grade classes with the same baffling mixture of accomplishments and demerits I had had in Glendale. During that year of 1934, old Gramps finally wore out, became ill and had to quit selling vacuum cleaners. Grandma tried her best, but I was too much for her and when it became apparent that nobody within the family in Los Angeles was able to take care of me, money was scraped together to return me alone by train to Pocatello where, they hoped, my father might have recovered enough from his own troubles to accept the responsibilities of rearing a son. He had not.

Austin Bucher lived together with a group of itinerant men in a shack located close by the electric power station on the banks of the Snake River and he took me in as a sort of amusing pet who was tolerated, even given certain rough affection, as long as it did not get in the way too much. I remember him as a tall, thin man with tousled dark hair and deep-set eyes that could quickly change from a brooding look to laughter and nervous excitement. His movements were jumpy and tense, but sometimes he would just sit and stare into space for a long time without moving at all. He laughed at me a lot, but I also often made him sad without knowing why. I was then going on eight years old and had learned how to adapt myself to a wide variety of circumstances, if nothing else. My father and his circle of rough characters were really lost children, so it was not specially difficult for me to fit myself in with their shiftless existence. They were a hard bunch including ex-convicts, derelict cowboys, alcoholics and even a gnarled old Nez Percé Indian named Tom Nine-Knots. Father was involved in many nefarious schemes, most of which never came to anything, and otherwise would spend his time swapping yarns with his companions over endless games of poker. It was at this time that I first learned the rudiments of that game and also various card tricks with which I still amuse friends and their children. Food was sometimes a problem solved by foraging over the countryside in a communal jalopy to rustle a sheep from one of the outlying ranches, truss up the luckless animal and return it for slaughter inside our shack.

I also had the companionship of other children, some of whom were as tough as my adult ones and formed a gang that roamed in search of mischief around the outskirts of Pocatello. Our main operating area was along the banks of the Snake River where we had our headquarters in a cave of a cliff rising sheer out of the rapidly flowing water. Access to our lair was by a rope ladder that could not have supported a fully grown man. Our leader was a girl who was the oldest and toughest member of our gang, and maintained her status with a sharp tongue and pair of hard fists; she could lick or outargue any of us. My own position in the gang was peculiar in that, as the only one who had learned to read without tracking each letter with a grubby index finger, I was assigned to entertain the group with dramatic readings from lurid pulp magazines we either stole from local cigar and drugstores, or salvaged from trash heaps. These sessions actually turned into theatricals where I directed a ragamuffin cast to take parts in plays created out of my readings, and even if the material was not culturally sound, it revealed to us (and mostly to me) the power of the written word. I must credit much of my lifelong interest in literature to those uninhibited performances in a secret cave on the banks of the Snake River.

A summer rolled by, then the rest of the year without any such formality as school being imposed upon my haphazard existence.

There were times when my father would be gone for several days and knowing that I was not always welcome at the shack, I would sleep in our cave or in a coalbin behind a cafe in town where I could usually get a handout from the cook or dishwasher. I learned to live on my own, and where something could not be had for the asking, I would find a way to steal it. One of my best capers was collecting bottles, selling them to one grocery store, then stealing them back and selling them again to another customer. I got into the habit of raiding the Five & Dime Store which seemed to me to have something available from the whole world, all ready for the taking by quick fingers. The only close honest association I had with my father was when he decided to become a lumberjack and took me with him to a camp in the northern forests of Idaho, a job that came to an end with the first heavy winter snows. Back to the shack on the banks of the Snake! At least it was warm. And when the other occupants got drunk and mean, I knew how to discreetly slip out of sight.

I ran loose all that winter, miraculously avoiding the police and truant officer. Then one day when I was raiding the Five & Dime and had managed to stuff my pockets with fishhooks and line in anticipation of angling for trout in the spring thaw of the Snake, I was suddenly grabbed by a huge pair of hands that shook all the loot out of me. A rough voice growled, "Come along, you little bastard!" I kicked and bit, but could not break away and was eventually turned over to a policeman who took me back to the shack. My father was, as usual, not there, but one of his fellow tenants was and he took over with a beating that made the policeman seem gentle by comparison. He made it obvious to me that my crime was not that of stealing—but of being caught at it. I was totally ashamed of myself, but at the same time perplexed over the strange hypocrisies of grown-ups. Father gave me a half-joking scuffing when he returned and heard about my inglorious arrest, then was again absent when a few days later, two officers and a lady welfare worker suddenly arrived at the shack and with the flourish of an official piece of paper, took me away. I never saw my father again. Nor was anything ever the same again. Things good and bad left my life in one confusing swoop, changing it forever.

The people who took me away were employed by the state and I was escorted by train to Boise and placed in the custody of a state-run orphanage. Within minutes of arriving there, I was given a bath, a decent outfit of clothes, a good hot meal and a clean warm bed—none of which I had seen during the past year. There were lots of other children there and I quickly made new friends (something I've never had trouble doing). Both recreation and study were organized, of course, and while I sometimes missed roaming the banks of the Snake River and my companions of its cave, I was kept too busy for brooding; home being only a vague notion in my mind, I never suffered from homesickness. My grandmother somehow discovered that I had been lodged in an orphanage and sent me some parcels of candy and toys, but they soon stopped coming and I completely lost touch with her and all my other adopted relatives for the next ten years. During that summer I actually enjoyed my new life and when schoolwork became tedious, I found relief in the library full of books by authors who wrote about adventures beyond my wildest imagination. I discovered on my own that Jules Verne, Daniel Defoe, and Robert Louis Stevenson were far more gratifying than the crude pulp magazine hacks I had read in the cave. I was soon up to my old tricks of reading aloud to my friends and directing them in taking acting parts in the stories.

The orphanage was run by people of the Mormon faith and I found myself enjoying their Bible classes and the tenets of their teaching. Then someone discovered that I had been baptized a Catholic and I was no longer allowed to join in their church services, but left outside to play alone in the yard. This was my first brush with religous prejudice and it had its effects. As the only boy of Catholic background in the orphanage, I was considered "different" and became a natural object for childish teasing—childish, but cruel. However, there happened to be a Catholic lady appointed to the Board of Trustees of the institution who became aware of my existence and took a special interest in me. Mrs. Clark was very wealthy and lived in a beautiful home where she invited me to do odd jobs in her garden for 25 cents per week—a munificent salary to an eight-year-old in 1936. I was also invited to dine with her a few times and discovered that she had a butler who could be summoned by pushing a buzzer under the dining-room table. I valued my friendship with Mrs. Clark very much, and although vaguely uneasy over the special privileges it brought me, took advantage of the fact that prejudice can be a two-edged sword.

By the fall much of what had inspired me at the orphanage became routine and my problems increased to the point where I decided to run away from them all. My most plausible justification was a sudden longing for Grandmother and the sea, but I knew I was doing a wrong thing and fully expected immediate pursuit by the officials of the orphanage. I lit out just the same, running and trotting toward a large table-rock mountain near Boise where I planned to lie low among the boulders until the heat was off and it was safe for me to proceed on the 900-mile journey to California. During my scrambling up the mountain, I spotted a small civilian airplane circling above and decided that the posse was hard on my trail, using the most modern methods of apprehending fugitives. Convinced that the pilot had spotted me, I dove into a thicket. When he departed, I was certain it was to report my position which I promptly changed to one in the next valley where I huddled until after dark. Then came hunger and the cold of the October night, neither of which I had pro-vided for in my otherwise elaborate plans. There were some farm-houses around winking friendly lights in the gloom, and swallow-ing my pride, I eventually wandered up to one and asked permission to sleep in the barn. I was, of course, invited inside, fed a proper meal, then put to bed with the children of the house-hold. The next morning I awakened to the smell of bacon per-meating the room and hoped that I would be offered some before resuming my flight. I was. But a policeman also arrived in time to partake in breakfast. Even before he washed down his gen-erous portion of bacon and eggs with a third cup of coffee and said, "Let's go, son," I knew that my break for freedom had come to an end.

Back at the orphanage I took the punishment due me and immediately began planning another escape, this time giving better attention to such details as the rigors of Idaho's severe winters. It occurred to me that I had failed in my first attempt largely because of having picked the wrong season in which to make it. Better wait until next summer when warmer weather made it pleasanter and easier to live off the land, and in the meanwhile make the best of it at the orphanage by pretending cooperation. That was a sensible decision. The cold winter passed with me grateful for shelter and regular meals, then a long wet spring which stimulated impatient daydreams of high adventure on the road to California. With the first hot days of summer I was about to put them into action when my friend, Mrs. Clark, suddenly called me aside and announced that she had completed arrangements to have me transferred to a Catholic Mission and Orphanage in the northern part of the state and near the famous Nez Percé Indian reservation. This astounding news made me abandon all plans of escape and turn into a model of genuinely eager cooperation.

When I arrived at the Mission, run by the teaching order of Catholic Sisters of St. Joseph, who were trying to tame one of the last great wilderness areas of the United States, dim happy memories of my grandparents' farm were rekindled. This too was a farm nestled in even wilder country, the nearest community being a sleepy outpost with the appropriate name of Slickpoo, the next nearest named Culdesac by some long dead and disillusioned "voyageur," and the county seat, Lewiston, lying thirty miles beyond a barrier of sawtooth ridges and deep canyons was barely emerging from trading post to a full-fledged small town. Our nearest neighbors were tribesmen of the Nez Percé and a handful of hardbitten ranchers working the lands bordering their reservation. The remoteness preserved a completely unspoiled atmosphere of the old Pioneer West, an inspirational one to an adventurous young romanticist such as myself. I was, of course, immediately subjected to the disciplines of organized studies and recreation that were even more stringently supervised than those of the state orphanage, but I was also allowed to expend my surplus energy in healthy farming chores and when the old restlessness set in, it could be soothed by expeditions into forested Indian hunting grounds, along rapid mountain streams full of trout, and over open ranges where wild mustangs still roamed. The good Sisters at the Mission were strict in matters of faith and practical scholarship, but their work in this frontier district had taught them not to overly restrict the freedom of their charges.

Under their tutelage, I breezed through the fifth, sixth, and seventh grades with better than average marks; even my deportment improved, though I could still get into mischief. Such as the time when my awakening interest in chemistry inspired me to create an experimental explosive which was secretly tested beneath the chicken coop with disastrous effects upon some of the Mission's poultry. But on the whole, the three years I spent there were more secure and happier than any I had known before.

Yet the restlessness remained. I became a curious admixture of activist and bookworm who, in between daily periods of furious activity, read every book in the library I was permitted to lay my hands on, and some that I was not. I also began reading the sports pages of old newspapers and soon found out that football—the game I loved best—had a lot more to it than the touch variety we played in the Mission's yard. And then I happened upon an article about a wonderful movie starring Spencer Tracy and Mickey Rooney which told the story of Father Flanagan's Boys Town of Nebraska. I wanted to see it for myself, of course, but important movies rarely reached Culdesac, let alone our isolated back-country mission. Yet the article told me all I really needed to know: that Boys Town was meant for boys like me and had a real *coached* football team whose games were reported in the newspapers. My first impulse was to sneak off to Nebraska on my own and present myself on Father Flanagan's doorstep. However, there was the formidable intervening barrier of the Rocky Mountains whose peaks were snow-covered even in summer. So I wisely decided to try an easier way first and wrote a carefully composed letter asking him to admit me to Boys Town.

It must have been a good letter because Father Flanagan was impressed enough to write back to the Sisters for more information. In spite of my intimidating and quite unnecessary threat to "light out" for Boys Town if they did not recommend my transfer, they agreed between themselves that Father Flanagan could do far more for my future than their small wilderness mission. The Mother Superior enthusiastically urged my acceptance and even went further than that. As I only recently found out, neither

Boys Town nor St. Joseph Mission had enough money for my fare, but the good Mother Superior used her influence on the Union Pacific Railroad and persuaded them to let me ride on a free pass. So it happened that in the summer of 1941 I made alone the long overland trip to Omaha. The conductor had been charged to keep an eye on me, but I maintained a most careful behavior on the train. I wanted no trouble to interfere with my enrollment in Father Flanagan's famous institution.

Boys Town was then emerging from a long struggle for existence that had barely survived the bleak depression years of the '30s. Father Flanagan's dedication and drive, combined with the publicity generated by two popular films about his life and work, brought a welcome flood of contributions. It also vastly increased the pressure of cases like mine, who were begging for admission. World War II had started and many plans involving buildings and expanded programs had to be deferred—the materials and manpower were simply not available in a war economy. But the institution was on its way to becoming the great school it is today, offering real opportunity rather than merely a haven for disadvantaged children. The student body had grown from the handful of ragamuffins Father Flanagan took into his fold in 1917 to over two hundred. I found myself among a varied lot between the ages of ten and seventeen, some orphans with nowhere else to go, some rejected or ejected from broken homes, some rescued with criminal records from harsh court judgments, and almost every one of them oppressed by years of neglect and privation. There were black and white boys, Protestants and Catholics and Jews, and some who had come with no traceable ethnic background or religious faith whatsoever. I soon discovered that many of them had been salvaged out of worse circumstances than my own, especially those who originated from the slum jungles of large cities. It dawned on me that perhaps I was among the luckier of this ill-starred breed and that helped me adjust to the school's strict discipline.

In my studies I did well with the subjects I liked (math, science, and geography), less well with those I did not (grammar, history, Latin), but by juggling my capabilities, I managed to maintain above average grades that kept me on the honor roll during most of my six years at Boys Town. I went in for all of the organized sports offered by an expanding athletic department which included basketball, track, baseball, swimming and, of course, football. That game lived up to all my expectations. I loved the teamwork of intricate plays and the rough body contact against hard-playing opponents. Because I was shorter and lighter than other players, I had to develop wit and speed as a substitute for weight and brawn in order to beat out several bigger and older boys for a place on the 1st Varsity Squad which I was eventually to captain.

Coach "Skip" Palrang became a great influence on my life. He had given up his promising position of coaching college football that might well have led him to big league professional clubs, to devote his life to Boys Town. There was nothing maudlin in his love for boys; like Knute Rockne, he knew when to encourage them with a kick in the behind or a pat on the back. He could bellow. He could cajole. He always inspired the best efforts out of his players, making the good ones better and the weaker ones feeling stronger just for having tried. Coach Palrang turned out championship teams that won most of their games on the high-school circuit, including two undefeated seasons during the mid-'40s. This was important to Father Flanagan who sent him and his players all over the United States to show what Boys Town could make out of orphans and delinquents. The results were a continued flow of contributions that secured his plans for expanding the scope of his work.

It was also important to "Pete" Bucher (I acquired the nickname that was to stick for the rest of my life on the Boys Town football field), because it forced me to keep up high scholastic grades in order to enjoy the privileges of a varsity player. I came to appreciate the rewards far beyond the exhilaration of rugged games played under exciting "big league" conditions in stadiums of cities as far apart as San Francisco and Boston, Detroit and Washington. It inspired me to work hard even over boring grammar and Latin and history when our railroad coach was turned into a perambulating classroom rolling across the country. It broadened my horizons beyond the dream world of books and pulp magazines, finally allowing me to perceive with my own eyes the reality of America's vastness, beauty and throbbing activity. My leisure reading acquired a more current nature, involving tales of the monumental conflicts going on at the time and which seemed to dwarf my personal ones on the high school football fields. These were the days of Guadalcanal, Anzio, Iwo Jima, the Battle of the Philippine Sea, and the beaches of Normandy, where boys only a few years older than myself were laying down their lives by the thousands. They were the real heroes every day of the week, while I was only an occasional Friday night or Saturday afternoon variety, reacting to a referee's whistle rather than bullets and shells. Satisfaction over my accomplishments was never complete; the old restlessness was still there, taking different forms, but as compelling as ever.

Thus all was not serene for me at Boys Town. High spirits sometimes turned into fits of temper, vivid imagination occasionally dissolved into black moods of depression. While I was being taught self-discipline and control, disturbing turbulences would occasionally break through the surface, aggravated by the physiological upheavals of approaching manhood. The greatest security for Boys Town's students was its complete lack of confining fences, but I was twice driven to break bounds and start off on aimless searches for the lost family I yearned to belong to (my father was by then a permanent patient in a Washington Veterans Hospital). Twice I returned on my own and accepted the punishment meted out by stern teacher-priests who were not in the least inhibited by the permissive "Spock school" of child rearing.

And there were violent outbursts like the one when a Brother sneaked up behind me during religion class, caught me reading a smuggled *Battle Aces* pulp instead of the prescribed Bible text, and clouted me so hard that I fell out of my seat. I bounced back to my feet, fighting mad, and shouted: "That was a lousy thing to do, you dirty son-of-a-bitch!" I then ducked the next blow from the outraged Brother and fled the classroom, initiating a pursuit that crisscrossed the entire campus. I had trained too well on the football field to be caught and tackled by a flat-footed monk hampered by his heavy cassock, but I could not escape the eventual punishment decreed by Father Flanagan himself: a thou-

sand word apology which to the miscreant seemed a novel-length
penance for a dozen ill-chosen words.

There were other incidents in the same general category and
some escapades during my senior year when I developed a compelling interest in the opposite sex, which tarnished my image as
a popular football star in the eyes of the faculty. When I was
elected Mayor of Boys Town by the less circumspect student body,
they voided the ballot on the grounds that I was unprepared for
such a responsibility.

However, I learned to accept rebukes along with honors in good
grace and the overall effect was of growing toward maturity with
more forward leaps than backward slips. When I graduated in
1946 among the top ten of my class, the recommendations of my
teachers along with my scholastic and athletic record, qualified me
to enter a good college. But I had absolutely no funds of my own
and Boys Town could not as yet provide scholarships for its most
promising graduates. The best they could do for me at the time
was to hand me my diploma, outfit me in a new store-bought suit,
and give me seven dollars cash with which to face the outside
world. I did not complain. It was enough to see me through to
the nearest Navy recruiting station where I promptly enlisted for
a two-year hitch.

Without seriously intending to make a career of the Navy, I
was at last off to the sea I had fallen in love with as a toddler
and avidly read about throughout my childhood. After my two-
year hitch, I'd decide what to do next. Maybe save up a nest egg
from my pay and go to college. Maybe buy back Gramps' lost farm
in Idaho. All that could be decided later and—best of all—from
here on out, I could decide for myself. Little did I know, as I
rolled westward toward boot camp in San Diego, what a compelling, clinging mistress the sea would be in my future.

When Monsignor Wegner finished his benediction, he gave me
a broad wink that brought me back to the reality of the present,
then with the formal part of the commissioning over, he joined
me and my family. He was at the time seventy years old, but
moved and acted like a man in the prime of life. When in motion,
he walked with long purposeful strides that made his followers

break into a trot if they wanted to keep up. When he was supposed to be standing still, he had a tendency to do a sort of stationary jig on the spot. He had a deeply lined craggy face, homely and handsome at the same time, but mostly reflecting a strong will and lively sense of humor. There was no trace of that sanctimonious flatulence which many clerics develop with advancing seniority. A lifetime devoted to remolding waifs and delinquents had left him with few illusions about the world, yet without in the least shaking his faith in God and humanity. Some of his students' rough qualities had rubbed off on their teacher, creating a two-fisted, no-nonsense kind of priest who knew—and could turn against them—their own profane jargon as well as the language of the Scriptures. He spoke in rapidly delivered, short sentences that drove directly to the point he wanted to make, usually emphasizing it with sharp cracks that sometimes bordered on the ribald. His worldly ways were mostly expressed by a cheerfully cynical wit that could either soothe with a joke or slash with irony, as the occasion warranted. But regardless of the temper of the moment, the seriousness of his mission as Director of Boys Town, teacher and spiritual father of over nine hundred boys, and principal fundraiser for their support and education, was always uppermost in his mind. "Well, Pete, I guess you may turn out a credit to the old school after all," he told me with a twinkle. It was his way of saying he was proud of me, and that made me feel very good.

"Come on, Father! I'll show you over my ship. You might as well get a good look at what you just blessed and know how badly it needed it."

All our other guests swarmed aboard *Pueblo*, jostling one another on her narrow decks, jamming up the companionways, and clogging the confined interior spaces where they were permitted to visit. Their most visible reaction was one of amazement over what they would politely refer to as our "compactness," trying to hide their shock over the Navy's sending us across the oceans in such a small cockleshell. They were not shown the SOD-Hut, of course, and to those who asked what was behind the locked steel door, we would answer "Delicate research instruments!" and press them on through the passage to look at something else. Some ladies inspecting our galley marveled over our optimism on having it feed eighty men with a cooking facility that was smaller than most of their own kitchens. A few wives and mothers looking into the berthing spaces with bunks stacked four high to the overhead, blanched and could only mutter the one compliment I had expected for my ship: "Well . . . it's certainly clean!" Father Wegner inspected my tiny stateroom and made some caustic comments about my having it all to myself, and when I took him up to the flying bridge from where he could survey the entire one-hundred seventy-six feet of my ship, he said something about having to look up more special prayers for the safety of seafaring men. My officers, crew, and I reassured everybody that *Pueblo* was really a very able little ship; that without all these guests aboard, there was enough room to get along, and that in any case, size had little to do with seaworthiness. Both Columbus and the Pilgrim Fathers had traversed the Atlantic to open the colonization of the Americas with vessels of less than half the size of *Pueblo*.

The crowd gradually debouched off the gangplank and streamed up to Bremerton's far more spacious service clubs. The officers escorted their guests to theirs, where a cocktail party and sumptuous buffet had been laid on. As we had intended, formalities relaxed completely as the captains of the two newly commissioned ships became hosts of a great party. The Admirals circulated among the VIPs and unbended over drinks with their subordinates, making a democratic effort to remember everybody's first name. Monsignor Wegner, as at ease at this cocktail party as in his rectory, charmed everybody with his tersely witty affability.

All the pretty wives, sweethearts, and dates received ardent attention, especially from Dave Behr who flitted among them like an ecstatic bumblebee buzzing from one gorgeous flower to the next. Steve Harris gradually shed his professorial dignity, began to glow, then have a good time of it without compromising any of the deep, dark secrets locked in his mind or behind his steel door. Our much abused ship's superintendent, Leo Sweeney, released his pent-up frustration over his job of putting us in shape for this glorious day by getting himself hilariously tipsy.

It developed into the kind of grand party I can never resist happily joining in, and as it kept going on past four o'clock, was myself getting into a very carefree mood. It took Rose to remind me that we were supposed to host a private dinner at a Bremerton restaurant for Father Wegner and *Pueblo*'s officers. That is where our party transferred the celebration and eventually ended it much later, not wholly sober, but with a warm afterglow of satisfaction over a very successful day.

Early the next afternoon, Rose, Mike, and I saw Father Wegner off on his return flight to Omaha, arriving at Seattle Airport in time for a few minutes of goodbyes that were to bridge a long parting with unsuspected trials in our lives. It is impossible to get overly emotional with Father Wegner, but I felt that way just the same as we exchanged cheery waves before he vanished into the crowd of travelers pressing through the boarding gate. After he was gone, we drove into Seattle to spend the remaining hours of the weekend alone together; Rose too was scheduled to fly away early next morning. We had a good steak dinner before checking into a hotel where we put Mike up in a room of his own, then retired to our own where we sat up for an hour, rehashing husband-wife fashion, the events of the last two days. When we had exhausted the trivia, Rose got around to the important matter that was on both our minds:

"So *Pueblo* is commissioned at last! But is she really ready to go out to Japan very soon?"

The answer to that was, of course, classified information. But, on the other hand, there was no official answer to it as yet, so I said without much hesitation "No—not soon."

"How long?"

I decided then and there as we lay in bed together that our separate lives had to be rejoined again even if for only a short time. I knew that *Pueblo*'s forthcoming sea trials and the inevitable deficiencies they would reveal for correction, had to keep us for at least another six weeks in Bremerton. Then would follow the trip down to San Diego and our predeployment training period there—at least another six weeks before proceeding to Japan. During most of this time our boys would be on summer vacation when a nomadic life would not hinder their education—only dent our bank account. So I answered Rose, "Long enough to make it worth-

while for us to try to live together again. As soon as you get back
to Jefferson City, start making arrangements to move out here."

"That's what I wanted to hear you say," Rose sighed with relief
and settled back on her pillow.

Lights out.

CHAPTER IV

"LEO, I AM ABSOLUTELY SICK OVER BEING TOLD FROM ALL DIRECTIONS THAT THE SOLUTION TO EVERY PROBLEM ABOARD PUEBLO CAN BE SOLVED BY MAKING HER LIKE THE BANNER, BECAUSE YOU KNOW AND I KNOW THAT BANNER IS BARELY SEA-WORTHY."—(CDR. *Bucher to LCDR Leo Sweeney USN, Ship's Superintendent for USS Pueblo's conversion, Bremerton, July 1967.*)

The warm glow of optimism kindled by our commissioning smouldered on into the following days even though the bunting was removed from *Pueblo's* superstructure and she reverted to her status of just another naval unit among the many awaiting finishing touches before being released from the busy Puget Sound Navy Shipyard. The difference was that she was now a live ship with Union Jack and Colors flying, regular watches set under a duty officer, and a constant humming of the electrical machinery that kept her breathing and alight, even when lying otherwise inert alongside Pier 5. I knew of many things that should still be done to bring her closer to perfection, but I had also come to realize that perfection was a will-o'-the-wisp in our case, and was concentrating on plans for our sea trials that were due within the next week. From these I not only hoped to squeeze out a few more concessions on minor physical improvements, but also to start some sorely needed training of our people in seamanship. I had myself not been to sea since leaving USS *Ronquil,* and most of my deck and engineering force, including officers, had been on the beach for as long, or longer; only four men besides myself had

solid seagoing experience and the rest varied from a few brief
cruises on much larger ships to nothing more than rides on the
Seattle-Bremerton ferry. The broad calm waters of Puget Sound
might be fine for trying out *Pueblo's* machinery and maneuverability under optimum conditions, and to gently introduce the
landlubbers among her crew to the feel of being under way. But,
once we passed through Juan de Fuca Strait, rounded Cape
Flattery, and started butting into those gray beard combers of
the North Pacific, circumstances might turn brutally different for
all but the most salty sailors among us. I did not doubt that
Pueblo would be seaworthy (I would not take her out there if
she were not) but I was equally convinced she would be an unusually rough-riding teacher of our greenhorns. This, along with
concern over anticipated crankiness of her antiquated machinery,
became my foremost worry as the sea trials became imminent.

Then Steve Harris dropped a bombshell.

I had noticed a worried frown on his thoughtful face during
the preceding day, but paid little attention to it as Steve tended
to take even small worries seriously. However, on the following
morning when I came aboard, he met me with a look of positive
agony and without any beating around the bush, informed me,
"Sir, all the work in the SOD-Hut has to be done over again from
top to bottom."

"You've got to be kidding me!" I exclaimed in disbelief. But
from his expression of misery, I knew he was not. Rushing below,
we passed through the steel door into the secret spaces where I
found a collection of agitated CTs and technicians of our civilian
subcontractor standing about studying rolls of electronic diagrams
with long perplexed faces. "All right! What's this all about?"
I demanded. "What's wrong down here?"

Chief Communications Technician Bouden shot an unhappy
glance at Steve, and, on receiving a nod from him, started answering in terms he hoped I would understand with my limited
electronic knowledge. "Well, Captain . . . it's simply that much of
this gear has been installed upside down . . ."

"Upside down?" I echoed in outrage. The whole thing was beginning to sound like a bad joke and I felt my temper rising.
"What the devil do you mean it's upside down?"

Bouden swallowed hard and said, "Just that, sir. That is, gear we hardly ever will use is accessibly installed at eye level, while that we'll have to constantly get at to operate has either been put out of reach near the overhead, or down on the deck." One of the CTs pantomimed his explanation by standing tiptoe in front of a rack of instruments and tried to reach a tuner at the top, while another got down on his hands and knees to demonstrate the difficulties of changing reels on a tape recorder located at the bottom. It didn't take an electronic engineer to see that the system would be unworkable when the cramped compartment was being tossed about by an even moderate sea. This was no joke. It was a disaster of bungled planning.

"How in God's name did you let this happen?" I asked Steve in anguish. "Why did you report to me that all the work here was being accomplished according to plan?"

"It was, sir," Steve answered, with a hopeless shrug. "It's the plans that are screwed up, not the work."

The civilian technicians flourished their rolls of diagrams at me and protested, "We installed everything the way the company Drafting Department laid it out for us. Every sheet of these plans has been approved by NAVSHIPSYSTEM Command. If we'd done it any other way, it would have been our ass, sir."

"And *ours* if we'd interfered, sir," Bouden interjected. "Our job was to learn how this system was being put together so we could service it, not why, so we could challenge it . . ."

"All right! Never mind who's to blame right now," I interrupted him. "The most important thing for me to know is how long will it take to fix it?"

There followed a long depressed silence in the cold fluorescent light of the SOD-Hut as CTs and subcontractors exchanged uncertain glances. One of the civilians tried to hedge by showing me his plans and explaining: "Well, sir, it's not just a matter of shuffling units around on their racks. There's all this wiring here that's got to be relocated, and . . ."

"Six to ten weeks, Captain!" Steve blurted out.

Six to ten weeks! That meant sea trials delayed until late July. Our fleet training period in San Diego until mid-September. Our arrival in Japan for operational duty until November. Allowing

for necessary rest and refit after a trans-Pacific trip in this small
ship, we could not look forward to taking part in Operation
Clickbeetle until January of 1968—ten months behind schedule!
A degrading delay for a supposedly high priority project. But I
realized that there was no use in cursing and screaming at these
men about it; my temper turned into cold anger as I stalked out
of the SOD-Hut to discuss in private with Steve what was to be
done.

It soon transpired that because we had been working from common plans, *Palm Beach*'s intelligence gathering equipment du-
plicated all the errors of ours. It was small comfort, but at least
we could now act in concert in dealing with the difficulty, which
we did by sending a letter directly to the officer concerned with
our project at Naval Security Group headquarters in Washington.
In the meanwhile, we locally kept the situation to ourselves in
order to avoid a premature uproar at the shipyard which was as
fed up with our long stay at their docks as we were. But without
going into any of the tiresome details, I informed Rose on long-
distance telephone to Jefferson City that she could now count on
spending virtually the entire summer in Bremerton and to be ready
to move out as soon as the boys' school ended its spring term.
The heavy expenses were now better justified and I hoped to reduce them by immediately applying for low cost housing on the
base. Rose was delighted, and the prospects of us living together
as a family through the beautiful summer season of the Olympic
Peninsula was one bright compensation for an otherwise dismal
week.

I also informed our ship's superintendent in strict confidence
about the developments as it had been my policy not to spring
surprises on this hard-pressed officer. Poor Leo Sweeney showed
signs of throwing a fit of apoplexy over having *Pueblo* and *Palm
Beach* on his work schedule for an additional six to ten weeks.
"What happened? What went wrong, for Christ sake?" he kept
asking in a daze.

Because of the closely held security of the spaces involved, to
which he was still not officially privy, I could only repeat the preposterous explanation: "The goddamned SOD-Huts have been
put in upside down, Leo. That's all I can tell you." He reeled away

with a crushed, vacant stare, seemingly torn between seeking sanctuary at the base hospital or the chaplain's office. But in the end he stoutly kept his and our troubles to himself.

Since our latest foul-up involved classified areas of *Pueblo* the word did not quickly penetrate the otherwise effective scuttlebutt system of the shipyard and I covertly took advantage of this to trap their Production Officer, a captain, into paving the way for work I wanted done besides righting the upside-down SOD-Hut. I inveigled him aboard my ship and gave him a personally conducted tour, pointing out such deficiencies as a useless warping winch whose massive power-train blocked our crew's mess, our antediluvian internal communication system, an unsatisfactory watertight integrity when considering we might be faced with ramming by harassing Communist forces, a defective windlass that could not be counted upon to handle our anchor when we might need it the most, and a lifeboat which could never be launched in heavy seas and was only adding two tons to our already critical topside weight (we were nimble enough to pick up any man-overboard without it, and were equipped with self-inflating life rafts for all hands, if we had to abandon ship). It was not difficult to get the captain to agree that these things were really quite intolerable, nor did he hesitate to say that he would be very happy to have them corrected—*if* he had six or eight weeks to do the work.

"I may hold you to that, sir," I warned him, feeling certain that much time would shortly be made available. In his ignorance of the latest developments in our SOD-Hut, he felt equally certain he would never be called upon to make good his promise. He left *Pueblo* with sincere assurances of his complete understanding and sympathy for my problems.

The reaction from our letter to NAVSECGRU, amplified by some long-distance calls between Bremerton and Washington, came with unusual promptness. NSG assigned the job of investigating our reports to Lieutenant John P. Arnold, USN who came winging out on the first available jet, conducted a whirlwind but thorough inspection of both *Pueblo* and *Palm Beach*, verified that our SOD-Huts had indeed been installed upside down, then flashed an encrypted brief of the disaster ahead of his return to

Washington, which followed within a day. The lieutenant pulled no punches and his report caused more than a ripple through the placid halls of headquarters, especially when they digested the fact that necessary revisions in *Pueblo* and *Palm Beach's* SOD-Huts would cost upward of $500,000 and weeks more delay in a program that was already months behind schedule. The people at NAVSHIPSYSCOM who were responsible for approving all our original plans, had some embarrassing explaining to do. The Vice Chief of Naval Operations, the Navy's second highest ranking admiral, lost his temper when the report came to his attention and bellowed something to the effect of: "Get those damned intelligence ships to sea immediately!" But he also must have realized that the recommended revisions were absolutely necessary if "those damned intelligence ships" were ever to redeem the time and money already spent on them. He directed they be accomplished forthwith and with no more stupid mistakes about it.

For the first time since I had been assigned to *Pueblo*, I began noticing strong command attention from Washington. Rear Admiral Roy Iseman, in charge of OPNAV-34, came out himself to talk to Doug Raper and me, inspected our ships, and promised all the help he could provide from his position; upon his return to Washington he promptly fired an assistant who had in his opinion heretofore merely been shuffling our affairs through the IN and OUT baskets on his desk. His replacement not only showed keen interest, but also made intelligent suggestions through frequent communications. I was encouraged by finding things moving in the right direction and my morale rose accordingly. If only this kind of interest and attention to detail had been shown by CNO from the beginning, I thought, we would have long since been in operation with a good ship. Well, better late than never! If they kept it up now, we would soon be in good shape. If . . .

Contracts were rewritten to provide the subcontractors the time and money to properly complete the SOD-Huts of both ships, and they went about it with a serious intention of doing a good job (they were really very competent technicians and engineers). Things were stirred up into productive activity and I had also gained those weeks I needed to put right items which had previously been denied me on the pretext of lack of time. By now, the shipyard had, of course, been jolted into full awareness of what was going on and its own chain of command (almost as complex as the one above us) proceeded to give me trouble from their level.

Conferences were convened around a huge table in the Planning Office which seated representatives of four different yard departments, as well as the officers concerned from *Pueblo* and *Palm Beach*—about twenty of us, all inclusive. All with the common goal of getting these little ships out of Bremerton and off on their mysterious missions before they attracted more lightning from Washington. But the difference of opinion raged over in what state this could be accomplished in good conscience. We avoided the whys and wherefores of the upside-down SOD-Huts as that embarrassing matter had already been resolved by higher directives and, as usual, security clearances were lacking to allow free discussion on the subject. Instead we concentrated on my long list of basic deficiencies which I wanted put right while our intelligence department was being rebuilt. The captain in charge of the Production Office gave me that aggrieved, accusing look of one who had been thoroughly conned, but had to admit to having personally determined my requests were reasonable and could be implemented with enough time, which was evidently now available. However, the civilian Director of Planning, who held a civil service rating that made him equivalent to a rear admiral, started nitpicking through my list, protesting each item with "Make it like the *Banner*, that's my orders!"—the same line he had been throwing at me for many weeks and so often I had come to doubt he knew any other in the language. But this time he added some platitudes about saving taxpayers' money and reminders about the Navy's "can-do" philosophy.

The discussion became heated. Leo Sweeney, who had recovered both his sense of humor and proportion, supported most of my demands although they meant more work for him. Doug Raper of *Palm Beach* backed me forcefully even though he had different problems; his ship had come to Bremerton with a different and somewhat better layout than mine. But other shipyard authorities (Ship Type and Commandant's Office) listened with a growing impatience that stemmed from their intense desire to be rid of a mess diverting their attention from servicing units urgently needed in the escalating, controversial Vietnam war. I could understand their position, yet refused to back down from mine, which I considered a clear responsibility to take my ship to sea in the best possible condition to meet her operational requirements. When I feel certain of being in the right, I can match the intransigence of any opponent, ungracefully so if hard pressed. So, when I argued the Civilian Planning Officer into asking in exasperation: "What the hell are you trying to make out of your old tub, Captain—some kind of marine silk purse out of a sow's ear?" I lost my temper.

"Don't you call my ship an old tub!" I shouted back at him. "She's a U. S. Navy ship in which I'm ordered to take eighty men halfway around the world on a damned tough mission. If you don't understand the importance of that, get the hell off the job and let somebody else take over who does!"

During the following shocked silence, Leo Sweeney pulled me out of my chair and out of the room for a long cooling-off stroll up and down the outside corridors. After regaining my composure, I returned to exchange apologies with the Planning Officer, but without too much sincerity on either of our parts. The end of all the noisy arguments was a compromise in which his views prevailed more than mine.

The useless warping winch was to be removed, allowing the crews' mess deck to be rearranged and the galley's scullery enlarged (cost $65,000). We were allocated wiring and telephone instruments with which to create an internal communication system on a "do-it-yourself" basis as best we could. The items involving watertight integrity of Pueblo were denied as impractical to her design even if desirable. The unwanted lifeboat remained with its excess topside weight because it was too expensive to remove. Our inefficient and cranky anchor windlass would have to make do even if it might be needed to keep us from drifting up on the Communist shoals. Many other items on my list were relegated to the "make-do" category. With this I had to be satisfied or otherwise clinch my dismissal as Commanding Officer (and ruin any subsequent naval career). My stubbornness in making

Pueblo the most efficient intelligence gathering ship in the Navy had evidently reached its limits and the time had come to roll with the punches. Otherwise *Pueblo* would eventually take off anyway, leaving me marooned and discredited on the beach.

It is difficult for me to write about *Pueblo* during her next two months. What can one say of interest about a ship which never moves from her dock? There was no lack of activity aboard her, but it consisted of the same work with the same ups and downs and dreary plateaus of marking time that had been going on for the past six months. As a commissioned ship, her watches were set and changed regularly around the clock, but they had little to do besides routine chores of maintenance and cleaning up behind the littering shipyard workmen; the enginemen started up the main engines occasionally to idle against the mooring lines just to keep them from fossilizing out of long disuse. Electricians puttered and experimented with the internal communication system we were supposed to install ourselves. Seamen chipped clean corroded spots on deck and recovered them with paint; cooks rubbed their refrigerators and ranges to a high gloss, but had to restrict their culinary art to brewing coffee. Our flag and commissioning pennant fluttered from the mainmast, but listlessly in the land breeze and turned shabby from soiling fumes swirling out of the shipyard basin. In many respects, *Pueblo* reminded me of those permanently shorebound mockup ships set in concrete by our naval boot camps (and usually named USS *Recruit*), whose gear and fittings are constantly being torn down and reassembled to familiarize the boots with their use, and whose watches are a make-believe rehearsal of the real thing. This created morale problems for me as well as everybody aboard and I sometimes had a difficult job of trying to keep up an effective pitch of enthusiasm.

Keeping everybody busy with meaningful work was one solution. That was not too difficult with Steve Harris and his gang of CTs who were watching things carefully as the subcontractors worked over their SOD-Hut; I had warned them to make use of this opportunity to make sure everything was installed to their satisfaction and not present me with any more unpleasant surprises from that department. But their activities were largely confined behind their steel door and isolated from the rest of the ship's company. Keeping up the interest of sailors, enginemen, commissary, and radiomen was not as easy when their shorebased status made most of their duties seem contrived and unnecessary. For how long can you expect a quartermaster to keep dusting off a wheel he never gets to use for steering his ship? For how long will an engineroom keep engines tuned up that never seem required to drive his ship to sea? For how long can you expect a cook who does not have to turn out regular meals for a hungry crew to remain interested in creating good food? For how long will a deck sailor be inspired to keep his ship ready for sea when, day after day, he is only asked to dab away at gathering rust while staring out over the same basin full of turbid water? The answer, as ever is leadership. This must come from the captain. But through him, it needs the support of his subordinate officers, and most important, of the enlisted chiefs who have the most intimate contact with the crew.

Of the latter I had three excellent men, Chiefs Goldman, Bouden, and QM1 Law; they sensed without explicit detailing what was expected of them. Among my officers, Steve Harris was immersed in his own specialized duties and kept his separate detachment busy; Gene Lacy with his unruffled, methodical ways kept up the Engineering Department, and my brash Operations Officer, Dave Behr, never flagged in his gritty enthusiasm of getting the most out of his men with sticks and carrots. Ed Murphy, as my Executive Officer, should have been an important driving force and my alter ego, but while he dutifully listened to all of my instructions and exhortations, he did so in a politely perfunctory manner that suggested to me that he was more concerned with his personal problems than those of his ship or shipmates. He was often absent in both work and recreation and I gradually became conscious of a widening gulf between us. Maybe I should have reacted then and there to a nebulous conflict of personality and manner of doing things, but then I instinctively shied away from adding to *Pueblo*'s difficulties. Let it ride and don't rock a sensitive boat!

As important as work was, recreation and relaxation from our daily travails was equally so. This became a matter of delicate balance under these very unusual circumstances wherein our ship was tied up for a long time within tantalizing reach of both the exciting metropolitan facilities of Seattle and the bucolic wilderness of the Olympic Peninsula. According to one's temperament, each one offered tempting avenues of escape. I tried very hard to be fair with all my people in giving them the opportunity to enjoy liberties in whichever direction they wished—sometimes both. I myself needed and enjoyed both. Rose and the boys arrived during the third week of June and we all moved into the only government housing I had been able to obtain—an old cottage that was substandard even for the chief's family it was intended for. In spite of being the Pacific Coast's largest and most active shipyard, Bremerton was making do with many inadequate facilities left over from World War II. Only the Officers' Club had aged with a certain elegant dignity. But Rose cheerfully adjusted herself to the conditions and as soon as we were settled in, we threw a combination housewarming and ship's party which was attended by *Pueblo*'s entire officer complement. Because of lack of room and furniture, most of our guests sat on the floor while drinking beer and eating lasagne off paper plates. It was perhaps not the kind of entertaining expected of a commanding officer, but it made for an informal, happy-go-lucky atmosphere that we all enjoyed.

From the Buchers' personal point of view, this turned out one of the happiest summers together that we can remember. Since there was a limit to how much prowling around the various projects on my ship I could do without becoming a disruptive influence, and the time had come to stem my flow of complaining memoranda and reports, I found time to spend with my family. We bought a secondhand car and used it to range out over this fascinating area of one of our most beautiful states. There were outings to Seattle where we had dinner in the revolving restaurant on top of its Exposition Space Needle with a breathtaking view of the city, its harbor, the glittering arms of Puget Sound, and the distant forested mountains, all aglow in the long twilight of a northern sunset. We took weekend trips along the Olympic Peninsula, penetrating the wilderness on precipitous mountain roads winding over the misty slopes of Mount Olympus, and picnicking on the banks of clear streams tumbling down from glacier springs. We drove out to Port Angeles and took the car ferry that crossed Juan de Fuca Strait to British Columbia and the town of Victoria, a quaint transplant from old England. We visited Vancouver and its bustling mixture of British-American atmosphere. And at frequent intervals, Leo Sweeney would invite us out to his charmingly rustic home located on a secluded lake, some fifteen miles north of Bremerton, where fat trout could be caught within yards of his doorstep and good cheer always reigned around his warm fireplace.

Our long separation of the past winter became an unpleasant fading memory as we lived closely together through a lovely summer, savoring each other's company all the more because we knew another parting loomed in the near future. For the time being, Rose and I were joined as husband and wife in fact, not just as a figure of speech, and my boys and I were able to develop a participating father-son relationship that benefited all of us. Mark and Mike were growing fast, but still young enough to take childish delight in their new surroundings and wholesome fresh-air life on Puget Sound.

I still had those Happy Hour sessions with my officers to informally talk over the work on *Pueblo*, but they were shorter as I could now look forward to a home-cooked dinner instead of eating alone in the club restaurant whose menu I had learned by heart. And I socialized with other officers whose ships were in the yard for refit, including old friends from the submarine service who would take me on nostalgic tours of their boats. I was entertained by the captain of USS *Gompers*, a huge destroyer-tender which had just been built and commissioned in Bremerton, and with whom *Pueblo* was destined to have a special relationship. The visit almost gave me an inferiority complex. The captain's bathroom was larger than my whole cabin and he could seat ten of us with room to spare in the salon section of his quarters. Everything aboard *Gompers* was brand new, spacious, automated and computerized, including the ship's laundry which turned out hundreds of pounds of spotless, pressed and neatly folded clothing, all sorted and packaged for the wearer to pick up, but with only a couple of laundrymen keeping the whole plant going by pushing buttons. It made me think unkindly about the cranky old home-appliance that sloshed and burped through the same job in *Pueblo*'s fo'c'sle.

And so passed the summer of 1967 for the Buchers, snugged down in the happily cramped togetherness of their cottage perched on the hill above the eternal racket of the busy shipyard. The din of cutting, shaping and welding steel was with us day and night, and within the discordant percussion could be heard occasional counterpoints of tinny squeaks and rattles which suggested that among the giants, little *Pueblo* was being hammered into shape.

The great day came in the latter part of July. With her SOD-Hut properly installed right-side-up and the few additional improvements allowed her completed, *Pueblo* was at long last ready for sea trials. These were, of course, to start with a daylight cruise in protected waters safely adjacent to Bremerton, but we embarked upon it with the adventurous spirit of sailors outward bound across the great deep. There were nervous tensions felt by those of us who suspected we had been landbound too long to keep a sure feel of a ship under way, and by those for whom it would be a new experience entirely. But everybody was eager to go, no less so the shipyard personnel who were to accompany us as official observers praying that their handiwork would not be found wanting. Among these was Leo Sweeney who covered up any forebodings with his characteristic Irish humor. As for my worries, they were the usual sublimated ones of a new commanding officer taking his ship out for the first time. When my Executive Officer reported to me on the bridge "Ship ready in every respect for sea, sir!" I felt at the same time an enormous relief of impatience and great weight of responsibility.

"Very good, Mr. Murphy. Engines will stand by to answer bells. Single up our lines. I will take the conn and get us under way."

I was conscious of a crowd of kibitzing workmen on the dock, watching us with ironic expectancy, like a bunch of disbelievers on the scene of an unlikely miracle. I could not hear what they were saying as they nudged each other with skeptical grins, but it had to be something like, "D'ya think that bucket is actually about to move by itself?" I also noticed that one of the shipyard tugs lying in the neighboring basin had lit off her engine and was idling with her full crew lining her rails, looking on our departure with the resigned expectation of soon being called to our assistance.

All lines were singled up except the after spring. I ordered right full rudder and rang up "Port ahead one-third." Hard on the answering bells came a belch of diesel smoke out of our stubby stack, a tremor of vibration, then the distinct feel of movement. The spring was cast free. *Pueblo* began slowly, surely creeping away from her long confinement on Pier 5.

Some exulting profanities floated up to the bridge from Dave Behr who was in charge of the line handlers. There erupted a mixed chorus of cheers and taunts from the dock, answered in kind from our lower deck. The tug in the neighboring basin saluted our progress with an encouraging shriek from her whistle, but remained on the alert as *Pueblo* glided, not majestically, but with a definite saucy confidence into the Bremerton channel. It was a narrow one and I hoped that we would not meet there the Seattle ferry whose beamy bulk her skipper usually handled with cavalier abandon as he maneuvered in or out of his slip lying hard by the naval shipyard. My luck held. We avoided tangling with the ferry schedule and only had to contend with the usual fleet of yachts and fishing skiffs which we left bobbing in our wake as we cautiously headed for the wider sea room of Puget Sound.

Once clear of the channel, we steamed northward in a state of euphoria for a couple of hours, making 10 knots over placid waters sparkling with sundance, and enjoying ourselves like a party of yachtsmen trying out their new toy. My self-confidence rose as I quickly discovered how easily *Pueblo* handled—much easier than the submarines I was used to and which were always clumsy and sluggish in confined surface waters. Leo Sweeney became completely lighthearted as soon as he convinced himself that neither an internal explosion nor sudden leak was threatening to smite us with shipwreck. We swept by the rugged shoreline with its deeply indented bays and rocky islands crowned by green spires of pines, passed a tiny tugboat dragging an enormous raft of logs against the tide, met a pair of freighters boiling along in a cumbersome race to deliver their cargo to Seattle, and re-

turned the waves of a lot of anglers blissfully trolling for salmon
without any particular regard for the right-of-way.

For this special occasion I relaxed the strict routine of normal
sea-keeping watches. People not otherwise occupied could come
and go as they wanted to visit every part of the ship. Everybody
qualified to steer was given a chance to get the feel of the wheel.
I kept the conn from the flying bridge located on top of the
pilothouse, taking advantage of the best visibility to check out the
gyro compass' accuracy against known ranges, calling down course
corrections through the voice-tube, and trying to keep under control my exuberance over finding myself involved in practical seamanship rather than bureaucratic wrangling. Ed Murphy, whose
duties included that of Navigator, looked up askance at my
exposed position in between uneasy glances at passing shoals and
otherwise busying himself with frequent bearings on prominent
landmarks and navigational buoys.

Down in the engineroom, Gene Lacy and his enginemen
watched and listened to the steady beat of their diesels, worrying
less and less as the revolutions kept churning without a protesting murmur, and finally settling down to puttering over the most
minor adjustments and making reflex swipes of rags over perfectly clean metal. Some of them popped briefly topside for a
glimpse of the magnificent Puget Sound scenery, then vanished
below again, gopherlike, to return their attention to their engines. It is amazing how this breed, in any and all circumstances,
can exclude any diversion to keep their whole being tied in with
the pulse of their ship's machinery. They make a lie out of the
old saw about constant feuding between engineroom and bridge.
Would that captains of the old hemp and canvas Navy had sailing masters as dedicated as today's Engineering Officers! Their
hearts are more constant than the wind!

Our most different individualists aboard, Steve Harris and his
detachment of CTs had little to do besides acquaint themselves
with a SOD-Hut that vibrated slightly with the turn of the
screws, and heaved even more gently as the ship cleaved the wave-
lets, but was otherwise no different an environment than when
alongside a dock. There was no meaningful "research" for them

to do. Their real trials would come later and in the meanwhile they just rode along, trying to feel and act like sailors.

But there was work going on in the galley where lunch was being prepared for eighty men whose appetites were whetted by the invigorating sea air. The accompanying shipyard technicians were extra mouths to feed and usually the Navy, in its unpredictable vacillation between extremes of parsimony and generosity, would charge them cash for their meal. I decided that they were to be our guests and we would somehow juggle the ship's accounts to cover the expense.

So, for a while, it was a grand waterborne picnic with everybody enjoying himself while glowing with pride and goodwill over *Pueblo*. But a sea trial is serious business which determines whether or not the captain will accept the shipyard's work as satisfactorily completed. Right after an early lunch I began putting us through a series of tests. I rang up ALL AHEAD FULL and determined our speed to be a shade over 12 knots; then ALL AHEAD FLANK, which had her working herself up with a lot of thumping and rattling to a churning 12.7 knots; then I tried the opposite to see how slowly we could jog along without seizing up the engines and that turned out to be 4 knots. Finding a wide expanse of the Sound which was free of other traffic, I put her through a series of turning maneuvers with different rudder settings at various speeds, engines changing from ahead to astern. I was pleased with the results and decided that while *Pueblo* was no speed demon, she was nimble enough for us to evade harassment by Communist ships of comparable class. There were reports of minor deficiencies coming to the bridge, but nothing that sounded alarming and unexpected on a first trial. Then, while in a sharp turn, the helmsman suddenly sang out in dismay: "She does not answer the helm, sir! Rudder frozen!"

I immediately rang STOP on the port annunciator while leaving the other engine running full ahead to straighten out *Pueblo's* uncontrolled turn. I next called the engineroom on the telephone (our only functioning interior communication), told them what had happened, to stand by for maneuvering by engines only, and to check and repair our steering engine. Gene Lacy reported that a repair party was already crawling toward the cramped spaces above the rudder, alerted by a sudden explosive noise. While he went to work there, Dave Behr rushed to the fantail with another party to activate the emergency manual steering, but in the meanwhile *Pueblo* slewed crazily from left to right as I jockeyed the engine bells, gradually bringing her to an erratic stop within reasonably safe distance of the nearest shore and shoal. There we proceeded to drift for the next half-hour, our carefree spirit ruined by the indignity of having to hoist the International Signal I AM BROKEN DOWN to our yardarm.

I received various advice, including calling for the Bremerton tug which was so obviously expecting to hear from us, and making ready our balky anchor windlass to keep us from drifting on the rocks. I resisted the idea of having my ship towed back to port from her first cruise under my command. As for anchoring out there, I had discovered that *Pueblo* could be steered fairly well with her twin propellers and felt confident of being able to keep her in deep water. "So this is good training for rigging emergency steering and repairing the steering engine," I announced, trying to sound unruffled, and proceeded to wait for one or the other to be accomplished.

From the fantail I heard the sounds of continuous grunts, groans, cursing and clattering as Behr and his men struggled with the complicated job of fitting a heavy cast-iron tiller to the rudder pintle and rigging the block and tackle system needed to swing it. Those sounds, together with the time they were taking, did little to bolster confidence in the outcome. Then Gene Lacy reported to me that as far as the steering engine was concerned, a cable connecting it to the main rudder-yoke with 30,000 pounds tension on it had snapped. There was absolutely no chance of repair then and there. I considered that with the engines and Behr's monstrous contraption we could limp up the Sound without endangering ourselves or other traffic, but then there was the narrow channel into Bremerton and maneuvering alongside Pier 5 with no room at all for mistakes. The only sensible decision was to swallow my pride and radio the tug to come to our assistance.

She met us an hour later, her crew passing across the towing hawsers with a smug efficiency and politely understanding "we-thought-so" look. As they towed us home, I withheld the bitter comments I felt like expressing to poor Leo Sweeney and his ship-yard technicians. They did not need them as in great dismay they scurried back and forth between the bridge and offending steer-ing mechanisms, observing and taking notes in anticipation of another session of work on their perverse gray beast. The last of the carefree picnic atmosphere evaporated in the gloom all sailors feel when they suspect the reliability of their ship's rudder. There was much worrying and fretting over the steering engine and manual system. Only our CTs found nothing different to do from what they had been doing all day—riding along—except trying to do it without acting too much like the helpless victims of a potential marine disaster.

The sunny skies of the morning clouded over. By late after-noon when the tug was nudging us back into our old berth at Pier 5, a chilling drizzly rain was falling. When she had us secur-ing our mooring lines, I made a last effort to boost our sagging morale with a bit of sardonic humor and exclaimed over our bull-horn, "That's all for today, tug! We're happy to have assisted you back to port." Both the tug's crew and my own laughed, but with a hollow ring.

Three days later Pueblo steamed out for another trial with a new cable replacing the broken one of the steering engine. As before, I put us through various maneuvers with different rudder settings, engine speeds, both forward and reverse. As before, every-thing went well for a while. Then, as before, the helmsman made the same dire exclamation "She doesn't answer the helm, sir! . . ."

For the second time that week we had to go through the whole miserable procedure of steering with the engines, sending Lacy and his repair party crawling into the steering-engine spaces, and Behr with his deck force sweating and cursing over the back-breaking process of rigging the manual system.

But this time the engineers completed the repairs before the seamen had wrestled their unwieldy tiller and block-and-tackle into operation. Both Lacy and Behr characterized their respective jobs as "a real bitch." Behr estimated that, with a little more prac-tice, the emergency steering could be put in operation within twenty-five minutes, given fair weather and no other complications. Lacy informed me that while no cable had parted on this occasion, our steering engine was a unique contraption that had been put together by a Wisconsin elevator company during the boom years of World War II subcontracting. It had little relevance to either hoisting loads from one floor to the next, or steering ships with any degree of reliability.

"Well, damn it all, Gene, it took *Pueblo* to the South Pacific, Korea, and hell and back several times before we got her," I told my Chief Engineer. "Can't she do it again?"

"Yes sir," Gene glumly answered, "if you don't mind stopping now and then to fix it up when it quits. Which it will."

"Okay then, let's see if we can handle it that way!" Gritting my teeth, I got us under way and resumed the trials. Somehow we got through that day without further complications and made it back to Bremerton without having to call for our friend, the tug. And that had to be considered a triumph of sorts, since it meant the first round-trip entirely under our own steam.

CHAPTER V

". . . MATÉRIEL DEFICIENCIES EXIST IN THE SHIP
THAT SUBSTANTIALLY REDUCE HER FITNESS FOR
NAVAL SERVICE, BUT ARE NOT OF SUCH MAGNITUDE
AS TO WARRANT RETRIAL OF THE SHIP.*"—(Extract
from report of Board of Inspection and Survey
for USS* Pueblo, *September 5, 1967.)*

Through the end of July and the entire month of August 1967, we continued *Pueblo*'s sea trials, the usual schedules being one day at sea for every two in the shipyard correcting deficiencies. The Naval Board of Inspection and Survey report, appended a list of deficiencies running to eighty-five pages. In fairness, the majority of the items in that list (which would make horrifying reading to a merchant or even yachting skipper) were either minor ones or deficiencies endemic to a ship of *Pueblo*'s vintage and class. It noted that a clock was missing on the mess deck, that there was a poor arc of visibility for the open bridge pelorus, buckled and deteriorated deck plates, and pointed out the fact that the Commanding Officer's stateroom only had forty-five square feet of clear walking space, rather than the prescribed fifty. The list included virtually all the items I had fought unsuccessfully to have remedied: poor watertight integrity, a lack of adequate emergency destruct system, and lack of stability due to excess topside weight accrued during conversion. Finally, the deficiency list singled out our steering engine which, in spite of every effort to make it reliable, failed us no less than one hundred eighty times in the course of our trials.

It may seem insane to a layman that a ship with so many flaws would be accepted by the Navy and her captain. I did so with a number of reservations and as much protest as I dared make. The standards of safety and comfort for our naval vessels have considerably improved since World War II, as reflected in fine new units such as USS *Gompers*, and our magnificent nuclear submarine and surface ships. But it is impossible to enforce these standards throughout a navy with world-wide commitments and so many ships that less than twenty percent of them are of modern new construction.

If every commanding officer refused to take his ship on operational deployment because of the list of deficiencies in his Board of Inspection and Survey, more than half of our fleet would lie moribund in home port, to the delight of our enemies, dismay of our allies, and negation of our obligations as the free world's last great seapower. Most of that seapower is made up of old ships like *Pueblo*, many of them retrieved from the boneyard and converted, like her, to cope as best they can with the growing complexities of modern naval techniques. In this respect, our Navy's "make-do–can-do" philosophy becomes valid, if for no other reason than stark necessity. After fighting the good fight to obtain the best available for his command, the conscientious naval officer must know when to quit protesting and start "doing"— for his own sake as well as that of his service and country.

Take the matter of *Pueblo*'s unreliable steering engine. After discussions with shipyard officers, including Leo Sweeney, with whom I had a close personal friendship, it became obvious to me that the problems were inherent with the design and that nothing short of total replacement would cure the trouble. The company that had built it was long since defunct so there was no recourse from them. Total replacement was almost as major an undertaking as replacing one of the main propulsion engines, a matter of many weeks and hundreds of thousands of dollars. *Pueblo* would be delayed to the point of compromising a mission which I had been told (and believed) to be vitally important to our defense posture. The Navy was unlikely to stand for that, could always point to *Banner's* success with identical equipment, then appoint a less finicky captain to take my place. In the end, *Pueblo* and her men would eventually go to sea just the same. By now I was too closely tied to her and them to let that happen without me, especially since I was learning during those trials how to live with the deficiencies and cope with sudden emergencies.

With every steering failure, my OODs and I became more adept at controlling the ship with engines alone, the deck force at rigging out the cumbersome manual system, and the engineers at wrestling the machinery back into operation. There was always much cursing and sweating involved when it happened, but then it happened so often that we took it for granted as an inevitable unpleasantness. A quirk of our ship we learned to deal with smoothly and quickly enough that there was no sense of danger —only annoyance. Of course, most of us, including myself, wondered what might be the result of losing our steering in a tight situation, like a crowded harbor, or in a narrow inlet with breaking seas, or when trying to claw off a hostile lee shore. I could only tell those who asked, and myself, "We must be ready to react twice as fast and well . . . and trust to luck."

I developed the same general attitude toward our other problems: overcome those you can with ingenuity, resourcefulness and training; otherwise live with them and trust to luck.

The officers and men of *Pueblo* entered into the gritty spirit of our ship with the usual grumbling and bitching that was more temper than sulk, gradually adapting themselves to her peculiarities. I began moving the crew aboard, especially those who had never experienced *living* in the confined quarters of a small vessel. Bremerton Harbor was a good place to break in on that before contending with rougher conditions of the open ocean. Officers made their staterooms livable and I required that we occasionally give up shoreside comforts to spend a night in them. We took stores aboard and the galley began serving regular meals. I rode Murphy about ship's organization, drills, bills, and training, which were his responsibility to keep in hand. Everybody aboard got to know me better and became aware that I had brought with me from eleven years' service in submarines, a manner of informal camaraderie in dealing with my people, combined with the highest expectation of performance and loyalty. There were a few who resented either one or both of these characteristics, but neither was an affectation on my part. In regard to informality, I considered that we were the same number of shipmates thrown as intimately together in a vessel actually smaller than the average submarine. As for performance and loyalty, it had become obvious to me that our survival depended no less on these qualities than it did among submariners.

Into *Pueblo*'s gradually improving state of organized confusion arrived at this time a twenty-one-year-old ensign, Timothy L. Harris, our long-awaited Supply Officer. In spite of the fact that having *two* Harrises of commissioned rank on our little ship could add to our confusion, I was very glad to welcome him aboard, as was Chief Engineer Gene Lacy who had been Supply Officer pro-tem for the past eight months. It did not matter that Tim's experience was, to say the least, marginal. Commissioned just four months previous to reporting to *Pueblo*, he had in the meanwhile tried his hand at naval aviation and quit upon discovering he hated airplanes. He then successfully completed four crash courses in the fundamentals of Storekeeping, Registered Publications, Cryptography, and Emergency Ship Handling. Never mind! He came to us without a mind full of preconceived notions, marching up our gangplank without lightening his step to keep from capsizing us with his weight, and saluting our flag without flinching over the short distance between it and the jack-staff on our bow. His demeanor was serious, his smile infectious. With a glance at him and his very thin record jacket, I suspected he might become the butt of the usual caustic asides by our senior chiefs about brand-new ensigns; but with the same glance I also decided he would know how to gain their confidence—and mine.

With Ensign Tim Harris's arrival, we were very close to being ready at long, long last to cut our umbilical cord to Pier 5 of the Puget Sound Naval Shipyard and take off on our own on a 1200 mile trip to San Diego where we were scheduled to run our final predeployment exercises before steaming across the Pacific Ocean to Yokosuka, Japan.

We were as ready as we would ever be, but there remained one more comedy of errors to bedevil us—one originating in an event which had taken place thousands of miles away in one of our most distant areas of naval operations.

In June 1967, the smoldering hostility between Israel and her neighboring Arab states flared into the Seven Day War. The Israeli Army, combining the best tactics of Rommel and Montgomery, swept across the Sinai Desert to the Suez Canal, from where they threatened to capture both Alexandria and Cairo and to soundly trounce the United Arab Republic. After one short week, heavy diplomatic pressure brought to bear on both sides resulted in an uneasy truce. The Soviet Union, who had backed and armed the Egyptians, could not afford to have its prestige in the Middle East besmirched by a total Arab defeat. The United States, who had backed and helped to arm Israel, quailed at the prospect of driving the Soviets to the brink of direct intervention by allowing a total Israeli victory. The United States also found itself intimidated by an incident involving the USS *Liberty*.

The USS *Liberty* was a naval auxiliary attached to our Sixth Fleet in the Mediterranean. Like *Pueblo*, she used her venerable configuration of a twenty-five-year-old merchantman as a thin disguise for her sophisticated electronic intelligence gathering capability. USS *Liberty* was larger than *Pueblo* by more than six thousand tons, and carried more than three times the number of CTs who operated several salon-sized SOD-Huts. The Seven Day War represented a tremendous opportunity for *Liberty* to "listen in" on the Egyptians who were Soviet trained and using Soviet supplied communication equipment under full wartime conditions. *Liberty* was cruising miles outside any territorial waters of the Suez area and going about her business of harvesting an intelligence windfall when a flight of Israeli fighter-bombers spotted her and, having been given no forewarning of her presence adjacent to the scene of hostilities, promptly attacked what they suspected might be an enemy commando transport with rockets and cannon fire. *Liberty* was riddled and severely damaged, but managed to limp away with thirty-four of her crew killed and seventy-five wounded. Sixth Fleet rushed in destroyers and aircraft to cover her withdrawal, all fully armed and ready to fight what, with their natural prejudice, they at first assumed to be a Soviet-Egyptian aggression against our ship. But the Israelis were honest enough to own up to their error (for which they later willingly paid a stiff indemnity) and any serious repercussions were avoided. Nevertheless, America's domestic press played up the story for all it was worth. For the first time it alerted its readers to the fact that the U. S. Navy was operating "spyships" in troubled foreign waters.

I read about the *Liberty* incident in the papers and news magazines with more than passing interest. While her mission was different in many ways from ours, there were strong similarities. I immediately thought about the requests I had made for destruct systems and better watertight integrity for *Pueblo*. *Liberty* was in fact lightly armed and large enough to carry specialists to man her weapons. Yet had the attack against her been pressed home by a determined enemy instead of broken off, she would have either been sunk or left an unmanageable hulk to drift ashore. Without adequate destruct and scuttling capability, much of her secret equipment and matériel could have fallen into the hands of a hostile power. It was not lost on me that *Liberty* got into trouble in an area where our Sixth Fleet was alerted by threatening war conditions and responded quickly. *Pueblo* would be operating in the Pacific, which is vastly larger than the Mediterranean, and could not expect even that sort of support in an emergency, since we were intended to operate in more distant areas, closer to unfriendly shores, with a smaller, totally unbattleworthy ship. Our need to be able to destroy our ship was that much greater.

I discussed my thoughts with Steve Harris and our opposite numbers on *Palm Beach*. We worried about them to a degree. But it is axiomatic that officers must have confidence in their service and the high command that issues the orders. I considered (as did my colleagues) that my letters on the subject and the *Liberty* incident, conveyed sufficient warning to high places. If they thought something should be done, it would be. Later I deeply regretted not following through on my initial recommendations of March 1967.

The only positive reaction to the *Liberty* incident came from an outraged admiral with CNO who made no bones about his feelings: "Arm every damned ship in the Navy!" he said, or words to that effect. "I don't want any more of our people coming under attack without being able to effectively defend themselves!" These are noble sentiments to most Navy captains and their crews, but the implications of the admiral's orders for *Pueblo* and

Operation Clickbeetle introduced some subtle considerations which, evidently, CNO did not think about. First and foremost, we were to operate on the high seas where tradition and International Law hold that we had a right to conduct peaceful operations without interference. Secondly, our ships would in fact be engaged in the collection of hydrographic and oceanographic information which, regardless of the fact that it would be a cover, had peaceful applications and connotations. With this in mind, it followed that ships like *Pueblo* should be entirely non-provocative and never appear hostile, or act aggressively. The justification for not arming the AGERs was, of course, that the Soviet Union had been sending unarmed trawlers near (and sometimes inside) our territorial waters for almost twenty years. They fish, but they also have electronic intelligence equipment. Our planners in Washington deduced that the Soviets would respect our rights to engage in similar operations in order to protect their own investment in intelligence-gathering ships, and would keep other Communist countries in line with this policy. Thus any order to arm the AGERs would represent a major change of policy, and a departure from one of Operation Clickbeetle's fundamental concepts.

So when I learned that CNOs orders specified that a 3-inch 50-caliber cannon be mounted on *Pueblo*, I almost threw a fit.

A 3-inch 50 is a piece of naval ordnance which, together with its magazine, fire control, and massive training mechanism, would take weeks to install, require a five-man gun crew which my solitary Gunners Mate 2nd Class was not qualified to train or lead, it weighed so much it was likely to sink us on the spot, and if not to capsize us with the firing of our first practice broadside. Obviously, there was no way to arm *Pueblo* with such a weapon and I did not have to consult the shipyard braintrust to prove it.

In the upsetting turmoil of the *Liberty* incident, CNO had either become confused over the relative sizes of *Pueblo* and *Liberty*, or, perhaps never had time to be bothered with such minor details of the Navy's intelligence gathering program. In any case, I diplomatically tried to explain that the weaponry he was ordering us to carry would be a greater threat to *Pueblo*'s safety than that posed by any potential aggressor and that it was entirely impractical for us to install such a piece and provide gunners for it. I respectfully pointed out that our little ship was already overburdened with men and equipment, making her both crowded and tender. But to show that I was not arguing against arming us on general principle (which I was not), I recommended that instead of the 3-inch 50, we take on a pair of light 20-mm automatic cannons whose weight would be more in keeping with our tonnage, and whose simplicity of operation more suited to the talent already available aboard. In the meantime, I concluded in my carefully composed communication, I would defer action on the original order pending reconsideration.

Within a few days I received an amended order from CNO which in effect approved my proposal to arm Pueblo with 20-mm guns and directed me immediately to proceed to do so. However, when I took this problem to the shipyard authorities, instead of outright derision, they protested that they did not have the items available on the spot, nor the available work force to install the cannon within a reasonable schedule. If I insisted on the 20-mm guns, I would be forced to accept another long delay. Since I knew that CNO had already expressed impatience over our interminable conversion period at Bremerton, I wrote another letter of carefully worded explanation, stating that it appeared impractical even to take aboard the 20s I myself had recommended. A terse reply came back, authorizing me to defer implementation of heavy armament until a later, less pressing time in either San Diego or Yokosuka.

At the time it happened, this business of the Seven Day War, the Liberty incident, and the subsequent confusion over arming the Pueblo did not really cause me as much concern as the space devoted to it in this narrative might suggest. In hindsight, they take on the importance of storm warnings which should have been better heeded. Perhaps I should have been aware that, contrary to my briefings, we could not entirely rely on International Law as a guarantee against unprovoked attack, and that CNO was neither taking a realistic view of the lawless mood of the world, nor paying careful attention to the details of a sensitive intelligence mission being sent forth into it. But this is a postmortem conclusion arrived at long after Pueblo became an em-

1. About four years old

2. Age six

3. Taken at the San Francisco USO while on football tour in high school at Boys Town; pre-game publicity.

4. My mentor, coach, and friend whom I greatly admire. Coach Maurice "Skip" Palrang at Boys Town.

5. "Pete" Bucher, regular starter on the Boys Town High School football team, is a three-year letter man.

My
favorite Aunt
uncle   Lloyd

6. 1945; taken at completion of Boot
Camp, U.S. Naval Training Center,
San Diego, California.

7. Signaling aboard my first ship,
USS *Zelima* (AF-49). I was a
Quartermaster 3rd Class at this time.

8. Wedding picture; June 10, 1950, to Rose Dolores Roling of
Jefferson City, Missouri.

9. When I was a lieutenant and guest speaker at the Boys Town Annual Athletics Awards Banquet, May 19, 1958, with Monsignor Nicholas H. Wegner, one of the truly great men in my life.

10. Weapons Officer and First Lieutenant aboard USS *Besugo* (SS-321).

11. While Operations Officer on patrol aboard USS *Caiman* (SS-323).

12. While Executive Officer and Navigator on patrol aboard USS *Ronquil* (SS-396).

13. USS *Ronquil* (SS-396), my duty station from July 1961 to July 1964.

14. Rose and I, taken in January 1967, two weeks prior to reporting to *Pueblo*.

15. USS *Pueblo* (AKL-44), commissioning day May 13, 1967
Within two weeks our designator was changed to AGER-2.

16. Taken May 13, 1967, Commissioning Day, on 01 level forward of the Pilot house. Left to right: Lieutenant Edward R. Murphy (Executive Officer and Navigator), Carol Murphy, Dr. Jack Osburne (President of City Council, Pueblo, Colorado), Monsignor Nicholas H. Wegner, Director, Boys Town, Nebraska, Rose, LCDR "Pete" Bucher, Commanding Officer.

17. USS *Pueblo* (AGER-2), shown here during pre-deployment training in the San Diego area.

18. The Soviet Ship Peleng, the Russian counterpart to *Pueblo* and other AGERs. She is much larger and has better riding characteristics.

19. Taken at the Yokosuka Officers' Club a few days prior to the last cruise of *Pueblo* at my "Wetting Down" Party celebrating my promotion to Commander. We are giving voice to the *Pueblo* theme song. *Pueblo's* officers left to right: Ed Murphy, Gene Lacy, Tim Harris, "Skip" Schumacher, Steve Harris, myself.

20. Mid-December 1967; first picture as Commander, U.S. Navy.

21. *Pueblo's* Operational Commander, Commander Task Force Ninety-Six COMNAVFORJAPAN Rear Admiral Frank L. Johnson, USN.

22. Lieutenant (Junior Grade) F. C. "Skip" Schumacher, my outstanding operations officer and valued friend.

23. Chief Engineman Monroe O. Goldman was one of the most exceptional men with whom I have had the pleasure to serve. He was a fine leader both before and after the seizure of *Pueblo*.

24. Quartermaster 1st Class Charles Law was outstanding as a leader during the period of captivity and deserves the highest award for valor.

25. Fireman Duane D. Hodges was killed by North Korean gunfire while carrying out my order to destroy classified material.

26. USS *Pueblo* (AGER-2), starboard bow, during training exercises in San Diego.

27. A North Korean Communist Modified SO-1. Two gunboat and submarine chasers of this class were used in the attack and seizure of *Pueblo*. Two MIGS were flown in in their support.

28. A North Korean Communist P-4 class torpedo boat. Four of these were used in the attack on *Pueblo*.

barrassing corpus delicti in the archives of our naval history. In August 1967 it was just another irritation among many that obstructed our progress.

By the first week of September we completed a last sea trial which revealed no further deficiencies other than those we had decided to live with or correct on our own after leaving Bremerton. I signed the documents releasing the shipyard from further responsibility, notified COMSERVPAC that we were ready to proceed to San Diego for our predeployment training and shakedown, applied for Sail Orders, and notified all hands to be ready for departure within a few days.

There followed a last flurry of liberties for our people to attend farewell parties and make arrangements with girl friends and families for a future that seemed less certain than that of most Navy crews. Even before taking us to sea, *Pueblo* had established herself as a capricious mistress. Yet we were looking forward to our long-awaited sailing date, if not with passionate excitement, at least with stubborn determination to meet her challenge and bend her to our will. There were the bittersweet goodbyes with Rose and my boys, telling them to be helpful to their mother and take advantage of whatever fractured schooling they might have to endure this year, telling her to sit tight in her shipyard cottage until developments indicated another move would not be wasted.

Our last party in Bremerton was with our good friends, the Sweeneys. *Pueblo*'s case-hardened Ship's Superintendent, among all the officers of Puget Sound Naval Shipyard, had the best reason to celebrate our departure with wild Irish glee. But he turned out to be rather subdued and prone to sentimental reminiscing about our preposterous experiences together. It was almost as though he would miss us, even though he kept muttering, "Well, thank God you're getting away at last!"

Just after dawn of the following morning, we did.

CHAPTER VI

"USS PUEBLO (AGER-2) IS CONSIDERED READY FOR UNRESTRICTED OPERATIONS"—(*Extract from COMSERVPAC report on Pueblo's pre-deployment training, October 1967.*)

The trip from Bremerton to San Diego was a coastwise one in which we were never far from land, yet far enough to get a feel of the open sea. From the start the weather was variably skittish with intermittent rain showers and a gusty breeze that put a slight chop on the otherwise gently heaving swells. *Pueblo* rolled snappily as she snorted along at a steady eleven knots, occasionally dusting herself with a burst of white spray, but generally acting considerately of her green crew. A few men felt squeamish and after we left the flat waters of Puget Sound, some of the meals were lightly attended or lost over the side. But most of us settled down to gain our sea-legs under what amounted to ideal conditions—not too rough, but not too easy. For me it was exhilarating to feel a moving deck beneath me and hear the wind singing in the rigging after my long stay on the beach. As I always have done, I tried to infect my shipmates with my own enthusiasm for the sea and our ship.

Sea watches were set for deck and enginerooms, four hours on, eight off, around the clock. Work parties tended to the unending maintenance chores, as well as the long list of improvement jobs we had assumed from our Board of Inspection and Survey Report. The Commissary Department provided hot meals out of a galley that no longer gently bobbed, but took occasional pot-rattling rolls. Yeoman Canales was squeezed into a heaving steel cubicle with his file cabinet and typewriter, isolated near the bilges just forward of the auxiliary engineroom, trying to catch up with *Pueblo's* paperwork, while wishing himself back in the office of Bremerton's musty but staid old administration building.

Our detachment of Communications Technicians, landbound office types by nature, braced themselves to dry-run watches in their SOD-Hut while their Officer in Charge, Steve Harris, tried his best to steel them and himself for far worse conditions he knew would come. He came up to the bridge and, squinting watering eyes into the spume, said, "My boys are finding out things may get rough down there."

"That's why we've got to make them seamen as well as CTs, Steve," I told him. "That's why I want them getting out of the SOD-Hut to work the ship once in a while. Some topside action and fresh air will straighten them out and give them confidence."

Making seamen out of everybody aboard *Pueblo* was one of my main problems and I knew it could not be accomplished just by spreading my own enthusiasm and preaching fresh air. They would have to learn by working like seamen at seamen's jobs.

On a small ship such as ours, there was no room for limited specialists who performed their bits on cue while otherwise riding along as passengers. Everybody had to pitch in and learn several skills and be prepared to relieve a shipmate who might either be incapacitated or needed elsewhere. From the moment we left Bremerton, I turned *Pueblo* into a schoolship with the purpose of producing just such a versatile crew. I considered my raw material good, but there were very few among us experienced enough to be effective teachers, and that included my officers.

Murphy as my Exec, should have been fully qualified, but he had served a long period of shore duty before joining us and was quite rusty in the sailor's arts. He needed a lot of seasoning in his job. Steve Harris was technically exempt from any duty besides Officer in Charge of our SOD-Hut, but he had qualified as OOD during the early part of his career and requalified on *Pueblo* while on sea trials and now volunteered to take watches on our bridge, setting a good example in teamwork for his CTs—but he was also long out of practice. Likewise, as our Engineering Officer, Gene Lacy would not normally be required to take bridge watches, but since his enginerooms functioned so smoothly under Chief Goldman, he had gone through OOD school to learn the fundamentals and now made himself available for this extra duty. Ensign Tim Harris, with just one week's course in Emergency Ship Handling, had to virtually be taught seamanship from scratch. This left Dave Behr, sometimes erratic and irascible, but his background as a Maritime Academy graduate, his fairly fresh shipboard experience, and a natural affinity for things nautical, made him generally useful. These were my officers.

However, there was an enlisted man to back them and me—Quartermaster 1st Class Charles Law, who demonstrated an unerring ability to pick out his navigational stars, take an accurate sight through the sextant, breeze through his calculations and correctly plot the ship's position with a superior facile ease. He was that rare bird, a natural-born navigator, a sharp-eyed star-gazer with a computer mind with which he could work miracles of precision with no more than high school mathematics. Chuck Law took pride in his talents which some mistook for arrogance, but I marked him down as a potential OOD.

Even though I was a brand-new captain taking his ship to sea for the first time, I found that years of service in submarines stood me in good stead and easily adapted to *Pueblo*. I let it be known how I wanted things done, then stood aside with the air of one who had no doubt his instructions would be followed. I expected those who did not know their jobs to learn from those who did, and those who knew to freely impart their knowledge to those who did not. I was understanding of mistakes, but not if they were repeated. I spent hours on the flying bridge, occasionally enjoying the comfort of my new captain's chair, keeping out of the way, but observant and available. On changes of watches I checked the chart and log, discussing progress with the OODs, advising, encouraging, correcting obvious errors, but otherwise letting everybody learn by doing. I emphasized my trust by missing no meals in the wardroom, nor any sleep due me in my stateroom.

There were many irritations connected with getting used to living and working aboard *Pueblo* at sea, especially her nasty habit of periodically shedding her rudder control and trying to take off in a wild buck-and-wing through the crests and troughs of the Pacific swells. Yet we had learned how to deal with the problem

and were only slightly slower in wrestling her back on course than
we had been on Puget Sound. She presented us with new ailments as quickly as we fixed her old ones, but not in a way that
suggested she was frail and weary. Rather she acted like a tough
little old lady who kept contriving devious tricks to keep her
family from taking her for granted.

Pueblo frothed along her southward course which I had laid
to parallel the coast from about forty miles off shore. After the
snowy peak of Mount Olympus dissolved in clouds misting her
rugged peninsula, there was no more land in sight, only the endless columns of gray swells marching along in lazy cadence from
horizon to horizon. To the uninitiated, the view became one of a
vast, dull, yet threatening, desert of restless water which shrank
their already small ship to complete insignificance. A bleak
monotony in daylight, a heaving black void at night through
which our progress seemed to have no more substance than the
fading hiss of our wake. Sounds acquired more substance than
matter. The constant, reassuring throb of the engines. The solid
thump of the bow shoving into a sea and parting it with a streaming rush of water. A lively clattering from the galley which, together with a whiff of sizzling pork-chops and French fries,
signaled that things are snug enough to keep catering to man's
eternal gluttony.

As to progress toward our destination, it is only the silent mark
of a pencil on a sheet of paper tacked to the desk of the chartroom of the pilothouse that gives a tangible hint of it. The thin
black line stretches along inch by inch, representing mile upon
mile logged over the sea, with X-marks to indicate fixes determined from sun, stars, or bearings taken by twirling the knobs of
those magic electronic boxes labeled LORAN-C, or SRD-7. There
are erasures here and there, creating bends in the theoretically
perfect penciled facsimile of *Pueblo*'s course and smudges of corrected X-marks that suggest a certain uncertainty in regard to our
exact position. If so, they probably represented very accurately
the occasionally wobbly effects of temporarily losing our steering-
engine, or the overreaction of a green helmsman chasing the
swing of his compass. With very flat zigzags, the courseline
crawls across the chart, passing in turn the invisible 90-degree

bisects of Westport, Columbia River, Coos Bay, Cape Mendocino, then angles inward to pick up a landfall, Puenta del Rey, which we sight very close to schedule. Our neophyte navigators draw sighs of relief and the seasoned ones hide their satisfactions with a shrug over the obvious result of their skill. The thin pencil line has run true all the way across the sheet of paper.

Just below the bald headland of the Marin hills lies the Golden Gate, entrance to one of the world's greatest liberty ports. Having decided to break in both my men and ship in easy stages, I had asked for and was granted permission to interrupt our trip south and turn in through the Gate for a weekend liberty call. You could feel a spirit of joyful anticipation sweep through *Pueblo* who cooperated by behaving herself perfectly as we entered San Francisco Bay.

"Make sure everybody gets a chance to let off steam and raise a little hell," I told Murphy. "You too, Ed."

A couple of hours later, we were safely tied up at the docks of Treasure Island Naval Base and our first liberty party swaggered ashore with all the determination of old salts about to make the best of great opportunities to forget for a while the hard ways of the sailor's life.

We had by then been at sea for just short of three days.

Beyond a genuine desire to give my men a well-deserved break, I had put into San Francisco because this was a city which held many fond memories for me, dating back to 1945, when I first visited it as a player on Father Flanagan's widely traveled Boys Town football team, and followed by a number of calls through the '50s when I was serving in submarines. I had always been intrigued by its wildly contrasting qualities of beauty and squalor, sophisticated culture and bawdy low-life, old-world elegance and new-world vitality. San Francisco, like a worldly patrician lady, maintained an air of respectability while at the same time allowing that a little sin was good for you. I always enjoyed her immensely, but I also suspected that the new promotion list for commanders was due to be published during our visit.

My first stop ashore was at the Base Communication Office of the Treasure Island Naval Base to ask to check through the list and find out if my sometimes obstreperous behavior in Bremerton had eliminated me entirely from the promotion list. I was informed that although the list was due momentarily, it had not as yet been received and, in any case, would probably not be released until after the weekend. So rather than fret about it, I took Gene Lacy and young Tim Harris in tow and headed for the diversions of the big city.

We had some drinks and a sumptuous meal we could ill afford, but thoroughly enjoyed. Then Gene split away from us when Tim and I decided to head for an old hangout of submariners, where I inevitably ran into some old shipmates from the "boats." Several of the people present had made the promotion list and were celebrating. My old friend and shipmate LCDR Ken Riley was there, he said they had found out by making a telephone call to SUBPAC Headquarters and thus getting the information before it was to be released. Not knowing we were to meet, they had not asked about me—but now I knew for certain the list was out. Was I on it? How I wished I knew! There was nothing else to do but wait until tomorrow. These old friends invited Tim and me to join them for supper at Fisherman's Wharf, but I declined. I did not want them to know how nervous I was over my prospects. So Tim and I went on to do the town on our own and were later joined by Gene Lacy. We ended the evening celebrating New Year's Eve at a bistro where New Year's Eve is celebrated every night of the year.

When I awakened next morning in my stateroom, I called Mullin, our Radioman 1st Class, and asked him to go to the base Communication Center to get the promotion list. In the meanwhile I steadied myself with some strong black Navy coffee. When Mullin returned with the list after an interminable half-hour, my heart was pounding with suspense. But there it was! My name on the first page. Among twenty others, I also spotted that of my good friend John P. "Woody" Wood just above mine. I was elated and immediately rushed to the quarterdeck where we had connected an outside phone, and placed a collect call to Rose in Bremerton from *Commander* Bucher. All the years of hard work had paid off. It took several rings before Rose's voice came on the line and even as she accepted the call, I shouted, "Guess what, honey? We made it! I'm on the Commanders selection list. How about that?"

"Whee-ee! Congratulations!"

It was a happy long-distance phone call which stretched into a pretty expensive one, yet one which boosted family morale. That evening, after a full day ashore, Gene and Tim Lacy insisted on a premature "wetting down" party in honor of their skipper's third full stripe. Gene opened up the galley and he and Tim prepared a late snack of bacon, eggs, toast and coffee. Before turning in, I made up a short congratulatory message to my old friend Woody and released it for transmission to his USS *Archerfish*, one of the most famous submarines of World War II, which was currently at sea.

On Monday morning, I delayed our getting under way until about 1000 hours. *Palm Beach* was arriving for a couple of days of Rest and Recreation and I wanted to discuss any problems which Doug Raper might have experienced on the way down from Bremerton. And, additionally, I wanted to congratulate him for his own selection as Commander. In fact, Chuck Clark of *Banner* had also made it, making all of us AGER skippers selected full Commanders. I found that Doug had not yet been informed about his promotion and only knew about it when I shouted my congratulations from the dock as *Palm Beach* was tying up. Naturally he was delighted and we had a brief, pleasant meeting. *Palm Beach* was also having her share of growing pains, but her skipper and crew were in good spirits.

Then came time for us to resume our own course toward San Diego. We cast off the lines from Treasure Island's dock and *Pueblo* slipped out of her berth to head down a mistily glowing San Francisco Bay, the fresh salty breeze sweeping her decks also began sweeping away the cobwebs of yesterday's liberty.

The hills of the white city with its skyscrapers sparkling in the morning sunlight passed to port as the ship skirted close to the Embarcadero with the ever-brooding Alcatraz Island looming to starboard.

Pueblo steamed on toward an ocean still hidden by green and yellow headlands of the Presidio to the south and the Marin hills to the north, then passing beneath the slender vaulted arch of

Golden Gate Bridge soaring more than three hundred feet above her stubby shape. She shuddered as the tide-rips of the Gate swirled and beat against her hull like the ghostly wakes of thousands of Navy ships who had preceded her to sail forth in harmsway through this channel of joys and sorrows. Here the sea always probes with a turbulence of cross-currents which both beckon and warn the outward bound sailor, somehow strangely complementing his own state of mind as he makes this passage out of San Francisco Bay. Beyond lie over sixty-three million square miles of deep ocean, sometimes as pacific as her name—sometimes more violent than any man has survived to tell, and always bounded by distant, fickle mixtures of friendly and hostile shores. For *Pueblo*, as she left Golden Gate astern, there waited as yet nothing but a peacefully benign sea stretching in long smooth swells beyond the foam of Point Lobos.

The pitometer log ticked off the 520 sea miles at the rate of ten and eight tenths per hour and with splendid weather all the way, *Pueblo* actually set a precedent for herself by rounding Point Cabrillo and entering San Diego's spacious harbor ahead of schedule. As a reward for this performance, we were signaled to put back to sea again as there was no berthing space available until tomorrow. So the only ones who got to go ashore then and there were Tim Harris and Storekeeper Garcia whom we landed in our whaleboat to make advance arrangements for supplies and provisions. The rest of us somewhat dejectedly turned away from another lively liberty port and headed toward a Naval exercise area off La Jolla where we used the spare time to conduct man-overboard and night-steaming drills.

Early on the morning of September 22, 1967, the USS *Pueblo* re-entered San Diego harbor and nosed into a vacated berth of the Navy's Anti-Submarine School's docks. Before being sent overseas for duty with any of our seafaring fleets, all Navy ships and their crews are given a period of Refresher Pre-Deployment training. A rigorous schedule of exercises is prescribed for each ship according to its type and its mission, culminating in graduation tests, which are known in the profession as Battle Problems. Inspectors from the responsible Training Command accompany you to sea throughout the training and prowl through your ship with note pads while you execute the various "problems," grading the efforts of every department from engineroom to bridge, galley to Combat Information Center. You have to pass a number of standard tests that apply to any Navy ship, plus those peculiar to your particular type. The curriculum you must assimilate and demonstrate proficiency in has been compiled in volumes of approved manuals which (theoretically) represent years of accumulated experience. The trouble with *Pueblo*'s Refresher and Pre-Deployment Training Program was that there was nothing in the huge library of manuals which even vaguely covered her class of ship. We were the first AGER-2 in their experience. Security had done its job so well that nobody on the staff of Training Command, Pacific (TRAPAC) had any notion of our true purpose.

No sooner had I reported in to TRAPAC to pick up our Pre-Deployment training schedule than I found myself facing the same galling confusion I had in Bremerton—the local authorities were handling us as an AKL (Auxiliary, Cargo, Light), the closest thing in their books with which we had any similarity. Our expensive, brand-new designation of AGER-2 painted in three-foot tall block lettering on our bows meant absolutely nothing to them. They had not been briefed by COMSERVPAC, COMNAVSEGRU or CNO in Washington and, as in Bremerton, I found nobody with the necessary security clearance to be given a full explanation of our unique status. When my face clouded as I read the schedule of standard exercises for an AKL which was handed me by an officer of TRAPAC staff, he asked, "Is it not germane to *Pueblo*'s mission, Captain?"

"Well, no . . . not exactly," I hedged. "You see, we have been modified for special duty and are not equipped for transfer of stores at sea, or any kind of cargo handling and delivery. We are actually a . . . well, a General Environmental Research vessel."

"Oh, well . . . I'm sure our inspectors will take that into consideration and scratch whatever doesn't apply in your case," he said. "It shouldn't affect all the standard drills too much. Right, Captain?"

I wanted to tell him that I had thirty Communication Technicians aboard who needed to practice their electronic intelligence arts in simulated enemy transmissions; that we should be exercised in countering harassment maneuvers, and in sneaking undetected along the edges of territorial waters where there was a lot of sensitive military activity. But I could not even hint at such a curriculum of training. The best I could say was, "Yes, sir. We'll make good your standard drills requirement for an AKL and try to handle any special stuff as we go along!"

The officer assigned by TRAPAC as our Liaison Officer for the duration of the training period turned out to be a tremendous asset to *Pueblo*. Lieutenant (jg) Paul Heubner, was a widely experienced young officer who had come up through the ranks. He went to sea with us each day during the training period and became a close associate of most of the wardroom officers. He was indispensable to us in every request for special and routine training. Before we were to leave San Diego, Paul was impressed enough with *Pueblo* that he applied for a job on board. I was sorry that Navy rules didn't permit him to immediately join us. I would have gladly traded Ed Murphy for Paul and I rather imagine that Ed would have welcomed the change as well. Ed was getting further and further behind in his work. The Ship's Organization Manual was not yet complete, even though I had spent several nights working myself to complete the basic publication. This job had been given him as a primary responsibility when he had first reported. He had not even scratched the surface. Other administrative problems plagued Ed and each increased growing dissatisfaction with him. I felt sorry for him, but I felt sorrier for the ship. Any ship without a good XO is in serious trouble. The problem is compounded when the XO must double in brass as Navigator and Personnel Officer, as is frequently the case in small ships. However, I considered the fact that he had not yet had a chance to demonstrate his ability. After all we had only been in commission for four months. I resolved to do my best to get along without a competent Exec, provided Ed could perform satisfactorily as Navigator. The other officers would be called upon to take up the slack until he found his balance and began to pull his weight.

Thus *Pueblo* entered a period of intensive Refresher Pre-Deployment training as an AKL, a class which has all but vanished off the Navy's list of active ships. It was another frustrating situation to contend with, but one in which I drew upon my experiences in Bremerton and saved a lot of wasted breath over protests and arguments with entrenched officialdom. If there was nothing in TRAPAC's books to measure an "intelligence-reconaissance" ship's readiness for deployment, there certainly was for ship-handling, seaworthiness, navigation, damage control and sea-keeping efficiency in general. In these areas I was determined to shoot for the highest marks, not only to make good grades in TRAPAC's AKL program, but mostly because I knew we would sorely need those skills when operating alone in the Sea of Japan. Toward this end I proceeded to drive myself and my crew throughout the next five weeks.

Since there would be no training in the area of electronic surveillance, and because Steve Harris wanted to update himself on the latest information available on possible missions for us in the Western Pacific, I gave him permission—providing COMNAVSECSTA concurred—to go for briefings in Washington. Orders taking Steve to Washington were received shortly thereafter and Steve departed *Pueblo* and San Diego for about two weeks.

Every morning between reveille at 0600 and 0800, we left our berth at the ASW School dock and joined the procession of assorted other naval units heading out to sea for exercises. Once clear of buoy 5 and Point Loma, we would break away from the crowd and go off on our own to conduct drills in our assigned area, either off the Coronado Islands or La Jolla. Fire drills, boat drills, damage control drills, man-overboard drills—every kind of prescribed drill, including emergency manual steering at which we had already become very proficient since *Pueblo* continuously presented us with *that* problem. The "research department" was not excused from participating and the CTs had to give up their intellectual reading and games of Monopoly or Bridge to learn how to become sailors. I insisted that every officer become thoroughly qualified as OOD, including Quartermaster Chuck Law. Sometimes we stayed out for night exercises, but usually returned to port in the late afternoon after a hard day's work, then worked some more with study periods over manuals or holding critiques in the wardroom. Liberties were handed out sparingly and could be measured in hours rather than long weekends.

There were days when the famous San Diego fog socked in the harbor with its thick gray pall, making most captains and sailors wish to remain snugly at their berth. But I took advantage of this for training with radar navigation under actual blind conditions, getting us under way when we could barely make out our own bow from the bridge. Ed's fog navigation team became quite an accomplished crew. Confidence in ship-handling grew along with increased proficiency. We began feeling ready to take *Pueblo* across the Pacific and probe into distant waters on our mysterious, lonely "research" missions.

Within a month of our arrival at San Diego, Lieutenant Dave Behr was to be detached for separation from the service. I was worried over losing Behr principally because I had no idea what kind of officer would replace him.

For once my worries turned out unfounded. The young man who reported to me, Lieutenant (jg) Frederick C. "Skip" Schumacher of St. Louis, Missouri, was barely twenty-four years old, but had accumulated considerable experience aboard another SERVPAC ship, an AF, and was a qualified OOD. I was quickly impressed by the lively humorous twinkle in his blue eyes and the alert intelligence suggested by his well chosen words. I instinctively liked him and felt he would fit in aboard our peculiar little ship. I lost no time in putting him to the test. "Okay, Lieutenant! Very glad to have you aboard! You will be our Operations Officer—our Communications Officer, Weapons Officer, and our First Lieutenant. Check out with Lieutenant Behr and settle yourself in as quickly as possible over this weekend. On Monday morning you'll take the deck when we go out for exercises."

He gave no hint of being troubled over plunging into his duties without further ado. On Monday morning he took the ship out as OOD and, as I expected, was taken by surprise over *Pueblo's* skittish reactions to her twin screws and sensitive rudder. I had to help him avoid making an impromptu 360 degree turn in the middle of San Diego's busy channel, but he caught on fast and I detected a touch of a natural shiphandler. "Skip" Schumacher, I decided, was a competent officer and welcome shipmate!

During our training period the officers and men of *Pueblo* only got ashore for brief liberties that were scarcely long enough for a meal, a movie and a few beers before having to report aboard again. The handful who had brought families to San Diego found little time to spend with them. But whenever a man had the opportunity to go ashore and unwind from the daily grind, I made it known that I expected him to take advantage of it. Whatever the individual's tastes, I believe in allowing him to satisfy them, giving the "hell-raisers" reasonably free reign, and the quieter types a chance to enjoy their own pursuits.

One night I was awakened around eleven-thirty to be informed that the Shore Patrol had arrested three of my men and had just delivered them in a paddy wagon. They insisted on being brought to me immediately, rather than to wait for mast the next day. They were CTs, Kisler, Wood, and Lamantia, who had enjoyed a movie in downtown San Diego and were looking for a bar where they could have a beer before returning early to *Pueblo*. An SP patrol car had pulled up to the curb and challenged them belligerently. After establishing their identity as naval personnel, the patrolman accused them of being drunk, which they were not. Nevertheless, they were racked back, searched, and hauled down to the "tank" and booked for violating an obscure 11th Naval District regulation which prohibits the wearing of "inappropriate" dress, in this case, levis and sports shirts. When I heard about this and noted that Kisler, Wood, and Lamantia appeared before me entirely neat and sober in appearance, I remembered my own days as an enlisted man in the Navy when overzealous Shore Patrols had ruined a sorely needed liberty. I got dressed in uniform, routed Ensign Tim Harris out of his bunk to join me, and went to pay an official visit of protest at Shore Patrol Headquarters.

The SP Duty Officer, a lieutenant (jg) was horrified at being confronted at the bleak hour of 0130 by an outraged ship's captain determined to redress the harassing of three of his crew. I began by bracing the arresting patrolmen and chewing them out for their bullying tactics. When the jg pulled out a thick file of 11th District regulations and read me the pertinent paragraph, I lit into him too.

The SP Duty Officer cringed slightly and said: "That is the word I go by, sir. Nothing else."

"Nothing else? Not even the morale of the men who make up this Navy? I'd like to talk to your CO about *that!* Get him on the line please."

The jg looked at me as if I were out of my mind. "It's zero two-ten, sir," he explained to me. "The District Shore Patrol Commander is at home, asleep."

His patronizing tone further infuriated me. "I know what god-damn time it is, Mister! I took the trouble to leave my ship in the middle of the night and come down here to deal with the harassment of my crew. So get your CO on the line right now, Mister!"

The outranked jg had to pick up the telephone and dial a number. When a voice answered, I took the phone and identified myself, gave a sharply succinct recapitulation of the circumstances of my men's arrest and my strenuous objections to its unfairness. The sleepily irritated voice of the District Shore Patrol Officer incredulously echoed back the details, said something to the effect that he resented being awakened out of a sound sleep over such a trifling case. I forcefully assured him it was not trifling to the members of my crew who had been arrested, and therefore, not to me. I rang off, signaled Tim to follow me, and returned to *Pueblo*. The Shore Patrol dropped the insignificant case against my CTs and decided to go after bigger game. Their captain.

The next morning, I fired off a letter to COMELEVEN, attaching to it affidavits from the CTs concerned, and including my own recommendation that the regulations about civilian dress be brought up to date. I promptly received verbal orders to report next morning to the Chief Staff Officer of COMSERVGRU ONE.

He was a grizzled senior captain ensconced in his shipboard office next to the one occupied by the commodore commanding COMSERVGRU ONE. He explained that the Chief of Staff at COMELEVEN had put me on report with the commodore after having his ear bent by the outraged District Shore Patrol Officer. What was my explanation? I stated it as forcefully as I had at the SP station, if in more restrained language. "I expect a lot of hard work out of my men, sir," I told him, "and I can't stand by and see them harassed for no good reason. If they'd gotten drunk and broken up some joint, I'd personally bust them. But for wearing levis and loud shirts?"

"The lieutenant (jg) who was duty officer reported to his superior that you were drunk when you barged into the SP Headquarters," the Chief Staff Officer said.

"Negative, sir!" I retorted.

The Chief Staff Officer drummed his fingers against the polished surface of his desk, nodding and shaking his head in one ambiguous gesture. "Well, all right. I can sympathize with your grievance. But on the other hand we can't compromise discipline by ignoring a dress regulation that does not suit us."

"No, sir. My point is that the regulation is unreasonable and should be changed."

The Chief Staff Officer again nodded and shook his head in one rolling motion. "Yes, you may well be right about it, but on the other hand, wrong when we consider that our Shore Patrol must enforce all the regulations in the book. I'll report our little talk to COMELEVEN and hope we can let it go at that. Well, Bucher, just show a little more discretion in the future. I know you are very busy on a refresher course for your ship. An AKL, isn't it?"

"No, sir, an AGER."

He seemed puzzled, but then exclaimed, "Oh, yes, of course. Oceanography and all that."

Hard by the ASW School docks lay the Ballast Point Submarine Base, home port of SUBFLOT ONE with which I had put in many years of service as a junior officer. Submariners being the loyal tight-knit clan they are, I found myself still welcome to use their Officers' Club, appropriately named the Ballast Tank. The privilege was extended to other *Pueblo* officers in my company and everybody took advantage of it whenever time permitted. They had no trouble at all in fitting in with the freewheeling atmosphere of this exclusive submariners' lair. It was not really out of ingratitude that we repaid their hospitality by pulling off a caper which must be recorded as one of the Navy's more notorious cases of "fine art" theft, entirely comparable, we thought, to the theft of da Vinci's Mona Lisa from the Louvre.

The Ballast Tank is a fairly modest establishment as Officers' Clubs go, being physically quite small and simply decorated. There is no opulence or stuffy formality. The only inspirational décor was a magnificently proportioned reclining female nude dominating the bar from a position above the row of bottles, hanging in tantalizing sight of every customer.

I remember suggesting one night that we steal the Ballast Tank's famous nude. We must have been struck by the sheer audacity of the scheme and, unable to resist the challenge, set about plotting its execution, perhaps jokingly at first, but then in all seriousness. The bar was usually well attended by members and, of course, always in charge of a reasonably alert bartender. Pool players would be playing or kibitzing in the adjoining game room. A well coordinated plan had to be worked out, followed by a couple of weeks of patient waiting for the right opportunity.

One slow evening Tim Harris, Gene Lacy, Paul Heubner, and I were among the few customers in attendance. We were playing pool, but actually alert to the great chance which seemed imminent. When the bartender left his post for a few moments to pick up empty glasses in another room, I followed him and delayed his return with some casual banter. Gene diverted the attention of some other club members. Paul watched the game room flank. Tim vaulted over the bar, deftly removed the painting from its hanger and scurried out with it through a side door. It took him less than a minute to deposit the loot in the trunk of our car and return with a look of dead-pan innocence. It was a perfectly executed operation. Nobody noticed what had happened, least of all the bartender who returned to his post without even missing the masterpiece which had left a gaping empty space above his shelves.

For two glorious days, Our Lady of the Ballast Tank adorned the bulkhead of *Pueblo*'s wardroom. For that brief time we enormously enjoyed her company, both from the point of view of her lifelike charms and our great sense of accomplishment in abducting her. All hands were permitted pilgrimages from the Petty Officers and crews for awestruck worshipful glimpses. Not since the days of Louis XIV's ornate ships-of-the-line had any Navy vessel carried such a lusty decoration! In the meanwhile, the theft had caused an uproar at Ballast Tank. The outrage spread from the Steward to the Club Officer, and upward through the entire command structure of Ballast Point Submarine Base. The next time I went to visit their Club, I found the conversation was about nothing else. I joined in the discussion with my own speculations about this brazen crime. But then an old shipmate from the submarines dropped me a pointed hint:

"The ONI sleuths have been called in on the case. They know Bucher is in port!"

So the nude was quietly returned to her rightful place, and the case was discreetly dropped, though well-remembered. The Ballast Tank's masterpiece was promptly wired with a sophisticated burglar alarm system which rang a bell if she were molested.

Meanwhile, *Pueblo* presented us with innumerable petty ailments and deficiencies which had to be taken care of by our Electronics Technician 2nd Class R. L. Berens, the CTP. Engineering, or Deck Force in order to make the old girl compatible with her assignment to the operational fleet. Our odd, ungraceful appearance may have caused caustic cracks along the waterfront, but as we completed our training, nobody could fault *Pueblo*'s performance. All the hard work paid off when we steamed out with a team of inspectors on our final "battle exercise." To quote from their official report:

Ship Control	79.00	(Good)
Navigation	93.00	(Excellent)
Seamanship	83.70	(Good)
CIC/Radar	85.00	(Good)
Communications	71.00	(Satisfactory)
Electronics	(Not observed due to classification of Department)	
Main Propulsion & Electrical	91.19	(Excellent)
Damage Control	70.49	(Satisfactory)
Final Average for Training; 81.28 (Good)		

These were considered high grades for a tough course which many ships flunked and the final notation on the report stated that "USS *Pueblo* (AGER-2) is considered ready for unrestricted operations." I was given to understand by the inspectors that we had attained the highest grades that had been won by a SERVPAC ship in the past six months. I was proud of *Pueblo* and my men at that moment. There were, however, many areas with which I was not myself satisfied. I comforted myself with the fact that our long trip to Japan would present opportunities for further seasoning of the men and ironing out a lot of the kinks. I congratulated my officers and men on successfully completing their training period but warned them that I expected even higher standards. We then moved away from the ASW docks to the Naval Station for final predeployment upkeep. The crew were given liberal liberties and once again, while technicians swarmed aboard to puzzle and curse over our obstinately contrary steering engine, my thoughts now returned to Rose and the boys.

I had had very little time to even think of my family who were facing the gathering gloom of a wet Northwestern autumn. I tried to write them a couple of letters a week and we talked on long-distance phone for a few precious minutes every ten days or so. Rose was carrying on like a good Navy wife, but I could tell that she was feeling restless and depressed. She would be far happier in Southern California where the weather was milder and there were more of our old friends from the Submarine Service. I was negotiating with BUPERS to have her and the boys join me in Japan, and although the mills of bureaucracy were grinding sluggishly, the prospects seemed good that the move would be permitted at government expense. Meanwhile, I alerted Rose to pack everything into the car and meet me at the Seattle Airport where I would arrive on a Friday afternoon, then drive them down on the long run South which had to be covered during my last weekend before deployment.

This move went according to plan and turned out a providential one. There was no Navy housing available in San Diego, but I put up my family in an apartment hotel beautifully located on Mission Bay and hoped that the drain on our finances would soon be eased by their transfer to Yokosuka, Japan. Mark and Mike threw themselves ecstatically into surfing. They appeared somewhat hippie-like, but at least they were fanatics in a healthy outdoor sport, and I had great pride and confidence in them. Rose blossomed out in beauty and buoyant spirit, settling into the little apartment (really meant for two, not four) and made those moments I could give her between preparations to sail, both warm and tender.

The last week flew past. There was plenty of work to be done up to the last moment, but I tried to give my men as much time as possible with their wives and sweethearts. The hour of parting came on the misty morning of November 6, 1967.

The women left behind on the dock faded out of sight but not out of mind. *Pueblo*'s bow turned toward the mouth of the harbor, quickly working up to her cruising speed of 11.5 knots, her propellers churning the steady 180 revolutions that were to continue for the next eight days and nights. Passing the Coronados and a couple of destroyers working ASW exercises, we plowed on toward deep placid open ocean, course 255 degrees, for Pearl Harbor, Hawaii, lying two thousand three hundred miles away.

The major reason for breaking our trans-Pacific voyage at Hawaii was, of course, that *Pueblo* did not have the range to safely make it all the way without refueling. But equally important were the briefings that I expected from COMSERVPAC and CINCPACFLT staffs headquartered in Pearl Harbor. They held some of the several strings that bound our forthcoming operations.

The passage turned out a pretty fair one with everybody adjusting well to working and living in the close quarters of a very small ship which kept ceaselessly bobbing and rolling as she cleaved through even the most placid sea. Routine watch-keeping and training drills alternated with maintenance chores. Our neophyte OODs seasoned themselves with serious celestial navigation. To them, *Pueblo* was a lonely plodding speck in the vast sea, moving hundreds, then more than a thousand miles from the nearest land. Quartermaster Law showed his usual competence and I knew he would be officially qualified to take the deck when we started the longer leg across the even vaster reaches of the Pacific between Pearl and Yokosuka. Our cook, cheerful black Commissaryman 2nd Class, Harry Lewis, turned out fine meals in his tiny galley. Our new Ops Officer, Skip Schumacher, gained my complete confidence and turned out to be a delightful shipmate with his competence, his wit and intellect. Things went so well that when we reached warmer latitudes, I took the time to come to ALL-STOP for a thirty-minute swim-call, traditional aboard submarines on long patrols. The *Pueblo* people were a bit hesitant at first about diving into the mid-ocean deep and mindful of the large sharks we had fought off La Jolla. But sharks are reasonably rare far from land and easily spotted in clear, calm seas. It was an exhilarating interlude of the kind not experienced by the crews of carriers, cruisers, or even larger auxiliary ships.

During the trip to Hawaii, our steering engine quit on an average of twice a watch, and although we were by now completely expert at quickly making repairs, the whole process became a bore. By the time we made landfall of Diamond Head, I had written out a Casualty Report on the system. This meant I needed major repairs before being able to proceed. The plan called for a two-day stay at Pearl, but I now was prepared to allocate whatever time was necessary for local Ship Repair Facility to repair the pesky steering engine.

We entered Pearl Harbor early in the morning of November 14 and I was very pleased to be allocated a berth at the Submarine Base where, once again, I would be near my beloved boats and expected to find friends waiting at the Officers' Club. I spent several hours on routine administrative matters, and in making certain we would be given immediate attention by Ship Repair Facility, before leaving for the various headquarters for briefings. These began with COMSERVPAC where I was not surprised to find that many of the key people did not have the necessary security clearance to be fully appraised of our purpose. Consequently there was little useful information they could give me. Because we were the first ship ever to call at Pearl under the mysterious new designation of AGER, there was tremendous curiosity about us. I invited all of those for whom I considered it important to get to know the ship to come aboard for a visit, including COMSERVPAC's Commanding Officer, Rear Admiral Edwin B. Hooper, who regretfully declined, but said he would send his Chief of Staff instead. Soon there was a steady stream of visitors aboard *Pueblo*, ranging in rank up to captain. I arranged in most cases for the clearing of our classified spaces to the extent where they could at least be shown them and given a broad picture of their function, including the SOD-Hut. This was justified in my mind by the obvious fact that some of these people had "a Need to Know" (one of the standard official reasons for revealing secrets) in their capacities as members of the staffs of Headquarters who shared responsibility for our operations.

I gave COMSERVPAC a rundown on our problems insofar as they could be openly discussed, but by now I had learned to do so with understatement rather than impassioned pleas. Among my requests, was permission to reduce our required load of classified publications and papers which I believed to be excessive. I felt "the Need to Know" doctrine of security should be supplemented by a "need to carry" corollary. It seemed logical that *Pueblo* should carry only a library of classified material absolutely essential to her operation. From Steve Harris's reports, and some of my own observations, I had already come to the conclusion that a lot of our classified documents were extraneous and would be a potential source of embarrassment, if not compromise, in case of some unexpected disaster. I was told to shoot off an official letter on this point, which I did. I later received a negative answer.

CINCPACFLOT is another Headquarters in our chain of command, and comprises a huge staff complex which exercised, directly and indirectly, control over every U. S. Navy ship operating in the Pacific Ocean, whether off Vietnam, in the Sea of Japan, or the far reaches of the Indian Ocean. Its area of responsibility in our global defense system is almost beyond conception. I was as courteously received here as at COMSERVPAC, and found the same curiosity about my little ship. Few within this staff seemed sure about what we were supposed to accomplish under their aegis. CINCPACFLT staff retains much of its old operational flavor and harbors some salty types with a keen understanding and concern for the problems of Commanding Officers of ships at sea. Among these was LCDR Irv Easton, a submariner filling an intelligence billet on this staff

and with whom I had been acquainted for several years. I knew
I could get straight dope from him, so I went to him first. It was
he who first told me that our initial operations would be off the
coast of North Korea, mentioning that *Banner* had touched there
on a couple of occasions and been totally ignored by the KOR-
COMs. (As opposed to her severe harassment experiences on
operations near Communist China and off the Soviet's Russo-
Siberian areas.) He would, he promised, make available all the
Banner patrol reports for my study and in the meanwhile asked
me to consider the assignment to be in the nature of a shakedown cruise, in which we could check out our intelligence-
gathering systems under optimum, minimum-hazard conditions.

This sounded acceptable to me. I knew very little about
North Korea beyond what I heard and read about the Korean
War which had ended in an uneasy armistice over fifteen years
ago. They had no navy worthy of the name, were armed with
obsolete castoff hardware. Yet, I was moved to ask Commander
Easton: "What happens if they attack us when on station outside
their claimed twelve-mile territorial limit? What kind of support
can I count on in such an emergency?"

He gave me a quizzical look which suggested that he had given
this question some consideration of his own without coming up
with any really positive answer. "From *Banner's* experience, which
is the only one we have, you can expect harassment, but actual
violence is considered highly unlikely to occur. They can be recklessly aggressive, but still smart enough not to challenge American seapower with a handful of subchasers and PT boats. That
would be quite different from a few infiltrations and firefights
along the DMZ. But you might as well hear what the thinking
about it is from higher echelon." He was not passing the buck,
but obviously understood my concern and wanted me as fully
briefed as possible. And so he escorted me to another office and
introduced me to Captain Charles M. Cassel (now Rear Admiral)
who was Assistant Chief of Staff for Operations for CINCPAC-
FLT. I put the same question to Captain Cassel and received almost exactly the same answer, except that he added something
to the effect that:

". . . in the unexpected event of a serious attack against

Pueblo, it would probably happen beyond the range of immediate assistance. We have just so many combatant ships and can't begin to cover every part of the Far East. But you can count on everything being done as quickly as possible to come to your assistance and that in any case a retaliation would be mounted within twenty-four hours. Contingency Plans for such an occurrence are written and approved. We consider the risk to be nominal if not nonexistent."

"I understand, sir," I told him. He also said, based on *Banner's* experience, that the possibility of getting into serious trouble was remote. Obviously they had plans for some form of help in case the unexpected happened. This was good enough for me.

Also based in Pearl Harbor, as a component part of CINCPAC-FLT staff, was the Naval Security Group (NAVSEGRUPAC), who had a direct interest in our mission, inasmuch as he was Steve Harris's immediate superior together with his SECGRU People working in our SOD-Hut. We both called on them for special briefings and I brought up the point about operating the intelligence-gathering function as a separate detachment as against an integral ship's department; I had been promised a department in Washington, D.C., but the former system still prevailed and it caused me considerable worry. They informed me that a "position paper" was coming out on our relationship soon, but when it did, it left matters exactly as they were. I found out that it was NAVSEGRUPAC itself who had objected to any change because they felt they had better control with Steve acting independently as Officer in Charge—the fact it left me, the captain, with *less* control over my own ship (for which I was ultimately, totally responsible) did not bother them. Of course, the cooperation between SOD-Hut and bridge had been excellent, but then we had yet to get into real intelligence-gathering operations and the decision was contrary to what the SECGRU parent organization in Washington had led me to believe it would be when I visited there early that year. However, I had no choice but to accept it in good grace for the moment. I planned to keep strong pressure on the Navy to bring *Pueblo* into the real Navy as soon as possible. Meetings, briefings and conducting official tours through *Pueblo*, made my three-day stay in Pearl extremely busy. I was constantly scurrying from one headquarters to the next with only tantalizing glimpses of Honolulu's glittering white waterfront. Only in the evening could I cut loose from my duties for a while and give vent to my natural sailor's yearning for a lusty fun and song-packed liberty. Maybe because time was so short, I lived a bit too well through those few hours I could permit myself. Even before leaving San Diego, I had flashed ahead a request for reservations at Duke Kahanamoka's famous nightclub where we threw a boisterous all-wardroom party on our first night in port. We were joined by an old submarine shipmate, Commander John Shilling and his wife, Angie, but otherwise it was a stag affair in which we could give over our full attention to food, drink, and the talents of the famous Don Ho followed by Tahitian dancers. Tim Harris took off his shoes to join in a Hula dance and permanently lost them, so that hours later, as dawn was dimming the bright neon lights of "the strip" with brighter strokes of pink and blue, he returned over *Pueblo*'s gangplank, barefooted. A bit later that morning when the first high-ranking visitors showed up to familiarize themselves in person with our strange AGER, I was grateful for Ed Murphy's abstentious ways. My Executive Officer did a good job of taking over as host while his Commanding Officer needed an extra hour to recoup from the effects of the night's revelry.

On the second evening of our stay in Hawaii I decided I would join the Chiefs' and enlisted rates' turn to go out on the town and I wanted to make certain they would fare no worse than the officers had. Gene, Tim, and I joined with their happy group of about twenty-five where they had picked out a lively spot on "the strip" where such a party was in progress with complete, frenetic abandon. Some naval officers are critical of others who join their men on liberty because they feel to do so, denigrates their officer status. They consider that officers, specially a skipper, must maintain a barrier of aloofness and detachment from their men in order to keep discipline; the premise is largely based on the old saw about "familiarity breeding contempt." Well, aboard diesel submarines and on 170-foot AGERs, familiarity is inevitable. I have always felt that I could only attain superiority of status by demonstrating superior ability. I look for an occasional camaraderie with my men (many of whom on the *Pueblo* had come under my command with far better social and educational background than my own) to increase mutual respect and solidify the team spirit of our ship.

At the end of the third day, after the men from the Ship Repair Facility came up weary and frustrated out of our main engine spaces with dubious assurances that the steering machinery would function long enough to get us to Japan, we cast off our lines from Pearl's Submarine Base, steaming out of the harbor and turning on a westward course in a losing race with the setting sun.

When you look at a chart of the Central Pacific, you will see a large sheet of blank paper representing the world's widest stretch of unbroken ocean before it eventually washes up against the islands of Japan and Asiatic Continent. In the right-hand (eastern) area of the blank space, there is a splattering of gray blobs which are the Hawaiian Islands chain, the links diminishing in size and growing farther apart before ending in a cluster of tiny atolls, among which is Midway Island. Most likely they named it Midway because it lies very close to the International Dateline. By the time *Pueblo* had come that far and Midway was only a half-day's steaming north of our position, we had had so many of our usual steering breakdowns that I considered aborting the voyage and putting in there for more major repairs. I discussed the matter with my Engineering Officer and there was little doubt in his mind or mine that there was good cause to abort; unreliable steering is among the few valid reasons a captain can give for refusing to continue his assigned voyage. But, on the other hand, Midway had minimal facilities, being a ring of coral reefs barely breaking the surface of the deep and able only to support a small naval base and the runways of an airport installation.

So my decision was to continue on, dealing as best we could with our cranky steering engine, and hoping that if the worst happened, we could wrestle *Pueblo* all the way to Japan on "manual emergency steering" from the fantail.

To keep up morale, and before plodding into colder water, I held a couple more swim-calls which had by now become a very popular form of recreation. On the last of these, Radioman 1st

Class Mullin was injured when one of his shipmates accidently landed on top of him while involved in horseplay. We carried no doctor aboard, but I had great confidence in the ability of our enlisted 1st Class Corpsman, Herman Baldridge, who was intelligent and through many years of experience at this job had accumulated a great deal of medical knowledge. He diagnosed Mullin's injury as a possible broken back—a case we had no way of dealing with effectively aboard *Pueblo*. All we could do was to strap the patient into his bunk, relieve his pain, then radio back to COMSERVPAC in Pearl for advice. We were instructed to rendezvous with the USS *Gompers*, the same brand-new destroyer tender we had come to know at Bremerton, and who had started her WESTPAC deployment a couple of days behind us, but was rapidly catching up to our position. She carried doctors and medical facilities that amounted to a small hospital. In the meanwhile we could do no more than continue on our course and wait for her superior speed to close with us.

As we proceeded westward, the smooth balmy weather turned into gusting rain squalls which quickly solidified into a steady downpour of rain out of leaden skies. The wind blustered around the compass and settled into an increasingly hard blow which warned of an approaching storm-front. *Pueblo*'s always lively motions turned violent and there came a sudden loss of interest in Cook Harry Lewis's fine food as many of our crew discovered they were not as yet the seasoned sailors they thought themselves to have become. In the driving rain and flying spume, visability was reduced to a couple of miles, but eventually *Gompers* showed up as a glowing "blip" on the outer range circles of our radar screen, then, a half-hour later, was sighted visually, a gradually swelling shape that appeared amazingly steady among the broken lines of the tumultuous seas. Soon she closed enough to appear as a massive gray block of steel, easily shedding the waves breaking against her towering bow and flanks, and only taking occasional ponderous rolls that made us look and feel by comparison like a cork caught in a maelstrom. Our combined navigation had brought us to an accurate rendezvous, but the foul weather was making hazardous the next steps to succor the injured Mullin lying in the wildly gyrating crew's forward berthing spaces, groaning with pain as he strained against the lashings of his bunk. We exchanged recognition signals, and then *Gompers* flashed to me:

STAND BY IN MY LEE TO RECEIVE OUR DOCTOR

I personally took the conn from the OOD on the exposed flying bridge from where I had always considered we had better control of the ship. Pray God that our steering engine would not pick this time to throw one of its fits! Some very critical shiphandling was imminent.

I cautiously maneuvered *Pueblo* into the lee of *Gompers'* starboard quarter, rising like a swaying wall above us, and jogging us on station there with just enough sea room to avoid a collision in case of steering failure. The big destroyer tender launched a whaleboat which came bobbing alongside of us, managing a close pass that allowed the doctor to make a perilous jump onto our welldeck before it had to veer clear. This in itself was a hairy piece of small-boat handling, but luck was with us. In a few moments, the doctor was below, giving Mullin as thorough an examination as he could in the wrenching, confined berthing space and with those basic instruments he had been able to carry aboard with him in his "black bag." He confirmed Baldridge's diagnosis of a possible broken back and ordered that in spite of the risks of the transfer, Mullin would have to be moved to *Gompers'* fully equipped sickbay for X-rays and whatever treatment a more thorough examination called for.

It was impossible to virtually throw the patient into *Gompers'* wildly heaving whaleboat without endangering his life. The only answer was to strap him into a stretcher which had to be loaded aboard our own small boat before attempting a tricky launch out of its davits. I only had a handful of seamen who came close to being qualified to do this with any degree of safety, but it had to be done. I nudged as close as I dared to the protecting (but still dangerous) bulk of *Gompers*. Miraculously, my prayers were answered! With Ensign Tim Harris in command, our boat crew performed admirably, the skill of the few supported by the sheer guts of others inspired to give their all to help a sick shipmate; far below in the main engineroom and on the exposed fantail, other men were poised instantly to leap into action if there came a sudden, critical, loss of steering—but even that cantan-

kerous mechanism decided to cooperate with the miracle. Our
boat cleared its falls without capsizing and made it across to
Gompers where it was expertly hoisted aboard, boat, patient,
crew and all, for safe delivery on her spacious deck.

Another tense moment came when our men were relaunched
for the return trip—but our luck still held. We retrieved them,
battered, soaking wet, but proud over their accomplishment.
Radioman Mullin was now in good medical hands. As soon as
the hazardous transfer was accomplished, the huge *Gompers* and
little *Pueblo* drew apart, exchanged complimentary signals of
thanks and mutual admiration, then became separated by a
widening gulf of churning sea as the giant left the dwarf behind, driving onward with majestic stability into the gathering
storm.

Within a couple of hours of our initial rendezvous, we were
once again a lonely tossing speck beating across the face of an
angry sea.

As we kept moving westward and angling to the north on a
course which gradually took us out of the subtropical zone, the
weather steadily deteriorated. *Pueblo*'s peculiar configuration (not
really designed for storms of the high seas) made her tricky to
handle in gale-force winds and heavy wave action; the helmsman
had to stay on the ball every second and anticipate the ship's
violently erratic reactions in order to avoid a dangerous roll. The
Norwegian whale-catcher or long-distance trawler designs (as
adopted by the Russians for their world-wide intelligence operations) are really the ideal small ships for taking the roughest
conditions of the open oceans, certainly far more resilient and
responsive to the helm than our old AKL which had been
originally intended for coastwise or island-hopping supply missions where shelter could be found in case the sea became too
rough. Once the Hawaiian chain of islands was left far astern,
there was no such shelter available in the Central Pacific for
Pueblo. We plowed on, carefully gauging each mountainous
graybeard as it surged up ahead, meeting its onslaught at exactly the right angle, going completely blind for a moment as a
cloud of spray exploded over the entire superstructure, shaking
off tons of water as we slid into the following trough, then

gathering wits and momentum to absorb the next blow. We found that by handling her carefully and never relaxing our vigilance, *Pueblo* proved herself seaworthy for all her age and obsolete design; worries about foundering in a fatal roll diminished, but not that of the consequences of loss of steering until a couple of them happened and we were able to cope with it. Then remained only that of the attrition of seasickness and the bruising wrenches of the violent rolls and pitches which was taking a fearful toll in all departments, first among our less experienced, then affecting even our few veteran seamen upon whose efficiency so much depended. There was havoc below decks, specially in the galley, when all sorts of gear broke loose and flew around with a clattering and clashing counterpoint against the constant roar of wind and water. As all exterior openings of our decks were dogged down, the interior living and working spaces became foul with the stench of vomit and humid from the many small leaks trickling in from constantly submerged decks. Cook Lewis gave up trying to put out hot meals and concentrated on sandwiches, producing a semblance of hot soup and coffee out of his sloshing urns. The CTs wedged themselves into their heaving bunks, leaving only to stagger to the heads and retch. The deck and engineering force stood their watches while fighting to keep their footing on the pitching decks and their nauseated stomachs from turning themselves inside out. The officers were no less affected and many an OOD had to make an undignified rush for the bridge railing and empty his guts into the wild wind and spume. Soon only Gene Lacy and I were attending "meals" in the wardroom.

Ironically, as a boy raised far from the sea in the Western plains and mountain country, I have never been plagued by seasickness. During my eleven years of service with submarines, I had experienced many wild storms in the Pacific when I had to stand watches in the exposed bridge tower of a boat which for some reason or other had to remain surfaced and absorb all the punishment of tumultuous waves; but as a rule, when the going became really rough, our skipper would order a dive into the always calm deep so we could proceed on our mission in reasonable comfort regardless of the violent weather raging above. Aboard

the *Pueblo* we had no such option. For us the deep was the enemy
and the surface, no matter how roiled, our friend. I felt terribly
sorry for my men who were loyally trying to function while in
the debilitating throes of seasickness and those who, if not constantly vomiting, were wrenched and buffeted against machinery,
bulkheads and railings as they tried to keep on their feet and
perform their duties. For the many aboard who had never before
experienced such conditions, it was a brutally hard introduction.
I required our OODs to forecast what lay ahead of our course by
tuning in the coded synoptic weather broadcasts transmitted
every six hours from Guam and from this information, to plot
our own weather charts. This was exacting work, involving the
breaking down of numbered codes and transposing them into
meaningful lines, arrows, and figures on the chart, particularly
difficult for our green OODs who had to accomplish it while
nursing their own miseries of nausea and bruises. But it was good
training and enabled us to pick our way around and through the
worst fronts blocking our course to Yokosuka.

In contrast to our fickle steering engine, the pair of old refur-
bished diesels never faltered even in the worst pitches and rolls.
Their reassuring vibration drove us through the worst of it. We
called them Gene's "Rockcrushers" and marveled over how they
kept churning away through gyrations which might well have
torn them loose from their beddings. They were the steady twin
hearts keeping us alive and moving ahead, a credit to our Engineering Officer and his enormously competent *alter ego*, Chief
Goldman.

As we fought our way closer to Japan, the weather grew worse
rather than better. It became impossible to conn from the flying-
bridge which was entirely open with no protection from cascades
of spray that grew colder and colder as we curved northward out
of our basic westerly course. The pilothouse was comparatively
snug refuge in spite of the crazy angles of 50-degree rolls and its
windows rippling and diffusing visibility through constant streams
of water with which the wipers could not cope. The clatter of
gear breaking loose below became alarming. Seasickness became a minor irritation as compared to the fear that a giant
wave would rise up out of the sea and finally catch us off guard,

bringing about a fatal roll from which we could not recover. In its painful way, it sharpened our senses in dealing with the peril. And in the end *Pueblo* and her men prevailed over the elements.

During the afternoon of December 1 we sighted the hills of the main Japanese island of Honshu. We soon came under the lee of Point Nojima Saki and the long headland which guards the entrance to Tokyo Bay. *Pueblo* shook off her last green sea, began to settle down, and steamed battered but unbowed through the narrow mouth of the broad bay, next to San Francisco, the largest natural harbor in the world containing three major ports and shipbuilding centers, Yokosuka, Yokohama, and Tokyo.

It was great to feel a reasonably steady deck beneath our feet once again, even though, after seven consecutive days of storms, our inner-ears played tricks on us so that we staggered about in a drunken fashion as if still subject to violent wave action—some call it *land*sickness after a long sea voyage, but its effects are mild and slightly comical as compared to the real thing. It was well after dark when the lights of Yokosuka glinted and drew closer off our port bow. As we turned into the channel, every man not on watch below turned out on deck, eagerly looking toward the brightening lights of our destination, some amazed, some already growing cocky over having made it. Even I was unashamedly feeling satisfaction over the accomplishment. I was determined to make a perfect berthing at our assigned dock, a worthy first entrance to *Pueblo*'s assigned home port.

But I blew it. I went past our assigned berth. When I realized it, I had to back down full. At this point, the steering engine threw its final fit and quit completely. Even though I was familiar with the port, I dared not risk my approach with engines and emergency steering alone. We were forced to make our entrance with the assistance of a tug. There were many familiar faces looking up from under the dock lights at my bridge, laughing rather than applauding.

CHAPTER VII

"I SUGGEST YOU KEEP YOUR GUNS COVERED AND POINTED DOWN, OR BETTER YET, STOWED BELOW DECK."—(*Rear Admiral Frank L. Johnson COMNAVFORJAPAN to CDR Lloyd M. Bucher during briefing at Yokosuka, December 1967.*)

Yokosuka is a teeming Japanese town which has been a naval base and shipbuilding center since the emergence of Japan as a major sea power at the turn of this century. The flagship of Admiral Heihachiro Togo's fleet, which decisively thrashed the Russians in the Russo-Japanese War of 1904–5, is enshrined here as a national monument. The largest Japanese carrier ever built, the 70,000-ton *Shinano*, was launched out of Uraga Dock at Yokosuka for her brief life before being sent to the bottom by the American submarine *Archerfish* during World War II. Many of the heavily populated and industrialized areas of Tokyo Bay were destroyed by air raids during World War II—but not Yokosuka. During the worst bombings in 1944–45, the hard-pressed residents of Tokyo and Yokohama used to say: "Move to Yokosuka and live!" The rumor persists that Americans deliberately spared the city and its waterfront because they wanted to take it over intact for use after the war, which is exactly what happened. For the last twenty-five years Yokosuka has been virtually occupied by our naval forces, first by right of conquest, then by provisions of our peace treaty with Japan. It has served for many years as our naval base in the Far East.

Yokosuka has a fine natural harbor lying close to the seaward exit of the beautifully protected Tokyo Bay. The waterfront is indented by basins lined with piers and graving docks that can handle anything from submarines to carriers. The structures of machine shops, warehouses, headquarters buildings, officers' and enlisted housing and clubs, hospital, detention barracks, and a department store-size PX, are tightly packed together between prominent steep, bushy little hills which poke up out of the shoreline to five or six hundred feet above the rooftops. These hills are honeycombed with underground galleries (a Japanese specialty) that were used as bombproof storage, hospitals, and command posts during the last war, some of which we still maintain for the same purpose. Immediately north of the enclave lies the huge shipbuilding yard known as Uraga Dock (where *Shinano* was born) where today skillful Japanese shipwrights are busily welding together supertankers for the world's oil trade. They would make that monstrous battleship look like a dwarf.

The whole area is bounded by high fences or walls which, in a way, seal it off from Japan proper. Beyond the impressive main gate, guarded by smart U. S. Marines who are invariably courteous but very strict in examining the credentials of everybody coming and going, lies the town of Yokosuka itself with its crowded warrens of streets, alleys, shops, bars, restaurants, honkytonk joints, and all residences.

The Yokosuka naval base evolved into a very desirable foreign home port and billet for American Navy personnel assigned to duty in the Western Pacific during the years since 1945. It developed magnificent facilities for work, living and recreation, the pace being relatively leisurely in between bursts of urgent activity when the Cold War heated up during the Korean War, the Quemoi-Matsu confrontation in the Strait of Taiwan, and the Vietnam conflict. Families of officers and men were allowed to join them at government expense and were provided quarters which ranged from comfortable to luxurious, according to rank. Even during inflation, the cost of living on the base was inexpensive. Everyone assigned to Yokosuka could buy anything in the local PX cheaper than at home, including such items ranging from Kansas City steaks to hi-fi sets.

I had first visited Japan and Yokosuka as a young enlisted sailor in 1947, then repeatedly after receiving my commission when submarines to which I was attached were deployed to WESTPAC, and finally for the two and a half year tour on the staff of SUBFLOT SEVEN's Yokosuka headquarter. When I returned as captain of *Pueblo*, I had been away for a couple of weeks short of a year with happy memories fresh in my mind and looking forward to renewing old friendships. I had come to love Japan and her people.

Pueblo had reported in to Yokosuka over eight months behind her original schedule and, in my opinion, she was far from ready to go on her first operational mission, which could not be more than a few weeks away. Besides repairing and refurbishing the ship after her long and turbulent passage across the Pacific, there were a lot of details to be attended to in preparation for that mission. We could afford no diminution of effort toward that end.

When I made the announcement, soon after securing at our dock, that liberties would be brief and strictly rationed, that no families could immediately be sent for, and that work, work, work, had to be the order of the day for the next several weeks, I could feel the rumblings of resentment running through the ship like the shudders of a sprung propeller shaft. I no more liked making the decision than those who had to accept it.

First on the agenda was the steering engine; Gene and I made it clear to the ship's superintendent of the base's Ship Repair Facility that his artisans were charged with its repair, and that we could not go on operational patrol until it was operable. Within the hour, a team of Japanese mechanics were crawling into cramped spaces examining the machinery with amazed and amused chattering among themselves. They emerged with optimistic gold-toothed grins. What they had seen down there had obviously greatly tickled them, while at the same time offering an opportunity to show off their skills. "Very strange machinery to steer," the foreman announced, obviously never having seen anything like the defunct Wisconsin elevator company's product before in his life. "Can do! Will fix!"

The Commanding Officer of any ship arriving in a new port, particularly her home port, for the first time traditionally pays a call on the senior officers in command of the many activities that make up a large base, and particularly those officers who will provide specific services to his ship. I therefore set up a schedule of personal calls, the first of which was made on my Operational Commander, Rear Admiral Frank L. Johnson, Commander Task Force 96. Admiral Johnson was also Commander Naval Forces Japan (COMNAVFORJAPAN), which was primarily a housekeeping command involving responsibility for U. S. Naval Shore Activities and small craft on the numerous islands of Japan and Okinawa.

I had met Admiral Johnson when I served on the Staff of COMSUBFLOT SEVEN in Yokosuka. He had once been a famous destroyerman, having commanded the USS *Fletcher* in a number of actions in World War II. He emerged from that conflict with a chest full of medals including two Silver Stars! His great war record brought him to flag rank at the early age of fifty. Some years later, when I reported to him as captain of *Pueblo,* much of the look of a professional destroyerman had given way to that of a genial banker.

Admiral Johnson had other commands that were activated from time to time, depending upon their need. Inasmuch as his staff contained a complete intelligence support section, it had been determined by higher authority that he was to have operational control of intelligence missions conducted within his sphere of operations, thus *Banner* and *Pueblo,* being primarily intelligence collection platforms, were always under the operational control of Admiral Johnson's CTF 96. In fact, now that *Pueblo* had joined *Banner* in the Far East, Admiral Johnson's Task Force 96 consisted of exactly two permanently assigned ships, AGERs 1 & 2, USS *Banner* and USS *Pueblo.* Very little was known by the average naval officer or enlisted man concerning AGER operations, nor by other commands of Yokosuka. We made every attempt to keep the fact of, and the details of, AGER operations quiet. I must emphasize here that the need for restricted knowledge of AGER operations was directed for efficiency *only.* At no time were these ships ever operated illegally. They were never ordered to break international laws respecting the operation of ships on the high seas. In fact, they were specifically ordered always to operate well outside the "claimed" territorial waters of any potential enemy.

Many questions involving missile-carrying submarines had been the subject of articles questioning the effect they, and their long-range missiles, might have on the principle of freedom of the seas under International Law.

I had read unclassified articles on this subject and discussed these matters with Admiral Johnson after we exchanged pleasantries. He was aware of the possibility that the AGERs might henceforth be armed. He was concerned about it and told me so. I agreed that visible armament would alter the basic premise of AGER operations. However, this was certainly not a problem for the captain of a small ship, whose concerns were much simpler and more immediate than debates over International Law and its interpretations. I told the admiral of my problems and he promised to have his staff investigate each of them and seek solutions where action was necessary.

I reported that work on the steering engine had already begun. Then I proposed a modification to *Pueblo*'s flying bridge. "Admiral, it's the only safe place to conn the ship from—particularly when we can expect to have shadowing ships assigned to us by whatever country we happened to be working. The pilothouse has just too many blind spots, and I am aware of the many close calls *Banner* has already had, in addition to the ramming incident she experienced at the hands of the Russians."

"What can we do for you to make it a safer operation?" he asked.

"I would like some kind of screen built of lightweight material that would protect the Officer of the Deck from the weather and afford proper visibility. Perhaps lucite or something like that, so as not to affect the ship's stability."

The admiral pressed a buzzer on his desk and called in his Chief-of-Staff, a Captain Forrest A. Pease, USN ordering him to look into all of my needs and make sure they were taken care of. I was given every impression of keen concern, even one of pride over his little fleet of intelligence-gathering ships. He several times mentioned the fine work *Banner* had been doing singlehandedly in the Sea of Japan and urged me to consult closely with her captain, my old friend Chuck Clark. "And I expect you to ask me and my staff for whatever you feel you need," he said as we parted. "I'll be inspecting your ship before you leave on your first mission and want her in every respect to measure up to our standards, yours and mine. Right?"

"Yessir! Thank you, Admiral."

It was a pleasant meeting and in the course of the next five weeks we were to have several more. Yet, I felt an uneasy feeling growing that his genial interest in my problems was not really backed up by a solid understanding of them. Perhaps Admiral Johnson had been too long removed from ship operations to think instinctively like a ship's captain. Since my *Pueblo* and Chuck Clark's *Banner* were his whole "navy" it was natural that he would give us more than cursory attention. Yet our peculiar function as intelligence-gathering platforms intended for operations close to hostile coasts was basically alien to his training: he would have preferred us to be a pair of destroyers assigned scouting patrols in the Sea of Japan. He must have been pleased that *Banner* had been extraordinarily successful in completing sixteen missions, despite severe harassment by Red Chinese and Soviet Russian naval units. The *Banner*'s successes had apparently lulled him and all others into a false sense of security as Operational Officer in Command of the project and would in the end become his undoing—as well as my own, since I had also become imbued with the repeated admonition: "*Make it like the* Banner!"

The steering engine was being taken care of. The lucite weather screen for the flying bridge was quickly approved and work started on it. I next tackled several other necessary improvements that were on my mind. Some form of de-icing system was essential for survival in the winter conditions in the Sea of Japan. Gene Lacy and I discussed the possibility of installing a system of steam-nozzles with which to melt ice, but *Pueblo* was a diesel-powered vessel with only enough boiler capacity to provide for normal heating and making fresh water. It proved to be impossible to generate enough steam to de-ice her through jury-rigged nozzles. This left chisels and mallets wielded by flesh-and-blood sailors—a trying and hazardous system of doubtful efficiency when the decks were constantly awash with freezing seas. But it could be supplemented with that age-old anti-freeze: rock salt. I asked Tim Harris, as our Supply Officer, to order six hundred pounds of it. A truckload of cumbersome blocks, which are commonly used as salt-licks for cattle and worthless for any other purpose, was delivered on Christmas Eve. Eventually these were exchanged for bags of the granulated variety.

About this time I became somewhat concerned over Steve Harris's detachment of Communication Technicians. Steve shared my concern. Most of them had been with the ship since the previous March without having any opportunity to practice their highly specialized electronic surveillance and monitoring techniques. While they had gained some experience in shipboard life, *Pueblo* may have shaken their confidence more than bolstered it. In any case, it was reasonable to suppose that a lot of our CTs had become rusty in the practice of their arts and could use some refresher training. Steve planned to make use of some special facilities for training his men which happened to be close by. In his pleasant and cooperative manner, he assured me this would be taken care of.

I eagerly awaited the return of *Banner* from one of her missions and as soon as she arrived, lost no time in getting together with her captain. Chuck Clark, who excepting Lieutenant Bob Bishop, was by now the most experienced AGER skipper in the Navy. In fact, he was the only captain who had been running consecutive missions during the past several months. Doug Raper's *Palm Beach* I discovered had suffered a total steering breakdown on her way to her Atlantic assignment, had to be towed into Panama for major repairs, and was by now even further behind schedule than *Pueblo*. I did not hesitate to attach myself to Chuck and have my officers and key chiefs do likewise with their opposite numbers aboard *Banner*. Here, far more than from the briefing teams of various Headquarter staffs, was the source of the first hand information we needed. It was freely given with a spirit of camaraderie that immediately made us feel part of the *team* in spite of our late arrival.

Chuck had written me personal classified letters about his experiences already during our pre-commissioning days in Bremerton, but now as I listened to him man to man in his stateroom (a duplicate of mine) the impact was far greater. During some of the harassment situations he encountered with Red Chinese and Soviet armed vessels, he carried a small tape recorder with a microphone attached so he could keep up a running account of the action as it developed; he let me listen to some of these tapes which retained all the immediacy of the incidents. *Banner* had obviously been coolly and skillfully handled, but she had also been lucky. One occasion which specially impressed me occurred in the China Sea, with hostile ships circling her, when *both* engines broke down, leaving her drifting helplessly while the engineers sweated blood to regain propulsion. A Seventh Fleet destroyer some four hundred miles away was started toward her assistance and Fifth Air Force fighter-bombers were on strip alert to provide air cover in case the CHICOMs made a serious attack. The support was comforting, but too far away for immediate effectiveness, one hour for the aircraft and nearly twenty for the destroyer to reach her position. The tension was agonizing until her engineers got her old "rock-crushers" going again and she was able to pull out of a very tight situation. Chuck confirmed the fact that on the one occasion he had passed along it, he had encountered no hostile reactions at all off the North Korean coast. Near the Soviet and Red China territorial waters (he *never* intruded) they invariably sent out shadowing units, either armed auxiliaries or destroyers, which did not hesitate to intimidate him with maneuvers which threatened collision and signals which included HEAVE TO OR I WILL FIRE backed up by guns manned and ready to shoot. In each case his only defense had been to stick as closely as possible to the rules of the road as they apply to International Waters and proceed on his course and business according to his orders: in each case, the hostile forces had stopped their harassment just short of outright attack. It was nerve-wracking, but I decided that with the detailed experience he was passing on to me, I could steel myself to play the same game of Chicken. At least I knew what to expect out there. What disturbed me more than the prospects of harassment, were his accounts of the great difficulties in establishing communications with Japan at times when there was urgent need to let our headquarters there know what was going on. On one occasion it had taken *Banner* over twenty-four hours to raise anybody on the communication circuits. In order to try and solve this problem we held joint conferences with specialists from Yokosuka's and Kamiseya's Com-

munication Center and attended by staff officers of COMNAV-
FORJAPAN. These brought out a lot of technical discussions in
the jargon of the science, a resolve to explore various improved
techniques, but resulting in my resignation to having to rely on an
imperfect system.

During these conferences I once again brought up the matter
of *Pueblo*'s enormous load of classified material, and formally
requested I be permitted to reduce it to a "hazardous duty allowance of cryptological publications." This staff turned out more
sympathetic to the idea and promised to endorse the request and
expedite authorization—which came through finally a day before
sailing time.

Meanwhile, I conjured up visions of serious predicaments which
might turn out very embarrassing to my ship and the United
States itself. My main propulsion engines had performed well, but
they were as old as *Banner*'s which had quit on her at a critical
time. If that happened to *Pueblo*, would we be lucky enough to
get them going again? We had learned to live with our balky
steering engine, repair it at sea and in the meanwhile steer with
the emergency manual, or by propellers alone, but without main
engines? . . . Without being able to raise help by radio? . . .
Without capability of avoiding harassment by Communist ships?
. . . What then?

It was at this time that I began thinking of providing myself
with some cans of TNT, with which to scuttle *Pueblo* as a last
resort in a hopeless emergency.

Gene Lacy provided answers to my questions about ways of
purposely sinking *Pueblo* by pointing out that there was no quick
way of doing it since she was not equipped with seacocks. A slow
flooding of the engineroom would first kill propulsion, then
electric power generators needed for communications, ending with
an hour or two of wallowing, unless the two fore and aft watertight bulkheads burst. The only solution I could think of was to
blow holes in her hull with explosive charges, insuring effective
scuttling within minutes. Recalling Admiral Johnson's offer to
help solve any and all problems, I took this one to him, explaining
my anxieties and the solution I envisioned. He listened with his

usual, courteous attention, but he seemed to become tense at the
mention of that ugly word *scuttling*, as if suppressing a horrified
reaction to the idea of losing one of his ships by such inglorious
means. Nevertheless, he made no direct objection. Instead he
pressed a buzzer which produced his Chief of Staff, Captain Pease,
and turned the whole unpleasant business over to him. Captain
Pease took me into his own office from which he telephoned the
Commanding Officer of Yokosuka's Supply Depot, passing me,
and the buck, on to him. The Commanding Officer of Yokosuka's
Supply Depot introduced me (again by telephone) to the Officer
in Charge of Azuma Island Naval Ammunition Depot who listened to my story with sympathetic interest and then told me he
would immediately send over one of his Explosives and Demolition
experts to survey the situation aboard *Pueblo*. The Explosives and
Demolition expert showed up without too much delay. He was
a young lieutenant (jg) who went over the ship and came up
with the recommendation that we install thermite bombs in strategic locations, including the SOD-Hut. My reaction was one of
doubt.

Thermite bombs are really incendiary devices which are virtually
impossible to extinguish once triggered off and whose 2000–3000
degree heat can burn through iron plate like a burning cinder
through a pat of butter. There would always be a worry about
accidental discharge, a misunderstood order, or the deranged action of a disturbed mind which could produce disaster within
seconds. But this was the suggestion of a supposed expert, so I
asked Skip Schumacher to check it through the various regulations
governing such devices on U.S. ships. My suspicions were confirmed when he came up with the answer that thermite bombs
were prohibited. This clinched my belief that TNT charges, stable
and safe to handle, and which could only be detonated with due
preparation, were our obvious solution for quick destruct and
scuttling. But when I asked the Officer in Charge of Azuma Island Ammunition Depot for TNT (easily available to most construction contractors everywhere), I was informed that he had
none in stock and no immediate way of procuring any—thermite
yes, TNT, no.

I did not quite give up on this. Recalling that 50-lb. TNT canisters were standard aboard submarines I had served with, I went to my old friends at SUBFLOT SEVEN to try and scrounge some from them. Lieutenant Angelo Di Filippo who was their Supply Officer and Lieutenant Phil Stryker, Engineering Officer, both tried to accommodate me by checking with submarines of their Flotilla being sent home to the States and who might spare their charges. They were unsuccessful in their effort. My final attempt was to consult with my colleague on *Banner*, Chuck Clark, and when he told me that he carried no scuttling explosives whatsoever, I decided it was time for me to give up. All I could accomplish by pressing it further was to upset Admiral Johnson and his staff by giving them the impression they had a skipper on their hands who seemed obsessed with the capability to blow up his own ship. I didn't want to cross the boundary between chronic worry-wart and outright nut!

Besides there were other matters for me to busy myself with. Part of our intelligence-gathering mission, quite aside from the electronic (ELINT) type conducted by the CTs of the SOD-Hut, was the visual observation and identification of Communist-bloc naval and merchant shipping that we might encounter along the way. To sharpen our eyes in recognizing various types of ship configurations, I required all officers as well as QM1 Law and our ship's photographer, PH1 Lawrence Mack, to attend evening sessions in our wardroom where we flashed silhouettes out of our library of ships identification manuals. I also spent some time with Photographer Mack to make sure he had the camera equipment necessary to record on film the visual contacts we would encounter. His darkroom which had to be jury-rigged in the 1st Class Petty Officer's head, was workable, but hardly an ideal laboratory set-up. But Mack, like most dedicated professional photographers, was extraordinarily adaptable.

I was concerned with navigation in the distant unfriendly areas where we were designated to operate and although Ed Murphy was officially my Navigator, I assigned to Quartermaster Chuck Law (now a fully qualified OOD and navigator) the job of obtaining all the special charts we would need. This allowed Ed to be relieved of the watch bill and to concentrate on all the administrative work and implementations of captain's instructions which are the normal duties of an Executive Officer.

I had received notification from the Bureau of Naval Personnel shortly after my arrival at Yokosuka that since my promotion to Commander, I was considered too senior in rank to command *Pueblo* and to expect reassignment by May of 1968, probably back in the United States. This meant that Rose and the boys could not join me in Japan for the short time remaining until then, and that we would have to spend Christmas and the next four months apart. It was a disappointment, of course, but then we were sustained by high hopes for the future and whatever my next assignment would bring. I now had the additional incentive of wanting to turn *Pueblo* over to my successor in excellent shape and expected that by May we would be veterans of at least three operational missions. We had already been in touch by letter (he was stationed in Vietnam) and I began informing him—to the extent that I could—about the ship and her work.

Then came Christmas, the main holiday of the year celebrated by Americans no matter where in the world they may find themselves. Our base at Yokosuka was no exception. The ships in port vied with each other in turning their masts and rigging into Christmas trees shining with strings of lights, the drab headquarters and depot buildings were festooned with decorations, genuine Christmas trees and wreaths appeared in the clubs where egg nog imported from the good old USA was served on the bars. The housing of those lucky ones whose families were with them became as bright with the Yuletide spirit as any community back home. Duty assignments and routine watch-keeping had to continue, of course, but commanding officers made sure they were as light as prudence allowed and that everybody would have a chance to attend a fair share of the many parties thrown around the base which more than ever was made to feel like a piece of America in her most nostalgic and festive season. Santa-San is now well known in Japan, and he came to Yokosuka and even aboard little old *Pueblo* where we invited a group of Japanese orphans to make his acquaintance and receive Christmas gifts from this strange round-eyed bearded gentleman in a funny red suit (played to perfection by Quartermaster Law). In the galley, Cook Lewis outdid himself in producing a Christmas dinner with both the traditional turkey and ham, and all the fixin's. A lot of us suffered pangs of homesickness, veterans of WESTPAC no less than those on their first overseas deployment, but with the prevailing spirit of cheer and goodwill among shipmates, there was no need for any man to feel lonely or left out.

I managed to put a call through the overseas-telephone service to Rose and the boys on Christmas morning from Flip and Sanna Di Filippo's house where I had been their overnight guest, and for a few minutes we bridged the five thousand miles separating us with an exchange of loving greetings and happy banter; for each of us it was a mixture of happiness and sadness to hear each other's voices from so far away. No matter how hard you try to sound jolly, there has to be a melancholy quality to the exclamation "Merry Christmas!" under such circumstances. But I could not allow myself to fret over it after the silence of hanging up the receiver. Instead I took a vicarious pleasure in sharing the celebration with comrades who had wives and children present to make it a real Christmas—the families of Lieutenants Di Filippo and Stryker and LCDR Jim Jobe took turns in graciously making me part of their own happy chaos around their trees on Christmas Day. That took a lot of the sting, but not all, from missing Rose, Mark, and Mike.

As I had expected, the arrival of dependents had its effects on the efficiency of my officers and men who had to be given time to arrange for their families to set up housekeeping. This was specially evident with Ed Murphy who suddenly made himself very scarce around the ship as he devoted himself more to his duties as a husband and family man than to his job as Executive Officer of *Pueblo*. Our relationship became more strained. My mounting dissatisfaction with his performance brought me to the stage of seriously thinking about having him relieved of his job, yet I kept hesitating to take such a drastic step which was bound to have a devastating effect on the career of a fellow officer. I procrastinated, telling myself I owed him the chance of proving himself on at least one mission before bringing the matter to a head. Meanwhile I came to rely more and more on Gene Lacy, Skip Schumacher, Tim Harris and Quartermaster Law to take up the slack.

Steve Harris and his "research department" concerned me, if for no other reason than that the success of the entire effort depended upon its efficiency. His SOD-Hut was *Pueblo*'s only reason for existence. Our relationship was cordial in spite of our being totally divergent personalities, and it was supported by a respect and understanding of each other's problems. From mutual acquaintances, I found out that Steve had done fine work in his field. For my part I was convinced that Steve was doing his best, was sympathetic toward my concerns, and tried to alleviate them in every way he could. He assured me that his men were receiving the refresher training they needed and were ready to perform their jobs. When I brought up the matter of obtaining Korean language interpreters in support of the ship's effectiveness, he agreed they were necessary to have while gathering intelligence along the North Korean coast and would get on the problem right away.

The productive cover for *Pueblo*'s primary mission was the collection of oceanographic data. This made her in actual fact a perfectly legitimate oceanographic research ship whose cruises were expected to produce useful scientific data from remote seas. Two civilian oceanographers reported aboard at this time, Dunnie R. Tuck, a cheerfully competent and witty extrovert who brought with him the experience of two trips on *Banner*, and a slight wiry young man named Harry Iredale, who was his assistant. I liked both of them immediately and knew they would have no difficulty in fitting themselves in with we Navy types. We not only had to provide them with bunks and lockers for their personal use, but a workable laboratory facility which, by necessity and design wound up in our auxiliary engineroom. We also found storage space on our cluttered decks for their Nansen cast bottles and Bathythermographic gear near the special winches provided to operate them. Dunnie Tuck and Harry Iredale had officer-status aboard by virtue of their respective high Civil Service ratings, but the only benefit they got out of this was the privilege of our wardroom.

After a New Year's celebration in Tokyo, I found myself, on the morning of January 2, 1968, back facing the realities of *Pueblo*. We were going to keep our assigned sailing date of January 5, 1968. Time was growing short and there were several loose ends that needed tying in order to make *Pueblo* as ready as she could be made. Quartermaster Law had obtained the charts we needed, and I had firmed up the track I intended us to follow in order to accomplish our primary and secondary missions. To accomplish these missions we were equipped with various sensitive electronic receivers and recorders, professional photographic equipment and personnel. I was doubtful that we would see much since we were restricted by our orders from approaching land or offshore islands, closer than 13 nautical miles. Our assigned operating area was bounded to the north by Chongjin (close to the Russian Vladivostok area) and to the south by Wonsan which lies several miles above the DMZ (Demilitarized Zone) which divides North and South Korea. My plan was to steam to Sasebo (Japan) where we would call at the U. S. Naval Base there to have our fuel tanks topped off and if he was then in port, I would report to our Administrative Commander, CONSERVGRU THREE, Rear Admiral Norvell G. Ward, then proceed through the Tsushima Strait, hugging the Japanese side so as to avoid Soviet naval units who we knew to be operating there. I then planned to work my way north through the assigned operation areas, respectively, Mars, Venus, and Pluto, remaining 30–40 miles offshore, then closing the coast to within 15 miles and working south through the OP areas. I informed our COMNAVFORJAPAN Staff liaison Officer Lieutenant Edward Brooks about this plan, but apparently caused some confusion when I requested that he and other staff members brief me, and other ship officers, on probable conditions and activities in the Sea of Japan. It turned out that COMNAVFORJAPAN had not been in the habit of briefing *Banner* in this way before sending her forth on her missions. Nevertheless, I insisted on it and suggested to Ed Brooks that the Staff brief us on current and expected weather and ice conditions in the Sea of Japan, navigational hazards and aids that were known, and commercial and naval activities of all foreign origin that we could expect. In particular I wanted my officers and myself briefed on all that was known about North Korea. We had been provided with a couple of books on the subject but I wanted to hear the latest information available from those on COMNAVFORJAPAN Staff who were current on the subject. This meant additional work for Lieutenant Brooks, but he scheduled the briefing.

I invited Chuck Clark to attend and all of my officers who were cleared for the type of information that might be discussed. The briefing commenced at 0900 on January 3 in one of the intelligence briefing rooms at COMNAVFORJAPAN Headquarters. The chief briefer was Captain Thomas Dwyer, USN, who was the Chief of Staff for Intelligence for COMNAVFORJAPAN. Other officers from the intelligence section of the Staff followed Captain Dwyer and all of their comments were pertinent. Then we were all surprised by a visit to the briefing by Admiral Johnson. "Any further questions, Skipper?" he asked me.

"Sir, I believe that we have been well briefed by these various members of your Staff. We have undoubtedly benefited from their words of wisdom. Thank you very much."

Then Chuck Clark mentioned, "Admiral, we still have the continuing problem of initiating communications from many of our operating areas. I feel that it must be improved or some day it could result in a terrible situation."

"Captain Dwyer, let's look into this problem in detail," Admiral Johnson said.

"Yes, sir."

Further discussion of communications problems ensued and I mentioned, "I would prefer operating with a hazardous duty allowance of publications."

"Look into that as well, Tom," the admiral said impatiently.

"Yes, sir."

Then Admiral Johnson brought up the subject of the .50-caliber machine guns then being installed aboard both *Banner* and *Pueblo*.

A few days earlier, a priority message from CNO had been received directing the arming of AGERs with .50-caliber machine guns as a temporary step toward the eventual provision of 20-mm guns. The revival of the plan to arm AGERs explained Admiral Johnson's attendance at our briefing. He was worried about having them aboard in visible places. They would, in short, be provocative and could cause serious problems.

"Have both installations of the .50s been completed?" he quickly asked of no one in particular.

"We are finishing up our installation," I replied.

Chuck Clark said his own installation was just beginning, but he wasn't sailing for a couple of weeks.

Admiral Johnson's eyes narrowed somewhat and he spoke very carefully.

"I am against arming your ships. It could lead to trouble for you which you are not prepared for. Where have you placed the mounts?" he looked at me.

"I have two mounts forward on the bow on either side of the anchor windlass and one mount aft on the centerline, O-1 level, but only two guns, Admiral," I said.

"I suggest you keep your guns covered and pointed down, or better yet, stow them below decks," the admiral continued.

Chuck Clark declared that he would stow his below. I thought about it and said nothing. I felt that if CNO wanted these guns aboard, then why the hell should we carry them below. I said as much later to Chuck, but he was of the opinion they could cause less problems if they were stowed below and I really couldn't argue with him. He had the experience and I had none.

"I'll be down to look your ship over tomorrow, Skipper," Admiral Johnson said, as he prepared to depart the briefing area.

"It will be a pleasure to have you aboard, sir," I replied. All hands stood to their feet as the admiral departed. The next few minutes were spent in consultation with Captain Dwyer and Chuck Clark while we discussed communications. None of us really could get too excited about two measly .50-caliber machine guns. Later I was to have plenty of time to think about that briefing and why Admiral Johnson put so much emphasis on the .50s. By arming the AGERs, CNO was in diametric opposition to the fundamental principle of these ships being operated as unprovocative, unarmed snoopers. Yet putting two .50s aboard hardly changed the *Pueblo* from what it was—a small non-combatant cargo hull not designed nor intended to fight lone pitched battles with anyone.

Well, CNO runs the Navy and it was certainly within his prerogative to arm the AGERs, or not, as he deemed best.

The briefing was over and Chuck and I scheduled to meet later in the day with officers from the Yokosuka Naval Communication Station to discuss the problems already aired.

Skip and I returned to the ship as it was close to lunch. I asked him to show me the progress on the gun mounts.

"Considering where you decided to place them, Captain, the mounts they've given us aren't much," Skip complained.

A .50-caliber machine gun is a relatively light weapon originally designed for use by infantry, then adapted to World War II aircraft and tanks, but otherwise not considered very useful as a piece of naval ordnance; in spite of its lightness, it required a fixed mount with permanently located ammunition boxes. It is also a very temperamental weapon when not handled by gunners who are thoroughly familiar with it, delicate in adjustment, and therefore subject to jamming under conditions of salt-water corrosion and icing as would be encountered on a small vessel operating in frigid winter seas. We had no .50 experts aboard *Pueblo*. My senior Gunners Mate, Kenneth Wadley, a 2nd Class Gunner, had no experience at all with them. A Seaman 1st Class, Roy Maggard, who at one time served a hitch in the Army's Tank Corps, had received a basic training in their use and retained a little of that knowledge.

Nobody on either *Pueblo* or *Banner*, or within the staff of COMNAVFORJAPAN, really took armament problems very seriously. Our ships were not capable of providing locations for the guns so that they would be readily accessible in an emergency. Nor could we offer any protection to the gunners who had to bring them into action. The fo'c'sle deck mounts could only be reached and manned after exposure to a considerable field of enemy counterfire if the enemy were already close aboard; the other, located on the O-1 level deck abaft the stack, was almost equally exposed, and also was limited in effectiveness by a more restricted arc of fire. As for training our people, Marine instructors followed with familiarization lectures, a visit to a target range where forty or fifty of us were each allowed to shoot off a burst of a half-dozen rounds. This failed to produce any confident marksmen.

In short, our non-combatant status had been compromised without providing us adequate means of repelling any serious attack. Both the Navy's high command and I myself as captain of *Pueblo* would come to rue the day we accepted this situation with so little foresight.

As promised, Admiral Johnson came to inspect *Pueblo*. He was piped aboard with due ceremony. He was his genial self as he made a thorough tour of our decks and interior spaces and expressed his satisfaction with what he saw. Critical expressions were few and mild, confined to pointing out some rust bleeding through the paint at a few spots topside and admonishing me to find better stowage of some items which he thought might otherwise come adrift in heavy weather. He threw a jaundiced eye over our .50-caliber machine guns secured beneath their canvas covers on brand-new mounts and while their shapes were not obviously those of weapons, they must have retriggered the uneasiness in his mind. "Remember you are not going out there to start a war, Captain," he told me. "Make sure you keep them covered and don't use them in any provocative way at all. It doesn't take much to set those damned Communists off and start an international incident. That's the last thing we want!"

"Yes sir, Admiral, I understand that completely," I assured him with genuine sincerity.

"Okay, Skipper. That's all I have to say except that your ship looks fine and I wish you the best of luck."

We shook hands and saluted at the gangway, then he departed my ship smiling with pleasure as Bosun Mate Klepac honored him with another ceremonial shrill of his Bosuns' Pipe. It had been a successful inspection by his lights and with this I had to be satisfied.

We were now supposedly ready for sea and operations with the blessing of COMNAVFORJAPAN. But there were a few difficulties to crop up in the last hours before sailing. For one thing we had not yet received our official Operation Order or our Sailing Orders because of some foul-up with COMNAVFORJAPAN staff; they kept being promised within the next few hours, and the next and next . . . until we found ourselves thoroughly irritated by the continuing delay in delivering to us these essential documents. A partial Sailing Order to Sasebo arrived on the morning of the day we were scheduled to depart. The Operation Order arrived at 0300 January 5; hardly time to review it prior to departure. The remainder of our Sailing Order was to be transmitted while we were underway to Sasebo.

During the last week the matter of our ship's 1st Class Radioman, an essential man in our communications department, suddenly became a problem. Radioman Mullin had been fully recovered from his back injury after transfer at sea to the Destroyer Tender USS *Gompers* (also now docked at Yokosuka) and had been put on an out-patient basis for the holidays, which he celebrated by getting himself into some serious disciplinary troubles. I had no choice but to have him replaced. In the rush of obtaining a qualified man at the last minute, I could not obtain 1st Class replacement to which *Pueblo* was entitled. So it happened that a lanky young man wearing horn-rimmed glasses over a beaked nose, Radioman 2nd Class Lee R. Hayes, got one of the fateful jobs of his life. He virtually had to jump aboard with his seabag as we were about to pull away from the dock. I was disgruntled at the time over not getting an experienced man, but Lee Hayes was to turn out a Godsend to our ill-starred complement.

The delayed arrival of two other important specialists—the Korean language interpreters—kept me on edge during our last days in Yokosuka. Steve Harris assured me that they would show up aboard at any moment . . . which they did at nearly the last one. They were two Marine sergeants, Robert J. Hammond and Robert Chicca, both attached to us from NAVSEGRUDET KAMISEYA and assigned to Steve's complement of "research department" CTs where their duties would be to listen in on North Korean voice transmissions and to provide me with close support intelligence of tactical importance and an instantaneous running translation of what Koreans in our vicinity were talking about. Although I only had time to get a quick impression of a pair of bright-looking men and relied entirely on the Navy to send me men with proper qualifications, I was greatly relieved to have them part of the independent SOD-Hut team. In fact I would not have sailed without them.

On the brisk and blustery morning of January 5, 1968, a small group of my friends from SUBFLOT SEVEN and COMNAV-FORJAPAN came down to say goodbye and watch us cast off from the dock. I felt that we were as ready as we could be to accomplish a mission which, in the strange and devious ways of intelligence staffs who are in charge of such things, had gone through three changes of code names, Clickbeetle and Pinkroot, and was now finally getting under way as Operation Ichthyic 1. The Japanese artisans of Yokosuka's Ship Repair Facility had virtually rebuilt our steering engine into a mechanism which promised to be far more reliable than the original; over the flying bridge they had installed a beautifully fitted weather screen of tinted lucite. We had installed our machine guns as ordered by CNO and some of us had acquired a smattering of skill in their use which we never expected to be called upon to demonstrate in deadly earnest. I had been unable to procure the TNT for destruct and scuttling purposes, but then had been reassured that *Banner* had never carried anything like that and was not really necessary and was satisfied to go forth with a halfway decent incinerator (*Banner* had only a 50-gallon drum) for burning classified papers and a shredding machine that could chew them up at the rate of about two reams an hour. We still carried an enormous unnecessary load of classified cryptological and technical material, but we had been granted authorization to offload some in Sasebo. The CTs of the SOD-Hut, Steve reported, had completed refresher courses and were ready to do their work when their electronic monitoring equipment was brought within range of our targets. Altogether we had eighty-three officers and men aboard, including our two civilian oceanographers, and even though very few of them had a really clear concept of the mission we were embarking upon, each supposedly knew what he needed to know and how to do his particular job. Any misgivings I may have felt as the time came to cast off our lines, I drove out of my mind as unnecessary worries over things which it was too late to do any more about now. I let Skip Schumacher take the deck for getting us under way while perching myself proudly above him under the brand-new weather screen of the flying bridge from where I waved farewell to my friends on the dock in between watching his maneuvering to clear the basin.

CHAPTER VIII

(A)-DETERMINE KORCOM AND SOVIET REACTION
RESPECTIVELY TO AN OVERT INTELLIGENCE COL-
LECTOR OPERATING NEAR KORCOM PERIPHERY AND
ACTIVELY CONDUCTING SURVEILLANCE OF USSR
NAVAL UNITS . . . (B)-ESTIMATE OF RISK:
MINIMAL, SINCE PUEBLO WILL BE OPERATING IN
INTERNATIONAL WATERS FOR ENTIRE DEPLOY-
MENT. . . ."—(*Extract from operations orders
to USS* Pueblo, *December 31, 1968*)*

I remember especially noticing, for no particular reason, the
Japanese skipper of the tug standing by us as he grinned up at me
with a mouthful of gold-capped teeth. They glinted beautifully in
the pale light of a winter sun, sending blinker signals which I
could not read. I attached no mystic significance to the sight of
him, rather was amused by it; but that golden smile of his was
the last bright light I was to see before plunging into a period of
my life unrelieved by the darkness of doubt, pain and despair.

Pueblo had only steamed a few hours out of Tokyo Bay when
she ran into heavy weather that steadily deteriorated. The wind
built up to a steady gale force and whipped the tops off mountainous seas. It normally would take less than three days to make
the coastwise passage between Yokosuka and Sasebo, but our speed
often dropped to bare steerage way as the helmsman struggled
to keep control when the bow began climbing to meet a hurtling
wall of water, burst through the crest, then started a crazy sleigh-
ride into the following trough. With our lurching, wrenching, in-

---

* See appendix for complete operations orders to *Pueblo.*

constant progress, it quickly became evident that we were once again falling far behind schedule. Most of my officers and men again suffered the debilitating convulsions of seasickness. Those who felt they had developed immunity after the Pacific crossing, were soon retching with less hardy shipmates. We again experienced frightening steep rolls which left the ship hanging with her lee railings under before staggering back on her keel, where she barely paused before whipping over on her opposite beam ends. As much as motion sickness, these violent gyrations generated fear among the unseasoned sailors that was a sickness in itself. I felt sorry for these victims of a brutally hard and unfamiliar environment, but I could not let them give into it and wedge themselves into their bunks. We were on an operational mission—the real thing—and they might as well get used to functioning under these conditions which might get much worse before getting any better.

I remember starting an arduous move from my stateroom to the bridge when there was a tremendous lurch and a body came hurtling down the companionway, crashed on top of me, and dropping us both in a sprawling heap on the deck. As we untangled ourselves and tried to regain our footing, the body acquired identity and I recognized our new Radioman Lee Hayes. His face had a green pallor which was accentuated by a look of horror at having fallen on top of his captain. "Jesus Christ, sir, I'm sorry!" he croaked. "Are you hurt?"

For a moment we clutched each other, trying to keep from falling again as *Pueblo* slewed over in another violent roll. I had received some bruises and so had he, but there was nothing to do but hang on and laugh it off. "I'm okay, Hayes!" I assured him. "How are you? I'm counting on you to stay on the job and have those URC-32s at max power at a moment's notice."

Hayes managed a wan smile as he adjusted his moistured spectacles. "Yessir, I'll be ready. But right now . . . excuse me, sir, but I've got to puke." He fled down the heaving passageway. Yet I knew he would fight his way back up to the radio-shack within minutes.

In the pilothouse the OOD and his bridge watch were hanging on for dear life to anything solid overhead or attached to a bulkhead in order to keep their footing. The helmsman clung to his wheel for support while simultaneously spinning it left or right to compensate for the wild buffetings of the seas, his eyes flicking from the click-click-clicking gyrocompass telling him his course to the window through whose obscuring steam of spume he had to gauge his reaction to the endless thrusts of the great waves. In the chartroom, Quartermaster Law seemed to be steadied by some mysterious gyrostabilizer operating inside his own stocky hull, rocking back and forth on his feet as the rest of the compartment pivoted around him while he calmly tuned the LORAN and transposed its signals into position coordinates on the chart. Up on the flying bridge above the pilothouse, the new lucite weather screen provided much more protection than before, but it was drenched by sheets of spray flying over the superstructure and the wild motions of the ship were exaggerated because of its greater height. It was still an untenable position for conning through a watch in this kind of weather. But I was satisfied that we were holding our own, and making headway against the storm. With a few words of advice and encouragement, I let the watch steel themselves to handle the situation on their own.

My other officers stood their watches and performed their duties by summoning all the pride and willpower they could, but when relieved, they bypassed the wardroom and headed straight for their cabins where they struggled sick and exhausted into their bunks. An exception was Dunnie Tuck, a veteran of the *Banner* who ate as though heavy seas didn't exist. We nicknamed him "Friar Tuck," for his raffish sense of humor. The quarters and interior spaces of the ship were fetid with the sour smell of soaked clothing and foul-weather gear and vomit. In spite of Admiral Johnson's earnest recommendation to securely stow everything for exactly these conditions, there came the periodic thump and crash of some item breaking loose and being hurled against a bulkhead, shortly mingled with the curses of sailors as they tried to chase it down and secure it.

We seemed to be trapped in a storm system that was stalled and yet moving as slowly as we were in our general direction, so that there was no way for us to claw our way clear of its violent center. I did not worry too much for the safety of the ship until we came abreast of Kyushu Island and rounded its point Sata

Misaki which sticks out in the sea like a rocky talon. From here, we had to turn north around the heel of the Japanese islands to make good our course to Sasebo and I was hoping that our new course would take us out of the worst of the storm. But, perversely, the storm turned with us and held us in its powerful system. The winds began gusting close to hurricane force and the irregular waves rose higher and broke more steeply as they butted into contrary currents sweeping around this part of the coast. During the night I was called to the bridge several times because our long bluff bow got caught "in irons" between wind and sea so that the ship was no longer effectively answering the helm. I thanked God that the steering engine was at last functioning and by combining it with the alternate thrust of our port and starboard engines, managed to wrest *Pueblo* back under control. But now we faced the hazards of shoals and skerries which litter the west coast of Kyushu--no place to find oneself when the sea is so rough that ship control is marginal. We took some rolls that alarmed me and made me decide to run for shelter in the lee of a nearby island. It was only by most gingerly using a combination of rudder and engines that *Pueblo* managed to slowly crab her way out of the turmoil to reach somewhat calmer waters where we could safely catch our breath while waiting for the storm to pass us by.

This came very slowly, but I had no time to waste and when after a couple of hours of being hove to behind our sheltering island there were signs of improving weather, I ordered *Pueblo* to get under way again and resume her fight to reach Sasebo— still lying some hundred miles to the north. The weather improved imperceptibly and as I was getting quite weary and battered, I called for the Navigator to set us a new course and I turned the deck back to the regular OOD Tim Harris and retired to my stateroom for a few hours' rest. It seemed that I had dozed for no more than an hour before the telephone next to my bunk buzzed me back into full consciousness. When I picked it up, Tim Harris' voice rattled out an electrifying report:

"Captain, we are on course, but I think I see breakers about a half-mile dead ahead!"

"Back down emergency full! And come dead in the water!" I shouted at him. "I'll be right up there."

It was only a matter of seconds for me to rush up to the pilot-house from my stateroom where I had been lying down fully clothed. Tim Harris, the OOD, had been following the course laid down by Ed Murphy, but had spotted in the nick of time from the flying bridge a pale ring of breakers marking a large rock as it suddenly materialized in the driving rain and spume screening our forward visibility. By the time I arrived on the bridge I could clearly see the ominous shape for myself over our bow and realized that we had come within less than a thousand yards of running *Pueblo* on the rocks. Only by quickly throwing the engines into reverse and turning the rudder to left full had total disaster been avoided. There is no more heart-stopping situation for a captain than this and for several minutes I sweated blood until I felt reasonably certain we were clear of the danger and had deep enough soundings beneath our keel.

I controlled my fear and anger for long enough thoroughly to check our position by LORAN and radar and give a badly shaken Tim Harris a new, safer course. I remained on the bridge for a while to make sure everybody had recovered their nerves after this close call. Then I returned to my stateroom where I ordered Ed Murphy to report in privacy and explain a stupid and potentially fatal mistake in navigation. He attempted to excuse away every part of it except his personal responsibility as the ship's Navigator. I became so overwrought by this culmination of all his faults, our fundamental personality clash, and the trying circumstances of the moment, that I lost my temper and yelled at him above the noise of the storm: "Jesus Christ, mister! Don't you think maybe you should get the hell out of this business? Haven't you learned that an Executive Officer is supposed to be able to take over a captain's job? . . . That he isn't there to have his captain pick up the pieces when he screws up? . . . Shit, man! After all the time and chances you've had, do you really expect me to take this kind of crap from you?"

Murphy's eyes boggled in moist distress through his spectacles and it was difficult to tell whether his strained expression was a result of my profane outrage or the sickening lurches of my cabin. "I laid out the course as carefully as I could in these conditions, Captain," he wheezed with a mournful defiance. "Maybe the

OOD, or Quartermaster Law, or somebody, kind of slipped up in following it. Perhaps . . ."

"You are my Executive and Navigation officer," I bellowed at him. "If I can't rely on you in those duties, what the hell use are you?"

His Adam's apple bobbed fitfully up and down out of a soggy collar. "Yessir, Captain. I'm trying my best, but . . ."

"It's not good enough!"

"Yessir. You are making that quite plain. I'm sorry, but . . ."

"Then think it over and get on the ball, Godamnit! . . ."

There followed a painful moment of the sort of silence which had come between us lately, now filled in by the urgent sound of green seas breaking over our decks. He made an attempt at a formal exit, trying to come to attention on the bucking deck and almost missing the door as he aimed his body through it. He left me with my anger and frustration unabated, still swearing under my breath that the time had come for relieving him "For Cause" from his duties as my Executive Officer, yet still feeling a great revulsion for such drastic action.

During the course of that night I kept occasionally going up to the bridge to make sure that things were under control and that our navigation was accurate. In between I tried to relieve my tensions by sitting at my desk with one hand clasped around my portable typewriter to keep it from sliding to the deck, and pecking out with two fingers of the other a letter to Rose:

9 January 1968

Dearest Rose and Boys:

This is being written at sea about 100 miles from Sasebo. We have had a hell of a trip. It has been storming since the evening of 6 January. We had to lay to today behind an island to get out of about a 50 knot gale. It hailed, snowed and rained today all in a driving rain. We were supposed to get to Sasebo this morning but will be delayed until tomorrow. The XO is some navigator. We will stay in Sasebo tomorrow until the evening and then . . . back out for about a month . . . Man it really has been rough here. This little ship really bounces around. This is the first day in three that you can even stand up on this ship. Everyone is sick as dogs and some haven't eaten since we have been under way. I really feel sorry for those . . . Well I trust the boys are doing well. They don't have much time left before they will have to be on their own. I do hate to be away so much. I am missing so much. I don't have my 1040 for income tax purposes as yet but will get it off as soon as I can figure it out. We will probably have to pay some this year unless I can figure a way to get some deductions . . . Take care of yourself and have fun . . .

All My Love:
Pete.

Pecking out the letter forced me to think of my family and took my mind off the worries that I so briefly described to them. I could tell from the muffled wail of the wind and slackening rolls of the sea that we were working our way clear of the storm. There were no more urgent calls from the bridge. The din of the waves dropped to a fitful rush through which the steady beat of Gene Lacy's faithful "rockcrushers" made a reassuringly constant sound. My aroused temper began abating along with the weather.

I sealed up the letter to Rose and my sons, feeling certain it would catch the afternoon mail out of Sasebo and give them news of me before we steamed on toward the coast of North Korea. After one last tour topside to make sure all was well with the watch, I dropped back into my bunk and slept hard for the next hour and a half.

Sasebo has a longer history as a naval base than Yokosuka and in many respects is a more picturesque old Japanese city. While we maintain very complete facilities here under the provisions of our Peace Treaty with Japan, it is not a very desirable port of call for American sailors because it is relatively small and isolated. It lacks Yokosuka's nearness to great metropolitan centers, which lie far to the northeast on the main island of Honshu. There is much of rustic old Japan to be found on the island of Kyushu, but Sasebo offers by way of liberty-entertainment little more than the usual waterfront establishments clustered around the fences of the base. This did not affect *Pueblo*'s people too much during their brief visit. We were there for only two days.

For the first few hours after tying up at the dock, all anybody wanted was to rest after the bone-wrenching, stomach-turning passage. But there was work to be done in order to get back under way as soon as possible. Steve Harris began "off-loading" some of our surplus classified crypto material, together with the necessary paperwork. We had had a failure in a particular piece of electronic equipment which required my telephoning back to COMNAV-FORJAPAN and asking that spare parts be flown down immediately so that repairs could be made before we left. Depleted bunkers were refueled. And there was a lot of cleaning up and petty repairs of damage sustained during the storm. I had planned to only remain in port for about twelve hours, but there were jobs to be completed before we were again ready for sea, and, in fact, all hands needed a breather before facing the next leg of the mission.

The second morning in Sasebo I made arrangements to call on my Administrative Commander COMSERVGRU THREE, Rear Admiral Norvell G. Ward, USN. He was a tough old submariner of whom I had heard many tales but had never met. I was met at the quarterdeck of his Flagship USS *Ajax* by his Chief of Staff and taken immediately to the Admiral's cabin and introduced to him.

"Have a seat, Bucher. I am the only one on this staff who is cleared for your operations. Do you have any big headaches I can help with?"

"No, Sir," I replied. "One antenna is being repaired before we sail on our assigned mission but I expect no problems with it."

"Guess you must have hit a little rough weather coming down from Yoko, eh?"

"Yes, Sir, we did, but these little AKL hulls take it well even if they do argue with every wave."

"Well, let me know anytime we can assist you, Skipper."

"I will, Sir." Then I invited him to inspect *Pueblo* if he could find time during our stay.

"I'll return your call this afternoon and take a short tour with you but the inspection will have to wait," he said.

My coffee cup was empty and I departed.

Admiral Ward called on me at 1400 that afternoon and Bosun Mate Klepac piped him aboard. He had coffee in our wardroom and went through the SOD-Hut asking questions, which I later found out from Steve Harris, I had given wrong answers to. I hoped the Admiral didn't know that.

During the evening of January 10, a number of the crew were given liberty and took off to sample what relaxation was available within a close proximity of the naval base. Officers who had caught up with their work had the same privilege, but through his own choice, this did not immediately include Ed Murphy. Ever since our clash over his latest navigation error he had held himself sulkily apart from the rest of us, going about his duties with a certain grim determination and then vanishing inside his cabin for long periods of solitude in which (I found out much later) he occupied himself by composing a letter of resignation from the Navy. I had also been agonizing over what to do about him, but against my own instinct, I found myself procrastinating over his case and deciding to keep him as my XO through the completion of this mission, clinging to a fading hope that he would show enough improvement so I could give him a halfway decent fitness report. Once I had decided on this course and was otherwise satisfied that *Pueblo* had been reasonably restored to operational capability, I cast aside these worries and joined Gene, Skip, and Tim for a last fling ashore. Surprisingly Ed joined us as well and I was truly happy to have him along. We had a very satisfying meal in a local Japanese restaurant followed by an unusual session of poker played in the demi-exotic locale of a Sasebo "girly-joint" and banked by the shrewd Mama-San who wound up raking in most of the pots. It turned out an interesting evening which ended somewhere around 0400 hours when we came back across *Pueblo*'s gangplank in joyfully resuscitated spirits. By 0600 hours of January 11, 1968, *Pueblo* quietly cast off her lines and slipped out of Sasebo's harbor in the predawn darkness.

Our destination was the northernmost of our intelligence-gathering area, code-named Pluto and lying close to the North Korean-Soviet Russian line near Vladivostok. It was nearly six hundred miles of steaming across the widest portion of the Sea of Japan; under optimum conditions which could hardly be expected this time of the year, it would take some sixty hours at our eleven knot cruising speed. The day started clear and cold and we passed through Tsushima Strait, hugging close to the coastline so as to avoid being observed by Soviet naval units we knew to be operating farther out, and relieved by the ship's comparatively normal rolling in a moderate sea. Toward afternoon, we changed course to angle up the middle of the Sea of Japan and by early evening found ourselves out of sight of land with lowering skies and freshening winds laced with snow flurries. What had at first appeared as improving weather quickly changed back to the same rough going. *Pueblo* was heading into another wild winter storm and by the following day was caught in the thick of it.

Now there was no handy island behind which to run for shelter and when the ship again threatened to become unmanageable in the steep breaking seas, my choice was to turn and either run before them, or butt directly against them. While trying to make as much progress as possible toward Mars it became a matter of holding our own and not actually losing ground. For hours we tacked from one course to the other like an old sailingship beating her way to windward. Some of our tacks were very frightening when huge waves caught us abeam and thrust *Pueblo* over in a 50-degree roll. As usual, seasickness was rampant and although many officers and men were gaining their sealegs and getting over it, it became chronic for a distressing number of the crew. Almost half of our complement seemed unable to adapt themselves to the rugged life aboard a small ship operating in an area of wild winter storms. The attrition was specially heavy in Steve Harris's SOD-Hut, upon whose men so much depended during the next three weeks.

The bad weather that plagued us from the beginning at first had the effect of bringing much of the administrative and paperwork to a halt. But we were becoming used to rough conditions. When it calmed just a bit I reviewed our past reports and assured myself that the administrative mill was grinding along as smoothly as could be expected. Based on the operation order under which we were conducting this mission there were a number of reports to be kept chronologically; I prepared detailed instructions explaining how the various contributors (navigators, OODs, photographer, ELINT Watchstanders among others) were to submit their data on a daily basis to Skip Schumacher, the Operations Officer who would compile the data into our official ships reports of Ichthyic 1. Each day's activities were thus recorded on the day following its occurrence. In addition to my own, there was a complete report of the operation that had to be submitted separately from Steve Harris to, and through, his own chain of command. His report was one which would be most carefully analyzed by the many elements within the intelligence community. My ship's report would be primarily of operational value, unless of course we would happen to photograph or observe something that was heretofore unknown, in which case it would also be of high intelligence value. In the field of intelligence it is impossible to gather too much information. Even an absence of activity is valuable to the analysts. Therefore, in addition to our many requirements to report Ichthyic 1, I included other data that would hopefully aid distant shore-bound analysts. The details that would go into Steve's report were primarily technical in nature and the vast bulk of his information would take weeks, months and maybe even years to decipher or unravel. It was *Pueblo*'s purpose to collect and report information which would later be carefully examined by experts and filed away for possible future use, or non-use, as our military or political exigencies required.

When I became satisfied that the organization of our patrol report was in good hands I called upon Ed Murphy to produce several routine reports that were to be filed in the ship's office. For some time I had been querying Ed about the checklist which executive officers use to keep up with the vast paperwork that must be routinely produced. Although he had never actually shown it to me, he constantly assured me that such a checklist was made up and that he was following it. I was eager to have everything in good order for my expected relief in May, so that when Ed was unable to produce or explain several missing reports and files

I became very upset and decided to go below to Yeoman Canales' office and conduct a thorough inspection there.

"Open every file and safe that you have in here, Canales," I ordered.

He complied with mixed surprise and hesitation. I became appalled when my inspection revealed an almost complete lack of organization. Incoming mail that had been onboard for months had never been routed; outgoing mail that had been signed by myself for dispatch several weeks, and even months, before had not left the ship. Then came the clincher—hidden behind a stack of paper was a fitness report that I'd signed on Gene Lacy last July. Gene was then being considered for a promotion into his next higher pay grade and one of any command's primary responsibility to an officer is timely filing of their fitness report. It was now possible that Gene might be passed over in promotion just because of our failure to get this report to the Bureau of Personnel on time. This made me so furious that I gave Canales a terrible tongue-lashing on the spot, while continuing my inspection and becoming more and more upset as I looked around and found more and more things that were being done improperly, or not at all. I promptly called Ed on the ship's service telephone and told him to place Canales on report and to charge him with dereliction of duty. I then quickly brought him to captain's mast and reduced him in rating from 1st to 2nd Class Petty Officer, with the commensurate cut in pay. Although Canales was a primary offender in this mess, Ed was the responsible party. He had been assuring me all these months that everything was fine where administration was concerned, and yet here was clear evidence that he'd never checked on it.

I called him to my stateroom where, in the relative privacy of those quarters, I chewed him out in a monumental fashion for his dereliction. Of course Ed quickly produced a dozen excuses. Ed always had excuses. But he could explain none of the deficiencies in the ship's administration, nor why he had on several occasions reported to me that all of Canales' office work was in good order. I bitterly pointed out to him that the really innocent victims of his negligence and of this inexcusable foul-up were the ship's crew in general and Gene Lacy in particular, whom I considered an outstanding officer—and one to whom he owed apologies and amends. These I ultimately had to make myself, after I calmed down.

Pueblo stubbornly plowed on toward our southernmost operations area Mars whose southern boundary was at 39° N. Lat. and extended seaward from land a distance of 60 nautical miles. It was my intention to pass through the operation areas in order (Mars-Venus-Pluto) heading north while remaining 30 to 40 miles from the shore and then when reaching the northern boundary of Pluto at 42° N. Lat. to bring *Pueblo* west toward the North Korean shore and follow the coast south at a distance of 15 to 20 nautical miles while hopefully collecting some worthwhile information.

The full fury of the storm was still with us as we entered the area Mars, I found it impossible to make headway and was forced to tack about—mostly on an eastward course as I was not anxious to close the hostile coast of North Korea. LORAN was fairly good for navigation in this area and we were occasionally rewarded with morning or evening stars peeking through the overcast to obtain a celestial fix, so there was never any question about our position. The wind howled through the masts and the ship fought each comber by wildly sloughing her bow, bucking her helmsman who grew quickly weary from the constant fight to hold her head and keep his own balance as we bounced, twisted, and wallowed in the troughs. Yet she gradually built up our confidence by consistently recovering from every onslaught of the elements. Even to those most sorely tried by her wild ways of riding the seas, it became evident that she was a most seaworthy freak of an archaic, unseaworthy design.

Since departure from Sasebo, *Pueblo* had been proceeding under strict electronic silence. To insure that we did not accidentally key a transmitter, certain vital parts were removed from these instruments, but they were easily reinserted in the event of an emergency. Radio silence is a requirement for this sort of operation because any electronic emission emanating from the ship would in all probability be heard by unfriendly ears and thus our presence would be announced and perhaps cause our target country to bring her own scheduled electronic operations to a halt thereby denying us knowledge of them. My orders were to remain under radio silence until we'd been detected, which meant such time when we had been probably identified as a U.S. naval ship. It became a question of judgment on the part of the commanding officer as to when that had happened. From the time of detection and as long as the target country kept the AGER under evident surveillance a regular daily radio report was transmitted to our headquarters which summarized the preceding day's activities in addition to our current logistics status. Two messages would actually be sent, one by the ship as prepared by the Operations Officer and released by the captain; the other, a technical report by the OIC of the detachment (Lieutenant Steve Harris in our case). So since we were in fact operating at the present time under radio and electronic silence and had checked out of the Navy's Movement Report System, there were none of our higher commands who knew exactly where *Pueblo* was at any given moment.

The storm finally broke and we angled back into Mars and headed north, again through the heavy swells that always follow a storm at sea. At night we steamed without the usual required ship's navigation lights. The switch to these lights was handy in the pilothouse and could quickly be energized in an emergency. Every evening I wrote explicit instructions for the night watches in the Captain's Night Order Book, including what to do in case of an unusual occurrence. In any case, I was to be called to the bridge in such instances, no matter how trivial.

As the winds moderated, the temperature began to drop lower and lower until by the time we'd completed the transit of Mars and Venus and neared the northern part of area Pluto, it was well below freezing. We began our battle to keep too much ice from forming on the superstructure and weather decks. By a rough computation I had performed before leaving Japan, I'd estimated that we could operate safely with less than four inches of ice on *Pueblo* and that figure included a J (Jesus) factor on her side. If more ice than that were allowed to accumulate, the ship would become unstable and could not recover from a sharp roll. This would mean foundering on the spot.

Before turning the ship westward and closing the coast to commence operations within sight of land, I called all the ship's senior petty officers down to second class for a meeting in the crew's mess deck. Only a very few of the crew, except Steve's gang of CTs, knew anything about the purpose of our mission, or even where we were. I knew there were many rumors floating around and decided that all senior petty officers who'd been cleared for SECRET, should know the bare essentials of our mission in order to keep rumors from getting out of hand.

When everyone was gathered, I left my cabin and went to the mess hall. "I know there's a great deal of curiosity among the crew and each of you has undoubtedly had occasion to wonder where the ship is going and what we're about to do. I can only tell you that we're in the Sea of Japan and will be conducting various operations along the coast of North Korea. These operations are required for the defense of our country. Let me emphasize that what we are about to do is completely legal under International Law. In other words, you are not in any way party to illegal activity." I let that sink in for a few moments. "Every man aboard must perform the duties assigned to him in an efficient manner if the goals of this mission are to be successfully met. We can't go anywhere if our engines aren't working efficiently. If our meals are not properly and tastily prepared, some of us will not do our jobs as well as we would otherwise. Therefore all of you in your own way will have to contribute your best effort if we are to successfully perform our tasks. Do any of you have any questions?"

Boatswain's Mate 1st Class Klepac looked quizzical and asked, "Sir, just what does our mission consist of specifically?"

"I can't give you the details, Klepac. I can only ask each of you to trust that I'm following my orders and that the Navy and our country would not order us to do things illegally or anything unusually dangerous."

The men seemed to accept this and as there were no further questions I returned to my cabin. When we arrived at a point of about 25 miles off the North Korean coast dawn was breaking. The weather was freezing, ice had formed on our decks. I was on the bridge. Reveille was held early and about fifteen men turned to with mallets, scrapers, and shovels to clear the ice from the decks and superstructure. I brought the ship about and laid to while we chopped our decks clear of ice. Since we'd installed the .50-caliber guns I'd written a standing order that their covers should be removed each morning and that they be placed in working order by Gunner's Mate Wadley, assisted by Maggard. Because of the storm it had not always been possible to put men on deck safely so this job had sometimes gone undone. However, this morning I decided to make sure that the guns were in proper working order before we moved close in shore to commence our work. I ordered that both guns be brought to readiness and test fired. I began timing as soon as the frozen covers were removed. The first one to be tested was the one mounted forward on the starboard bow. It took both Wadley and Maggard working as well as they knew how over twenty minutes to get the first round off that forward gun and over twelve minutes to get the after one in action—a very long time. The problem was head spacing which needs constant adjustment. I myself fired a few rounds from each gun. Then we had a session of impromptu gunnery practice. As a target we threw over the side a 50-gallon drum brought along for that purpose. I never knew whether the drum sank from hits or because we scared it to death.

After the guns were secured, we headed on in with our navigator and Quartermaster Law doing their best to cut accurate bearings on the snow-covered peaks rising out of the haze shielding North Korea's craggy coast. We were closing the mainland at a point just south of the great Soviet naval complex of Vladivostok which lies a few miles from the juncture of their border with North Korea. The area I intended to put under surveillance was outside of Chongin, the northernmost of four KORCOM ports suspected of being centers of naval activities. No other shipping was in sight and we'd encountered none after seeing a few commercial tramp steamers and fishing boats just outside of the Tsushima Strait. The only aircraft we'd seen since then was a U. S. Navy P-34 Orion, making a routine ASW patrol in the Sea of Japan near Honchu. It had been alerted to our probable track and had flown low alongside us and given the traditional wing wave salute as it flew away in the opposite direction. On this wintry noon when we penetrated area Pluto to within a point fifteen miles off Chongin there was no visual activity to be seen and except for the magnificent snow-capped mountains, Steve

Harris reported that no significant information was being picked up by his thoroughly keyed-up men.

Since starting this our first operational mission, Steve Harris and I had been having a running discussion that often resulted in sharp words on my part concerning his attitude aboard with respect to decision making. I was bitterly disappointed that the Naval Security Group had reversed themselves on making Steve and his detachment a ship's department wherein there would be no question of authority. During our transit to WESTPAC we had received a poorly written and ill-conceived document that attempted to spell out our relationship. The document referred to several instructions and to one General Order, but never were Naval Regulations mentioned. Steve had one interpretation of our relationship, while I had another. Well, I was captain and I was going to comport myself as one. I made an attempt to inspect Steve's office in the same manner as I'd inspected my own, including the contents of his file cabinets. Steve explained to me as patiently as he could that they contained material that I was not cleared to see. I decided to wait and bring the matter up with higher authority when an opportune moment arose. In the meantime, he interpreted his orders as giving him the authority to originate message traffic whenever he deemed necessary to keep his bosses informed. I was against this practice, and let him know it in no uncertain terms. A ship can have only one captain, but I had frequently to remind Steve of this fact, often in language heavily interspersed with invectives.

We laid to for all the remainder of the day waiting for something to happen. Officers and men of the deck watch peered intently toward the haze line shrouding the bases of the coastal range, alert for any speck which might solidify into unfriendly patrol vessels coming out to devil us with harassing action. Down in the SOD-Hut, Steve Harris kept his racks of electronic instruments fired up and all his men were expectantly braced at their consoles. Our oceanographers came up on deck bundled against the cold and took one of the many hydrographic measurements which would take place during every four to six hours of daylight for the rest of the mission. Their Nansen bottles and Bathythermograph paid out on their winches down to 600 fathom depths to obtain water samples and record temperature gradients. *Pueblo* offered no more comfortable a ride for being stopped, or slowed to her minimum speed. If anything, she seemed to acquire a novel and sickening motion as she wallowed in the swells which was as hard to take as when she was snorting along at cruising speed. I suppose we were overly keyed up after our long preparation and voyage, expecting to have something happen at once to make it all worthwhile. Nothing did, and it somehow seemed disappointing. At nightfall, I moved *Pueblo* farther out to sea to night-steam 25–30 miles from land, and instructed the OODs to move back into position by 0700 of the following day to resume our surveillance.

That night another problem came to a boil, this one involving Chief Engineman Goldman, *Pueblo*'s Chief Master at Arms. I had appointed him to this important job some two months ago when it had become clear that he was the best man to bring together our two divergent groups, ship's crew and detachment personnel. I hoped he would maintain discipline as senior enlisted man, and prevent the feuding that had occasionally erupted between them on our sister ship *Banner*. It was with some difficulty that I had convinced Gene Lacy to release Goldman for this duty, but Gene had acceded in the over-all interest of the ship. Now Chief Goldman came knocking at my stateroom door and respectfully asked a word with his captain.

"What can I do for you, Chief?"

"Captain, I'll come straight to the point," Chief Goldman said with his face clouded with his problem. "I want you to relieve me of my duties as Chief Master at Arms."

"Chief, I don't think I quite understand. You're doing a great job as far as I'm concerned. And Blancet and Scarborough are doing good jobs in honchoing the enginerooms."

"Captain, I've tried my very best to carry out your wishes as Chief MAA, but, sir, I just can't get Mr. Murphy to back me up. My biggest problem is bringing the CTs and the balance of the crew together so they will work as a team. Unless the XO backs me up it makes my job impossible. He doesn't, and has been unwilling to help at all. So, Captain, I want to be relieved."

"Chief, you're the only Chief Petty Officer aboard who has any real idea of what is involved in running this ship. I really need you to hang in there."

Chief Goldman looked more troubled than ever but also quite adamant. "Captain, I'm sorry but I've made up my mind."

It seemed obvious that I could do nothing to convince him otherwise at this time. So I told Chief Goldman, that I would sleep on it and ask that he do the same. After he left I called Ed Murphy to my cabin and asked him for his side of the problem. He made the round of excuses which I had grown to expect from him, but nothing came out that was productive or remotely connected to solving the problem. I called Gene Lacy, Goldman's department head. When he arrived in my cabin I explained the situation to him.

"Captain, I already know all about this."

"Well, Gene, the ship really needs Goldman as the Chief MAA; there just isn't anyone else. Now I need your help. Convince Goldman to stay on at least for the duration of this first mission. Then we'll take another look at it." I knew, of course, that it was entirely likely that I would have Ed Murphy replaced before the next mission and fully expected that whoever they sent me as his replacement, would be an improvement.

Gene noticeably tightened his jaw, the inner struggle of loyalty toward me and to his chief engineman was quite apparent. Then, after a long silence, he said: "Captain, I don't think it will do any good for me to talk to Goldman. His mind seems to be made up."

"I'm fully aware of his complaints and understand that Chief MAA is one hell of a tough job here on *Pueblo*, which is a ship that's both in and out of the Navy at the same time. But unless we have the strongest possible enlisted leaders from the troops, there is no way we'll ever accomplish the harmony between the detachment faction and the ship's crew. Unless we do accomplish it *Pueblo* can never become the ship that I want it to be, and what it must be to accomplish its purpose."

Once again Gene fought with himself for the right words and finally said: "Yes, sir, I'm sure you're right, and I'll talk to him right away and do my best to convince him to stay on."

As it happened, Goldman did stay on. I never did find out how Gene convinced him.

One place where good rapport had to exist was between my ship's radiomen (Hayes and Crandall) and their opposite numbers in the detachment (Bailey, McClarren, Layton, and Karnes). The reason this was necessary was because the ship's receivers were located in a compartment adjacent to the SOD-Hut. Since only CTs had the necessary security clearance to enter there, my radiomen could not. Although a small problem in a sense, it turned out to be not only ridiculous, but also created an unworkable situation for *Pueblo*. My radiomen resented the fact that they couldn't enter the receiver spaces and the CTs seemed to enjoy their privileged status. The biggest problem, however, was that all incoming messages had to be copied by the CTs and then given to my radiomen who would route the traffic in accordance with the ship's procedure. But because the CTs had so much of their own work to accomplish, they frequently neglected pulling incoming messages off the teletype that were addressed to my attention. Whenever that happened I became furious and heated words would be exchanged between Steve Harris and myself. It must be understood that even though *Pueblo* was operating under conditions of radio and electronic silence, we nevertheless continued to receive messages addressed to the ship which are placed on a separate broadcast that we could copy it without making any signal of our own. One message that I looked forward to receiving was the daily intelligence report made up by COMNAVFOR-JAPAN for my personal current information. Most important were items that concerned what, if anything, was going on in Korea that might affect my plan of operations.

After we had been surveying Chong-Jin for several hours of the next day, I called Steve to my cabin and asked him if he'd got any positive results. "If anyone actually lives in the area, Captain, we sure have no sign of it. We are confirming many of the known KORCOM radar sites but otherwise there is nothing new."

"O.K., Steve, that's all I wanted to know," I told him. "We will pull out to about 25 miles this evening and then head down to our next target, Song-Jin."

Later that day we sighted a couple of freighters emerging from Chong-Jin and Mack got some good photographs of them through telephoto lenses from a minimum distance of 8000 yards. He immediately developed them and together with my intelligence team of Skip Schumacher and Steve Harris, we carefully analyzed the two ships and, with the aid of publications designed for that purpose, identified them as specific Japanese and Red Chinese freighters. As we were heading back out toward the safety of the open ocean that evening, we relaxed with a movie in the wardroom for the off duty officers and Dunnie Tuck and Harry Iredale.

The run down to our next surveillance point, Song-Jin, was accomplished without incident during the night. We did see the distant lights of several ships but we always took the optimum course to open our track, which made it impossible to identify them and, as we were traveling without navigation lights, they never saw us.

Song-Jin turned out to be the same disappointment that Chong-Jin had been. The CTs were bored to death. Many of them answered every call to remove ice and I was delighted that they did so. The ship's spirit was building and I was intent on raising it to a high level and keeping it there. A day and a half passed and our only significant contributions were the readings and the oceanographic samples that Friar Tuck and Harry Iredale were recording and bottling. During daylight hours Korean mountains would materialize in stark outline between shredded veils of snow squalls. My mood was one of futility and frustration.

So we moved on to the vicinity of Myang Do, which lay south in operation area Venus. My primary interest in Myang Do was the possibility that we might sight and photograph KORCOM submarines of Russian origin suspected of operating in these waters. Accomplishment of this task would pay for the whole operation. I asked the navigator to fix our position accurately and when the LORAN failed to produce a good fix I ordered the radar energized for a few sweeps. We were then able to cut ourselves in with pinpoint accuracy. *Pueblo* was lying to in waters adjacent to Myang Do 15 miles distant. But my computations showed that we had less time than I'd originally thought before we had to end the first part of Ichthyic 1, the surveillance of the KOR-

COM areas, and then head down to Tsushima Strait for a look at the Soviet navy units.

It was just about twilight that evening when my phone rang in my cabin. "Captain here," I spoke into the phone.

I recognized Skip's voice but someone else came on the line at the same time calling another part of the ship. How I wished the Navy had authorized the installation of a couple more sound powered phone circuits. We had the one circuit only and everyone on the ship used it. It made me furious when I was in conversation with an OOD and someone else would cut in from some other station.

"This is the captain. Get the hell off the line!"

"Yes sir!" came a quick embarrassed reply.

"O.K., what's up, Skip?"

"Captain, there is a ship bearing 048, about 8 miles, that looks like a warship coming over the horizon. Angle on the bow, starboard 20, the bearing is drawing right and he will pass clear."

"Be right there," I quickly replied. "Skip, get hold of Steve and tell him I want him on the bridge pronto, also get Mack to break out his camera equipment."

I grabbed my heavy weather jacket and bounded up the ladder to the O-1 level and then climbed to the flying bridge where Skip was peering intently through the "big eyes" (22-inch binoculars mounted on a pedestal). I followed his general gaze and brought my own binoculars to bear. It was in fact a warship, the range was now about 12,000 yards and he had a sizable bone in his teeth.

I rapidly applied a formula, taught to me by one of my former submarine skippers, and came up with a close estimate of his speed. He was doing about 25 knots. I checked his bearing through the pelorus and indeed he was drawing rapidly to the right which told me that unless he should turn toward us quickly, he would pass well astern of my present location. There is also a quick formula for deriving distance to the track (the closest distance which an approaching ship will pass if he continues on his present course). I estimated from these calculations that our approaching "friend" would pass at the closest point of about 1500 yards, over a half mile. But it was quite well into the evening twilight and he was almost clothed completely in silhouette. Steve arrived and quickly took in our first sight of a KORCOM warship. Photographer Mack was ready with his cameras and shouted over to me that he thought his film was too slow to pick up the pictures, but he would try anyway. "Captain, I think it's an SO-1 class subchaser," Skip ventured.

"I agree, sir," Steve chimed in.

"I don't see his radar antenna rotating," I stated, "but I agree it certainly looks like the pictures we have of that type of ship. How about a modified SO-1?" I queried.

"Can't see any rocket launchers, sir. The area where they would normally be carried is in complete shadow," Skip volunteered.

I stared intently at the dark form as it continued to close us. It didn't change course but merely knifed its way through icy waters as if on a mission from which it could not be diverted. I thought for certain that his hull number was a double digit and after much staring was quite sure the last number was 6. As he drew closer, Steve said he could make out what appeared to be rocket launchers and we concluded from this that she was indeed a modified SQ-1 subchaser of Russian build and design. But most certainly part of the KORCOM navy. Well, I thought to myself, it makes sense that a subchaser would be in the Myang Do area if there are in fact submarines based there. They were probably here for training. Mack made several exposures while the ship approached and as it passed its closest point before drawing away. None of us ever saw a single person aboard; not even a deck watch was present. I went to the chartroom and laid down our visitor's approximate position and his angle on the bow. By extending this line I could see where he was heading. He was making for Wonsan, our next area for surveillance. I then called a conference among the officers who had observed the SO-1 and quickly drained them of everything they could remember seeing so that our report would be complete and accurate. Steve went below to his SOD-Hut and questioned his watch about any possible electronic activity they may have picked up from the subchaser. They had none, but would have had if he had been radiating or emitting any signal. I concluded he had not seen us or at the very least had certainly not identified us. After a quick conference with my officers we all agreed that we were still undetected within the meaning of our orders.

That night we proceeded to the Wonsan area, arriving in the early morning. A couple more freighters were sighted and identified, photographed and included in our report. It was January 22 and I planned to spend just one more day after this one and then depart area Mars and head for what at least had some promise of productive activity if we could locate the Soviet ships in Tsushima Strait.

About 1000 hours, Steve came to my cabin where I was examining records.

"Well, Captain, we are finally getting some interesting signals and are recording them."

"That's great, Steve. I'm delighted that you've finally hit some pay dirt."

"I've got my best people in there now," Steve said.

"Is there anything I can do to position the ship more advantageously?" I asked.

"Not that I'm aware of, sir, but I'll keep you cut in."

"Notify the OOD to the extent that he's cleared," I ordered.

"Will do, Captain." Steve hastily departed with real purpose in his stride for the first time since we commenced Ichthyic 1.

Just after our noon meal, Gene called me from the bridge and reported two trawlers in the distance who were heading our way. I went immediately to the flying bridge to join him. He was using the big eyes to look them over carefully.

After checking myself, I told him: "Those are Russian-built, Lentra Class, trawlers."

"Yes sir, I can see that now."

"Call Mack and Lieutenant Schumacher up here and alert the SOD-Hut so they can be prepared to look for this type of ship."

As the fishermen drew closer, I began to suspect they might not be exactly what they appeared. They were painted a uniform gray color and outfitted with exactly the same superstructure and fishing rig. Could it be then that they were coming out to shadow our operation? Ships not too dissimilar from these had been described to me by Chuck Clark of *Banner*. In any event they continued to close and then circled *Pueblo* slowly at a range of about

500 yards. What must have been their entire crew appeared on deck in typical fishing clothing. They were pointing at us and jabbering among themselves excitedly. Several of my own crew came out on the open welldeck forward and began gazing back at them. I became concerned that some of my men might get carried away with the excitement and shout or gesture some obscenity at the KORCOMs; also I did not want them to get any clue as to the actual number of people that were crowded into my small ship. So I ordered the weather decks to be cleared of all personnel not actually on watch. After the two ships had completed their circle of *Pueblo*, they began steaming in a northeasterly direction at what must have been for them about standard speed of 10 knots. When they had retired to a distance of about two and three-quarters miles, they drew close together and lay to while apparently discussing what they had just seen. I immediately prepared my first situation report (SITREP) to be filed as soon as all information necessary could be included. In addition to the fact that I'd been obviously detected by what were apparently KORCOM ships, I had to include in this initial message all the worthwhile information that I'd collected thus far on our mission. This included such items as the number and type and where possible the position of coastal radars, also the number of visual contacts we'd made and the percentage of fuel and lube oil remaining in our tanks. Therefore this first message took considerable pain and preparation but Skip Schumacher was quite equal to the task and had all the necessary information compiled very quickly.

While the preparation of this SITREP-1 was in progress the two fishing ships parted and headed directly back to us. As we were lying to I feared an intentional ramming from one or both, so I passed the word to the engineroom to light off the main engines and stand by to answer bells.

The senior watch captain in the engineroom, Blansett, quickly reported: "Ready to answer all bells."

I could see our exhaust boiling from out of our stack and the color looked good. The engines were running efficiently. By the time the KORCOMs came abeam of *Pueblo* they were making a maximum of 3 knots. They circled us once more, this time at a distance of only about 25 yards with all hands out on their decks and gazing intently at what they were seeing. I made notes of their deployment and all visible gear they had on deck. I further noted that they were apparently unarmed. Considerable relief came over me after I drew this highly probable estimate of the capabilities. As they circled I had Mack take photographs of them at this very close range. I kept notes and a running account of the affair on my cassette tape recorder slung to my shoulder. After things calmed down I would replay the notes and summarize them into my official report.

One highly distinguishing feature that I considered important was to decipher the individual ship's names which appeared in large Korean characters on the side of the ships. I called Steve to the bridge together with one of his Marine interpreters. I asked Steve's opinion, and he agreed that these were government fishermen. The interpreter he brought with him to the bridge was Sergeant Chicca.

"Chicca, do you see the Kongi Marks on the bows of each ship?"

"Yes, sir, I can see them clearly."

"O.K., what do they mean?"

"I'll get my Korean dictionary and find out right away." A few minutes passed and the ships were still with us when Chicca returned and gazed intently at them. "One of them is *Rice Paddy* and the other is *Rice Paddy*, 1, Captain," he announced.

"Thanks, Chicca, you may return to your other duties."

I included the interpreted names of the two ships in my report and they were by this time under way toward the north again and soon became small vanishing specks dissolving into nothingness. I returned to my cabin and smoothed up the first SITREP I had filed. I called the OOD to get Hayes to light off the transmitter and to key it to the dummy antennae. This permits the radioman to set up his transmitters without emitting external signals. Steve was writing up his own technical message which would go to different addresses than mine. His message was written in a language all its own, which could only be clearly understood by another intelligence specialist. It annoyed me that he was reporting to a different commander and that he had the authority to release messages that might wittingly or unwittingly reflect adversely on *Pueblo*. In view of the fact that neither of the KORCOM ships had opted to remain with us, I decided I would insert a line in the message to the effect that, in view of the fact we were no longer under surveillance, this would be my final SITREP of this incident. In other words we would go back to radio silence. I was happy and relieved that those two KORCOM boats had not been bent on mischief.

The messages were both released at about 1645 (4:45 P.M.). Radioman Hayes had the transmitter set on the proper frequency of the day, I know this because I personally checked it out. Then began a long disturbing frustrating night and early morning while the best communication talent aboard were unable to get a response to our signals to Kamiseya.

The night dragged on and I plagued the responsible CTs every hour and sometimes more often. I even took three to four more looks at the transmitter and told Hayes to try the spare one, because maybe the output meter on the transmitter we were using was in error. But it performed no better than the first one.

"Keep on trying, Hayes," I admonished him. Then told Steve Harris, "I want you to stay on top of establishing communications. Let me know the minute we have a solid signal."

There was no feeling of apprehension aboard, nor even tension among those of us who were directly concerned with what was going on—rather a feeling of irritation over the very unsatisfactory communications with headquarters when we finally needed them.

CHAPTER IX

"30 INFILTRATORS FROM NORTH KOREA KILL POLICEMAN AND 5 OTHERS IN SEOUL—3 SOUTH KOREAN ARMY DIVISIONS AND ELEMENTS OF US 2ND INF. DIVISION PARTICIPATE IN SEARCH OPERATION"—(*New York Times, January 22, 1968*)

"REMEMBER YOU ARE NOT OUT THERE TO START A WAR!"—(*Rear Admiral Frank L. Johnson's parting advice to Commander Bucher, January 9, 1968*)

I rolled out of my bunk shortly before 0700 hours of the morning of January 23, feeling stiff and unrested after having stayed up for most of the night, checking contacts and waiting for my radioman to establish communications with Japan to report our inquisitive visitors of the previous day. My awakening cup of coffee in the wardroom tasted bitter, like the one I had drunk just a few hours earlier. I noticed a humid, sour smell permeating the interior of the ship and decided that if the warming fair weather held, we would hang out our bedding for a good airing when lying to while the CTs checked the ether outside Wonsan. Going to the bridge, I was struck by a cold that seemed a comparatively mild 20 degrees, noticed the light 4-knot wind out of the northwest, the sea heaving with gentle swells, and a high thin overcast reflecting the first pale light of dawn. The rugged Korean coast was still hidden in darkness through which a few faint lights glimmered on higher ridges. They were just clear enough to establish our position and confirm it as 25 miles offshore by checking the bottom contour with our depthsounder. I ordered the OOD, Gene Lacy, to close that distance to 15 miles and put us on station within effective range for monitoring any electronic traffic in the Wonsan area, then returned to the wardroom for breakfast, feeling this was going to be a routine day with relief from the usual bitter weather of the Sea of Japan.

The watch changed at 0745 but Gene Lacy had relieved an hour early as OOD. The sun burned through the patches of stratus clouds and details of the coastline began to emerge out of its dark sawtooth silhouettes, enabling us to take accurate bearings on prominent features shown on our charts. By 1000 hours we could clearly make out and identify the craggy headland of Hado Pando and its pendant islands of Yo Do and Ung Do lying across the northern entrance to Yong Hung Bay. These landfalls gave reliable fixes, but as had become my habit since his fiasco off Sasebo, I double-checked Murphy's navigation before ringing up all-stop and going dead in the water exactly 15.5 miles away from the nearest North Korean soil. There was no other shipping in sight as Friar Tuck manned the hydrographic winch for a Nansen cast and Harry Iredale ambled back to the fantail to take a BT reading. A work party went on deck to clear the night's small accumulation of snow and ice. From the fo'c'sle came the slurping clatter of our washing machine being fed its first load of laundry, the noisiest equipment aboard since the main engines were shut down. Below decks the CTs sat before their consoles in chairs that rocked rather than wrenched as they concentrated on their intelligence watch. Steve Harris reported to the bridge that their sensors were picking up the emissions of two distant search-radars conducting normal sweeps and that, for an interesting change, there was some "chatter" on nearby Korean voice communication frequencies.

"Anything indicating an interest in us?" I asked him over the phone.

"Not that we can read, Captain. Probably routine traffic, but we're recording and will go back over the tapes."

Going back over the tapes and extracting coherent translation might take anything up to four or five hours and I wished that Sergeant Hammond and Sergeant Chicca had come to me with more than a long-past sixteen-week course in the Korean language, enabling them to pick up the gist of radio conversations without time-consuming playbacks and references to a dictionary. But I knew they were doing the best they could with the training they had been given for this assignment, and in the meanwhile reassured myself by carefully searching the empty sea and deserted coastline with my binoculars. We might as well have been adrift in a virtually uninhabited part of the world. The only faint suggestion of human activity was a barely visible smudge of smoke hanging over what I knew to be the location of Wonsan; the town and harbor itself were hidden behind spits and islets of its deeply indented bay. There was absolutely nothing to suggest we were some fifteen miles off the entrance to North Korea's principal east-coast commercial and naval port; not a single patrol craft, coastwise tramp, nor even a lowly fishboat. I was in a way disappointed, deciding that yesterday's flurry of excitement had been a passing thing. They had come out to let us know they knew of our presence, and having decided we were irritating but harmless capitalists conducting oceanographic research in the Sea of Japan, were now ignoring us and had withdrawn into their hermetic Communist isolation. It moved me to make up another SITREP to supplement the one we had been trying to send all night, the meat of this message being:

". . . No significant ELINT . . . No longer under surveillance . . . Intentions remain in area . . . This is last SITREP this incident. UNODIR reverting to EMCON."

This was meant to convey to higher commands in Japan that the situation had cooled off since my last message, I was peacefully proceeding with our mission, and reverting to our status of radio silence. Radioman Hayes, red-eyed and weary from his efforts to establish a workable frequency with headquarters throughout the night, roused himself with equal dedication to overcome the difficulties in finding a suitable frequency for this less critical, but necessary, reassuring signal of the morning. The noon watch-change was reporting to the bridge when these messages were finally receipted for by our headquarters in Japan.

Hayes staggered down to the mess deck for a hot lunch, anticipating to digest it through a long afternoon nap in his bunk.

Quartermaster Law relieved Gene Lacy as OOD, taking over *Pueblo*, which was still lazily rolling within a few hundred yards of the spot where she had stopped two hours earlier, the slight southeast current butting against the northwest breeze to hold her position which, nevertheless, Law carefully checked with bearings on Hado Pando and Ung Do. Gene made his prescribed tour of the ship upon leaving the bridge, inspecting the decks and interior spaces, including his own main engineroom where he found Chief Goldman and Engineman 1st Class Blansett keeping themselves busy with maintenance and sprucing up of their inert diesels, and the auxiliary engineroom where Engineman 1st Class Scarborough was watching over humming banks of generators which were never relieved from the demands of electrical power from the SOD-Hut. The crew's mess was into its second sitting with twenty-five men hungrily digging in to ample portions of meatloaf, succotash, potatoes, and gravy. In the galley our cook, Harry Lewis, and his assistants were making certain that they would have second helpings, plus double portions for the third sitting due in twenty minutes. The quality of food and service was still amazing when considering it all originated out of a space measuring eight-by-thirteen feet. In the wardroom, Gene squeezed himself into our table where we were receiving the identical fare as the enlisted people with the slight refinement of having it served on a tablecloth by a steward. Anemic rays of sunlight focused through the double portholes, throwing wandering spotlights on stains of soup, coffee, and catsup that our wheezing laundry machine had been unable to deal with since the last violent seas.

"Everything okay on your watch, Gene?" I asked him.

"Yessir," he answered with his cheerful smile, "and we're catching up with some housekeeping in this nice weather."

"Yeah. Almost like the balmy winters on Newfoundland's Grand Banks," Skip quipped. "Like the man said at briefing—a real milk-run."

"At this time of the year, the Grand Banks average fourteen-point-five degrees warmer than the Sea of Japan," Steve Harris answered. "Gulf Stream, you know."

Our luncheon chatter was interrupted by a call from the bridge, Quartermaster Law reporting that a vessel had been sighted about eight miles to the south of us and appeared to be approaching. I told him to keep her under observation and let me know if and when she closed to within five miles. Eating and conversation resumed. The sighting was routine and worried nobody.

But I had just started my second portion of meatloaf when the telephone buzzed again and Law reported the ship was now five miles away and rapidly closing. It had covered three miles in four minutes, indicating a speed of better than 40 knots. It was no longer a routine sighting. I excused myself and hurried up to the bridge. As I departed the wardroom, I heard Gene make a last casual crack:

"Maybe this won't be another dull day after all!"

Topside I found the weather unchanged except that the bite of the air suggested the temperature was suddenly reversing itself and sliding back down into a hard freeze. The sun glowed without warmth through wintry clouds and the visibility was still good enough for me to spot from the pilothouse the distant dark shape bobbing toward us through flashes of white—the foam of a powerful bow wave. I climbed on up to the flying bridge where I trained the "big eyes" on the approaching vessel which showed me enough details for a tentative identification: a submarine chaser flying the North Korean ensign bearing down on us at flank speed.

I was not alarmed, only slightly annoyed that he would show up at lunchtime. I told Quartermaster Law to call Lieutenants Harris and Schumacher to the flying bridge with their identification book, and Photographer Mack with his cameras. When the subchaser kept coming on without change of speed or course, I decided to make sure we looked in every respect what we wanted to appear to be—an oceanographic research vessel operating on the high seas. The international day signals indicating such activity were hoisted and I called my oceanographers from their meal to put on an extra Nansen cast for the benefit of our visitors. Then I scrambled down the ladder to the pilothouse and checked our position to make sure we *really* were in international waters. Our cross-bearing fixes on the coast were still clearly visible, but Law had confirmed them with radar when he first sighted the subchaser. *Pueblo* was now a tenth less than sixteen miles off the island of Hung Do, still lying dead in the water with a slight southeasterly drift. There was no doubt in my mind that we were completely legal and that all I had to do was match my orders to any situation that might develop. I was joined by Steve Harris who climbed back to the flying bridge with me, took a long careful look at the much closer subchaser, flipped through his identification book, then announced his conclusions:

"She's a Russian-built, modified SO-1 class submarine chaser. One hundred-thirty feet overall by twenty-one feet beam. Speeds up to forty-eight knots through sea-state two. Normally armed with depth charges and automatic cannons, but other configurations, including missiles, may be encountered. Normal complement is three officers and sixteen crewmen."

"That's what I make her out to be, Steve," I agreed with him. "Now, get below and find out if your CTs can eavesdrop on any talk with her base. It might be fun to know her impressions of us."

"We'll do our best, Captain. Our circuits are still open to report her presence."

"Okay, but don't get everybody in an uproar. Remember that another one like her just peacefully steamed past us the other evening," I reminded him.

"Yes sir, I'll keep you informed," he answered.

Word had spread through *Pueblo* that something more interesting than a routine contact was afoot and a number of off-duty people were drifting out on deck to take a look. Bearing in mind that we should not show more crew than the normal thirty-odd carried by a legitimate oceanographic research vessel, I had the order passed over the ship's 1MC that everybody was to remain below and out of sight unless engaged in official topside business. Those remaining visible were the oceanographic people on the foredeck and personnel assigned to the bridge, all dressed in the conglomerate non-regulation cold weather clothing that I permitted on this distant independent mission. I was myself wearing a heavy leather flight jacket and a woolen ski-cap crowned by a fuzzy red tassel.

The SO-1 closed to a thousand yards and I was able to see through my binoculars that her bridge was not only crowded with men scrutinizing us through their own, but that her twin automatic cannon was fully manned and aimed at us. She was charging us in a state of General Quarters—Battle Stations! But that did not signify to me that battle was imminent. Only the same kind of harassment that *Banner* had endured many times and that I had been briefed to expect for my own ship.

I did not want an enlisted man in charge of the deck during a potentially sensitive situation, so I called for Gene Lacy to relieve Quartermaster Law as OOD. Then I ordered the engineroom to start up our diesels and be ready to answer bells.

As the SO-1 began cutting a wide but tightening circle around us, she broke out an International Signal flag-hoist that read: WHAT NATIONALITY? and to which I immediately answered by having my signalmen raise our American flag. I noticed that this caused a flurry of activity on the Korean bridge and decks, bringing me through my binoculars a silent pantomime picture of surprise and momentary confusion. However, this in no way changed their belligerent show of challenging us at Battle Stations.

By now, Skip Schumacher and Ensign Tim Harris had joined me on the bridge, looking over the situation with an eager, youthful curiosity which neither could hide beneath attempts at acting unperturbed. To both of them, the sight at close quarters of a Communist naval vessel swarming with genuine Commie crew, was still a novelty. But I reminded them that they were participants, not just spectators in the confrontation. To Skip, I ordered: "Get going on the message-form for a JOPREP PINNACLE report. Contact is a KORCOM, modified SO-1 subchaser, challenging and receiving confirmation of our nationality." To Tim, I ordered: "Make yourself at home in my bridge chair and start keeping a running narrative log on whatever show they decide to put on."

At this moment, Gene Lacy suddenly sang out: "Three high-speed torpedo boats, bearing 160, range short ten-thousand yards with zero angle on the bow!"

Grateful that he had had the foresight to keep a sharp lookout beyond the diversion within our immediate vicinity, I aimed my binoculars toward the sighting which was in the general direction of Wonsan, confirmed it, and called after Skip: "Add that to the JOPREP PINNACLE! Ask them to keep the circuits open for more."

I meant by that a full-fledged harassment operation appeared to be imminent, as opposed to the surveillance by a single unit of the North Korean navy I had initially anticipated. But no additional tension became evident on *Pueblo*'s bridge. Our sister ship *Banner* had on several occasions been surrounded by several intimidating Red Chinese or Russian vessels and apparently we were about to be given the same treatment by the KORCOMs. It flashed through my mind that here was the unexpected opportunity to really test, according to our orders, their reaction to our presence near their territorial waters. *Near*—not inside them. Of this I had to keep myself absolutely certain, and ordered Murphy, who was in the pilothouse beneath me, to again check our position with radar fixes, then sent Quartermaster Law down to doublecheck his results. Still 15.8 miles off nearest land.

The SO-1 was making its second circle around us and had closed to within five hundred yards so we could clearly see her crew wearing their peculiar foot-soldier uniforms. They now raised a second hoist of signals which read: HEAVE TO OR I WILL FIRE!

"What the hell does he mean by that?" I wondered aloud. "We are already lying dead in the water!"

"Maybe he can't think of anything else nasty to say to us," Tim suggested as he recorded the development in his narrative.

It was true that *Banner* had received the same unfriendly greeting on previous missions, but I called down the voice tube to Murphy and asked him to look up the signal in the "dictionary" and make certain there was no other meaning. There wasn't. Then I hurriedly dropped down the ladder to the pilothouse where I personally checked the radar for range and bearing to nearest land: 15.8 *miles* . . . 3.8 beyond North Korean claimed territorial waters. It was impossible that *all* of us were making a mistake. This was pure intimidation of the Communist kind. So I confidently climbed back up to the flying bridge and ordered my signalmen to make the International flag-hoist: I AM IN INTERNATIONAL WATERS.

Three torpedo boats were now within a mile and still approaching at full speed to join the larger SO-1 subchaser who continued circling with her signal fluttering from her yardarm, her cannons training directly at us with guncrews ready. Photographer Mack, busy snapping pictures through his telephoto lens, found himself looking right down their barrels. But if the atmosphere aboard *Pueblo* had changed, it was one of bracing for a test of nerves, not battle. And there was a perverse element of luck developing out of our previous communication difficulties with Japan. Because of delays in transmitting our last SITREP, the channels had not been secured when this incident started and were being kept open as it developed. Steve Harris, secluded in the SOD-Hut with his CTs was visually blind and trying without enlightening results to interpret excited Korean jabberings that were filling their voice-communication channels; I had him instructed to keep his teletype going with casual "chitchat" to Japan, revealing we had unwelcome company and to keep the circuits open for further messages. Skip then urgently asked me if we should upgrade the priority of our JOPREP PINNACLE message from FLASH to CRITIC. CRITIC was a new priority that had been devised to flag important messages that were to go through immediately to all echelons of higher command including the White House. As this was a brand-new system, only just promulgated to the fleet, it had never been used by anyone to my knowledge, so I asked Skip for a quick review of the purpose of the use of CRITIC. He gave me a quick rundown and I immediately decided to go with CRITIC and ordered him to make it so. CRITIC would indicate a possible international incident was impending and it would be passed all the way up the chain of command to the White House in Washington. It was by no means a matter of pushing the panic button. Only alerting high-level authorities to a situation where serious trouble might, if it deteriorated, require their immediate attention. I fully intended, even at this stage, to remain in the area and stated so in the JOPREP.

However, it was at this time that a certain uneasiness began to bother me, at least subconsciously, over my old worries about an inadequate destruct system that would require a couple of hours to dispose of all our classified publications and equipment. As the four torpedo boats closed in, broke their loose formation, and deployed themselves to cover us from all sides, near enough for me to see with the naked eye that they had fully manned machine-gun mounts aimed at us, I became aware of how rapidly things were happening. It had only been a little over twenty minutes since the SO-1 was first sighted. Another disquieting thought intruded upon my mind, one quite contrary to my previous concern about *Pueblo*'s poor reserve buoyancy in case she was accidentally holed in a collision during wild harassing maneuvers by Communists; I expressed it by suddenly asking Gene Lacy:

"Could we scuttle the ship quickly if we had to?"

He gave me a searching glance that was more thoughtful than startled, then calmly answered: "Not quickly, sir. About two hours to flood the main engineroom after unbolting and disconnecting the saltwater cooling intakes. Then she would not sink without breaching the bulkhead to the auxiliary engineroom. Another tough long job."

"And in the meantime we'd wallow without power for maneuvering or communications."

"That's right, sir."

I surprised myself by pursuing the matter farther and calling down the voice tube for soundings by our depth recorder. "Thirty fathoms, sir!" came the immediate reply. That drove all scuttling considerations out of my mind. Too shallow depth to justify an extreme destruct action that would take too long, and too easily canceled out by Korean divers who would eventually recover the ship's contents. Besides, I told myself, the situation was not that critical and was unlikely to become so. Instead I reminded myself of a recent special order from Chief of Naval Operations to the effect that no U.S. ships operating on the high seas were to permit themselves to be intimidated by the actions of Communist-bloc ships. I had to henceforth rely on my briefings and sweat out an unfamiliar predicament without betraying the slightest personal doubts to my officers and men. They were beginning to show some nervousness (I noticed Tim smoking a cigarette, which was unusual for him), and I could only steady them by keeping under control any of my own. Calling down the voice tube again, I ordered the Navigator to get together a plotting team to record all hostile movements of the harassment "for future study by the desk jockeys at Staff!"

We were now completely covered by four North Korean warships. The three torpedo boats were circling us within fifty yards with their machine guns aimed at our bridge and their decks filled with what looked like soldiers or marines armed with Russian-type automatic carbines. I could clearly see their oriental features scowling under the brims of their fur caps. The SO-1 was jogging a little farther off our port quarter, its 57-mm cannons ready to fire at point-blank range and her threatening signal of HEAVE TO OR I WILL FIRE still fluttering from her yardarm. Presuming she was the flagship of the pack, I added to my answer of AM IN INTERNATIONAL WATERS the International Signal for INTEND TO REMAIN IN THE AREA. Noticing that my signalman was a little shaky as he tied in the flag-hoist, possibly as much from the intense cold as from the mounting tension, I breezily exclaimed for the benefit of all the personnel on the flying bridge:

"We're not going to let these sons-o'-bitches bullshit us!"

No sooner had I spoken that encouraging defiance than I heard the sudden sibilant swoosh of jets overhead, and looking up, saw the unmistakable shapes of a pair of Russian-built MIGs flashing by on a low pass over my ship. Then I spotted a fourth torpedo boat appearing out of nowhere and bearing down on us from a distance of less than a mile. And to further complicate things, there was another small but swelling shape cutting a white wake over the leaden seas outside Yong Hung Bay—another KORCOM subchaser coming out to join in the fun!

Gene Lacy showed his mounting concern by asking me: "Should we think about going to General Quarters, Captain?"

While I am not known to back away from a fight when challenged, my instructions to not act provocatively, together with Admiral Johnson's parting admonition specifying that I was not out here to start a war, had to remain a primary influence on all of my actions. "I don't want to go to General Quarters," I answered him, "because that would give these bastards the impression we're here to conduct hostile operations. All they'd need to turn a harassment into a full-fledged international incident."

Gene accepted my decision without question, but with worry still clouding his handsome face.

Skip Schumacher returned to the flying bridge after taking my first JOPREP PINNACLE down to the cryptographic room for transmission and there came a sobering look of consternation when he found that during his short absence below, *Pueblo* had become boxed in by a total of six Korean naval units with two MIGs providing air cover. "I guess there is no doubt we've been detected," he exclaimed with a gulp.

"So they are honoring us with special attention," I told him. "Did you get off that JOPREP?" He nodded, still staring with some shock at all the activity around us. "Okay! Then get set to plug in number two!" I ordered, and started rattling off the bare facts of the developments over the past ten minutes to supplement our first report. But even as I did this, things were happening too fast for me to keep up with the message content.

One of the torpedo boats drew close alongside their SO-1 flagship, communicating first by semaphore, then by megaphones which amplified their gibberish loudly enough for us to hear it echoing across the three hundred yards of slow swells. They drew close together, bumped for a moment, while a dozen armed, stocky figures jumped across from the larger vessel, then the smaller one started backing down toward us with the obvious intention of putting a reinforced boarding party aboard *Pueblo*. I shouted at Skip to include this unexpected action in the message, then swore:

"I'll be Goddamned if they are going to get away with it!"

The sight of this brazen attempt had me more furious than worried, but I instantly realized the time had come to remove ourselves from a harassment situation that went beyond my briefings and seemed on the brink of getting out of control. *Banner* had never experienced a serious threat of seizure on the high seas, but these KORCOMs seemed crazy enough to try it. I did not want to test them that far, and lost no time in calling down the voice tube: "All ahead one-third! Navigator! Give the best course to open from land!"

"Zero-eight-zero, sir!" came Murphy's reply, sounding a bit thin.

"Steer zero-eight-zero," I confirmed. "Build up speed to two-thirds, then full. We are making a dignified withdrawal, not a run for it." I happened to glance through the lucite windscreen down at the welldeck where poor Friar Tuck was looking quite perplexed while standing by his hydrographic winch that had some 30 fathoms of Nansen cast paid out over the side. "Belay all oceanographic activity!" I shouted down at him. "Haul in those damned bottles on the double!"

Gene Lacy left the flying bridge to conduct his duties as OOD from the pilothouse and Tim followed him to continue his narrative down there, both grateful to get out of the biting cold.

A series of catarrhic coughs erupted out of our stack as the engineroom answered the bells by throwing the idling diesels into gear and advancing the throttles. The rumbling and belching of smoke was out of proportion to the very slow reaction to overcome *Pueblo*'s inertia and get her moving. For a moment it looked like the torpedo boat foaming full astern with fenders rigged and decks crowded with armed men was going to touch our sides. She actually came within a few yards of doing so and the boarding party was braced to jump over our railings when we at last began gathering speed and the gap between us widened again. *Pueblo* moved ahead in a wide turning circle toward the open sea, leaving behind the torpedo boat with its boarding party looking somewhat foolish, but then her sister ships began cutting back and forth across my bow in the old game of "chicken." I still hoped to get clear, but I had to consider now the eventuality that I would not. I ordered the word passed over the ship's IMC to prepare for destruction of all classified material, then had a long signal hoisted which I hoped would cause a stall while they broke it down: THANK YOU FOR YOUR CONSIDERATION—AM DEPARTING THE AREA.

There followed a slight—very slight—relief of the pressure against us. Just enough to sustain my hope that we could yet get out of this mess without further complications. The SO-1 hauled down her signal of HEAVE TO OR I WILL FIRE and appeared to jog along indecisively in our wake, dropping behind more than two thousand yards. But the torpedo boats still kept up their unwanted company. Two of them stuck close to our stern, the other two porpoised around our bows, zigzagging as close as ten yards with the obvious purpose of blocking our withdrawal. And I noticed that the second SO-1 subchaser had caught up and was joining the fray, making *six* hostile vessels confronting us! Ironically, the good weather for which we had been so grateful earlier in the day, was now playing into the enemy's hands because the calm seas allowed them full use of vastly superior speed and maximum stability for their otherwise tipsy gun platforms. They were having no trouble at all in keeping up with *Pueblo*'s plodding 12 knots, nor in training their weapons on an easy target. But we kept stubbornly pressing along a course of escape and for a few moments it looked like we might bluff our way through.

Lieutenant Murphy's voice rattled out of the tube with a less than confident tone: "Captain, shall I try to raise Kamiseya on the HIGHCOM circuit and let them know about this?"

The emergency had reached the point where the use of the HIGHCOM voice communication with Japan was justified. "Affirmative—go ahead and get them on the line," I agreed.

The first SO-1 began speeding up and rapidly regaining the distance she had lost during her brief hesitation. A now familiar hoist of signal flags shot back up her yardarm: HEAVE TO OR I WILL FIRE! I ignored that beyond an instinctive reaction to present as small a target as possible, just in case her intentions were serious, and shouted down the voice tube to our helmsman: "Come right ten degrees!"

The SO-1 easily countered this maneuver by pouring on more speed and turning outside of me to give her gunners a broadside shot.

"Come right ten more degrees!"

Again the SO-1 adjusted herself to the evasion and during the next few seconds while I was considering that any more right rudder on our part would inevitably bring our heading back toward North Korea, she suddenly opened fire with a long-sustained burst from her automatic 57-mm cannon.

I heard the shells screaming overhead, exploding with peculiar crackling sounds against the radar-mast, the whine of splinters drilling through the lucite windscreen of the flying bridge. Even as I threw myself down on the deck to dodge the lethal hail of shattered steel and plastic, I felt pieces slashing into my legs and buttocks. A sliver of shrapnel seared squarely up my rectum with a red-hot shock of pain. For an instant the agony and humiliation almost overcame me, but then the adrenalin of rage took over, dulling all physical pain while sharpening every other sense of awareness. The muzzle-blast of the SO-1's cannon came as a delayed series of dull popping concussions, but were intermingled with a rattle of machine-gun bullets hammering against the metal of our stack and superstructure, telling me that the torpedo boats had also opened fire on us. The salvo lasted for perhaps five or six seconds, blasting to shambles not only my bridge—but also all the high-level briefings which had been my guidelines for this mission. At that moment, if Admiral Johnson had been present, I might well have cursed him as roundly as I found myself cursing these Communists! But when the din of their opening attack ceased, I had to belay my temper even against them and keep acting as rationally as possible in the face of a situation that had literally blown up in my face.

"Commence emergency destruction of all classified pubs and gear! Be sure the word is passed on down to Lieutenant Harris in the SOD-Hut!" Then I looked around the flying bridge and shouted the next most important thing on my mind: "Anybody hurt up here?"

Gene and Tim had gone to the pilothouse a few moments before the shooting and only Leach, my signalman, and Robin, manning the telephone, were with me. They had also hit the deck and were lying among the shards of the windscreen, but scrambled to their feet with stunned expressions a couple of seconds after I did. They shook their heads in answer to my question, but I saw that both had been hit by shrapnel. Robin was bleeding from a neck wound and Leach had splinters in a leg. Quartermaster Law came bounding up the ladder, exclaiming: "Is everybody okay here, sir?"

"A few nicks we can survive without the corpsman. How about below?"

"No casualties reported yet, sir," he answered, then cut loose a stream of profanities at the Communist vessels.

My own feelings were of an almost overwhelming need to retaliate by shooting back, to bring my ship to General Quarters and Battle Stations. This command was on the tip of my tongue, but I choked it down. There were in fact no Battle Stations on *Pueblo* and General Quarters really meant nothing more than manning Damage Control. Our 50-caliber machine guns were no match for 57-mm automatic cannons, could only be reached by crossing exposed decks that would be raked by many machine guns from 30-yard range concentrating from both sides against our mounts while our gunners unlashed frozen tarpaulin covers, opened ammunition lockers, and attempted to bring into action their totally exposed weapons. It was certain death to even try to shoot back. So I shouted down the voice tube:

"Set a *modified* General Quarters! Nobody to expose themselves topside! I have the deck as well as the conn. Left full rudder, all ahead full!" Even if I could not fight back, I was damned if I would give up. As futile a gesture as it might seem, I ordered Leach to haul a protest flag to our yardarm, and pressed my ship on toward the open sea.

There was a roar overhead as the MIGs made another threatening pass at *Pueblo* and as I glanced up at them, I saw the lead plane fire a rocket. Whether the pilot intended it as a warning shot or had accidentally triggered his missile I could not tell; it streaked high and far ahead of the ship, exploding in the sea a good eight miles away. But it was obvious the KORCOMs air cover was fully armed and ready to support their surface action. I remained more concerned with their subchasers and torpedo boats.

Perhaps forty seconds had gone by since the first salvo, and now came the second. A stream of shells yowled through the rigging, some of them bursting against the masts and scattering another shower of shrapnel downward; others could be heard slamming through the stack and superstructure. And the torpedo boats cut loose with their machine guns at the same time, stitching through the pilothouse from both sides. All four of us flattened ourselves on the deck and as soon as the cannon fire let up, I shouted: "Clear the flying bridge!" When I raised myself to scramble for the ladder, I noticed a large hole in the deck where my chin had just been and wondered how the hell I had escaped having the piece of shrapnel go through my head.

Machine guns from two of the torpedo boats were still shooting long bursts at us, propelling Law, Robin, and Leach to jump for the lower bridge where they landed, unhurt, in a heap. My own attempt to make a more dignified retreat via the ladder was given a precipitous impetus by bullets that missed me by inches. Even as I dropped down, I had a glance at the torpedo boat firing at me and saw that it had also unmasked its port torpedo tube and was training it outboard for a shot that could hardly miss blowing *Pueblo* sky-high.

Inside the flimsy protection of the pilothouse, I found the entire bridge-watch lying prone on the deck with the wheel tended from that awkward position. I had to cringe myself while ricocheting bullets and bits of window glass flew around as I entered, but when the machine guns stopped firing, I yelled: "Everybody on your feet!"

Berens, the helmsman, was the first one up, muttering angrily to himself as he grabbed the wheel and steadied *Pueblo* on her course. Tim, who had hurled himself out of the captain's chair, picked up his pencil and narrative log, sat down again and resumed a furious scribbling. Everybody got back on his feet—ten or twelve people rising after having fallen all over each other in a 14-by-8 foot space crammed with conning and navigation equipment—everybody except my Executive Officer, Lieutenant Murphy, who remained prone on the deck, his spectacles askew on his nose as he whined at me:

"But, sir . . . they are still shooting at us! . . ."

"No kidding, Ed! So get off your ass and start acting like my XO!" When he did not instantly react, I gave him a kick that brought him more or less upright. He fumbled for the microphone of the HIGHCOM receiver which he had dropped when diving for the deck and complained: "I've been trying to raise Japan, sir, and they said to shift frequency, but . . ."

Now that some order had been restored to the bridge, it came uppermost in my mind to make sure the emergency destruction of the especially sensitive material kept in the cryptographic room and SOD-Hut be accomplished with all possible speed. But I suppose that I was becoming rattled myself, not from my wounds, which I hardly felt at all beyond the soggy trickling of blood, but from the first tangible evidence that some of my key people, myself included, might buckle under the stress of this confrontation. I picked up the wrong receiver while ringing the right telephone of the two located next to each other. Thirty seconds were lost while I kept ringing the wrong circuit and a distraught CT tried to answer me on the right one. When I finally realized my mistake and switched receivers, I was somewhat relieved by Steve Harris's report:

"Emergency destruct is in progress, Captain, and our communications are open with Kamiseya."

"Good! Keep up the destruct, but don't destroy today's crypto codes until I give the orders. I'll have another CRITIC message to go soon."

"Yes sir." His tone was a little shaken, yet sounded as if he understood what had to be done and was prepared to do it.

Temporarily reassured that matters were being taken care of in the SOD-Hut, I returned my full attention to the bridge, checking our course (still angling out to sea at 135 degrees) and our speed (all ahead, full) and our soundings (still 30-35 fathoms which was too shallow according to accepted standards for effective dumping over the side of classified material in weighted bags). A quick glance through star-burst holes of the pilothouse windows confirmed that all the KORCOM aggressors were staying with us and threatening further violence with complete impunity. Our radiomen, Hayes and Crandall, were initiating their Destruction Bill by carrying out files from their cubicle and rushing them to the incinerator located behind the stack; swirls of smoke smelling of burning paper told me that primitive destruct equipment was functioning. Quartermaster Law, Signalman Leach, CT Robin, together with the now useless lookouts and photographer were helping them pass out an amazing amount of classified matériel and documents from our cramped spaces, all of them aware of the importance of keeping these from falling into Communist hands. "Watch yourselves out there and take cover behind the whaleboat if the shooting gets hot," I warned them. "But keep that stuff burning . . . burning . . . burning to ashes!"

"Sir, the HIGHCOM has gone dead!" Murphy screeched at me, waving the mike as if he could shake a response out of it.

Radioman Hayes overheard him while passing by with his arms full of pubs and paused a second to say, "I've rechecked the frequency shift, sir, and the output of the HIGHCOM. Maybe the antenna has been shot out."

"Well, never mind the goddamned HIGHCOM," I said to Murphy. "What about the plot of this action that I ordered a while back?"

Gene Lacy was returning to the bridge after checking in with his General Quarters station at Central Damage Control. His face was ashen, but his voice steady enough as he reported to me: "No damage below, sir, except minor hits above the waterline."

"Okay, Gene. We're still afloat and under way. We'll keep trying to bull our way through." I picked up some papers off the chart table and shoved them into the arms of Crandall as he rushed another load toward the incinerator.

Then the KORCOMs opened up another salvo that was accurately aimed directly at *Pueblo*'s bridge.

The 57-mm shells came ahead of the sound of their thumping muzzle blasts, and one of them passed through the pilothouse, drilling through the remaining glass of one window and out through the next, passing within inches of Gene's head and scorching Tim's left ear before zinging into the sea a hundred yards beyond the ship. If it had exploded, we would all have been killed then and there. But we hit the deck completely alive and unhurt, listening for the following pizzicato of machine gun bursts to let up before returning upright. I was stunned by Gene Lacy's wild-eyed look as he dragged himself back to his feet and suddenly yelled at me:

"Are you going to stop this son-of-a-bitch or not?"

There was only a fraction of hesitation before he reached out himself and yanked the handles of the annunciator to ALL STOP. The blindly alert engineers isolated three decks down instantly

rang the answering bells. There followed an abrupt break in the
wheezing exhaust throb of our perforated stack, then a rapid de-
celeration downward of our 12-knot speed. I kept staring at Gene
in utter disbelief for another fifteen seconds. Fifteen seconds that
brought the stark realization that my most experienced officer,
my most trusted friend aboard this ill-starred little ship, had
robbed me of the last vestige of support in my efforts to save the
mission, leaving me alone with an Executive Officer who had
proven to be unreliable and two very young and inexperienced
junior officers on my bridge. Suddenly the complete uselessness of
further resistance flooded my brain. It would only result in our
being shot to pieces and a lot of good men killed to no avail, because the North Koreans would in the end get most of our secret
documents. Instead of lunging for the annunciator and racking it
back to ALL AHEAD FULL, I turned my back on it and Gene,
and walked out on the starboard wing of the bridge.

The shooting had stopped. From 40 yards off our starboard
quarter, the KORCOM torpedo boat was bobbing along, its machine gunners staring back at me with grimly impassive oriental
faces over the sights of their weapons. Farther behind them, their
SO-1 subchaser dropped apace as we coasted to a stop, its smoking cannon still aimed at our vitals, and a new signal rising to her
yardarm:

FOLLOW ME—HAVE PILOT ABOARD.

CHAPTER X

"WE STILL WID U AND DOING ALL WE CAN EVERY-
ONE REALLY TURNING TO AND FIGURE BY NOW
AIRFORCE GOT SOME BIRDS WINGING UR WAY
BACK TO U."—(*Message from NAVSECGRU,
Kamiseya, Japan, to* Pueblo *while she was un-
der attack.*)

". . . FOUR MEN INJURED AND ONE CRITICALLY
AND GOING OFF THE AIR NOW AND DESTROY THIS
GEAR."—(*Last message from* Pueblo *received by
Kamiseya, 1450 local time, January 23, 1968.*)

I stood there in the starboard wing of *Pueblo*'s bridge for perhaps ten seconds without doing anything. But it seemed like a
prolonged agonizing purgatory for all the sins of omission, all the
half-measures and make-do's, all the misplaced trusting to luck
and equivocating orders which had dogged my ship since the first
day I had taken command of her, and had now come home to
roost in one sudden swoop of stark disaster. The feeling of utter
loneliness and complete severance from any reliable support became suddenly so overwhelming that I wanted to cry out for help
from anybody with a sensible suggestion about *what to do!* Four
of my officers were on the bridge with me, but none of them came
forward with a single word of advice.

Gene Lacy remained by the annunciator, rubbing his hands
together as if they had been burned when he rang up ALL STOP,
and glowering vacantly through the shattered pilothouse windows.
Ed Murphy was swaying unsteadily by the dead HIGHCOM

set, silently blinking through his spectacles while alternating fearful squints with ferocious frowns that signified nothing but indecision and total lapse of initiative.

Tim Harris had stopped his scribbling and was staring at me with a lost expression which asked *me* to give him something more significant to do than keep up a narrative log that would now be unlikely to serve any useful purpose. Likewise, Skip Schumacher's eyes pleaded with me for something more positive for him to do than plug in another PINNACLE-CRITIC message and burn publications.

None of them came forward to advise even the simplest alternatives: to go down fighting or strike our flag then and there. None of them said a word to me. There was, during those critical ten seconds, no communication between us whatsoever. It was all up to me, and me alone.

With more than a score of automatic weapons, including an unmasked torpedo tube, all aimed at us from point-blank range, it was far too late to put up a fight. The KORCOMs were in a position to kill most of us in a matter of minutes, then board the hulk of *Pueblo* and capture her secret material before she sank. The sacrifice would be useless. Protecting that secret material was now the paramount and only possibility remaining to us, and to accomplish this, we had to stay alive. "We will stall as long as we can so as to complete destruction," I announced. "Everybody not needed to work the ship will bear a hand at burning—*everybody!* What can't be burned goes over the side. Never mind the shallow water. Now move! Mr. Lacy will take the deck."

Gene roused himself out of his torpor and said, "Yes sir, I have the deck!" with a voice that sounded almost normal.

"Hang in there and do the job right," I admonished him. "I'm going down to the SOD-Hut and make sure they are also destructing completely. Let me know when those bastards make their move to board us."

A board and search operation was what I expected next from the KORCOMs. Outright seizure where we now were located, a good twenty-five miles off shore, did not strike me as their intentions. I did not acknowledge their signal to follow them, and just left the protest flag flapping from our yardarm. They seemed again to be hesitating as their torpedo boats and subchasers slowly circled us where we lay dead in the water. Perhaps the smoke pouring out of the incinerator behind the stack and seeping out of doors and ventilators from pyres of publications below deck was giving them the impression that they had disabled us with their shooting. That might give me more time, and my principal objective had become to gain all the time I could. With this in mind, I rushed off the bridge, only vaguely conscious of surges of pain from the wound in my rectum and the soggy feeling of blood soaking my right sock.

I was shocked by what I found below . . .

The passageway outside the SOD-Hut was thick with smoke from piles of burning paper. I bumped into men who were fumbling in the dark, coughing and sputtering curses as they tried to feed the fires that were smoldering rather than brightly flaming. Inside the threshold of the steel door, I found the deck of the SOD-Hut littered with files and publications which had been dumped out of drawers to be shoveled out into the passageway, but among them were lying the CTs where they had flattened themselves during the last Communist salvo. Steve Harris had wedged himself behind the protection of a rack of radio receivers whose dials still glowed through the suffocating gloom. "Everybody, on your feet!" I yelled. "The shooting has stopped, so get off your asses and get on with the destruction down here! Come out from there, Steve, and make your men move, damn it! We're about to be boarded and every second counts. Destroy everything you can, any way you can!"

Steve squeezed himself out from behind the rack, his face gray as he coughed and wheezed "Yes sir, Captain . . . we're getting it done!"—then began frantically yanking open more file drawers and dumping their contents on the deck. His actions were dazed and uncoordinated, like those of a man on the brink of panic, and it forcibly struck me that here in the SOD-Hut, as well as on the bridge, leadership was failing me in the emergency. But at least the CTs were back on their feet and scrambling all over each other in the confined space to resume tearing apart the secret publications, or throwing them whole out of the door toward the belching pyres, or trying to stuff them into weighted sacks to be jettisoned over the side. "Jesus!" somebody sputtered as he gagged on the smoke. "We must have a ton of this crap! How can we get rid of it all?"

"You've got to get rid of it," I shouted, "so keep going until it's all gone!"

"Yeah . . . keep going boys," Steve croaked.

One of the men picked up a sledgehammer and started pounding in the faces of a pair of electronic devices which should have shattered with his blows, but did not. The Navy's specifications for rugged equipment was working against his efforts, but he kept swinging away as hard as he could.

I interrupted our two Marine language experts, Sergeants Chicca and Hammond, who were monitoring the North Korean's tactical communication network for the purpose of keeping me informed as to their intentions against us. I had so far received no such intelligence whatsoever out of our supposedly sophisticated capability. "Well, what about it?" I asked. "Haven't you guys been able to make out anything they are saying out there?"

They both shook their heads and Chicca made an aggrieved confession, "It's nothing but a lot of fast gibberish which we can only identify as Korean. We're just not proficient enough at the language, sir . . ."

"You can't understand a word of it?" When they helplessly shrugged, I exclaimed in disgust to Steve, "Some damned linguists they sent us. If they'd been qualified, they could probably have warned us out of this mess hours ago. You might as well turn them to destructing."

I shoved my way through the confusion toward the Crypto Center which was a separate compartment from the main SOD-Hut and where some measure of order still reigned. The buzz of the coding machines and rhythmic clatter of the teletype were steady normal sounds beneath the uproar and banging outside. CT1 Don Bailey was seated at his console trying to pay attention to a message appearing on the roll of paper flaking out of the teletype. He jumped when I tapped him on the shoulder and asked, "Are you on the line with Kamiseya?"

"Yes, Captain," he answered and nervously flicked the long sheets of paper. "All our messages have gone through and been acknowledged. I am keeping up the circuit with chatter, as you ordered, sir."

My mind flashed to the string of admirals posted over the thousands of miles between Japan and Washington who were being jolted by a chain reaction originating from this Crypto Center. They were responsible for my being here in this predicament. I was responsible to them and to my country for my actions at this moment. I thought about getting on the line myself, but before I could do it, somebody shouted to me that I was being urgently called from the bridge.

Groping through the smoke, I found the telephone and heard Gene say that the KORCOMs were ordering us to get under way and follow them. I told him I would be right up. I could not be everywhere at once. In an emergency, a captain's place is on his bridge. So I left the SOD-Hut to Steve, hoping he would keep the destruction activity going at full blast.

When I returned to the pilothouse, I saw that the KORCOMs were impatiently threatening us with their guns and pointing at the flag-hoist of their lurking subchaser which still commanded FOLLOW ME. Destruction on the bridge seemed to be proceeding better than in the SOD-Hut as paper materials were passed along a sort of bucket-brigade to the incinerator and more solid objects—including Mack's camera equipment—were being dumped over the side. Clearly this phase of stalling had to be substituted with another to avoid more prodding bursts of lethal fire. So I ordered a slow ALL AHEAD, ONE-THIRD and a course to drag along behind the leading KORCOM subchaser. At least we had not been boarded as yet, and at the bare five knots of one-third speed I calculated we should have enough time to complete destruction of all the secret pubs and gear before we could be herded inside North Korean territorial waters—perhaps enough to allow Seventh Fleet to react and come to our assistance. But I had to now face the prospect of total capture—seizure—because the KORCOMs were obviously forcing us toward their naval base of Wonsan.

"Keep destroying everything!" I urged. "All the logs! All the charts! Clean everything out that's classified, Murphy! All the codebooks and recognition manuals! Hayes! Make sure you don't leave a scrap in the radio shack."

The bridge was a frantic bustle of activity as everybody tackled the amazing amount of material stored in such a small area. I lent a hand myself, carrying an armful of papers back to the incinerator which was belching smoke, but had to be carefully stoked so as not to actually smother its fire with fuel. Pages had to be ripped out and fed in a handful at a time and it was frustrating to discover how incombustible large amounts of paper can be. There always seemed to be more accumulating outside the little furnace than was being consumed inside of it. God! If we were having this much trouble on the bridge, what was happening in the SOD-Hut which had to dispose of fifty times the amount of even more sensitive documents? Time! We needed more time!

"Captain, they are signaling us to put on more speed," Gene called out to me.

"To hell with 'em," I shouted back, but went to the starboard wing from where I could see Koreans on the closest torpedo boat giving me imperious waves that plainly indicated they wanted me to go faster. I answered with the old "Amphibious Salute"—a shrug of the shoulders with palms flapping upward, indicating total incomprehension of what was expected of me. They kept angrily waving and I kept stupidly shrugging, walked back inside the pilothouse as if to consult with somebody there. The cannons of the subchaser and the machine guns of the torpedo boats were trained upon us, but they did not back up their request with another burst of fire. "To hell with 'em," I repeated and leaving the annunciator on the ONE-THIRD mark, returned my attention to the most urgent matters at hand. "Keep running all classified stuff out to that incinerator, men!"

Ed Murphy shuffled out with a load of charts, his lips set in a grim thin line that was disturbed by neither curses nor prayer, but a kind of trancelike resolve.

Yeoman Canales emerged from below, puffing and sweating in the cold after his long climb upward from the ship's office with both arms full of thick file folders consigned to the incinerator. He cursed the volume of *Pueblo*'s administrative paperwork which continued to weight him down to this bitter end and his vicarious delight in sending it all up in smoke was dampened by the enormous effort required in virtually dragging everything from keel to top deck. "Christ! To think I gotta make many more trips like this . . . and maybe get shot at too!"

Somebody—I think it was CT1 Barrett—retorted, "Well, so that's one reason why we're out here—to find out how these red assholes will react to us!"

Radioman Crandall staggered up from below with files of radio schedules precariously wedged between his chin and forearms, hissing through clenched teeth, "This should be the last of it, godamnedsonofabitchtohell!" But Quartermaster Law was shoving close behind him with a load of his own and huffed, "No good just stacking it by the incinerator. We gotta burn it—burn it up to ashes! Move, god damn!"

Radioman Hayes stopped with a horrified look on his lean face and shouted at a sailor heaving something overboard, "Hey, that's my tools you're heaving over the side, you dumb sonofabitch!" Then quickly belayed his outrage with a strident giggle, "Okay—Okay. So I won't need them any more!" and rushed back into the radio shack to gather up whatever else was left to be destroyed in there.

I noticed Photographer Mack as he paused to stare disconsolately into the deep where all of his expensive cameras and lenses had just sunk into eternity and gave him a part comforting, part encouraging prod, "Hey, Mack! What about your files of prints and negatives? Better get rid of them too!" He gave me a look of startled realization, then rushed down to his lab on the lower deck where those compromising items were stored. His action made me think of what was stored in my own cabin and those of the other officers. All of us had some confidential papers and personal records that could be of value to the enemy.

"Each of you men take turns going down to your quarters and cleaning out any compromising stuff in your possession," I ordered. "I'm going down to my stateroom to take care of what I have right now. Let me know if anything happens up here."

I found much of my crew milling about the mess deck and connecting passageways, shadowy figures in the smoke as they worked on setting fire to fresh piles of paper which were being passed up from a seemingly inexhaustible supply in the SOD-Hut. Some of them were stuffing the material into ordinary mattress covers which they weighted with anything handy, even galley utensils, before dragging them out to be heaved overboard. There was no sign of panic and surprisingly little shouting and cursing, but with more than half of our eighty-three people jammed into this part of the ship, the press of bodies, clutter of torn and smoldering trash, and thick atmosphere, all created a demoralizing feeling of confusion and futility. While some men struggled with their assigned tasks of destruction, others waited uselessly at their Damage Control station, or were getting in the way by stumbling around in the smoke, uncertain of how to help. Being confined below deck, suppressed fears were compounded by not knowing exactly what was happening. This became evident when I appeared among them, shoving my way toward my stateroom, and somebody shouted at me, "What's going on out there, Captain? What's the real scoop?"

"We're being forced back toward North Korean waters," I answered, trying to sound as steady as possible. "There we'll probably be boarded and searched. So keep helping our CTs destroy all their classified stuff, men. That's the most important job at present."

I tapped a man to follow me into my stateroom and help carry out my papers to the pyres. A billow of smoke swirled in with us as we burst through the door, quickly obscuring the small cabin in a sooty pall. But its smallness had the advantage of having everything within reach with only a couple of steps in any direction. All of my Top Secret orders were stored in Steve Harris's safe in his SOD-Hut. I knew Peppard was destroying that material. In my own desk and file cabinet there were only some confidential publications, my personal record jacket, and files of personal notes and correspondence. It was only a matter of minutes before I emptied out everything, ripping it up and passing it out into the passageway. Letters from Rose, from friends in the service, photographs of home and family—all went together with anything official. When the drawers were emptied, I took a pair of .22 pistols that were my own property which I did not want confiscated by the KORCOMs and ordered them thrown over the side.

Then I started back to the bridge, noticing in passing that the Crypto Storage Compartment (close by my stateroom), seemed to have been cleaned out as both its safes gaped open and empty. Bales of paper were still being hauled up from the SOD-Hut and fed into the fires or scuttling sacks; crunching blows of axes and hammers smashing equipment resounded through the murky interior of *Pueblo*. Destruction was proceeding and I was encouraged to think that with a little more time, the Koreans would find nothing aboard but ashes and pulverized shambles. "Hang in there troops! Keep smashing and burning! Don't leave those bastards anything they can use."

When I reached the pilothouse, I was astounded to find that the annunciator had rung up ALL AHEAD, TWO-THIRDS and we were now making 8 knots in the wake of the KORCOM sub-chaser leading us toward Wonsan. I felt my temper boiling over, and did not try to belay it as I furiously asked, "Who the hell ordered more speed?"

Gene Lacy met my accusing glare with a glassy stubborn look of his own. "The Koreans ordered it, sir," he answered with a dead flat tone of voice.

"Those fucking Koreans aren't commanding this ship, Mister Lacy—I am!" I yelled in his face with no consideration for his obviously overwrought state. "Now, ring down one-third and keep your goddamned hands off that annunciator until I give you orders differently."

Gene racked the handles and recoiled away from me. I could sense how everybody on the bridge was beginning to freeze up before the disintegration of all discipline. Murphy stood behind the helmsman, transfixed, with his jaw hanging slack as his eyes darted from my livid face to the KORCOM warships boxing us in. Tim Harris wavered over his narrative, hesitating to record verbatim my outburst. Quartermaster Law and Radioman Hayes faltered in their rush toward the incinerator with more loads of documents to be burned. Electronics Technician Nolte, aiming a hammer against the IFF set, struck a couple of fitful blows that almost missed, then stopped. Everybody was badly shaken, but I was not about to calm them down. "Our only chance is to stall all we can and keep stalling, dammit," I shouted. "Understand that we need time to complete destruction. And we need time for help to get here," if any was coming, I thought.

In a desperate attempt to emphasize my point and to take back whatever time the Koreans had just gained, I reached out for the annunciator and rang up ALL STOP. It was becoming as difficult for me to keep a hold on myself as on my key officers and it took a tremendous effort to control my rage and fear so that I could act like the trained professional I was supposed to be. I tried to think of something meaningful to say that would bolster their resolve, but all that would come out was a repetition of my endlessly repeated order, "Get on with the destruction!"

The passing out of paper to the incinerator, dumping overboard of material, and smashing of equipment resumed as *Pueblo* lost headway and drifted to a stop. I tried to cool off with several deep breaths of fresh air from the side of the bridge. I noticed the air had turned searingly cold.

Then the KORCOMs reacted to my latest maneuver without even bothering with any warning signals.

The subchaser opened fire with its cannon from off our starboard bow, pumping a long salvo of shells which could be heard bursting inside of our hull. Simultaneously, the two closer torpedo boats began raking our sides and superstructure with machine-gun fire. Ricochet and shrapnel flew all over the ship, hammering against her plates and zinging over the decks before splattering into the sea. The machine guns kept shooting while the gunners on the subchaser rammed in another clip of shells, then fired five more rounds which made *Pueblo* shudder as they slammed through her thin skin.

Everybody on the bridge flattened down before this hail of fire and when it finally let up, I was sobered by the realization that it was useless to remain stopped there, letting them shoot us to pieces. ALL AHEAD ONE THIRD! I ordered. "Follow the sonsofbitches at one-third. Otherwise they'll kill us all before we can complete destruction." I was still clinging to the idea of trying to follow them as slowly as possible and made sure no higher speed was rung up to the engineroom. "Help *had* to be on the way." As soon as *Pueblo* started moving again, the shooting stopped. There were some muffled shouts from below and Robin, who was crouched with the telephone head-set clamped over his head, announced:

"Sir, there are casualties reported from Damage Control Two! One . . . *two* men hit!"

"All right, Robin. Tell them I'll be right down," I answered, then gave Gene a long hard look. "You've got the deck and the conn, Mister Lacy. Have you understood my orders and can you carry them out?"

"Yessir—we follow them at one-third."

"Right. I'll be back in a few minutes."

Complete havoc had been wreaked in the passageways of the mess deck and staterooms when several Korean cannon shells exploded there. Two men carrying up loads of documents from the SOD-Hut had been hit, blowing paper, chunks of human flesh and blood all over the place. One of the shells must have burst in Fireman Hodges' groin, virtually tearing his right leg off and ripping open his lower abdomen so that the intestines were hanging through the shreds of skin and clothing. He was being supported upright by Stewards Mate Aluague and another shipmate, while Corpsman Baldridge tried to stem the blood spurting between his dangling leg and crotch. "You'd better amputate that leg," I told the corpsman.

"Then he'll only bleed to death faster, sir," Baldridge answered.

Hodges was conscious, but his head was lolling backward, his eyes glazed by shock. I could see that he was dying. "Well, do what you can for him!"

A stretcher was passed up with some difficulty and the mortally wounded man was lowered into it, completely blocking the crowded littered passageway. I noted Engineman Woelk supporting himself against a bulkhead, blood flowing from a rip in the crotch of his trousers. Excited voices spoke of other wounded men. Others gagged on the acrid smoke and fumes which filled the air.

"I've got to have morphine, sir!" Baldridge exclaimed as he worked on Hodges. He shook his head and said to me with a lowered voice, "Jesus! Penis and testicles are all gone. The whole urinary tract is blown apart." That meant there was no hope even if a skilled team of surgeons had been available.

Lieutenant Murphy was the ship's Narcotics Control Officer and I ordered the word passed to the bridge to have him come down and issue morphine which he kept under lock and key. I reminded Baldridge to take care of the other wounded as soon as he could and use the wardroom and officers' staterooms as hospital wards. Then I left the scene of carnage and hurried down toward the research spaces, nauseated and heartsick, yet somehow numbed with a determination to keep doing what remained to be done.

The SOD-Hut was still the scene of frenetic destruction activity with fire axes and hammers pounding equipment to pieces and piles of discouragingly large amounts of pubs and papers being shoved toward the fires. CT1 Peppard was in the Communications Office stoking a pyre of documents in a wastebasket. Steve was ripping apart whole files with fearful, nervous bursts of exertion, his face flushed and grim. What appeared to be two large mattress covers stuffed with paper were laying in the middle of the deck.

"There's still too much stuff left, Steve," I admonished him. "Get all of it out of here over the side."

"We're doing it as best we can, Captain! We're doing it!"

"Never mind the shallow waters now. The fires can't keep up with these mountains of paper, so don't hesitate to throw the rest overboard."

"We're doing it! . . ."

I pushed my way through to the Crypto Center where CT Bailey was nervously concentrating on his teletype machine whose lively clattering told me we had maintained contact with Kamiseya. From over his shoulder I could read a message coming in: . . . LAST WE GOT FROM YOU WAS 'ARE YOU SENDING ASSIST?' PLEASE ADVISE WHAT KEY LISTS YOU HAVE LEFT AND IF IT APPEARS THAT YOUR COMM SPACES WILL BE ENTERED.

"Key lists" referred to our classified communication. Evidently the Naval Security Group had awakened to the danger of these falling into unfriendly hands. I tapped Bailey on the shoulder and told him to tell them I was coming on the line. Bailey was too nervous, so McClarren manned the keyboard. His fingers flew over the keys, alerting whichever high-ranking officer who had the deck at Kamiseya that the captain of *Pueblo* was sending the following personal message, then waited for me to dictate what I wanted to say. I had no time to compose any dramatic verbiage, only compress into a very few words all the essential information about the situation and my intentions in dealing with it:

HAVE O KEY LISTS AND THIS ONLY ONE HAVE, HAVE BEEN REQUESTED FOLLOW INTO WONSAN, HAVE THREE WOUNDED AND ONE MAN WITH LEG BLOWN OFF, HAVE NOT USED ANY WEAPONS NOR UNCOVERED 50 CAL. MAC . . . DESTROYING ALL KEYLISTS AND AS MUCH ELEC EQUIPT AS POSSIBLE. HOW ABOUT SOME HELP. THESE GUYS MEAN BUSINESS. HAVE SUSTAINED SMALL WOUND IN RECTUM, DO NOT INTEND TO OFFER ANY RESISTANCE.

Within a few seconds, Kamiseya's answer came back:

ROGER, ROGER. WE DOING ALL WE CAN. CAPT. HERE AND CNFJ ON HOTLINE. LAST I GOT WAS AIRFORCE GOING HELP YOU WITH SOME AIRCRAFT BUT CAN'T REALLY SAY AS CNFJ COORDINATING WITH I PRESUME KOREA FOR SOME F-105. THIS UNOFFICIAL BUT I THINK THAT WHAT WILL HAPPEN.

I could see in my mind's eye Admiral Johnson on the "hotline" trying to rouse action out of the Fifth Air Force to scramble fighter-bombers to our assistance. Unless a carrier happened to be handy at sea with her aircraft armed and spotted for launch—very unlikely—the nearest naval aviation available was based at Okinawa, over six hundred miles away. The Air Force's 105s were much closer in South Korea, and even if not on strip alert and armed for this kind of mission, they might conceivably reach us in time to be effective—*if* there was instant reaction to the request from the Navy. In any case, there was no use in my wasting time with more urging. I had to rely upon the various headquarters concerned to stay on their hotlines and get done whatever possibly could be done. So I answered ROGER YOUR LAST. ROGER YOUR LAST. and after reflecting on nothing for a moment, hurriedly left the Crypto Center.

Finding the passageway outside the SOD-Hut blocked with destruction activity, I left through the forward access hatch and returned to the bridge via the O-1 deck. Along the way, I expressed my agonizing frustration by kicking at several fittings and throwing curses at the KORCOM ships bobbing along close to our quarters as they herded *Pueblo* toward their lair like a fat cow to the slaughterhouse.

The bleak ramparts of the Korean coastal mountains were reappearing solidly ahead after having almost vanished during our abortive run to sea. The cold had become intense, probably plunging down to zero degrees during the past fateful two hours. The light breeze barely ruffling the swells cut through my clothing with icy thrusts into the tepid moisture of sweat and blood.

In the pilothouse, the last stages of destruction were being accomplished. Murphy had left, I presumed to break open his Narcotics Locker and provide succor for our wounded. Gene Lacy was standing by the annunciator which was set at ALL AHEAD ONE-THIRD, his face showing a tense expression that betrayed the terrible struggle for control going on inside his mind. Boatswain's Mate 3rd Class Berens worked the wheel with a steady competence that was entirely unaffected by whatever turbulent feelings he was experiencing. Radioman Hayes was turning inside out the remaining contents of his radio shack while Crandall kept demolishing equipment with his hammer. The traffic from below to feed the incinerator was continuing and Yeoman Canales staggered up with a final load from the ship's office, his tenth long tortuous trip from the bilges to the bridge. Tim Harris noted my return in his narrative report, then gave me a questioning look which made me nod my head with a sardonic smile. "Okay, Tim! Now put down there that the captain orders the narrative log destroyed—then destroy it!"

He almost cheerfully ripped up the sheets of his pad, tearing them lengthwise, folding them over and tearing them again, then again into yet smaller pieces before throwing them through a shot-out window to scatter like confetti in our wake. I noticed that there was a long trail of other jettisoned trash littering the sea behind *Pueblo*. Surprisingly, the KORCOM torpedo boat covering our stern steamed right through that flotsam of secret documents without paying any attention to it.

A call came to me on the telephone from the SOD-Hut. It was Steve Harris. "I request permission, sir, to send a message to Kamiseya," he said, sounding stiffly formal, "telling them we will be unable to destroy all our classified publications, that some of them may be compromised."

"Like what?" I barked.

"Mostly technical pubs and such. We simply can't get to them all, sir, but . . ." his voice faded into an agitated whimper ". . . but I think we've gotten rid of everything else."

"Permission granted to send the message if that's the situation as you see it," I shouted back at him. "But we've still got time, so don't let up on your destruction."

A couple of minutes later, the leading Korean subchaser ran up a new signal which ordered us to stop. One of their torpedo boats swung into a sharp turn to cut in alongside of us with an armed boarding party deploying on its deck. The other KORCOM warships kept their guns aimed and ready as they slowed down and allowed the distance between us to close. I had no alternative but to order Gene to ring up ALL STOP and to stand by to receive boarders.

He racked the handles of the annunciator, waited for the answering bells from the engineroom, then turned to me and asked, "Captain, shouldn't we remind the crew about the requirements of the Military Code of Conduct?"

This pertinent suggestion calmly spoken took me somewhat by surprise after the way he had been acting during the past hour. It was in its way reassuring that he was yet able to function rationally. "Yes—remind them about it, Gene. Pass the word over the 1MC!" I agreed. "You've got the deck and the conn. I'll greet the bastards in person."

He nodded as I departed from the bridge, picked up the microphone and spoke into it with a completely controlled voice: "Now hear this! Now hear this! All hands are reminded of our Code of Conduct. Say nothing to the enemy besides your name, rank and serial number. Repeat: Nothing besides your name, rank and serial number! Deck watch will now lay aft to receive boarders!"

I estimated that it would take another three or four minutes for *Pueblo* to come dead in the water and for the KORCOM torpedo boat to maneuver itself into position to board us. I used that time to make another dash to my stateroom with the purpose of exchanging my tassled ski cap for regulation headgear that would mark me as a senior officer of the U. S. Navy and captain of my ship. I also took the opportunity to hastily pull on some heavy woolen underpants as protection against the increasingly bitter cold, and to wrap a sock around my blood-soaked ankle. The doors connecting to the bathroom I shared with the Executive Officer's quarters were open and I saw Murphy standing in there, sort of listlessly fumbling about over nothing in particular, then looking surprised at seeing me, said, "What shall we do now, sir? What happens next?"

I thought it had been a long time since he left the bridge without being specially missed. I felt almost sorry for him and wished to hell that for both our sakes I had requested his transfer "for cause" and sailed into the Sea of Japan with one officer short. But there was no more time left for another of our private talks. I could only tell him, "I am going to meet the KORCOMs who are now making to board us. You had better go topside and stand by for whatever develops. You might as well brace yourself for the worst, Ed, and try to measure up."

Then I rushed out into the passageway which was a slippery slime of cinders and blood, making my way through the littered messdeck whose crowd had fallen strangely subdued, and passing out the door leading to the fantail where a party of sailors under Boatswain's Mate 1st Class Klepac was making ready to receive the lines of the approaching torpedo boat.

Its fenders thumped against our stern and suddenly a detachment of eight or ten Koreans swarmed over the railing, brandishing automatic weapons with fixed bayonets. They were led by two officers with red and gold shoulderboards attached to their dark green jackets. One of them came right at me with a pistol aimed at my head.

"I protest this outrage!" I shouted at him. "We are a United States ship operating in international waters and you have no damned right to attack us like this. As captain, I order you to get off my ship at once and let us go our way in peace."

There was not a flicker of understanding on his sullen face, nor did he speak a word to me in answer. But his gestures with his weapon made his intentions amply clear. He was capturing USS *Pueblo* and all her crew were forthwith being made prisoners of Democratic People's Republic of Korea.

CHAPTER XI

"RECOMMEND THIS LATEST MOST FLAGRANT DIS-
REGARD OF U.S. PROPERTY AND LIVES ON THE HIGH
SEAS BE MET WITH STERN PROTESTS AND DEMAND
FOR IMMEDIATE RELEASE OF SHIP AND CREW,
FULL EXPLANATION THIS BRAZEN ACT OF PIRACY,
AND INDEMNITY ALL DAMAGES."—(*Excerpt of
message from U. S. Commander in Chief,
Pacific, to Joint Chiefs of Staff, January 23,
1968, U.S. date.*)

"YOU ARE CRIMINALS WHO WILL BE TRIED IN OUR
PEOPLE'S COURT AND SHOT."—(*North Korean
General's statement to Pueblo officers shortly
after their capture.*)

Although the Korean Communists who boarded us looked more
like ground troops than sailors, they did not act out of their element or hesitate in their actions. Some, with Russian style sub-
machine guns, forced my men on the fantail to sit down on the
deck with their hands above their heads; others immediately
moved through the rest of the ship, looking for more of the crew
whom they roughly herded forward and made to sit on the welldeck in the freezing cold. They produced lengths of rope to tie
the prisoners' hands and tore up strips of sheets with which to
blindfold them. Not everybody submitted meekly. There were
furious American profanities thrown at the KORCOMs, even
some scuffling, followed by the first thumps of gun butts and boots
cracking against flesh and bone. Right from the start, it was being

driven home to us that we were in for some brutal treatment, perhaps the kind of inhuman torture techniques we had all heard that these people used against Americans during the Korean War.

The two Korean lieutenants did not let me linger to protest the treatment of my crew, but shoved me ahead of them toward the bridge with a pistol pressed hard against my back. Only Berens was allowed to remain up there, standing glumly, faithfully at his post by the wheel; the rest of my bridge watch was forced below to be trussed and blindfolded with their shipmates. One of the Korean officers pointed at their subchaser who was again flying its FOLLOW ME signal and then indicated the annunciator with some vigorous motions ahead. I rang up ALL AHEAD ONE-THIRD and ordered Berens to steer in the wake of the subchaser. The other officer had entered the radio shack which was in shambles except for one transmitter that had been left intact and still turned on. When he indicated to me that he wanted it turned off and I adamantly shook my head, I received my first blow, a sharp crack with the barrel of his pistol to the side of my head. Yanking me out of the way, he tore out the transmitting key from its base and the power connectors out of their jackboxes, thus severing our last communication with the outside world.

Neither of these officers could speak any English, but it turned out that one of them could write a few words of it. Picking up a scrap of paper among those littering the deck, he printed the words MANY MANS, thrust it in my face and made a querying gesture. This gave me a chance to stall by having a shouted conference with Yeoman Canales whom I had spotted among the prisoners on the welldeck. After we decided there were eighty-three men on our roster, I scribbled down that figure and showed it to the lieutenant. He stared at it with an incredulous expression that turned into irritated disbelief.

"I need help for my wounded, damn you!" I said to him and pointed to the last signal hoisted to my mast, a request for medical assistance. I noticed with a certain satisfaction that our ensign was still flying up there.

He shrugged, then gave me a shove out of the pilothouse, leaving Berens with a single enlisted guard as *Pueblo* got under way again. I was prodded at pistol point along the O-1 deck, passing the still smoldering incinerator behind the stack with its jagged holes of cannon shots, on back to our after 50-caliber machine-gun mount. There I was given the sign to unlash the tarpaulin covering the weapon. It had, as usual, frozen solid in the intense cold and that gave me an excuse to again adamantly shake my head in refusal. Again I received a blow from the pistol barrel. The lieutenant then assigned the job to two enlisted troopers who, I noted, immediately ran into great difficulties in trying to untie the rock-hard knots and pry off the stiff folds of canvas. They were still struggling at it long after I was escorted back to the bridge.

One lieutenant left to take over things below while the other remained in the pilothouse with me and Berens, and an enlisted Korean trooper who kept a finger on the trigger of his submachine gun. *Pueblo* was moving along at her one-third speed of 5 knots, following her escorts of KORCOM warships toward the walls of Korean mountains which were turning a reddish purple in the early winter twilight; the island of Hado Pando stood out sharply with its distinctive shape that reminded me of Rio de Janeiro's famous Sugar Loaf. We were getting close to the hostile mainland, but I had learned during the past twenty-four hours to fairly accurately estimate the ranges of this area and judged us to be barely within the Korean's own twelve-mile territorial limit, and still a full twenty miles from Wonsan harbor. Maybe there was still time for our dismal fortunes to change! Time! I still had to stall for time! SOME BIRDS WINGING YOUR WAY was the last word I had gotten from Kamiseya before being boarded. God! Give us time for them to get here!

Even with the two pairs of suspicious eyes watching my every move and keeping me covered with a pistol and a cocked sub-machine gun, I still had some freedom of movement on my bridge. The Korean lieutenant urged more speed, but somehow accepted my gestures of refusing to comply without administering any more punishing blows. Perhaps, after all, he was an infantry-type who had been thrust into an unfamiliar role by his Communist superiors and could not really judge what could or could not be done by a ship at sea. Perhaps he had to still rely on *me* to a certain extent. I took advantage of it by pacing my bridge as a captain who was concerned only with the operation of his ship. J moved from one wing to the other, my ears picking up the muffled curses of my crew as they were corraled and trussed up in the welldeck and on the fantail, my eyes desperately sweeping the darkening southeastern horizon for any small spark of hope that might flare into rocket-firing F-105s of our Fifth Air Force. I was determined that if I spotted them, I would lunge for the microphone of the 1MC and order my crew to break their bonds, try to overpower the Korean boarding party, and regain control over *Pueblo*. There might follow a bloodbath, but I thought we could make it and the risk would be worth it.

I did get to use the 1MC to address my men for one last time, but not to tell them to make a break for freedom. Word was evidently passed up to the Korean lieutenant on the bridge that we really did seem to have the astounding number of eighty-three men aboard our small ship; that prisoners were clogging the fantail, and many more were being ferreted out of the interior spaces. Like the famous act of circus clowns, wherein a score of them tumble out of a single small Volkswagen, more and more people were erupting out of *Pueblo*'s relatively equal capacity. The lieutenant's stonily impassive demeanor became ruffled by uneasy amazement. Then he put his pistol against the back of my neck and pushed me toward the microphone, flourishing his piece of paper on which he had written MANY MANS, then pointed to the welldeck. I knew that he knew I understood what he wanted. I didn't want those bastards to panic and begin shooting at my crew. I had no alternative but to pick up the instrument and speak into it.

"All hands muster forward and stand by on the welldeck." I thought of adding a hopeful word, but decided against it. The sky and sea to the southeast remained coldly devoid of any sign of help and even if the Koreans had not understood my words, there was no use in raising false hopes among my bound and blindfolded crew.

Pueblo chugged along helplessly toward her ignominious fate with all but four of her able bodied complement—myself and Berens on the bridge, Goldman and Blansett in the engineroom —bound and blindfolded. I prayed that Baldridge had been left to tend our wounded, especially the dying Hodges, but had no way of establishing this. I could only see a huddled mass of unidentifiable bodies shivering in the exposed cold between our fo'c'sle and forward superstructure. There were still defiant curses as the Korean soldiers tried to cower that unexpected number of prisoners with savage kicks—and somebody—sounding like Russell—gave a yelp of pain and snarl of humor: "Jesus! Some of these cruds should punt for the Packers instead of kicking my ass! . . ."

Twenty-thirty minutes went by. Then signals were blinked to our prize crew as we drew within about nine miles of their coastline and the Korean lieutenants grabbed the annunciator and placed it at STOP. One of the escorting torpedo boats swung around our stern, nudged up close and deposited another contingent of boarders on our fantail. This was a high-level personage and his staff who had evidently decided the situation was now secure enough for him to make a personal intervention on the scene. He swaggered up to my bridge with red shoulderboards reflecting the rays of the setting sun from clusters of gold stars. I didn't know what they signified—a full colonel, at least. His face and neck were disfigured by the prominent scars of a veteran campaigner. He had in tow an interpreter who addressed me with a letter-perfect textbook English that was devoid of any courteous preambles.

"You will conduct us through a complete inspection of this ship at once and without any tricks of concealment. At once! Go now!"

"Tell your colonel I demand that all his people leave my ship immediately," I answered.

The interpreter mumbled a few words in Korean to which the colonel gave nothing more than a blank completely ignoring look. "Go now! Complete inspection without any tricks!"

"My government knows where we are and what is happening here. It will quickly react to this outrage!"

"Go now!" This time his order was backed up by an automatic pistol jabbing my ribs and a kick in the lower back. The scarred Korean colonel maintained a steely businesslike detachment which warned me he did not give a damn whether I lived or died. Among the reinforcements he had brought with him was a civilian pilot who barged into my pilothouse, unceremoniously rang up ALL AHEAD FLANK SPEED, then shoved Berens away from the wheel and took it himself while my helmsman was turned over to a Korean guard who promptly escorted him below to join the rest of the prisoners. I too left the bridge as the unwilling conductor on a tour of *Pueblo* for the benefit of Colonel Scar. I regretted that I had not ordered my enginemen to answer only 1/3 regardless.

I first led him to the passageway where Hodges was still lying in his stretcher, unattended and apparently unconscious, just outside the wardroom where Baldridge and Reed watched over the badly injured Woelk. "I need medical attention for this man and several others whom you wounded," I told the colonel through his interpreter.

He listened to the translation, but gave no reaction or answer, barely wasting a glance at the dying sailor. The accompanying trooper kicked me on toward the mess deck.

The quarters which had been so crowded with activity just a half hour ago were now deserted with only piles of ashes and scorched scraps to tell what had taken place. Colonel Scar took note of this and asked through his translator, "What were you doing in here? Burning your secret orders?"

"Oh, just making ice cream," I replied.

The flippant answer earned me a kick which knocked me sprawling against the bulkhead with stars shooting before my eyes. I discovered, as had several of my men, that these Koreans use their feet as expertly as some occidentals use their fists. They could throw a kick anywhere between your kidneys and jaw with lightning speed. I also discovered that they did not hesitate to kick a man when he was down. But in this case, Colonel Scar intervened before the third blow, indicating I was to be jerked to my feet to resume the tour.

We next went through the engineroom hatch and climbed down the ladder toward the throbbing diesels which were being tended by Chief Goldman and Engineman Blansett. They were working under the threatening muzzle of a submachine gun held by a watchful Korean trooper. Colonel Scar looked around without making any comment, and after only a minute's inspection, made it known he wished to go on to other parts of the ship. Chief Goldman and I were barely able to exchange glances

of understanding over each other's respective helplessness, trying to make them convey more hope than despair. Then the
bayonet of my guard's carbine drove me back up the ladder.

We looked into the abandoned galley where remains of lunch
were still on the stove, and into the officers' staterooms showing
a state of disarray after the occupants' scramble to destroy personal or confidential documents. We waded through thick ashes
in the passageway leading to the SOD-Hut, but I received a shock
when we reached it. Large amounts of unburned papers blocked
the open steel door and inside it a mattress cover stuffed full of
what must have been classified publications had been left lying
in plain view on the deck. Although I did not know what the materials were, my heart sank when I saw how much Steve and his
men had not been able to destroy.

Colonel Scar showed his first reaction of surprise when he
entered the SOD-Hut, his hooded eyes popping as he took in all
those racks full of smashed electronic equipment. He quite obviously never expected this small ship to carry such an elaborate
electronic intelligence system. He even made some exclamations
about it in Korean to his subordinates that were not translated to
me. We stepped inside the Crypto Center where I was relieved
to notice all the visible coding equipment had been smashed. But
the power was still on and the teletype machine was faintly humming with an occasional random twitch of its keys that left odd,
meaningless letters typed on the teletype paper. I was ordered to
shut it down and when I refused with an ignorant shrug, received·
a hard blow to the back of my neck (there was not enough room
in there for kicking).

The interpreter proceeded to kill the teletype by yanking out
its power connector and Colonel Scar looked around with interest
while a couple of enlisted Korean troopers began clearing the
SOD-Hut door by shoveling the piles of torn publications and
file folders back inside. I had been knocked down and lay there
sneaking a hand inside my trouser pocket, fumbling for a lighter
which had not been taken away when they frisked me. I was
grasping at the idea of somehow setting a fire as we left and spinning the lock of the door so that they could not get back in to
put it out. But Colonel Scar must have sensed what I was plan-

ning, because he had one of the guards pull me to my feet and pin me against the bulkhead with a bayonet against my chest. Then they inadvertently locked the door themselves as we left. I heard the automatic mechanism click home and knew that the only way they would ever get back into the SOD-Hut would be by burning their way in with a cutting torch.

The last part of our tour was the forward berthing spaces where I found that most of the crew, including all my officers, had been transferred to get them out of the bitterly cold welldeck. This had doubtlessly been done more out of consideration for the guards than the prisoners. As everybody was bound and blindfolded, they could not see me come in to their presence, and since I could do nothing to help them, I did not raise my voice to let them know I was there.

Colonel Scar snapped out orders to his enlisted subordinates that stopped them from pillaging the private lockers, but not from freely administering kicks and jabs with their weapons. I heard somebody out of the battered but unbroken crowd of Americans growl in defiant outrage, "One of those thieving bastards just ripped off my watch!"

"Share the wealth! That's communism," another muttered.

I wanted to stay there with my crew, but I was taken back to the passageway outside the wardroom and made to sit down on the deck next to Hodges' stretcher and left there under the guard of two enlisted troopers while Colonel Scar and his interpreter went back to the bridge. There was no motion at all from Hodges. But I was relieved to see that Corpsman Baldridge and Reed, the cook, had been left to tend the severely wounded Woelk who was lying on the wardroom deck with his legs propped up on a chair while they tried to stem the bleeding from his crotch and hip.

"What about Hodges?" I hissed at them.

"He's dead, sir. Died about ten minutes ago," Baldridge answered. He put a restraining hand on Woelk who heard our voices and tried to sit up with a drugged reaction brought on by the dose of morphine he had received. "Woelk is pretty badly torn up and needs a surgeon."

Our guards punished us for talking with hard blows with their boots and butts. Mine kicked me in the small of my back which was getting very sore by now. Baldridge and Reed received chops against the neck, apparently another favorite Korean assault. The pain was excruciating yet somehow numbing. It did not stop us from more talk. "It's all up to you, Baldridge," I said. "They've refused any medical help. Anyway, you probably know more than any of their pill rollers."

"I'm just a goddamned corpsman, sir . . ."

"But with lots of experience, so use it! . . ."

Our conversation was again cut off by more blows, these so hard that we could speak no more while trying to catch our breath. I kept silent even after recovering myself so that Baldridge and Reed would be left free to do what they could for Woelk. The two guards kept alternating with occasional kicks and jabs against my ribs which were beginning to feel like they were breaking to pieces. I could only hunch down next to Hodges' dead body and take it. The pummeling let up briefly when Colonel Scar came back through the passageway with his interpreter —giving us no more than a passing glance—then resumed as soon as he was gone.

An hour dragged by as my whole body seemed to turn into a mass of bruises and welts throbbing with the diesels that were driving *Pueblo* at flank speed toward Wonsan. Out of the corner of one eye, I could see a porthole in the wardroom. It revealed nothing but darkness of night enveloping the ship. Too dark now for the "birds winging our way" to save us. I accepted the realization that if any help was still contemplated by our Seventh Fleet or Fifth Air Force, its objective could no longer be rescue, only retaliation. This was the next prospect I began to cling to and even though its implementation might mean the death of us all, I found myself looking forward to it. Pain, shame and desperation produces a fatalistic euphoria of its own.

It was about two and a half to three hours after the seizure that I saw outside lights flashing through the porthole. The engine-room bells clanged below me and I could feel the ship change speed and begin berthing maneuvers. Old *Pueblo* showed her resentment over foreign handling by banging hard against a dock. I could hear commands and shouts in Korean from the deck, then the thump of many boots jumping aboard. Colonel Scar and his interpreter suddenly appeared with several senior Korean officers, including a general and what looked like an admiral. I was prodded to my feet and shown off to the newcomers as a prime catch among the prisoners, then shoved inside my stateroom where I was thoroughly searched. This time they cleaned me out of everything but my clothes; wallet, watch, ring—everything was taken. I kept loudly protesting, of course, for the benefit of the general and admiral who had squeezed themselves into my tiny quarters together with Colonel Scar and the interpreter who translated my words to them without coming back with anything but accusing questions:

"Why are you spying on Korea? You are a CIA agent bringing spies to provoke another war?"

"Absolutely not!" I answered. "We were conducting oceanographic research in international waters. This is a research ship that has nothing to do with the CIA or any kind of armed aggression. What are you going to do for my men you have wounded? . . . I demand you at least give them decent medical attention. And I demand that you let us leave in peace, or the United States will never let you get away with this."

Their response was a couple of jabs to the jaw and neck. "You will all be removed from the ship, tried and shot," I was told. The guard grabbed my hands and tied them with a very hard knot and proceeded to blindfold me. Before my vision was totally cut off, I had a glimpse of Goldman and Blansett passing through the passageway, also bound and blindfolded.

My men were being taken off *Pueblo* and there were now so many Korean guards available that they outnumbered the Americans. As I was forced ashore over a crude gangplank with a bayonet guiding my steps, my blindfold slipped just enough to give me a half one-eyed view of what was happening. The ship had been berthed at a pier that was located outside of Wonsan whose lights glowed in the distance, about five miles away. The cold was intense and the night very dark. Lampposts made pools of light around the docks and reflected on the faces of a large crowd of Korean civilians who were being held back by soldiers keeping them in line almost as roughly as they did us. The mob was yelling insults and spitting at my crew as they were led toward some wait-

ing buses, and they acted as if they would have delighted in tearing us to pieces if it had not been for the restraint imposed by
their military who did not hesitate to knock down the overzealous.
Yet I had the impression that this was in a way a put-up job. How
else could such a controlled vociferous reception be waiting on
short notice without advance organization?

I was shoved into one of the buses and had barely sat down
before being yanked out again. It was Colonel Scar's interpreter
who had singled me out to open the accidentally locked SOD-
Hut. "You will open it or be shot at once!" he shouted when I
feigned ignorance of the combination. I did know it as well as
Steve Harris and several of his men but hoped we could both
keep the secret so that they would have to perform a complicated
feat of safe-cracking. I was taken back to the *Pueblo*, this time
the sole object of the spectators' venom which literally spurted
out of them in globs of spittle. When we returned aboard and
reached the passageway outside the SOD-Hut, my blindfold was
ripped off and I saw several Koreans fiddling with the securely
locked steel door. "Open it!" I was commanded as they untied my
hands.

"How?" I shrugged helplessly.

An automatic pistol pressed against my ear. "Open it or be shot
right now!"

I still refused.

There followed some excited, frustrated jabbering between
them in Korean and from the anger in their voices I fully expected
the pistol to go off in my ear. It would at least be a quick death,
I thought. No torture! But instead I received a hard infantry-boot
in the stomach and the pain felt as if my intestines had burst. My
hands were tied again in front, the knot drawn even tighter than
before, and my blindfold replaced, this time completely obliterating all sight. From then on I was in a complete darkness and
could see nothing as I was dragged off *Pueblo* for the last time.
I heard the curses of the mob and felt splatters of their saliva,
but my optic nerves registered nothing but weird psychedelic fire-
works which flared with the throbbing hurt in my belly.

Back on the bus! There I could tell from the protests of my
crew that they were being searched again with more emphasis on

looting personal possessions than collecting intelligence materials. I recognized the voices of our Filipino and Mexican-American men, Aluague, Abelon, and Rosales, crying out above the others and realized why when Colonel Scar's interpreter threw out the accusation:

"You have been trying to make infiltration of North Korea with South Korean spies! You are criminals who will be tried in our People's Court and shot!"

I decided it was time to let my men know I was among them and shouted as loudly as I could, "Bullshit! There is nobody but Americans in this crew."

That caused me to be instantly removed from the bus for the second time. Even though I could not see where they dragged me, I sensed it was into a staff car where I was wedged in between two guards who kept up a steady pummeling. Colonel Scar might have been in the front seat, but I know that his interpreter was there because when I demanded that we be treated in accordance with the Geneva Convention and that the crew be kept together, it was his voice that answered:

"You capitalist dogs and Korea are not at war, so no Geneva Convention applies. You have no military rights at all. You will be treated as civilian espionage agents of CIA. You are criminals and will be tried in our People's Court and shot."

As the automobile rolled along a rather bumpy road, I kept protesting above the grind of its noisy engine, repeating over and over our cover story that we were an oceanographic research vessel and that on this day we had been conducting observations of sunspots in cooperation with the International Geophysical Year program. The only answers were counterdemands to confess that we were assigned to land South Korean agents on the North Korean coast. "It is best for you to say why you do such criminal action!"

The ride lasted perhaps fifteen minutes without any let-up in this dialogue of accusations and denials. Then we lurched to a stop and I was pulled out of the car and hustled inside some sort of building. Apparently the buses carrying my crew had preceded us there because I could hear them being beaten up. The sound of blows mingled with shouts and groans that were turning strident with desperation. I became particularly worried about my Filipino and Mexican-American men whom they were obviously taking for South Korean spies. "Stop this brutality! There are only Americans here who were on a peaceful oceanographic mission on the high seas!" I loudly insisted.

"Spies! Saboteurs! Criminals!" More blows and groans.

I felt myself roughly shoved into another room. A door slammed shut behind me, cutting off the sound of the beatings. My bound hands were completely numb; my eyes could see nothing but blackness under the tight blindfold. I was now isolated from my crew and when I protested this too, received a couple of hard cracks from rifle butts which reminded me I still had the company of my guards. And there was the voice of the ubiquitous interpreter hammering away at me with his accusing questions about espionage, and my constantly repeated denials.

Then I was conducted out of the room and building, shoved into a bus, and taken for a short ride that ended in what I identified as a railway station from the smell of steam and chugging wheeze of a waiting steam locomotive. My feet were guided up the steps of a coach, led on by my tied hands down an aisle and thrust onto what seemed to be an old style coach seat. I could sense the presence of my men, but the beatings had momentarily ceased and they were very quiet. I must have been the last one brought aboard the train, because as soon as I was seated, it lurched forward with a shriek of the locomotive's whistle and started moving toward—God knew where!

The train rattled through the night making several short stops with jerky starts for the next six or seven hours. My body ached far more from the blows I had received (and continued to receive) than from the sting of shrapnel in my leg and rectum. My blindfold was not removed and the rope tying my hands cut off all circulation in them until they felt like amputated stumps. One of the guards must have noticed that they had turned black and did me the small charity of loosening the knot a little and massaging some life back into them. My whole being was numbed by shock and weariness, yet remained acutely conscious of every mental and physical pain, every sound, every jolt of the rough roadbed which the iron wheels transmitted to my body through the hard seat. I could not have slept even if my turbulent thoughts had permitted it. The Koreans were not about to give me any rest.

I had begun to lose all concept of time which seemed both prolonged in an agony of suspense and contracted in a tumble of stunning events. But very shortly after our train left Wonsan, I was pulled from my seat and steered down the aisle, made to cross the rattling couplings to the next car which must have been a later, more luxurious model because it was warmer and smoother riding. There the crude but persistent interrogation technique resumed, Colonel Scar's interpreter throwing his now familiar accusations at me while I threw back retorts that by now poured out of me almost like conditioned reflexes:

"No, we were not spying—we were conducting oceanographic research! . . . Observing sunspots! . . . Taking electromagnetic measurements . . . Cooperating with the International Geophysical Year! . . . No, we were not putting South Korean agents ashore—we have nothing but American citizens aboard! . . . I demand you take care of my wounded men! . . . No, I have nothing to do with the CIA! My name is Lloyd M. Bucher, my rank is Commander, United States Navy, my serial number is 582154 . . . My men and I are entitled to treatment according to the Geneva Convention! . . ."

The interpreter's voice drummed back into a counterpoint that had the same steely ring as the wheels rushing along the rails:

"You are a spy! You are a spy! You must confess! You must confess! . . . You will be shot! . . . You will be shot! . . ."

These repeated sessions lasted anywhere from ten to twenty minutes before I was taken back to my seat in the other car. Then again a half hour later, and regularly throughout the rest of this journey through darkness.

In between the interrogations when I was trying to collect myself in my assigned seat, I could hear other members of my crew being hauled off for their turns with Colonel Scar and his interpreter. In the meanwhile, some Koreans who spoke broken English, passed up and down the aisle asking each man their name, rate and function aboard the ship. I thought I heard Tim Harris passing himself off as a chief petty officer, and remembering the way he had been dressed, decided he might get away with it.

Voices were muffled and broken up by the noisy rattling and creaking of the railroad coach and periodic shrieks from the chugging locomotive, but I got the impression that everybody aboard *Pueblo* was representing himself as a petty officer assigned to either the ship's laundry or galley departments, making us the cleanest, most culinary excellent ship in the Navy. The Koreans only reacted with some scuffings against a few wilder exaggerations, but otherwise seemed to take the statements quite seriously. In my blindness, I could only tell that my boys were still showing some defiantly humorous American moxie in their misery, and that raised my own sagging spirits.

We were not allowed to talk between ourselves and any attempt to do so was met with blows. Some men were suffering from thirst and hunger by now, but their complaints were met with terse announcement that they would be fed breakfast when we reached our destination—which told us that we were in for a pretty long trip. For some reason I was given the privilege of a midnight snack which I did not want. Some water was forced down my throat and a greasy glob of what tasted like sugared butter was shoved into my mouth which almost choked me before I could swallow it.

At long last the train slowed down and I could hear the wheels break their rhythm as they clattered over switch points of a railroad yard. A voice speaking broken English announced:

"You now come to destination! You will be untied and made to see. You will leave train in order of rank with heads down and hands up like prisoners!"

As the train stopped, my hands were freed and my blindfold removed. I saw the coach as one long compartment in which I could only dimly make out my crew and their guards by the few electric overhead lights. All the windows had been covered with sheets and blankets so that nothing could be seen outside. With prods and butts, we were organized in a single file along the aisle, with me in the lead, followed by Gene Lacy, Tim Harris, and Skip Schumacher who were the only others in the group who could be identified as officers. Then they herded us toward the exit.

When I stepped outside, I was instantly blinded by the glare of brilliant kleig lights and the flare of photographic flashbulbs. When I tried to shield my eyes from the intense bursts of light which actually caused great physical pain after long hours of absolute darkness, riflebutts knocked my hands back above my head. Batteries of movie and still cameras whirred and clicked as we were lined up on a platform for propaganda pictures and held there for several minutes while the photographers took their shots. "Heads down, hands up, like prisoners!" was the pose we were directed to assume. With sidelong glances through watering eyes, I could barely catch a few details of what appeared to be a large railroad station that was deserted in the predawn darkness except for the concentrated bustle and lights of official press people who had been alerted to meet us. This was, I guessed, Pyongyang's central station and the time about 0600. I also had a glimpse of two stretchers among my men as they were kept in line behind Gene, Skip and me, making me wonder if the Koreans had bothered to bring along Hodges' body, or if somebody besides Woelk was badly wounded too and if any had been killed by the beatings.

When the photographers were finished they marched us in single file past the station into buses waiting outside. The windows were not covered like those of our railroad coach, so that one could catch glimpses of the city we started driving through—greenish pools of light flashing by as we passed mercury-vapor street lamps illuminating the façades of modern but starkly plain, dark four-story buildings. Then the guards patrolling the aisle forced us to bow our heads and keep our eyes on the floor, but I could tell from the change of tone of the tires that we evidently were driven beyond the asphalt streets of the city into a suburban dirt road. The bus was terribly cold and the only warmth came from huddling close together in the seat I shared with Skip. None of our bodies had much to spare and we were, of course, forbidden on pain of more beating to talk to each other so we rode in silence for the next forty minutes.

The end of our long journey was reached in the cul-de-sac of a broad gravel yard flanked by grim looking concrete barracks which loomed black against the flat gray predawn light. Icicles hung from the eaves and puddles filling the wheel ruts were solidly frozen. As I stiffly staggered off the bus, I had the impression of what I always imagined any Asiatic-Siberian Communist concentration camp would look like. And my reception there was also up to expectations. No sooner had my feet touched the frozen ground when I received one of those expert Korean kicks in the small of my back, followed by another behind a knee. This time both my body and mind rebelled at the punishment they had received and I pulled myself up, reeled around at my assailant, a small moon-faced Korean soldier, and went for him with fists flailing. Before I could connect, four of his comrades tackled me and we fell in a struggling heap. I cursed with pain and rage as they pinioned me and started dragging me toward one of the barracks buildings. I could hear Skip and Gene getting the same treatment behind me before they faded from sight and hearing as I was manhandled by the four guards through an entrance and up three flights of stairs. A Korean officer bounded along with shouts that sounded like orders to belay the beating I was receiving along the way, but which did not stop my own wild outburst of resistance.

When we reached the third landing of the staircase, I was dragged down a dark corridor with closed doors on both sides, then hurled through one of them into a small barren cubicle and slammed down on a bunk. The hard judo grips let go of my limbs. The soldiers backed out. The door shut with a bang.

As I lay there gasping for breath while staring up at a naked lightbulb glowing from the end of a cord dangling from the ceiling, I heard an angry voice below from the corridor: "Will learn to be sincere—or die!"

I wheezed out a few more profanities, some inane babblings about the Geneva Convention, about oceanographic research, about sunspots (which seemed to be dancing before my eyes), then sat up with my hands wrapped around my neck, trying to regain control of my reeling senses. Jesus! Dear God! What had happened to me? To my *Pueblo*? To my men? Only a few hours ago we had been a United States ship with her complement going about their legitimate minimum risk mission in international waters of the Sea of Japan! And now? . . . Jesus, God! What was left to betray us in that bulging mattress cover sack I had seen lying on the deck of the SOD-Hut? . . .

CHAPTER XII

"THE STYLE AND WORDING OF THE DOCUMENT
BY NORTH KOREA PROVIDES UNMISTAKABLE EVI-
DENCE IN THEMSELVES THAT THIS WAS NOT
WRITTEN BY ANY AMERICAN."—(Asst. Secretary
of Defense, Phil G. Goulding's comment to
press, January 25, 1968, about CDR Bucher's
"confession".)

"OUR OFFICIAL BIRD IS NOT AN EAGLE, HAWK
OR DOVE. IT IS A CHICKEN."—(Editorial in Mil-
waukee Sentinel about Pueblo incident, January 25, 1968.)

I was not left for long to collect my thoughts or rest my battered body in the solitude of my cell. It was really a fairly spacious
one, measuring about twelve by seventeen feet, furnished with a
straight-backed wooden chair, a small table, a bunk with crude,
hard bedding, and a steam radiator that was either shut off or
broken down. The single window was sealed with canvas on the
outside and brown paper on the inside; its top pane was broken,
letting in an icy draft. No sooner had these details registered than
the door flew open and two Korean troopers escorted me out at
bayonet point, taking me down the now silent and empty corridor, down a flight of stairs, and into an interrogation room
where four officers whom I had seen before, waited. This team
was served by an interpreter who interspersed his translation
with a lot of wheezing and coughing to give himself time to figure
out the language. The questions and accusations were the same

as before; so were my retorts and protests. The session lasted for
ten minutes and ended in the usual draw, discounting a few
more bruises added to the many I had already accumulated. Back
to the cell!

Faint daylight seeped through my covered window, fainter than
the sickly yellow glow of the electric lightbulb, but helping me
estimate the time to be between seven and eight in the morning.
I looked around for electronic "bugs," but besides that bulb hanging from its old-fashioned cotton cord, there was nothing electric
in the room. The floor was made of poorly fitted tongue-and-
groove boards. The walls appeared to be thick concrete that
gave a solid impression, yet I could hear and feel the icy winter
wind whistling through the entire building. Its poor insulation
was testified to by a bucket of water standing in one corner which
had a cover of ice frozen over it. The door was made of wood with
nine panels, heavily timbered, but with many cracks through
which I occasionally noticed an eye peering at me. It suddenly
burst open and a junior KORCOM officer stormed in, sputtering
in a high-pitched voice his full repertoire of Communist insults
in a fractured English:

"Sonabichi! You are Imperialist sonabichi! You be sincere sorry
Imperialist sonabichi . . . or sonabichi be shot!" He glowered
with hatred and stamped his feet and flapped his arms, slapping
the holster of his pistol as he worked himself into a lather of
venom. "Imperialist aggressor! You better make sincere confession, or we shoot spying Imperialist liar! . . ."

I probably showed more genuine amazement than contempt
over his excited performance, and because he used the word so
often, promptly dubbed him the "Imperialist." He had brought in
with him an enlisted guard looking like a boy of fifteen playing
soldier, but who clutched a real loaded carbine with a sharp
bayonet in his nervous hands as he stared at me with an uncertain mixture of fear and revulsion. It was obvious I was the first
Imperialist-American beast he had ever seen with his own eyes
and the experience was quite unnerving.

The door to my cell was left open during the Imperialist's prolonged tirade, and I had a glimpse of a female KORCOM officer strutting by as she passed down the corridor, a stocky

Amazon in green twill uniform and a pistol on her belt, glancing at me with her bulldog face screwed into a grimace of disgust. "Iseekee!" she snarled before vanishing.

The Imperialist kept bawling over me for the next couple of minutes while I tried to remain stolidly unaffected, resisting equally my underlying fears as well as a temptation to laugh in his face. Then he suddenly turned off his torrent of curses and trickled forth a polite, inquiring "How you feel? Perhaps need to go to toilet, yes?"

Well, that was an offer I could not refuse. So I nodded yes.

"Follow me with no tricks! Come now!"

Before allowing me to step into the corridor, he peered out to make sure it was clear of any other *Pueblo* people, then motioned the nervous young guard to escort me to the latrine. I took the opportunity to really look over the layout outside my cell. There were closed doors spaced on both sides, suggesting that at least a dozen or more cells like mine were located on this floor. How many and who among my crew were imprisoned here, I could not tell. Besides the measured footfall of a couple more young enlisted guards patrolling the corridor, it was totally silent. My greatest surprise was to discover that the floor out here was made of finely polished marble—a peculiarly luxurious material to mix into the construction of a cement and wood prison! But I found the latrine located at the far end of the marble hall to be far from luxurious.

The Imperialist checked it first before allowing me to enter. The place had a horribly pungent odor, but I lurched toward the trough of a urinal because I had a painful urge to relieve myself. What came out of me was mostly blood and I noticed that there were other splatters of blood in the filthy receptacle besides my own—that of my crew who had obviously been beaten as badly, or worse, than I with damage to their kidneys. I wheeled on the Imperialist and shouted at him, "Where are my men? I demand to speak to them right now."

My sudden outburst made him uneasy, but he quickly recovered his scowl and hissed, "Sh-shs-sh, goddamned sonabichi prisoner, be quiet!"

But somebody among my people had heard my voice and recognized it, because when I was escorted back down that marble hall, an unmistakable American voice called through one of the doors:

"Good luck, Captain."

I don't know who it was, but he gave my spirits a tremendous lift. Some of my crew were close by and still alive, and now they knew that I was, too. Only that skittish guard's bayonet pressed between my shoulder blades kept me from shouting back encouragement.

Soon after I returned to my cell, I was brought a breakfast tray containing a platter of boiled turnips, bread, butter and sugar, all swimming together in watery juice. A chronic feeling of nausea from untreated wounds, multiple abrasions, and mental anguish combined with a determination to in no way cooperate with these KORCOMs made it easy for me to refuse to eat that mess. The guard who brought it looked insulted as he removed the tray, then returned to prod me with his bayonet toward another interrogation.

This session brought me face to face with a new, and most disturbing development. The interrogating officer, a squinty-eyed senior major, had some folders on his desk among which I recognized my own service record jacket. Oh, God. The same jacket I had passed out of my cabin to be jettisoned overboard! I pretended not to notice it, but when Major Squint began formulating questions out of the information it contained, there was no use in denying them. I was stunned to find this official document out of my personal files had not been destroyed, yet at the same time comforted by the knowledge that it contained no military secrets, only such items as the date of my commission, the vessels I had served aboard, duty assignments, and service schools attended, etc. He made no particular comment about my being a submarine officer, but took special interest in the fact that I had once attended the Navy's CIC School in Glenview, Illinois. When I admitted that was true, he triumphantly exclaimed through his interpreter:

"That proves you are a trained spy! Counter Intelligence School—part of infamous CIA!"

I was not about to put him straight on the meaning of CIC

in our naval parlance (Combat Information Center, a centralized plotting and weapons control system carried by all our armed Navy ships). At least I now had some idea why they were persistently accusing me of being a CIA agent, but I simply denied it categorically as I had before.

"You deny what is here written in your own official documentation?" he furiously shouted at me.

"I deny your interpretation of it," I answered and then launched into my standard protestations of being a peaceful oceanographer, a sunspot-gazer, etc., who had been wrongfully pirated off the high seas, and demanded the immediate release of my ship and crew.

There followed the expected rain of blows, kicks and karate chops, all accompanied by furious invectives from the senior major which were translated in simultaneous outbursts from his interpreter "Sonabitchi criminal! Goddamned liar! Spydog! . . ."

As I balled myself up on the floor trying to protect my vitals, I may well have given the inept interpreter a good lesson in more eloquent American profanities.

When I was dumped back in my cell, I felt myself on the ragged edge of total collapse. It had now been twenty-eight hours since I had risen from my last restless night of sleep aboard *Pueblo*, twenty since I started agonizing over the worst predicament of my life, and sixteen of almost constant physical beatings, compounded by pains of the wounds I had sustained in the first burst of the North Korean attack. They knew nothing about those wounds because I had never mentioned them out of fear of being separated from my crew in some North Korean hospital ward. Keeping us together so I could exercise my responsibility as their commanding officer was still a forlorn obsession. Another was the security of the classified material which might have been compromised with *Pueblo*'s seizure. I had been severely shaken to find the senior major in possession of a portion of my service record. What other documents had they salvaged from our incomplete destruction? And how well were the rest of my men bearing up? Like gentle, intellectual Steve Harris with his brain crammed full of vital naval intelligence secrets? And how about his sensitive CTs who knew all about Operation Ichthyic? And

the completely innocent ones, like my two Filipino Stewards
Mates, Abelon and Aluague, who knew absolutely nothing about
our mission, but were suspected of being South Korean infiltrators? And what about myself? How long could I keep functioning under constant beatings that were likely to escalate into
outright torture? Was I—were we all—in for those horrible bar-
barities which had become legendary among the living generations of servicemen of the past three wars in the Far East?

These things preyed on my mind and became an insidious torture of its own, giving me little opportunity to recuperate and
collect myself before time came for the next confrontation with
our captors.

It was about ten o'clock when I was roused out of my cell
again. In the corridor, all my officers were lined up in the enforced abject head-bowed position the Koreans required of their
prisoners. Ed Murphy, Steve Harris, Gene Lacy, Tim Harris, who
had escaped identification before because of their conglomerate
nonregulation clothing, were now included in the group. Had
their service records too been recovered? Without being allowed
to exchange a word, we were all marched off in a shuffling single-
file of six dejected Americans guarded by twice as many armed
Korean soldiers.

In a large conference room, about thirty officers were seated
at a U-shaped arrangement of tables before which they had placed
five chairs for us to sit on. This looked almost like a formal tribunal, complete with a presiding judge in the person of a splendidly
uniformed general who chain-smoked cigarettes and kept toying
with a silver lighter. He was flanked by several colonels and other
senior officers among whom I only recognized Colonel Scar and
the squinty-eyed major who had grilled me only an hour ago. The
interpreter was the same one who had boarded *Pueblo* yesterday
evening and accompanied us on our long trip to this place of
detention. He must have been almost as weary as we prisoners,
but did not show it as he rapped out: "You will each stand in
turn, identify yourself by name, rank, serial number, and duty
with your spyship. To start with Captain! At once!"

We complied, each giving correctly the information requested, except for Skip Schumacher who equivocated slightly by describing himself as *Pueblo*'s "First Lieutenant."

Translations of our answers were duly noted down and then the general launched into a long speech which gradually turned into an impassioned tirade that the interpreter had some difficulty in keeping up with. He could only convey fractured verbiage about American imperialist aggressions . . . provocations . . . espionage . . . intimidations of peaceful democratic peoples of Korea . . . sabotage of their efforts to develop the world's most advanced social system, and an ad nauseam repetition of all the standard Communist slogans and Marxist platitudes with which we were becoming boringly familiar. The performance ended with a question thrown directly at me:

"Why does your government of the United States keep fifty thousand American troops inside our South Korea? Say why! At once!"

I answered: "Because the government of South Korea found it necessary to ask our help in defending their country. That's why."

The colonel seated closest to me reacted to this statement by slamming his fist on the table with a torrent of Korean invectives that were spontaneous enough to completely befuddle the interpreter. It was the general who restrained him when he became so beside himself that he seemed ready to spring at me with a hand cocked karate-fashion, for the attack. The colonel managed to regain control and allow the Comrade General to complete his part in the proceedings which was to emphatically reiterate the already familiar statement: "You have no rights under any Geneva Convention rules as criminal spies and agents making provocations in time of peace between us! Do you not admit this be why you are here? Answer now!"

Each one of us was asked that question individually, and each one individually denied it.

The Comrade General made certain that his next words were carefully, precisely translated to us:

"If that is your persist . . . then you will all be shot this afternoon." After a pause to let that sink in, he sighed deeply and asked, "How would you like that? Each shot alone? Or all together? . . . Make choice!"

I yelled: "Shoot me! But let my officers and crew return to our ship and take it home."

"No, Captain! Because we caught you spying, ship now belongs to us."

"You seized us in international waters where we had every right to be—damn it! . . . You've committed an act of war against the United States!"

"It is you who commit act of war by spying! You will be shot this afternoon!" I was told and when my officers refused to confess, each of them was told in turn, "You will be shot this afternoon!" Then we were all herded out together in the same fashion we had arrived, each of us wondering if we had just attended what passed for a Communist trial and all received our death sentence.

We had no chance to discuss developments between ourselves and were quickly separated in solitary confinement. I was not to see any of these men again for several weeks.

Shortly after being returned to my cell, a tray of warm milk and cookies was offered to me. The condemned man's last meal? Perhaps. The Korean general had seemed entirely serious about our impending executions. But, in any case, I refused to eat or drink. A junior lieutenant came in and surprised me with a sudden show of concern which he expressed in halting English, "Best eat or ruin health, yes!" and even tried to encourage me with a smile of sorts. But the effect was spoiled when one of his companions tried a more characteristic technique which was a persuasive clout to the head. Neither of them could make me touch the food.

Within a very short time I was again removed from my cell and escorted down the corridor thinking that now my destination might be the ultimate one of this Communist prison's cellar. But it turned out to be just another interrogation and that raised my hopes slightly because if they wanted to continue to talk and were showing interest in my appetite, then they must also have something in mind for me besides immediate execution. Possibly worse than immediate execution? That grim idea dimmed hope to a feeble flicker. And it became dimmer yet when I found myself facing the same hatefully excitable senior colonel who had seemed ready to fly at me during the last session.

He had not calmed down at all and now there was no general to restrain him as he cut loose with a fist pounding, foot stomping tirade which he screamed out in Korean at the top of his voice. The effect of his interpreter trying to keep up with him in gesture, volume, and meaning would have been farcical under different circumstances. But in mine they became grotesquely terrifying. It was all I could do to face up to the performance without cringing and I could only do it by forcing myself to take a really good analytical look at the colonel. It struck me that for all his overacting, he was pacing his furious gestures within bounds of careful rehearsal. For all his yelled insults and profanities, their wording had been carefully memorized. In spite of his show of unbridled outrage, he was not, I decided, really losing control of himself. His intemperate posturing did not entirely compromise an underlying intelligence and natural aura of authority. I had a feeling that I was now confronted with the most influential authority in our prison and when he completed his tirade with a vociferous assurance that he had all the proof he needed that I was truly a spy, I calmly asked him "May I ask a question?"

"Ask it," he answered with a flash of expectation through his tinted glasses.

"What is happening to my wounded men? Are they being taken care of? I demand the right to see them."

The interpreter translated and the colonel put on a hard disappointed look, shook his head, and shoved toward me a sheet of paper with typewriting on it. "You must sign confession now."

"I will sign nothing," I answered, shoving it back at him without reading it.

I expected this would trigger another long outburst. But he merely snapped: "Then must take the consequence of refusing to cooperate!" The colonel left the room and Imperialist came in. The consequence was the worst beating yet, administered by the guards when they delivered me back to my cell, and with such force that I was slammed from one wall to the other and left half-conscious on the floor. But I noticed that they had avoided hitting me in the face. And I was still alive. When yet another tray of food was brought me within a few minutes and they tried very hard at coaxing me to eat, I knew they wanted to keep me alive for a while longer—for better or for worse!

My next grilling came sometime between noon and 1300 hours, the fifth one since being delivered to the prison early that morning. I was held in the dingy concrete conference hall where the Korean general had informed me and all my officers that we were to be shot that afternoon. The place had been rearranged somewhat and was now occupied by only a few interpreter officers, armed enlisted guards, and the squinty-eyed senior major who presided from behind a long table on which were piled documents that I instantly recognized to have come from *Pueblo*. I tried not to react to them as I was conducted past the table to a chair, strategically placed just beyond easy reading range of the evidence, and forced to sit down. I had been told by the choleric senior colonel during the preceding session that proof of our spying would be produced and I was almost overwhelmed by shock over what they had collected on that table.

Most of the material I could not identify, but by straining my eyes I could make out the special Navy stamps that were always affixed to classified material. Much of it looked like publications for our ship's technical library—hopefully pretty standard stuff carried by most naval vessels without necessarily including secret information. But I did identify copies of *Banner*'s cruise reports which I had received last month at Pearl Harbor from Commander Eastman and realized with a sinking heart that these would be very compromising, if not for the United States Navy as such, very much for us as a ship's company. I also noticed one of my own narratives of *Pueblo*'s current part in Operation Ichthyic which had been in Steve Harris's custody to be typed clean and prepared for multilith distribution to interested intelligence authorities upon our return to Yokosuka. My first reaction to it was one of impending disaster. But I quickly recalled what I had written in it: observations about an uneventful cruise where the greatest excitement was bad weather, severe icing conditions, Nansen casts, and the photographing of a few innocuous merchant ships and trawlers met along our lonely, stormy way. If anything, it might support our cover story of being a casual oceanographic research ship. Certainly there was nothing there to suggest intrusions into North Korean territorial waters or the landing on their soil of agents. Yet the possession of these documents, which we had failed to destroy, put the Koreans in a position to intimidate us and Major Squint proceeded to take subtle advantage of it. He picked out sheets of paper at random from the pile, and waved them in my face while being careful that I received no more than a glimpse of their content, asking, "Do these belong to you or your ship?"

"Yes—obviously. So what?"

"Are they official American Navy documents?"

"Yes—obviously. We are an official U. S. Navy ship operating on the high seas."

"Do you deny they prove you were spying?"

Since I glimpsed my signature on one of the papers, I said, "They prove nothing beyond that I collected incidental intelligence while conducting oceanographic research on the high seas. Which is perfectly legitimate, as you Communists well know and have taken full advantage of."

"Ah, then you will sign this confession!" He switched our document for one of their own which I recognized as the same pretyped confession that Super-C, our Super Colonel, had presented me with earlier that day.

This time I took advantage of the opportunity to glance through it, catching among the rest of the stilted English-Communist composition some specific reference to my admitted association with the CIA in provoking North Korea into a new war. And to promises of great rewards to myself and my family if I succeeded in this infamous mission. If I had not been so thoroughly beaten and weary, physically as well as mentally, I should have realized that this was the confession I should have signed then and there. It would have made the Koreans look completely ridiculous if they had publicized it to the world as justification for their piracy against *Pueblo*. But as it was, I angrily refused to sign it, exclaiming, "This is nothing but garbage. You know you have no proof to support such a confession on my part."

I braced myself for a painful pummeling, or at the very least a blast of the interpreter's oddly colorful translations of verbal abuse. But Colonel Squint merely made another deft switch of documents and waved my undoubtedly authentic narrative report before my eyes.

"Are you denying truth of this paper?" he asked with a doubt that struck me as entirely genuine and indicating he might be suspecting it to be a deliberate plant to throw his kind off the track in case we were captured.

"No, I don't deny it," I answered. "Like it says, we've been doing nothing but our assigned oceanographic research, observing what's to be seen in international waters of the high seas and nothing else. That's all!"

"All lies, then, you sonabitchy! We know you are a Imperialist capitalistic liar and spy!" The interpreter repeated several times what seemed to be their favorite version of a common American insult: "Sonabitchy"—spewed out in a splatter of saliva.

Colonel Squint ordered my removal from his presence and I left feeling almost victorious except for a lingering apprehension over the effect of his tableful of evidence which I felt certain would be shown many members of *Pueblo*'s crew. I prayed that it would not demolish them as it almost had me.

I was led back to my concrete cell on the third floor where once again I was tempted with food and coaxed to eat it by several officers-of-the-guard who tried to charm me in their basic Korean-English. This time I was given a fair amount of time without any violence before being hauled forth for the next interrogation. The supposed recuperative period was marred by my hearing faint but distinct screams of agony coming from somewhere down the corridor outside my cell. I could not eat, lie down on my bunk, nor sit on my chair. Only pace back and forth from one corner with occasional deviations to the green wooden panels of the door to yell, "Stop beating my men, you bastards! Stop beating my men and let us out of here!"

Jesus God, Bucher, you've got to get hold of yourself. At least don't let them know you're cracking. That's what they're waiting for—for you to crack completely. Get away from that door and shut up! God help me to hang in here. God help my men. . . .

There followed only one more interrogation session during that afternoon, one in which my service record card was used in the

questioning and where I denied nothing in it except their interpretation of CIC School. For the rest of the time I was left pacing alone in solitary confinement, listening to occasional screams
of pain coming from the far end of the concrete building, meanwhile trying to keep a grip on myself in the irrational hope that
those cries were staged effects to break my will. They had not
beaten me for a couple of hours, so perhaps they had also stopped
beating my crew. But then I was sure I recognized one of the
agonized voices as belonging to Ed Murphy. Regular bursts of
scuffling, of doors opening and slamming shut in the corridor,
clearly told how all of my men were being worked over in turn.

My helplessness gnawed like a malignant cancer in my breast.
I trembled with cold and frustration. I prayed. I cursed. And all
the while, the faint slivers of daylight seeping through my padded
window faded into another black Korean winter night. A silent
closing curtain of darkness undisturbed by the faintest whine of
avenging jets of our Fifth Air Force. Why in hell was the United
States not retaliating? Well, perhaps they had at least pulverized
Wonsan and did not know we were here in Pyongyang—or wherever this prison was located.

It must have been about eight o'clock in the evening when my
next turn came with the interrogators. I was taken out of my cell
to the floor below where the Super-C awaited me in a dingy
room with a couple of officer-interpreters and several enlisted
guards armed with automatic rifles with fixed bayonets. One of
the interpreters was hefting a drawn pistol. The Super-C was
seated behind a plain wooden desk that contrasted with the
luxurious material of his heavy military greatcoat and fur cap
which he kept on as protection against the cold seeping through
the dank clammy walls of this prison. A strange touch was a pair
of fancy civilian shoes. He was calm, almost chattily pleasant as
he explained to me that North Korea wanted nothing but peace,
and if world peace was to be preserved, it was absolutely essential that I sign a confession. I was then presented with the same
typewritten one I had seen twice that day, but he now offered
additional incentive. "Sign it and you will all shortly be returned
home without more unpleasantness between us."

The temptation was great, but I nevertheless refused, repeating all my previously stated reasons and protestations.

"So, you deny that you had materials aboard your ship for spying on our country. And that you were provoking the peace-loving Koreans to another Fatherland Liberation War?" he asked.

"I have seen documents you took from my ship," I answered, "including a narrative log with my comments in it. I'm sure you know the contents by now."

I was hoping to increase his suspicion of that narrative, but after a few more tries to reason me into signing the confession, his manner switched back to the one of abusive rage which he had used against me that morning. The cold cement walls of the little room reverberated with his blistering insults and the wooden desk jumped and rattled as he pounded on it. He was really quite an actor for an otherwise imposing, almost handsome, military figure. But was he just acting? "You have exactly two minutes to decide to sign, sonabitch!" he climaxed his histrionics. "Or then be shot!"

Two of his subordinate officers wrenched me out of my chair, forced me to my knees facing the wall. The one with the drawn pistol cocked his weapon close to my ear. "Two minutes to decide, or be shot!" Super-C repeated, his voice suddenly coldly measured.

I found myself quite prepared to die, almost looking forward to it because all the pain in my body was telling me that I could never withstand prolonged torture. Yet those two minutes became an agonizing suspense of pure terror in which I could only keep myself from collapsing in a heap on the floor by repeating over and over again "I love you, Rose! . . . I love you, Rose . . ."

One of the Korean lieutenants was standing in front of me and as time ran out, he was ordered to move aside so that the bullet passing through my head would not hit him. Then I heard the colonel rasp out something which was translated as "Are you ready to sign?"

I shook my head and whispered for the last time, "I love you, Rose! . . ."

"Kill the sonabitch!"

The brittle metallic snap jarred my whole body as much as

the expected obliterating explosion it had been braced to take.

The colonel let out an exclamation of surprise that was hardly necessary for his interpreter to translate, "Well! That was a misfire. Very lucky! So then take another two minutes—a last chance to confess without trusting to luck again!"

The pistol was still poised behind my head, but when the slide was racked to reload a new cartridge into the chamber, I did not hear the ejected dud hit the floor. There was just enough left of my reeling sense to realize the pistol had not been loaded; that I was being made the object of an age-old interrogation technique. It made it easier for me to withstand the suspense of the next two minutes and when they were up, to stubbornly keep up my refusal to cooperate. My supposed executioner did not even bother to click his weapon again, but Super-C howled a new threat:

"You are not worth a good bullet. Beat him to death!"

This one he came to within an inch of making good.

All but the colonel fell upon me with kicks, chops, and blows with rifle butts. They kept up their violent assault without let-up, knocking me all over the room and driving with vicious force for the pit of my stomach, the small of my back, and my testicles. When I tried to protect my lower body, they hit me around the neck and head, and when I tried to cover those parts, hammered away at my crotch and kidneys. They drowned out my screams with furious curses and kept beating, beating, beating until I was a retching, winded wreck being whipped back and forth between them like a rag doll in the hands of a gang of frenzied psychotic children. Then, mercifully, I blacked out.

I regained consciousness back in solitary where I had been dumped on my bunk. When I opened my eyes, the single bulb dangling from the ceiling turned into a crazy chandelier glowing through a red-tinged yellow haze. With the return of consciousness came the return of pain, shooting in fiery jabs through what felt like broken bones and torn flesh, but concentrating a sustained pressure of agony around my kidneys and testicles. Only my face seemed relatively free of pain and I tried to attach some meaningful significance to that—perhaps they did not want me to *look* like I had been severely beaten. Perhaps I was still being spared for some purpose. My face had not been disfigured and I also found that my bones were unbroken when I rolled off the bunk and was able to stagger to the door and pound on it, croaking, "*Benjo! Benjo!*" ("Toilet! Toilet!")

A guard let me out and kept me covered as I lurched toward the latrine at the end of the corridor to relieve the excruciating pressure on my kidneys. When I tried to urinate into the filthy trough, all that would come out was blood. The pain did not lessen and it was all I could do to drag myself back to my cell. Yet, there must have been some fight left in me because I defiantly shoved aside the guard when he tried to make me march with the prescribed head-down lock-step of Korean prisoners. To his yelled instructions, I snarled, "F—— you, bud, leave me alone!"

They did leave me alone for the next half hour, slumped in my chair by the table with all my contusions and deeper hurts stiffening to a near paralysis, until a stocky little lieutenant with teeth and jowls that made him look like a malign chipmunk, burst in on me with drawn pistol, shouting: "Get up! Out now! Move quick!" It was all I could do to move and the two Korean soldiers which Chipmunk assigned to guard me found themselves required to give more support than restraint as we went down the three long flights of stairs to the ground floor of the prison. Down there Super-C was waiting, immaculately dapper in his tailored uniform and coolly flicking the ashes off his cigarette as his interpreter said to me, almost apologetically:

"Now we must show you how we treat spies in our country!"

He then stepped aside to let me be dragged out of the building through a side entrance. I felt a searing blast of freezing night air that turned my cold sweat to ice before being hustled into the protection of an automobile—a sort of convertible command car whose plastic windows had been covered and its rear seat curtained off from the front one by an opaque screen. I was compressed between the hard quilted bodies of my guards in the back seat without any way of knowing where we were going after the driver started the engine and racked the gearshift to get us moving ahead. There were lots of bumps and wrenching turns during the next ten minutes, like we were traveling over a rough, winding country road. But as far as I could tell, we could also have been just driving around the barracks' compound to confuse me. At any rate, when we finally stopped and I was taken out, it was to be led inside a cement building very similar to our prison. But we did not go upstairs in this one. I was conducted down into one of those sinister cellar areas that have earned Communist police headquarters their gruesome reputation.

We entered a barren room with a small casement window located close to the ceiling and a pair of strong spotlights focused on one gray wall where a human being was hanging from his chest by a leather strap attached to an iron ring embedded in the concrete some six feet above the cement floor. The man was barely alive, stripped to the waist so that all the black bruises covering his torso were exposed, as was the compound fracture of one limp arm with a jagged piece of bone protruding through the torn flesh. His face was a pulp in which one eyeball dangled out of its socket in a dark ooze of fluid coagulating on his cheek. He had completely chewed through his lower lip that hung in shreds from between clenched teeth. With the first shock of seeing this horribly mangled wretch, I was stunned by the thought that he might be one of my own men, but then one of the interpreters announced: "This is a South Korean spy we have caught! Look at his just punishment!"

I could not take my eyes off that tortured pulp of humanity and saw through the torn and battered features that he was indeed a Korean, yet the shock remained and even intensified as I took in the details, completely overwhelming me with revulsion. It threw me into a sort of mental blackout that was like finding one's self in a horrible nightmare in which one consciously fights against a totally unbelievable experience and struggles to awaken to normalcy—but cannot! The dying South Korean hung there before my eyes from his strap, bleeding, twitching, frothing through his torn mouth. The voices of his torturers dinned my ears, boasting of their infamous craft. I tried to yell, but my vocal cords as well as the rest of my body, seemed to have been severed dreamlike from any controlling impulses of my brain.

I have no memory of being returned to our cell block and suspect that I had to be bodily carried out of that torture chamber, dumped back in the command car and delivered into the custody of Super-C. When my blackout eventually dissipated in a gray daze, it was his face that dissolved into focus through the haunting spectre of the South Korean's eviscerated eyeball, his eyes staring at me through tinted spectacles with a hooded smoldering intensity. "So now you have seen for yourself how we treat spies," he had his interpreter remind me. "Perhaps you will reconsider your refusal to confess?"

It was pure stubborn reflex that made me shake my head.

"You must realize we are not playing games and may lose patience with you," the colonel continued in measured words. "You must surely remember you are responsible for the lives of your crew."

That struck a sensitive chord which jolted my mind back to full awareness. "Yes, I know I am," I blurted out. "But *you* are responsible for what is happening here. *You* are responsible for the atrocity of not caring for my wounded. *You* are responsible for the murder of one of my men."

I don't know if the interpreter was able to fully translate my faltering, slurred accusations, but the colonel got the gist of them and reacted with a gesture that turned his subordinates loose on me. I was knocked out of my chair, kicked across the floor and bounced off the wall. But he was more bent on talking than beating and quickly ordered the guards to drag me back into the chair and prop me up in it.

"You must be sincere. You must sign this confession as proof that you wish your crew to be treated leniently and humanely. The evidence is complete. Why do you not sign?"

"Because of all the lies it contains about my country," I gasped.

"The world must know about the United States' imperialistic warmongering," he answered with a genuine note of agitation in his voice which warned me that he was really getting desperate for a confession to justify the North Korean's act of piracy.

"No, I won't sign it."

"We will see," he angrily shot back with an absolute conviction that made it quite different from any previous outbursts. "We will now begin to shoot your crew. We will shoot them one at a time, right here in front of your eyes so that you can see them die. We will shoot them all, starting with the youngest one first and so on, sonabitchy, until you sign confession. And if you have not signed when they are all dead, then we still have ways of making you do it, and all your crew will be dead for nothing. So that's what we mean about you being responsible for their lives. You are not sincere. We now bring in the crew member Bland to be shot."

The name was read from a list of names he held. One of the guards left the room, presumably to fetch Fireman Howard Bland who I did not remember as the youngest crew member, but nevertheless knew as a boy of not much over twenty years. Would these animals dare kill him before my eyes? The vision of that tortured South Korean hanging from a strap with his compound fracture, blinded eye and multiple contusions reappeared on the wall of the room in full, horribly vivid reality. Yes, this breed of politics did not give a damn about the life or death of their own kinsmen—let alone any round-eyed Americans! They were well molded beasts with the bare strappings of civilization. I could not even contemplate leaving Bland's life at their mercy for the sake of my signature on a scrap of paper containing nothing but blatantly obvious lies and propaganda. This dilemma was beyond my training as a naval officer, as captain of a ship, as a human being with deeply ingrained sensitivity for his fellow men. I had resisted as long as I could, but now I could do none other than finally give in to a totally foreign brutality. I made up my mind:

"All right . . . I will sign."

Super-C gave a start and let out a snakelike hiss and thrust a pen into my hand, eagerly directing his minions to support me while I leaned over his desk and scrawled a trembling signature across the bottom of the paper. I could feel the triumphant relief of my tormentors who suddenly became very concerned with my state of health, and after helping me back to my cell, offered me a tray loaded with their warm milk, cookies, an apple and boiled eggs. I sat and stared at the tray, wanting to eat, but unable to.

I was too emotionally wrung out, too physically battered to stay on my bunk and try to escape into sleep. No matter in what position I lay on the hard, musty mattress, one bruise would jab me into tossing against another. No matter how much I wanted to surrender to a numbing weariness, the torments in my mind kept fighting on. It became easier to pace my cell under the glare of the electric bulb which they never turned off, my shuffling steps keeping knotted insides and aching muscles from congealing in the bitter cold, and my mind from stalling over one unanswerable question by diverting to another equally unanswerable one.

How much classified material had the KORCOMs captured besides that which I had been shown? Who else had cracked under the pressure of beatings and intimidation? I was certain then uncertain that the United States would see through my confession as a phoney given under duress. But why had there been no attempt at retaliation or rescue? Were we abandoned? Disavowed? Would the KORCOMs wrest all the information they needed out of us, then return us home? Or let us linger indefinitely in this prison? Kill us all? My God, what will become of Rose, Mike and Mark? Had I remembered to write them before we left Sasebo? Yes, but the letter would be followed by the terrible news about *Pueblo* and start their own particular kind of agony over not knowing whether I was dead or alive. I wanted to reach out across the Pacific and hold my Rose, telling her not to worry, that I was still alive and would somehow get back to her, and in the meanwhile she had to carry on. But I wanted to hold her, comfort her, and in turn be held and comforted. Self-pity mingled with self-reproach. How had I gotten myself and my shipmates into this damnable hole? What fatuously negligent echelon of our Navy was responsible for allowing me to blunder into this kind of predicament without the slightest forewarning, and without training or equipment to properly contend with the situation? They had not even heeded my own expressed doubts, refusing me destruct equipment, scuttling equipment, effective armament, or permission significantly to cut down on *Pueblo*'s great overload of printed secrets. It's a "minimum risk" I was told over and over again, so stop worrying about it! During the several hours that lapsed between confrontations with the six KORCOM warships and two MIGs, the attack and capture, I had let COMNAV-FORJAPAN know what was happening and what action I was taking. When no specific orders were flashed back, I had to take this as tacit approval of that action since they had been given plenty of time to tell me more than WE ARE ON HOTLINE and ALL AUTHORITIES ALERTED. In the meanwhile my "minimum risk" mission turned into sudden disaster. One sailor had lost his life, several were wounded, our ship with all hands were prisoners. Why? How had this thing that could never happen, happen to me? With all our admirals safely beyond hearing of my distress, I directed an accusing prayer of woe to even higher authority: "Why me? Why me, oh, God!"

God's answer was a faint sublimated message in my conscience "You are responsible, Captain! This is your test and trial!"

But had I not already failed the test? My ship had fallen almost intact into enemy hands, and worse, so had some of her secrets. One man dead, doing his duty, perhaps others by now, either allowed to die of their wounds, or beaten to death by these barbarians. Perhaps I was the last one kept alive, only because I had made a partial confession and so might go all the way. Maybe they were planning to wring every last secret out of me, real or imagined, bit by agonized bit. They had already proven to me that there were limits to both the mental and physical torture that I could stand. Death did not frighten me anywhere nearly as much as torture, so was not death preferable? Death, now, before I caved in over something more harmful to my country than that ridiculously contrived confession. And the terrible thought struck me . . . that death now was better than waiting for Soviet Russian intelligence experts to arrive on the scene and back up the crude methods of the North Koreans.

Suicide is totally contrary to both my religion and my nature as a man, but in the terrible stress of this moment, it suddenly seemed to me forgivable as a last resort to protect my own honor and my country's trust. I had no weapon for self-destruction. I was too weak to bash in my head against the wall. Glass from the window to cut my veins was thickly padded by a screen of paper, and the noise I would create by tearing and breaking out a sliver would alert the guard whose steps I could hear outside my door. There remained nothing but a bucket of water standing in a corner of my cell. I had heard that drowning was a pleasant acquiescent death, once one gave in to it. I remembered when at Submarine School in New London, during a free ascent in the

110-foot escape tank, I had nearly drowned because of malfunctioning underwater glasses. The sensation was not as terrifying as I had previously thought.

But could it be done in a bucket? I was desperate enough to try it, but quickly found out it could not be done. For one thing, most of the water slopped out; for another, the room was so cold that I had to break through a sheet of ice and the freezing liquid jolted me back to my senses. Suicide was not only impossible—it was wrong. I had to hold out and live, taking what I had to—alive.

I must have finally slumped into the chair with my head on the table and sunk into a semiconscious torpor that lasted for the two hours between 0300 and 0500, when a junior lieutenant entered my cell and shook me fully awake. "You come now for talk!" was his familiar greeting. "Sonabichee be sincere with no lies. Come now!" I had hoped that with the signing of the coerced confession, Super-C would leave me alone for a while, but he had either had second thoughts about its completeness during the night, or, more likely, intended right along to browbeat me into allowing more compromising details to be inserted under my already affixed signature. He was waiting for me in the interrogation room, looking immaculately military, purposely fierce and alert in spite of the early hour, and after inquiring whether I had rested, explained that while my admitted intent of committing espionage was satisfactory in itself, the matter of actual intrusion into North Korean territorial waters had to be specified and included in the confession. I wearily denied this and pointed out that the U. S. Navy had been told our true position when we sent them our SOS on being attacked.

To this he replied through his interpreter, who was the hem-and-haw wheezing one, "Well, it's not so much about where we took you under attack. But you did follow us toward Wonsan, did you not?"

"Yes, I did—under protest."

"Then where finally did we board you?"

"Well, I don't know exactly where."

"But would you not estimate you were inside our twelve-mile line when we board you?"

"I am sure it was inside your twelve-mile line because I noticed islands about ten miles away, but . . ."

"So, that's all you have to tell, then!" he pounced. "Just that you were inside it and we captured ship in our territorial water."

When I dazedly tried to argue my way out of that trap, his eyes flashed angrily behind his spectacles and he sharply reminded me of what I had gone through yesterday, adding, "Your men are just as vulnerable now as they were last night." So I agreed to the technicality that we had been boarded inside their territorial waters, feeling sure that the Navy would know from my several JOPREPS that this too was a coerced admission. He seemed quite satisfied and after ordering the addition inserted, allowed me to be returned to my cell.

But Super-C did not remain satisfied for long and sent for me again within a very short time. Now he wanted it made clear in the confession that our intrusion had been for the specific purpose of committing acts of espionage; the wording would have to be changed and amplified accordingly. His technique of getting concessions piece by piece became clear to me, but I resisted it as best I could by continuing to protest regardless of what I had already signed. He countered with the same threats he had before and then added that my denials were useless because my Executive Officer and Navigator had already confessed to such intrusions.

So they had worked over Ed too! My heart sank. Poor Ed, I thought, but I shrugged at Super-C and said "Regardless of that, *Pueblo* never entered North Korea's claimed territorial waters to spy, and no matter what confessions you get, that is the truth."

"Are you calling your Executive Officer a liar, Captain?"

"Certainly not. If we had intruded, it would have been on my orders."

"Ah, but your Executive Officer told us he was afraid to inform you about something involving direct disobedience of your orders. That would make you very angry."

I knew this to be a hoax and even if Ed had said or signed anything like that, it was too ridiculous to be taken seriously in the United States. For all the troubles there had been between us during the past months, I was sure that he would only cooperate with these people under extreme duress—as I myself had done. Anything we signed would be judged at home as a transparent, coerced fraud. So when Super-C asked me if I wanted to see my Executive Officer's confession, I answered, "No. I don't doubt that you have some kind of paper with his signature, just like you've got one from me. So what?!"

"Then you confess you intruded especially to spy on peaceful Democratic People's Republic of Korea?"

"I confess nothing of the sort," I flatly stated.

Super-C turned on his act of rage and began chopping at his desk with the heels of his hands, and stamping his fashionable shoes against the floor. "You think we were fooling last night?" he shouted through his interpreter. "Well, you will see if we don't shoot your men, sonabeechy, especially all insincere liars! You sign or be responsible for them dying now!"

So I signed the amended confession, but then demanded for the hundredth time that we be kept together as a crew and that my wounded men be taken care of. For the first time he acknowledged that there were wounded among us by calming down and pleasantly reassuring me: "Since you cooperate with us, we will certainly give attention to your wounded. You will see we are humane. All we want is sincerity, you see!" I doubted his "sincerity" but was hardly in any position to test it.

There was breakfast waiting for me in my cell which I could not eat. All I could get down was a mug of water, served hot because evidently all drinking water in this establishment had to be boiled before consumed, while wash water was always ice cold. I was escorted to the latrine by a nervously scowling young soldier who watched me like I was a dangerous monster from another world. My urine was still full of blood. I did not dare try a bowel movement because of my painfully festering rectal wound. The long marble corridor was cleared of other prisoners during my passage, their cells silent behind closed doors. Within a half hour I was taken back to face Super-C again in the interrogation room and I found myself grudgingly admiring the man's endurance. His appearance was not in the least disheveled or fatigued after some twenty-four hours of supervising an unrelenting grilling of *Pueblo*'s crew.

I expected him to demand yet another addendum to my confession, but he surprised me with a different gambit in the Communist technique of dealing with Imperialist criminals. "You will be present at a press conference exactly thirty minutes from now," he informed me, then unwittingly betrayed its stage-managed nature as he handed me some typewritten sheets of paper, saying, "These are the questions you will be asked and the answers you will give. Read them over now to make sure everything is in accordance with your confession so that you are prepared to make a sincere appearance."

This was so ludicrous that I could not see how he was able to make the proposition with a straight face. But he was perfectly serious. I read through his script for my impending press conference and found it to be nothing more than a verbatim breakdown of my confession into question and answer form. I decided to purposely interject words and inflections of my own to subtly destroy the effect desired by the KORCOMs. However, when my study period was over and I was about to be led on stage to give my performance, I was warned to read off my answers exactly as written, "sincerely with no tricks." To make sure I had no excuse for any deviations, they sacrificed the last illusion of spontaneity by requiring me to perform with script in hand.

The setting was the same conference room where I had starred before, once with all my officers whom I hoped would be there again in supporting roles so I could see how they were holding up. But they were not. This was to be a solo for me. The audience consisted of Korean officers which included Colonels Super and Scar occupying a center loge in the form of a long table. Flanking them at smaller tables were the North Korean press corps, civilian "journalists," including one moonfaced woman, all properly provided with "programs" and note pads. As for me, the villain of the piece, I was marched to a podium, center-stage, by my somewhat jumpy platoon of bayonet carriers. The audience dutifully greeted my entrance with cluckings and hisses of disgust. I knew that I looked the part they expected of me, red-eyed and unshaven, wearing my leather jacket with its infamous *PUEBLO* insignia over the left breast and my name on the right, and rumpled khaki trousers with the right leg stained with dried blood, and clumsy thermal boots which made me stiffly shuffle like a Frankenstein monster in my weakened condition.

The show opened with Wheezy acting as interlocutor-interpreter, making an entirely unnecessary introduction which I was required to confirm (as in the opening statement of the confession) by loudly stating: "I am Lloyd Mark Bucher, Commander, U. S. Navy, Captain of the USS *Pueblo*."

The balance of the act followed the script to the letter, the questions being screamed at me by each "journalist" on cue, translated by Wheezy, answered according to my own copy of the script, then translated back so that everybody could scribble down on their note pads what they already knew the answer to be. Sample:

JOURNALIST: (Jumping up from table with wild gestures, yells) Were you captured while carrying out espionage activities after intruding deep into the territorial waters of the Democratic People's Republic of Korea?

BUCHER: (Reading from script) I was captured while carrying out espionage activities after intruding deep into the territorial waters of the Democratic People's Republic of Korea.

(Gasps, snorts, growls of outrage from audience)

ANOTHER JOURNALIST: (Checks program, jumps up from table with wild gestures, shouting) Had your ship conducted espionage activities on a number of occasions for the purpose of detecting the territorial waters of the Socialist countries?

BUCHER: (Reading from script) My ship conducted espionage activities on a number of occasions for the purpose of detecting the territorial waters of the Socialist countries.

(Gasps, snorts, and growls of outrage from audience)

FEMALE JOURNALIST: (Checks program, jumps up from table with wild gestures, screeches) Did the United States

Central Intelligence Agency not promise that if this task was done successfully, a lot of dollars would be offered the crew members of your ship and particularly yourself would be much honored?

BUCHER: (*Reading from script*) The United States Central Intelligence Agency promised me that if this task was done successfully, a lot of dollars would be offered the crew members of the ship and particularly I myself would be much honored.

(*Gasps, snorts, and growls of outrage from audience*)

And so it went until we had gone through the whole script, they speaking their lines with great emotion and dramatic flourishes—I delivering mine with a dull, unfeeling monotone which I feared might trigger an accusation of "insincerity" from that accomplished actor, Super-C, who watched my entire performance from front-row-center through the glitter of his lightly tinted glasses. It was hard for me to tell whether he was satisfied or not. No matter. I did not expect him to lead a claque of ovation. Suffice that he merely stood up at the end and waved at my bayonet-carriers to escort me off stage.

I shuffled off, hoping that if this so-called press conference was actually used to influence opinions beyond the confines of North Korea, my own performance, as well as theirs, would reduce it to its true status—a complete farce.

CHAPTER XIII

"TO SEND POORLY ARMED SURFACE RECONNAIS-
SANCE SHIPS INTO DANGEROUS WATERS WITHOUT
AIR COVER, NAVAL ESCORT, OR EMERGENCY PLANS
FOR ADEQUATE SUPPORT WAS A SERIOUS ERROR IN
JUDGEMENT."—(*Senator J. Strom Thurmond
[R, S.C.], statement to press, February 5,
1968, on* Pueblo *incident.*)

"A CLAMMY SPIRIT OF FEAR AND TIMIDITY SUR-
ROUNDS OUR EFFORTS TO REGAIN OUR SHIP AND
HER CREW."—(*Senator Everett M. Dirksen [R,
Ill.], statement to press on* Pueblo *incident.*)

The wind howled almost ceaselessly around our prison, making
the building give out moans and shrieks with a disconcerting
eerie effect of human cries. Snow squalls rustled against my
covered window and flakes seeped through the broken pane and
paper padding, trickling into my cell like grains of salt that would
not melt. Sometimes when the blustery weather calmed down for
a few moments, I could hear the tramp of boots outside, crunching through drifts, sentries patrolling their beat. A more regular
sound was the footfall of the guards passing up and down the
corridor on the other side of my closed door. At least once an
hour, regardless of the time of day or night, there would come
flurries of more violent noises, scuffling, curses, and muffled
screams that were definitely not caused by the wind. The ordeal
of interrogations and beatings was continuing without let-up for
the men of *Pueblo*.

In spite of the constant yellow glare of the electric bulb, I had a feeling of being isolated in a black void of loneliness. A loneliness entirely stemming from being deprived of any contact with my fellow prisoners beyond the sound of their muted cries. Although my own beatings had temporarily ceased, I did not look forward to the periodic visitations by my KORCOM jailers. Junior officers would burst in on me and belligerently ask a single, insignificant question in their fractured English and mull over my answer for a moment before departing with a snarled "Imperialist sonabeechy. Better be much sincere!" It left me with a feeling their visit was only an excuse to look in and check on my condition. They were evidently becoming more concerned about that since I still refused to eat and perhaps suspected me of the "insincere" gesture of a hunger strike. That gave me a certain satisfaction, but the fact was that even their fresh milk (a North Korean luxury) made me sick to my stomach; besides pains from beatings and shrapnel wounds I was suffering from a constant nausea that was aggravated by the mere sight of their food. As I continued my fasting, my guards brought what they thought to be more and more tempting trays of their best fare, like fresh apples, buttered bread, and fresh boiled fish swimming in turnip juice. My only reaction was an urgent need to vomit and the guard would remove the tray with a mixture of disgust, perplexity and salivating gluttony, muttering under his breath something which I imagined to be reproaches against an insolent Capitalist who dared turn up his nose at these fine delicacies from the People's kitchen.

Time settled into an interminable drag which I had no way of accurately measuring. The gloom of the snowy winter daylight could barely penetrate the seams of the paper covering my window, making little difference between short gray days and long black nights. I could best tell the passage of time by the changing of the guard, which manifested itself by changed faces among those who came into my presence, as close as I could tell, about every eight hours. I tried sleep to gather strength for what I was certain would soon be a renewed effort by the KORCOMs to break me completely. But sleep only came in fitful snatches filled with dreams of exploding shells, bleeding bodies lying on stretchers, or hanging, writhing, from butcher hooks on cement walls, and the screeching accusations of a schizophrenic Super-C. My waking moments were easier to take because I could maintain some degree of discipline over my mind by forcing it to busy itself with rational thoughts, no matter how dismal and bleak.

I considered others besides those which had been plaguing me ever since our capture. For instance, I began worrying about not having specifically flashed my superiors that *Pueblo* never at any time intruded into North Korean waters; that we had double-checked our position when challenged and were absolutely certain of it. It had never occurred to me at the time, but since being forced to sign that ridiculous trumped-up confession, including the admission of intrusion, I reproached myself for not having stated to the contrary in one of the JOPREPs sent to Kamiseya before enforced silence. I knew the agony of doubt which must be pervading responsible headquarters between Japan and the United States as they tried to evaluate the incident and could only count on my record for carrying out orders to stand up against the false confession. How I wished that I had foreseen this problem and given them the answer while there still was time. Now I could only tell them in person much later . . . too late . . . if ever.

I puzzled a great deal about the nature of the questions the interrogators had concentrated on so far, wondering why they had asked so little oriented toward obtaining technical information—military intelligence. Instead they had seemed completely hung up on a propaganda line for purely political purposes when dealing with me. Had they found out that Steve Harris was the real repository of sensitive intelligence knowledge aboard *Pueblo* and handled him accordingly? I somehow convinced myself that he was dead, either beaten to death during interrogation, or executed after having tortured everything out of him, or perhaps, protected his secrets by committing the suicide in which I had failed.

Not knowing the answers to these questions was a terrible strain, yet I was somewhat reassured by one fact: no Soviet Russian NKVD types had yet shown up on the scene to take over or contribute more sophisticated methods to those of the crudely brutal KORCOMs. I had not spotted a single occidental face among our interrogators ·or observers attending the sessions. The thought that Soviet Russians might be present in the persons of Mongolian race nationals crossed my mind, yet nothing in their questioning suggested this. It seemed an entirely North Korean show run in the narrow spirit of nationalistic bombast.

Why then had the KORCOMs perpetrated this flagrant act? I brooded over this at great length while either pacing my freezing cell or tossing restlessly on my bunk. I decided that they had most likely done it to provide a pretext for resuming their war against South Korea whom I knew they had vowed to conquer. If this fitted into broader international Communist strategy, it would be to divert and dilute the United States' efforts in Vietnam. In either case, we would be fully used as the excuse—then discarded—probably by firing squad. (I hoped by firing squad rather than the kind of torture I had seen them inflict with my own eyes and knew could make me lose all touch with sanity and reason.) With their obtuse singleminded purpose, they might expect no other benefits, such as technical intelligence, from us. In this respect the pieces of the puzzle fitted together, all the questions about intruding upon their territorial waters, espionage, provoking the "peaceful" Democratic People's Republic of Korea by landing South Korean infiltrators on their shores, violating the armistice . . . everything they intended doing themselves! The United States, I hopefully surmised, had already taken the bait of having the first of its Navy ships seized on the high seas in over one hundred fifty years, and smashed Wonsan with a massive airstrike. Perhaps the threat of full nuclear retaliation was keeping some of us alive.

Among the junior officers who burst in on me every hour or so during the second day and night of my imprisonment, there were the sadistic Imperialist, surly Chipmunk, and one I dubbed Missile, the only one who asked questions that were remotely connected with military intelligence. He seemed to have an amateur's knowledge about U.S. rocketry, like a missile buff who had read up on the subject in *Popular Science* magazine or the Sunday supplements, and was eager to be briefed about it by somebody he imagined to have firsthand knowledge. In spite of recognizing his mispronounced names from our missile arsenal, Hercules,

Regulus, Sparrow, Polaris and Terrier, all these were outside my ken as a former diesel submarine officer and captain of a small intelligence ship, neither of which were equipped with such weaponry. I did not even know enough about it to intelligently lead him astray with false information. So I could truthfully tell him I knew nothing about it and that only a select few in our Navy were privy to such secret weapons. Such an answer would temporarily satisfy him and he would leave with the contrived thoughtful frown of a pseudo intellectual. Sometimes he destroyed the effect by asking "When did you leave Sasebo?" for which he already had the obvious and accurate answer in our captured navigation charts. But repeating himself did not inhibit Missile in the least. Nor could I relate his repetitions with anything but ineptness. As he pursued this course, his performance become sort of a joke.

I was troubled by the constantly recurring worry about how my wounded men were being cared for, or if they were receiving any care at all. How many more had been badly hurt since our capture? Had any been killed while resisting interrogation? Were we still being held together in this icy wind-swept prison, or had my crew been scattered among the many similar places of detention maintained by this Communist society. Every time an officer like Missile, or Chipmunk, or Imperialist came into my cell, I demanded information about these things—*demanded* as befitting the captain of an illegally detained United States ship; not pleading as the civilian criminal they insisted I was. I never received anything but blank stares or indifferent shrugs in answer. The young enlisted guards gradually lost their fear of me as an unspeakable monster from an alien Capitalist-Imperialistic world and dared to show their courage with a snarled *"Keesee!"* and a kick with their boot when their superiors were not around.

They always accommodated my wishes to go to the toilet which I made known as often as I thought I could get away with. The trip down the marble corridor to their stinking urinal offered a break in the monotony as well as a possible opportunity to run into some of my crew on similar missions. But the guards invariably cleared the way ahead of me so that I would meet none of my own people. The bleeding from my injured kidneys became less severe even if still very painful. I remembered noticing a detail of their plumbing at this time: the drain of the urinal was not connected to the main system, but allowed everything to dribble out and collect in a puddle on the concrete floor that only gradually seeped through a clogged separate scupper hole. I could not help laughing at this system of People's sanitary engineering even as I was forced to stand in a miniature cesspool formed around the filthy urinal. Since I had eaten virtually nothing over the past forty-eight hours, my needs for a bowel movement only gradually became acute, but when I finally had to give in to it, it was such excruciating agony for my injured rectum that I almost fainted in the foul slop lapping against my boots. I never felt so weak and degraded as when I staggered back toward my cell after that painful experience. Yet it was then that something went wrong with the KORCOMs carefully scheduled toilet visitations and I finally did run into one of my men. I do not know to this day who he was. His guard had jammed him up against the wall while I passed, so his back was turned and his face hidden from my dazed gaze. I did not dare call out to him because I knew this would result in terrible beatings for both of us. So the meeting was no more than a brief consciousness of each other's presence, accomplished in silence and the most fleeting chance contact, yet I hoped it gave him as much of a boost in spirit as it did me.

By the third day I had become very weak, barely able to drag myself to the toilet or even pace my cell, and whatever medical authority was in charge became more worried that their prize prisoner might die on them. A female who was dressed in the same uniform as the men and could only be identified as a nurse by a Red Cross armband, came in and took my temperature by sticking a thermometer under my armpit. I was running a high fever, aggravated by violent chills from the freezing room. Hot paraffin packs were applied as treatment for the severe bruises on my back. Then I was moved to another cell across the corridor. It was identical to the first, except the steam radiator was putting out some heat which relieved my suffering from the cold. For the first time since my capture I took off my thermal boots and examined the shrapnel wound in my right leg. The sock was solidly glued to my foot with dried blood and after peeling it off, I found the wound itself to be slowly healing with discharges of oozing pus. I cleaned it off with water out of the bucket, then put the sock back on. I still wanted to keep the fact that I was wounded from the KORCOMs and since they had not given me anything like a thorough medical examination, figured I had a good chance of doing so. My trouser leg was blood stained. but they probably thought I had picked that up in *Pueblo*'s gory passageway where poor Hodges had been killed.

I do not know if the medical officer looked in on me at this time. If he did, it was only for a quick glance and there was no way to tell him apart from other officers. In spite of my efforts to keep a grip on myself, my mind would sink into periods of dazed confusion in which reality and illusion would blend into a continuous nightmare. I was probably delirious at times. Hazy figures and faces of my tormentors swam into my vision, came into sharp focus with grimaces and loud abusive voices, then vanished, leaving me wondering if I had really seen and heard them. But usually I did not care and shouted my protests and demands whether they were there or not. I was vaguely aware of the nurse giving me an injection. The wind stormed around the building and I could not tell its cries and moans from those of my crew as they were being beaten. Acute anxiety alternated with dull stupor, my feverish mind fighting against both. The nauseated rejection of any kind of food mingled with sudden pangs of hunger. All I had been able to take were sips of hot water, but then I managed to hold down a little milk, regaining some strength for my starving body. I became conscious of my appearance which, for lack of any mirror or reflecting surface I could only imagine to be one of a filthy, unshaven, emaciated derelict. I could smell my own uncleanliness in pungent whiffs of stale sweat permeating dirty clothes, mingling with the sickly sweet odor of pus. To all the other demoralizing factors was added the insidious one of wallowing in a degrading state of grime.

It was Chipmunk, or Imperialist or Missile who returned the watch they had stripped off of me when I first arrived. I was given it like a bad child being handed back a toy confiscated for punishment and with a threatening admonition to behave myself and "be sincere." Like a child I eagerly accepted it, and for a while gave it my full attention, listening to its tick and trying to make it tell me how long it had been since all these terrible things had started happening. Its hands pointed at ten minutes to three—but whether in the morning or afternoon, I was not sure. I tried to regain a concept of time by watching the second hand crawl around the dial, but each turn seemed to take longer, and the minute hand barely moved at all. The dial turned into a Korean face with hateful hooded eyes glowering, and a familiar interpreter's voice ranting at me, "You no prisoner war! You political prisoner caught criminally spying! You be tried in People's Court and made guilty with penalty of death!" I countered with the usual protests and accusations of my own: "I demand you release us at once! You have murdered one of my men, damn you!" When the Korean face faded and turned back into a watch, the second hand was still turning its endless circle, twitching second by second with a perceptible pause between each one. The minute and hour hands had barely moved. Eight minutes to three. Morning or afternoon? The watch would not tell, nor the paper padded window rustling with the faint patter of snowflakes. Time in purgatory becomes immeasurable and meaningless.

"How is your life these days?" Wheezy, the interpreter, translated the question from a politely benign Korean inquiry spoken by Super-C who faced me from across his desk in the interrogation room. I had been seated before him in a hard wooden chair and was trying to collect all of my wits for another session with the man I was now certain to be in charge of the North Korean end of the *Pueblo* affair. I was feeling slovenly and weak and full of pain, so obviously that it made his question patently cynical; but I was not about to concede this to him.

"I am only interested in the condition of my men," I answered. "Especially the wounded ones."

Wheezy conveyed this and came back with, "Your wounded are being treated and well cared for. We are humans. What other interest?"

"I want to see and speak to them."

Super-C made a long rambling speech delivered in pleasant conversational tones as he puffed on a cigarette and watched me earnestly through those red horn-rimmed spectacles of his. Wheezy sputtered and coughed in his efforts to translate, not so much over his supply of vocabulary (which was considerable), but rather to convey his chief's nuances of inflection which were, for the moment, subtly subdued. However, it contained no trace of an answer.

"You must be aware of the tortures which the Korean people suffered during the Fatherland Liberation war with the United States . . . cough-wheeze) . . . every Korean lost relatives in the war . . . (cough-cough) . . . CIA tortured them . . . killed them . . . (cough-sputter) . . . Koreans hate the lackeys of Imperialism . . . not the American people (sputter-cough) . . . You must be sincere. Forty million Korean people hate Americans . . . (sputter-sputter). Our brothers in the South are kept away from their mothers and fathers in the North . . . (cough-cough) . . . Johnson is the murdering enemy of Koreans . . . The CIA controls the Johnson clique . . . they are the murderers of thousands of Korean people . . . (wheeze-cough).

My condition was not such that I could easily sit there and pretend interest in this propaganda spiel, but I tried not to irritate him by showing it. Rather I decided to meet him on his own chosen grounds since he refused to discuss in detail the condition of my men. "I have read that North Korea only has a population of ten million," I told him, basing that information on a lead article I remembered reading in *Time* magazine.

Super-C bristled slightly, but maintained his patient attitude, refusing to be diverted by challenges of his statistics, and continued with the earnest conviction of one who had learned his lines to perfection and is determined to deliver them:

"The peace-loving people of Korea," he said through Wheezy, deliberately leaving out any North or South designation, "do not recognize any other leader than the beloved Father of the Workers Party of Korea, Kim Il Sung . . . We do not hate the American people who are in the clutches of the Johnson murder clique . . . and the Rockefeller gluttons and hobnailed boots of bloody-handed Wall Street warmongers . . . and kept oppressed with vicious murder by paid running dogs of CIA! We know that American workers are whipped slaves of Morgan Steel! We know that Americans will be our friends when they overthrow the CIA. But first the Johnson dogs must be dealt with! . . . If President Johnson had been aboard your ship we would not be so humane as we are with you. We would drag him through our streets like a fascist dog to die a thousand deaths."

He paused to let Wheezy collect himself from the strain of properly emoting the translation, then proceeded along more personal lines: "You must show your gratitude and sincerity to the Korean people by honest confession of your crimes . . . Then you may go home to your loved ones. You will soon see what I mean. You see, I have a message for you from your wife, Madam Rose!"

I was stunned by the mention of Rose and incredulous that she would have been able to get a message through to North Korea in such a short time. More likely he had gotten her name out of my service record and was concocting something to break down my resistance. With great difficulty I ignored the ploy. "Morgan Steel became U. S. Steel many years ago," I told him, "and you are also wrong about President Johnson. He has a great record in public life and has been responsible for much social legislation."

Without contradicting me, Super-C delivered himself of another lecture which in essence stated that he would give me logical proof that his charges against President Johnson and others were true, that the American public was being tricked and cheated, that the real ruler of the USA was the Central Intelligence Agency, and that he knew all American ships carried CIA agents aboard to keep the crews in line and mete out punishment to those who dared criticize "Johnson and fascist dogs." He asked: "Who is it on your ship?" When I denied any such person had been aboard *Pueblo*, he said he knew very well who it was and was only waiting for him to give himself up. Then he addressed himself directly to Wheezy who rose and left the room.

I found myself alone with Super-C who was unarmed. With the interpreter gone we could not communicate, but he offered me a cigarette out of the pack from which he had kept chain-smoking. I accepted my first cigarette since being captured and found myself enjoying the strong Korean tobacco. He was really turning on his most charming manner and even tried to reassure me with a smile, revealing a set of protruding teeth that somewhat marred his handsome features. For ten minutes we sat alone together and when Wheezy returned, I was asked if I needed to go to the toilet. To my surprise, I was allowed to go by myself without a guard.

This earned a great opportunity to meet one of my men and exchange a few words. But, of course, both the hall and latrine were empty. I looked around the urinal and crude plumbing for any messages that might have been hidden there, but found none. It was disappointing, yet I felt that if I and maybe other prisoners were to be permitted unguarded trips to the latrine, it would sooner or later develop into a clandestine message center for us.

Back in the interrogation room, Super-C and Wheezy were waiting. As soon as I was seated, the colonel began reading from a sheet of paper and even from his Korean I gleaned Rose's name and another which sounded occidental. But Wheezy had so much trouble with the translation that he finally had to ask his chief for the paper and work directly from it. With much coughing, sputtering and back-tracking, a news release emerged about Rose giving an interview to the American press, telling of her ordeal of uncertainty over my capture, but hopeful in the belief that I was alive and would somehow be returned safely with my crew. She had been accompanied by a friend of mine, the release stated, by the name of Hemmel. I searched my mind in vain for anyone I knew by the name of Hemmel and remained suspicious.

Noticing my doubtful expression, Wheezy tried another pronunciation of the name and this time came up with Hempil. Then it suddenly dawned on me who he was talking about. Alan Hemphill, indeed an old friend and shipmate whom I had not seen for about three years. Alan was a lieutenant commander and Annapolis graduate who had served under me when I was Executive Officer of the submarine *Ronquil*. As there was nothing aboard *Pueblo* to connect me with this American naval officer, the news release had to be genuine!

I asked that it be read to me again and this time I eagerly listened to every word. A terrible longing for my beloved Rose flooded my whole being, my heart going out to her in her trial, and filling with gratitude toward Alan for standing by her. The news release was brief and dry and badly translated, but at this moment it took me home again with a tremendous emotional impact.

My reaction did not escape the notice of Super-C, who looked very pleased with himself and began talking again through his interpreter. "Very nice message from Mrs. Rose and your friend. Now we will help you every way to be sincere and make forgiveness from peace-loving Korean people so you can go home."

That jolted me out of my reverie and I was suddenly furious and shouted at him: "How about my man Hodges whom your people murdered? What have you done with his body? We did nothing to provoke your ships into firing on us—nothing! It was pure and simple murder!"

As Wheezy translated, the colonel's face began turning beet-red beneath his slick black hair. Losing all his previous calm manner, he erupted into one of his livid performances, chopping the desk with the side of his hands, stamping and yelling the favorite Korean invective "Keessseee!"

I was ordered to stand up.

With his phenomenal endurance, Super-C ranted and raved through the next three or four hours in an endless diatribe which ran the full gamut of Imperialistic sins, the Korean War, the Vietnam War, the CIA, the South Korean traitors, the miseries of the workers being caused entirely by the United States, and the punishment of death which was about to be meted out to all those supporting her infamous policies of Imperialist aggression. He paused only long enough to light himself more cigarettes while poor Wheezy struggled with the translations. In my weakened condition, I found myself close to fainting while having to stand there in one spot, taking motionless his torrent of threats and abuse. But finally, when I was reduced to a numbed pain of mind and body and Wheezy was sputtering along hopelessly behind in translating the marathon soliloquy of vituperations, the colonel abruptly ended the session by snapping: "Back to your cell and think it over sincerely!" Then he squashed his last cigarette in a tray brimming with butts and stalked out with hardly a strand of his slick hair out of place.

When I was led staggering with exhaustion back to solitary confinement, I collapsed on my bunk and sank into the first oblivious, nightmare-free sleep since our capture. There were only two conscious thoughts before slipping away. Not a single sensitive intelligence question had been asked of me during the whole gruelling session. And I had had news of Rose and knew that she was bearing up in her own agony with the help of a good friend! God bless and sustain her and that friend!

By carefully studying my watch and making tedious calculations, endlessly rechecked, I was able to reduce eternity into approximate fractional measures of hours and days. Solitary confinement is a torture-machine in which time is the screw exerting a relentless pressure on the mind. A strong, sound mind resists the atrophy which inevitably afflicts the body, exercising itself with thoughts about events that culminated in disaster, about escape, revenge, resistance, and nurturing hope of deliverance from every red thread of rationale it can unravel out of a nightmare tapestry. Given too free a reign, it will tend to escape completely from reality into wild flights of fancy, making the prisoner suspect he is slipping into a state of insanity. The four walls of the prison cell are the reality and the mind must be forced to accept the fact— yet this can in itself become an obsession which carries its own virus of madness.

I caught myself constantly dwelling on wishes for a massive retaliation by the United States against North Korea's act of piracy, including visions of cataclysmic mushroom cloud sweeping the nuclear debris of Wonsan and Pyongyang into the stratosphere. My briefings at CINCPACFLT had led me to believe that some sort of forceful reaction was part of their contingency plans—surely more than forcefully worded diplomatic protests! And then I became more and more aware of a special kind of nervousness on the part of the KORCOMs, one expressed by constant attention to the tightness of the material sealing my window. It gradually occurred to me that they were not so much worried about my looking out on whatever view lay outside the prison, as in complying with some very strict black-out regulations. They had to be expecting an air raid!

This expectation was emphasized by constantly repeated threats of my immediate execution in the event of the United States attempting any armed intervention. Since I was convinced they were serious about this threat, the wish for that intervention also contained the bitter taste of a death-wish. Yet as time went by, it became a forlorn one with a steadily diminishing probability of becoming actual. As our KORCOM jailers gradually calmed their fears of a devastating air-strike, I had to divert my own mind into other, more realistic channels. There was first of all hope—hope that if we were not to be extricated or avenged by armed retaliation, then it was probable the United States contemplated other means, perhaps slower, but more certain. Secondly, and most immediate, was to prepare myself to cope with those interminable interrogation sessions which by now had become fixed in a set pattern; to not get lulled into a sense of false security by their blatant propaganda line; to protect the far greater secrets locked in my mind that had not been betrayed by captured documents; and remain alert to any surprising changes the interrogators might pull out of their bag of tricks. Finally, to remain braced against the mental agonies of solitary confinement and physical tortures of beatings and deprivation. Of the three, the third was the most difficult because it entailed the endurance of acute pain with no prospects of relief—coupled with a corroding uncertainty of what the next day, hour or minute might bring, and thus stirring the imagination into dwelling on the bleakest, bloodiest imagery. The agony of "not knowing" was really the worst of all in the long run.

Self-recrimination and remorse over things done or not done before and during the capture became a constant source of brooding in my loneliness. I was still angrily heaping a lot of blame on the Navy. Why, when they decided to arm us with those 50-caliber pea-shooters, had they not considered the impossibility of bringing them into timely action under their nonprovocation rules? Why had I allowed myself to be fooled into believing the nonprovocative, minimum risk nature of a mission which turned out being so obviously flaunted in the face of a totally unpredictable, violence-prone untested Communist government. I continued blaming myself more as my brain sifted through an endless procession of details. I should have heeded my own instincts and taken precautions independent of naive superiors. I should have obtained those TNT charges for scuttling even if illegally by "midnight requisition." I should have poked my nose into Steve Harris's research spaces and thoroughly acquainted myself with the volume of classified material in his care—many times the amount I had suspected, and arbitrarily gotten rid of far more of it than we had before leaving Japan, whether authorized to do so or not. That would have been a far lesser risk to my country, my ship, my crew and to my career than what I now faced. The painful thought occurred to me that even in the eleventh hour, much more could have been done to destroy those bales of secret papers, like dumping them into the head across the passageway from the SOD-Hut, dousing them with diesel oil or gasoline, and risking a fatal conflagration to make sure of their total destruction. I cursed myself for not having thought of that even in the confusion of the moment, for not having had the presence of mind to have taken a stronger hand with Steve and his CTs when they reacted with the partial paralysis of shock to a completely unexpected development. It was my fault that the emergency had culminated in the disaster of loss of life, injury and compromised national security. Blaming others was of little comfort. I was the captain. And was the captain still, regardless of my ship having been seized, my men imprisoned, and myself reduced to a guilt-ridden captive. But I must not give in completely to self-recrimination and self-pity. I was still responsible for salvaging whatever remained salvageable, to remain responsible to whatever bitter end awaited me. To remain *Captain*.

Both dreaded and welcome were the breaks in my solitude when a junior officer and guard would suddenly burst into my cell and rout me out of my introspective isolation for another interrogation session. In a peculiar way, these became intellectual exercises which kept my mind from foundering to bottomless pits of quicksand. Some interrogators, like Major Squint, provided little mental challenge as they endlessly droned questions about personal history obtained from my service record. Sometimes I had to be made to pay attention to them with a swift kick with a boot. By far the most stimulating were the confrontations with their chief inquisitor, that peerless military thespian, Super-C. It was a constant challenge for me to decide whether he was a buffoon in colonel's uniform, strutting through a routine in which he had thoroughly rehearsed—or a genuine sinister genius in the technique of breaking down a prisoner with a subtle mixture of cruel comedy and sardonic brutality.

"How is your life today?" he invariably opened the session when I was brought before him as an emaciated, scabrous wreck, smelling of filth, cold sweat, and the pus suppurating out of my wounds. "Sit down! Let us exchange a little sincere talk!"

I would sit down, accept the cigarette when offered, but invariably counter his invitation with the question, "How are you taking care of my wounded men?"

He ignored that, of course. Instead he launched into one of his usual diatribes, raving against the United States and accusing her of being solely responsible for the Korean people being divided into two separate countries. From this premise he worked into details of bestial treatment of North Korean patriots who fell into the hands of American troops occupying South Korea, giving full vent to his dramatic talents as he did so. Placing his left fist against his forehead, he pounded it with the other while describing how Korean women were tortured by having nails driven through their skulls by slavering GIs. He showed a considerable contortionist's ability by grabbing his own foot (wearing a luxurious Western-style shoe which had probably originated from a fashionable shop in Hong Kong), hauling it above his head to pantomime a torture victim being suspended upside down from the ceiling. "This is what you did to our people!" he fulminated, "hanged them by their heels and cut out their tongues so that they could only uh . . . glapshsh-glop . . ." His description of the torture turning gibberish as he wound up his performance by trying to grip his own tongue with thumb and forefinger while pretending to slice it to pieces with the heel of the other hand. Most devastating of all was his interpreter's antics as he tried simultaneously to translate and pantomime this Korean version of a Chinese opera.

In my decrepit state of mind and body, it was all I could do to keep from bursting into spontaneous or hysterical laughter. Not for a moment did I believe that American troops had been guilty of the atrocities Super-C and his interpreter were turning themselves inside-out to describe. I forced a dead-pan, even bored, expression through the performance by reminding myself of its underlying sinister implications: that he was actually implying all these tortures would be freely used against us because we had used them against them. I had carefully to check my reactions, either by deprecating word or gesture, because I noticed how in pauses between his outbursts he carefully studied me, watching for the slightest sign of cracking up or breaking down. And then I had to remain alert through hours of nonsensical propaganda histrionics for any sudden switch into something more pertinent, usually thrown at me without any warning preamble, such as "Why you use insincere, unusual English language in your confession, Captain? Do you not think we are aware of such tricks?"

That came as a jolt. Had they actually released that phoney confession full of stilted Communist verbiage which my family, friends, colleagues—anybody at home would know that I as an American naval officer would never use? Had they already monitored the reaction of the American press to such a release—or had some of their more knowledgeable language specialists checked it over and warned them about it? I did not know. And I could not react with anything more than an indifferent shrug, yet was comforted by the fact that he knew the confession had actually been dictated by himself for my signature. If he had been so stupid as to release it—then so much the better.

But was he really that stupid? Something warned me that he was not. Not even when he failed to pursue the point and contorted himself and his interpreter into another tirade of dogmatic Communist accusations against Yankee Imperialism, which they managed to drag out for another full two hours, finally ending it with another sudden non-sequitur:

"So, who do you think killed your President Kennedy?"

By then I was completely numb and had to really exert myself in order to give a cogent reply to one of his answerable questions: "Who killed President Kennedy? . . . Some kind of psycho . . . that is, a disturbed misfit in our society who knew nothing about what he was doing beyond the simple act of loading and aiming a rifle. The act of a maniac!"

Super-C wagged his head with a smug smile as the exhausted interpreter wheezed and spluttered through the translation of my answer, then quietly, deliberately, transmitted back his own retort:

"Not so at all! The assassin Oswald was engaged through your running-dog CIA by then Vice-President Johnson to specially kill President Kennedy. That way to make sure wars and provocations against peace-loving peoples of Socialist Republics continue into bloody future. You think over such fact which we can prove. You go back now with yourself alone and think sincerely about it."

With that sort of incongruous ending to a five-hour marathon exhortation, I was returned to solitary and the grind of its oppressive loneliness. The strain on me had been tremendous even though Super-C had used no pressure at all to extract any secrets. Why? Why? His methods of interrogation puzzled me, seeming so senseless and unproductive that I began fretting over some hidden purpose which must have escaped me. For a long time I would lie on my bunk, reviewing what he had said, what I had said, trying to recall any sentence, any word, which could have some kind of intelligent significance. None came to mind. Then, to keep myself from becoming completely addled by the problem, I tried to think of something else for a while. Something to let my mind escape the four walls of the cell . . .

Rose.

Thoughts of Rose came as both an added pain and a soothing relief. It pained me to think about what she must be going through with uncertainties over my fate and many questions about my conduct. Super-C had revealed the fact that the press had already reached Rose for interviews and I could easily imagine hordes of reporters beseiging our home, eager to find out through her what sort of man is this Commander Bucher. Poor Rose! This would be a frightening new experience for her and I thanked God that an old shipmate like Alan Hemphill was trying to help. Surely the Navy itself was giving her more support than the usual visits by wellmeaning chaplains and CACO (Casualty Assistance Calls Officer) types who pay routine visits to distressed Navy families. But in any case, I was certain that if Rose had been shown my "confession," she would have instantly proclaimed it as false . . . yet, in doing so, certainly also agonized over the tortures which she realized had made me sign such a spurious document. Did she

know that the wounds I had reported in my last message to
Kamiseya were not serious? Had there been retaliations which
made her certain I had been executed? Tortured more? What comforting words was she forcing herself to tell our sons before putting them to bed—then crying herself to sleep toward morning?
These speculations about Rose's own personal hell only added to
mine and I could not allow myself in my complete helplessness to
dwell on them too much. Some trust had to be put in our love and
prayers to bridge the awful void separating us. Better for me to
slake my yearning for her with memories far beyond the present
—back through eighteen years to when I first met a vivacious beautiful girl who set me to tingling with excitement, and could leave
me tingling still when I thought about her in this pest-hole of a
Communist jail.

It all started with a blind date in Omaha, Nebraska, on a warm
spring evening in 1949. I was a brash young man of twenty-one
who considered himself very much a man of the world after having served a hitch in the Navy taking him to such romantic ports
of call as Sydney, Australia, Saipan and Yokosuka, Japan. Since
my honorable discharge of last year, I had in addition been supporting my own college education at the University of Nebraska
with a variety of lucrative jobs, including that of a meatcutter in
a slaughterhouse for 93 cents an hour, a bartender in an Elks'
Club for slightly more, and an ambulance driver with an undertaking establishment for slightly less. While cash resources always
seemed low regardless of this diversified employment, I had few
debts, owned a 1939 Plymouth coupe, was making passing grades
as a sophomore student at the university, and only otherwise suffered from a smug sense of superiority contrived out of my vast
accumulation of experience since setting forth from Father
Flanagan's Boys Town somewhat less than three years previous.
I was, in short, far too sophisticated to be in the least flustered by
a routine blind date with the roommate of my buddy's girl-friend
who wouldn't go to a college dance with him without her. My attitude was in truth more condescending than gracious. But then,
all of a sudden, there was Rose.

I managed to keep an outwardly cool composure when I saw
how stunningly pretty she was, but everything inside of me be-

gan dissolving into a sort of delightful weakness when our eyes met and I caught a humorous glance which clearly said to me, "Well, don't look so surprised! You're not bad looking yourself." Her lips smiled, but more formally spoke a greeting, "Nice to meet you, Mr. Bucher."

Her roommate giggled and exclaimed, "His first name is Lloyd, Rose. Spelled with a double-L yet!"

"But everybody calls him Pete," my buddy injected. "What else can you call a guy with a double-L 'nitial?"

"Yeah—call me 'Pete'," I said, feeling myself turning scarlet.

"Okay, Pete. Let's go!" Rose merrily exclaimed and hooking her arm into mine, led me toward my prize possession, that 1939 Plymouth coupe which at the moment looked to me like a battered pumpkin which absolutely refused to turn itself into a royal coach. Yet the only magic that mattered was the electric touch of the girl holding my arm.

Rose Dolores Roling was born and raised on a farm near Jefferson City, Missouri, the daughter of Mr. and Mrs. Frank H. Roling. Her two brothers, Leonard and John, had both served in the Armed Forces during World War II and were now back in Jefferson City doing farm work, at the time we met. Only the youngest of the family, her sister Lola, was still living at home. Rose had decided against continuing a college education at the University of Missouri and had spread her wings toward wider horizons. In those days, the Bell Telephone Company provided the best opportunity for a respectable young woman to become self-supporting, while at the same time living away from home. With her strict farmer father's tacit approval, Rose and her other sister Angie had taken jobs as telephone operators in Omaha, a city of the Midwestern plains which seemed far more exciting than Jefferson City, Missouri. To make sure that excitement did not intrude on propriety, the girls boarded with an established family whose home was located in a pleasant suburban section. Mr. and Mrs. F. W. Martin treated them like their own daughters, and as my courtship with Rose turned serious, accepted me as her ardent swain with the sympathetic watchfulness of good parents. A lasting and warm relationship developed between us and Nita and Fred Martin which makes the old-fashioned ways of handling such things seem well worthwhile.

It was a couple of weeks before Rose and I dated again after our first meeting. She had her work schedule with the telephone company. I had my studies at the University of Nebraska, my moonlighting activities to supplement the meager stipends of my GI Bill of Rights and modest football scholarship, and then there was the cost of gasoline (18 cents per gallon) to run my Plymouth coupe back and forth over the seventy miles of highway separating my campus in Lincoln from the Martin home in Omaha. But I was badly smitten and threw myself into earning the necessary funds (no less than $5) for another date—then another—and another. Those were golden days, not entirely carefree because young ardent love never is, but filled with the ecstasy of growing ever closer in body and spirit with my beloved. The simplest pleasures of that summer courtship, holding hands in a movie, nestling close together while driving over a sunny countryside fragrant with ripening wheat, picnics and swims on the willowed banks of Lake Merritt, all took on the impact of great emotional involvement for me. I realized that I had fallen hopelessly in love with Rose. And finally, on a Sunday afternoon in late September, I proposed to her. It required all the courage I could muster, because even with all the intense desire and love I was feeling for her, my former self-confidence seemed to have deserted me and been replaced by a sense of unworthiness and inadequacy. It made me desperately add to my proposal, "I'll quit school and get a good full-time job if you'll marry me, Rose."

Her adamant "No!" came as a stab in my heart—until she made her meaning clear by firmly and tenderly saying "I mean no, you mustn't give up your school, but yes, I'll marry you just the same, my darling Pete! So why should you worry about supporting me? I've got a good job and I'll keep it until you're ready for the one you really want."

I could only hug her tightly and kiss her over and over again with my spirits swimming in a delight I had never known before.

But we did not get married at once. We were secure enough in our love to be able to wait through the winter while we built up our bank balance so we could afford a proper honeymoon and begin our married life with a decent household of our own. Also, I had to meet Rose's parents, so they could get to know their prospective son-in-law. I worried about this because of my orphaned background. How would they accept a waif from Boys Town with no family of his own as the husband of their daughter? It struck me that I knew very little about myself—who were my real parents? I could only dimly recall supposed relatives who cared for me in my early childhood before I was turned over to a series of institutions. Until now, I had been able to cope with these doubts and uncertainties about my origin. But when I fell in love with Rose and started making plans for our life together, it suddenly became very important for me to explore my past. For the first time I made serious inquiries through letters to various offices of public records in Idaho and what they dug up out of their musty files and transmitted to me came as a shock. In a state of total dejection, I had to tell Rose that because of the circumstances of my birth, I was not worthy of her and her family. Her reaction made me love her all the more.

"It's what you are that matters to me, Pete, and that I love you and want you as my husband. Nothing else matters."

Somehow we got through that long winter's unofficial engagement with its mixtures of joys and worries, joys as intimately warming as a softly glowing hearth, worries building up like the towering snowdrifts of the plains, coldly menacing at first glance, then blowing away in smoking flurries that quickly vanished into nothing. I do not know what Rose told her parents about me in her letters home—maybe not everything yet—but enough so that there were tensions when we first met on a weekend visit to their farm. But a mutual liking soon got the better of fears and prejudices. I felt I had cleared that particular hurdle, and kept studying hard toward my degree with greater confidence. We both worked, sometimes giving up dates in order to earn overtime pay. Our nest egg grew, slowly but surely. In the early spring, I finally had enough money to make a down-payment on the engagement ring I had been unable to afford when I proposed over six months ago. I carried the diamond around in my pocket for several days, waiting for a dramatic moment to surprise Rose with it. But neither of us had the time to arrange for carefully staged trysts, having to take advantage of every opportunity to get together. Rose thus received her belated engagement ring in the waiting room of the dentist's office where I was having a tooth filled. It was not the romantic setting I wanted for the occasion, but fortunately for me, Rose had a great sense of humor and the moment was made bright with love and laughter.

We were married almost exactly a year after we had first met, on June 10, 1950, in Jefferson City's St. Peter's Cathedral. It was a formal wedding attended in full splendor by the entire Roling clan with Angie, Lola, and Rose's sister-in-law, Jennie acting as bridesmaids. My best man and other male attendants were fellow graduates from Boys Town, loyally making up for the absence of any Bucher family. I was as jittery as any young groom facing the altar in a new suit, but when Rose came down the aisle, radiantly beautiful in her white gown, my whole being became aware only of my overwhelming love for her. Practically everything else during the ceremony is a blur in my memory. The congregation of family and guests shuffling and whispering in the pews, the priest's vestments glittering as he intoned the sacrament, the loaded banquet table crowded with happy, flushed faces, flashbulbs flaring the huge cake into a blinding whiteness as we started cutting it. There were cheers, jokes, laughter, well-wishes, showers of rice, then the fading tumult when we finally escaped in the old Plymouth with its rattling garlands of tin cans. We honeymooned for five days at the nearby lakes of the Ozarks. Only Rose's loveliness remains indelibly impressed upon my mind, as vividly now as when she came toward me on her father's arm to become my bride.

Had I ever really let her know how deeply I felt at that moment? How much in my heart had I wanted to tell, that I let go untold? Was the chance gone forever as I moldered in this prison with only a vision of her appearance in a feverish recurring dream of days long past and lost.

The door to my cell burst open with a resounding crash and Rose fled from my mind. Raising myself off my bunk, I faced the reality of the Imperialist as he snarled, "You come now! For sincere talk!"

Ten days had gone by since *Pueblo*'s capture according to my crude way of calculating time, based in part on my increasing state of filth and growth of beard. I was still wearing the clothes I had worn on January 23 which were impregnated with blood, sweat, and slime. I could smell my own strong smell, which seemed of a sub-human beast. It was a miracle that my fairly superficial wounds did not become infected with the virulent microbes I knew were incubating all over my unwashed body. I also noticed small gray bugs which emerged in swarms out of the rice-husk stuffing of my mattress and pillow to feed on me with pin-prick bites. What sort of disease would they infect me with? Typhus? Bubonic plague? Plague, I seemed to recall, was transmitted by rats, but rats infected by lice who were the real carriers. My bedding was full of lice and I had seen rats scurrying down fissures in the latrine. Foreigners often joke about Americans' obsession with cleanliness and hygiene. I can testify that filth is a subtle form of torture for most of us. I remember hoping that my immunization shots would be effective.

After another week I felt physically and mentally improved. I had previously been so ill from my wounds and beatings that I felt close to death. But some of my strength was now returning. I even developed a faint appetite for the food I was offered. As soon as the KORCOMs noticed I was getting better, the special rations of hot condensed milk and cookies were stopped and the fare returned to monotonous offerings of turnip soup, bread with rancid butter, and a sardine-like fish. The fish I rather liked. The rancid butter kept coming up throughout the day and gave me the opportunity to eat the meal over again unless, of course, it came up all the way. As the palsying weakness of fever and hunger left my body, my mind also regained its strength. I began more carefully to analyze my situation and to begin to cope with it. Paramount was the protection of those secrets locked inside my brain. Next I planned to re-establish contact with my officers and crew in order somehow to maintain the *Pueblo*'s chain of command and naval discipline: I knew that at least some of them were alive and nearby because I had heard their cries and moans, and on the way to the latrine I had briefly seen prisoners in the marble corridor. The guards either shoved them to face the wall or pushed them back into their cells. I also hoped to get some kind of message back to the United States which would say that *Pueblo* had never intruded into North Korean waters and that any statements or "confessions" released by the KORCOMs were false. It soon appeared that the KORCOMs themselves had opened up this tenuous line of communication through their propaganda to the outside world. I began concocting codes out of peculiar American idioms and odd twists of the infinitely flexible English language which might get by the rudimentary linguistic talents of their interpreters' staged "press conferences." I was wracking my brain to find complicated subterfuges to thwart the KORCOMs. Devious plotting could, I knew, be one of the symptoms of the deranged mind of a prisoner long kept in solitary confinement. Yet I felt it quite the opposite—a means of preserving my sanity. It gradually became obvious to me that they were meting out physical violence, at least in my case, in strictly controlled measures—not too little, not too much. If a guard became too rough, he would be restrained by a Junior Duty Officer. If a junior officer let his fists or feet get too wild, a senior major or colonel would bring him up short with a sharp word. I got the impression that none of them was authorized to beat me to death, or even cause anything like severe injuries. While their blows could hurt like hell, I found a relief in suspecting they were not permitted to kill me. I was encouraged enough to think that I was being spared for the time being, or for some devious purpose as yet unknown.

This did not mean that the atmosphere of terror did not continue. The Koreans had a way of creating it without violence. For example, one day an officer suddenly burst into my room and started bawling at me in fractured English: "Speak Korean? You speak Korean?" I had never seen him before. He was a major who wore a strange badge over his left tunic pocket, not unlike an American police badge. His question, which sounded more like an accusation, frightened me because I had been hoping they would not discover that we had people aboard *Pueblo* who spoke either their language or Russian. I knew they would consider this as *prima facie* evidence of our intention to commit espionage. I feigned difficulty in understanding him, but Imperialist followed him into my cell and proceeded to grill me with his slightly better English: "Who in your crew speak Korean?"

"No one," I lied. It was really a half-truth, I thought bitterly, remembering how limited Sergeants Chicca and Hammond were in Korean.

"Who speak Russian?" he demanded.

My heart sank at this one, remembering that Steve Harris and several of his CTs were quite fluent in that language, but I lied again.

"Researchy?" the Major barked at me with excitement. "Researchy speak Korean, Russian?"

For a moment I was genuinely confused until I realized he was asking about Steve, our "Research Officer." I wondered whether they had his service record, too. Nevertheless, I tried to appear contemptuous of the whole line of questioning: "Of course not! We are Americans, not Koreans nor Russians. I've told you that many times before, and certainly you should have found that out for yourselves by now."

They glowered at me. (Later someone dubbed the Major "Deputy Dawg" because of his bark and impressive badge.) The questions were repeated and I stuck with the same answers, trying to give the impression that I thought they were amusingly far off the track. Then they departed, abruptly, leaving me to brood and worry over the fact that they were at last close to a sensitive intelligence area. My concern became agonized the following night, when I heard more activity than usual in the hall outside my door: scufflings, thumps and slams, groans and suppressed cries of pain. Were they giving poor Chicca and Hammond the full treatment to get some Korean words out of them? Were they working over Steve to make him admit he was fluent in Russian? I prayed that they would hold out, and suffered along with them. I knew that it was unusual for a ship to carry qualified interpreters aboard, but I hoped that the KORCOMs would not make too much out of it even if they established the fact *Pueblo* actually carried language experts. When the matter was not pursued farther, my hope grew. But that evening I caught a glimpse of someone from the crew being carried past my cell on a stretcher, badly beaten.

One evening I was taken for the usual interrogation session and was surprised to find myself facing a strange officer wearing a blue uniform. He was the first naval type I had seen since my imprisonment. He looked me over with a grim scowl and sternly announced through his interpreter that he was about to read me *The Rules of Life*. This was something new. There was something comic about the way he tried to impress me with stiff formality, but he left no doubt that he was serious by warning me to pay strict attention as any infractions would be most severely punished. He proceeded to read *The Rules of Life*, rattling them off one at a time in Korean, then pausing while the interpreter gave a translation from a prepared English version. There were nine in all:

"One—the daily schedule will be strictly observed. Two—you will always display courtesy to the duty personnel when they enter your room to deal with you. Three—you must not talk loudly or sing in your room. Four—you must not sit or lie on the floor or bed except during prescribed hours but should sit on the chair. Five—you must wear your clothes at all times except when washing your face and in bed. Six—you must take care of your room, furniture and all expendables issued to you. Seven—you will keep your room and corridors clean at all times. Eight—you will entertain yourself only with the culture provided. Nine—if you have something to do, ask permission from the guards, who will escort you to the appropriate place."

He paused to observe my reaction, mistaking my incredulous expression for one of rapt concentration. He then continued with a dramatic rise in tone to emphasize the importance of the next part:

"You will be punished severely and unconditionally if you commit one of the following: One—in case you make false statements or refuse questioning or hint to others to do so. Two—in case you attempt to signal other rooms by this or that means. Three—in case you show disrespect to any of the duty personnel. Four—in case you make another offense." Having completed the reading he again sharply scrutinized me and asked: "Have you understood your *Rules of Life* and the otherwise if you disobey them?" Then he further cautioned me about not talking with other prisoners while eating.

I resisted asking any of the questions which came flooding into my mind, realizing that I would hardly receive any enlightening answers on the spot. So I nodded that I had understood and was curtly dismissed from the naval officer's presence. I was never to see him again. As I was being escorted back to my cell by a dour-faced guard, I concentrated on the implications of *The Rules of Life*. The fact that they had been put down on paper and formally read to me (and probably to other prisoners) must mean that, far from intending to execute us soon, as they had so often threatened, they planned to keep us alive. While this suggested an indefinite imprisonment without any prospects of release in the near future, it also largely removed the fear of sudden or deliberately slow extinction. We might shortly be gathered together in a *mess hall* for our meals. This opened up tremendous possibilities.

Ironically, I was soon subjected to my next experience of terror. It happened shortly after 2230 hours. I had just undressed to try for a night's sleep, when the door to my cell flew open and Lieutenant Chipmunk blew in together with two enlisted guards. They were all dressed in heavy winter greatcoats and Chipmunk had his pistol drawn and pointed at me. "You must dress," he snarled, "must hurry!" I was terrified. Something about their grim, hard demeanor and the threatening pistol told me that I was about to be taken out in the night and put to the wall. Chipmunk must have noticed my look of terror and without in the least moderating his scowl, snapped: "You will go now for bath."

That clinched it. A bath? At this hour? All the frail signs of hope I had been nursing were illusions, after all. I was convinced I was about to be executed. As soon as I knew that this was about to happen, I managed to shake off the terror and maintain a certain resigned calm as I put on my clothes. I was also plotting desperate action. If there were any sign of preliminary torture that I knew I would be unable to withstand, I planned to force them to shoot me. I resolved to provoke it by actually attacking them, or by making a wild break for freedom. My sole objective now became to avoid a slow agonizing death. Even when Chipmunk picked up my rag of a towel and small piece of soap and handed them to me with a command to hurry, I refused to believe that anything but death was in store for me.

"You must not look!" I was told when we reached the foot of the stairs and marched on toward the front door. But I did look—upward toward the starry vault of a magnificent clear winter night. Up there were Polaris and Betelgeuse and Orion, old friends of the heavens who had guided me in years past over the great oceans, tiny steadfast beacons now winking their last farewell. They were more beautiful than I had remembered them, tightening my heart with a fervent wish to cling to life a little longer. But our boots crunched through snow and then I was hustled into a waiting bus whose windows and driver's seat were screened from outside view. There were two more armed guards seated inside it and as soon as the door slammed shut, the driver threw the idling engine into gear and we lurched forward. Chipmunk sat directly opposite me, holstering his pistol but watching me intently as he kept his right hand close to the weapon. I stared back into his face, trying not to show the frantic thoughts of fear racing through my brain as I gauged the bumps and swerves which I expected were returning me to the dungeon where I had witnessed the last moments of that tortured South Korean agent.

But when we stopped, the bus did not seem to have traveled as far as I had been taken on that occasion. Chipmunk stepped out for a moment, then returned and ordered: "You will come now! Hurry!" I moved to follow him, hoping I was stepping onto an execution ground, not being led into a torture chamber.

There were three cement buildings, plain structures with a few lights illuminating the windows of their gloomy façades. I was escorted in between two guards. We passed several KORCOM officers and armed troopers who were stamping their feet to keep circulation going in the bitter cold. It did not look like an execution ground. As we approached the entrance to the third building, I was steeling myself to make a break to invite quick, merciful death. But then Chipmunk said to me as he threw open the door: "You must off your shoes!" That made me hesitate long enough to catch the unmistakable whiff of moist steam, a familiar scent I remembered well from my days in Japan when I often enjoyed their famous hot baths, the *ofuro*. My God in Heaven. I was really being taken for a bath!

The shock of relief was almost a greater strain than the anticipation of death. My knees grew weak and it was all I could do to keep myself from breaking into hysterical laughter, especially when the anteroom, where I was directed to strip myself nude, was suddenly invaded by uniformed members of the KORCOM press corps. Instead of the muzzles of rifles, I was suddenly faced with cameras, lightmeters, floodlights and flashbulbs. The customary scowls were replaced with grins to coax me into a proper expression. Even Chipmunk worked his formidable jowls into a smile and exclaimed: "You must stand so pictures can be!"

In a daze which ignored any sense of modesty, I let them photograph me in the "altogether" as I delightedly strode inside a white tiled bathroom toward a beautiful sunken tub filled to the brim with clean hot water. I almost forgot the strict Japanese bath etiquette which requires that you wash your body clean *before* immersing yourself in the communal tub. There was a standard wooden bucket for that purpose and Chipmunk threw me a bar of soap while he stood aside as the cameramen bustled against each other to take photographs of me going happily through the time-honored Oriental bath ritual. I may have giggled with foolish pleasure, but I still had enough wit left to realize that this was another staged propaganda ploy. As shutters clicked and flashbulbs popped, I smiled and extended my index and little finger with thumb closed in the vulgar sign recognized by any American student or serviceman, signifying: bullshit. It was not only difficult to manage while soaping myself, but also probably dangerous. But the KORCOM press corps, jammed into the bathroom to the point of bursting its tiled walls, seemed oblivious to it and kept clicking and grinding away with their cameras. In a moment of wry comedy, we exchanged buffooneries, each trying to fool the other. At this point, their Producer-Officer, a nervously chortling, wizened little major, ushered them out. I was left alone with Chipmunk, whose smile vanished as soon as his countrymen were out of sight. I expected him to order me out of the bath to return to my cell since I had now sincerely performed my act. I was wrong. "Now you clean your body!" he snapped and then wheeled out the door with his usual slamming exit.

I was alone, submerged to the neck in soothing hot water which magically drew all the pain and filth out of my aching, dirty body. I wondered whether they would release the pictures for worldwide publication. Pray God they would! The most obtuse intelligence analyst would spot the finger-sign and perhaps draw the right conclusion from it. So might some KORCOM analyst, but that was the chance I had to take.

When Chipmunk popped in to ask if I was ready to get out, I replied with an imperious: "No! Not yet!" He vanished for a half-hour longer, giving me a total of nearly one hour of complete bliss.

Back in my cell, I had the drowsy feeling of well-being that follows a good "*ofuro*" and as soon as I dropped onto my bunk, I fell into a deep sleep. At about 0200 hours a junior lieutenant made a typically noisy entrance and routed me to my feet, shouting:

"Come! Stand up! Must shave face!"

I had not seen him before, so I promptly gave him a name that described his most striking characteristic. In this case, it was a severe case of post-nasal drip. Snotnose spoke through stuffy sinuses with a high pitched voice, and looked very mean. Behind him appeared a guard carrying a bowl of water which turned out to be ice-cold. "I can't possibly shave off this beard in ice-cold water," I protested.

Snotnose looked agitated and wiped his nose on his sleeve while trying to understand what I had said. When my gestures failed to make my objection clear, he angrily stomped out and was shortly replaced by an officer of more senior rank to deal with the situation. He also was new to me; a squat little major with a wizened face who at first paid more attention to the floor of my cell than he did to me, indicating with grimaces and mumbled expressions of disgust that he found the place disgustingly dirty. After pantomiming a vigorous scrubbing and mopping of the deck, he indicated that he expected the floor to be cleaned up as soon as possible. Then he turned his attention to my beard. Although his English was no better than Snotnose's, he understood the problem of the ice water and had the guard exchange it for a bowl of water close to the boiling point. Then he produced a small box from which he assembled an old-fashioned safety razor while I sat on my chair, dabbed my face with the scorching water, and tried to work up a lather with the piece of soap I had been issued for daily use.

The major turned out to be a very rough barber and his razor extremely dull, so much so that he finally gave up and let me shave myself. The major let me take my time and turned his full attention to inspecting my cell, carefully pointing out all the soiled spots and indicating they must be cleaned. By the time I had finished and he had left, I dropped on my bunk, exhausted, sleepily wondering about these screwy KORCOMs. The major was later dubbed "Clean Floors."

The clanging reveille bell awakened me at 0600. I felt a sort of guarded optimism. Yet, all that happened was a finishing touch to my "sprucing up." I was ordered to shed the malodorous remains of my uniform and issued with prisoner's garb. It was at least clean. It consisted of coarse under-shorts without a fly and secured with a drawstring, a white cotton shirt. There was also a jacket and trousers of blue padded material, and a pair of socks (but no shoes, presumably to discourage escape across the snowbound countryside). I was left shivering naked in a freezing room down the corridor for a half hour before being outfitted with clothes which hung like sacking on my emaciated frame. The interpreter whom I had first met during the seizure of *Pueblo* (we named him Max, because of an Oriental likeness to Maximilian Schell), impressed upon me that I should be grateful to the Korean people for receiving this wardrobe and pointed out that I should take the best care of it.

One day I was summoned to another soiree with Super-C and Wheezy, a break in the tedium, yet boring because the line of interrogation had already been repeated ad nauseum.

It started with the usual: "How is your life these days?" and then degenerated into a harangue which in turn exploded into a rage of theatrics. Super-C was indefatigable in his performances, which never lasted less than two hours and often three or four. Wheezy's ability to keep up with him both in translation and mimicry was also astounding. They always rehashed a full list of alleged crimes in detail, those of the United States in general, and then picked on some particular propaganda aspect chosen as the central theme of the evening's program. Tonight Super-C returned to that of American atrocities in the Korean War and told me that he was actually protecting us from the wrath of the Korean people who would tear the *Pueblo* crew to pieces if they could get their hands on us. In that respect I tended to believe him, remembering the slavering mob who had greeted the ship when she was brought into Wonsan. He said that the hatred against Americans was so great that none could survive for an hour outside this compound. My thoughts had been dwelling a great deal on escape when I could determine with some accuracy where we were located in the country, but his implied warning had its effect. Could Occidentals have any chance to escape through this rabidly anti-white country? Had any Americans succeeded in escaping from prison during the Korean War? I could not recall of hearing about a single successful case and realized what a terribly hazardous undertaking it would be for us. Yet I remained determined to keep planning on it, as a support of morale if nothing else. If we only could get out one of our Filipino or Mexican Americans, who had the best chance of passing unnoticed among the Koreans, it would be a tremendous triumph. The DMZ might be within a couple of days' march and certainly the sea was no farther from any point on this narrow peninsula. The *sea* where a boat could be stolen and make a concealed passage south along the heavily serrated coastline. I had to keep thinking about it! My mind wandered into a maze of plotting in the middle of Super-C's endless ranting, but now he caught my attention by suddenly switching off his tirade and rather pompously announcing: "Tomorrow you will be given a special treat!"

"Oh? How so?" I asked, forcing myself to look interested.

Wheezy, who was growing weary from the prolonged session, spluttered and wheezed the colonel's explanation: "Tomorrow is the great Korean Holiday. The anniversary of beginning of the Korean People's Army!"

"So?"

"You too will have free day! (Cough-splutter) Will be allowed to celebrate with special food. Apples. Cakes. Candies. Much good food."

As my appetite had returned, this sounded downright mouthwatering, but I merely shrugged and was eventually dismissed with the customary admonition to be sincere.

The reveille bell jarred me awake the next morning at 0500, signaling that additional sleep was not to be part of our Korean

Army Day treat. A surly young guard came in and made me swab down the deck with a rag and bucket of cold water, a chore which I had to do on my hands and knees, then was escorted to dump the slops in the latrine urinal. The slops dribbled back onto the latrine floor, from where it sluggishly filtered through a scupper to the floor below, thence, I supposed, to the ground floor where it must have backed up into a dirty cesspool because of frozen drains. Breakfast consisted of slices of turnip and bread, some rancid butter and a teaspoon of sugar. This was served by a moonfaced Korean girl, who wore a long skirt and a baggy blouse. She never allowed her eyes to give me the slightest glance of recognition. When she came back for my tray, she brought one of those tasteless but juicy apples found in great quantity in the Far East. I decided to save it just in case Super-C's promised feast never materialized, and hid it under my bedding hoping that the vermin living there were exclusively carnivorous. Then I settled down for another long, lonely morning of pacing, sitting, thinking, waiting.

The banquet was real. It turned out to be quite a production.

Sometime after 1000 hours, my little cell was suddenly invaded by the same group of photographers and movie technicians who had recorded my bath scene. At first they paid no attention to me, as they inspected the premises and peered around through joined thumbs for camera angles. Their leader was the nervous, preoccupied major, whom I recognized as the director of the last production. I dubbed him Jack Warner and his busy minions, the Warner Brothers. It became difficult for me not to act as a temperamental star as they fussed around, chatting in excited Korean whispers, measuring and blocking out their shots, but I remained rigidly seated in my chair and puffed through my daily allotment of cigarettes. I was given no script, no direction. They left as suddenly as they had arrived. One of the Warner Brothers left me with an encouraging grin. I returned my most disinterested scowl.

Next came a pair of "maids" who set the stage under the stolidly watchful eye of an armed guard. They put a tablecloth over my table, laid what passed for a formal setting with a bowl of apples as a centerpiece, then brought in platters of steamed rice, boiled fish, and bread and butter. Imperialist entered and inspected the arrangement, gave me a sickly grin and indicated that I was not to attack this sumptuous feast, but await further developments. I remembered reading about staged propaganda meals like this for American prisoners in the Korean and Vietnam Wars where the food had been snatched away as soon as the pictures were taken and was fully prepared for this.

The main show started at about 1300 hours. Jack Warner and his Warner Brothers pressed into the cell with lights and cameras. The "maids" had exchanged their drab uniform dresses for colorful native costumes and while one served me a bowl of rich potato and pork soup, the other filled my glass with sparkling beer. The cameras whirred and clicked, the photographers and their director indicating some dismay over my glum face as I stared in stupefaction at the food spread before me. They frantically signaled for me to start eating, but it was not their direction which finally broke my willpower—it was all that food. The best I could do was to act and to look so famished that it would compromise their desire to depict a wellfed, pampered prisoner. I picked up the bowl of pork and potato soup and wolfed it down in eager gulps. I guzzled the beer. I stuffed myself with bread and fish and rice, then washed it down with more beer. My table manners were atrocious, but I ate as much as fast as I could because I still suspected that when the Warner Brothers had the pictures they needed, the banquet would end.

When they finished shooting I was surprised to be left alone to enjoy the rest of the meal. My stomach was not used to so much food and I knew I would probably make myself sick by overeating, but I didn't care. I ate everything but a couple of apples, which I squirreled away in a secret larder in my bunk. My only unselfish thought was a hope that my shipmates were being similarly feasted.

As I sat there in bloated euphoria, Major Clean Floors waddled in with a bottle and small glass. Evidently the meal was to be topped off with an after-dinner liqueur. He filled the glass and I cautiously tasted it, then gulped it down. It was Ginseng, a powerful spirit distilled from a root common throughout Asia. Clean Floors refilled the glass and let me sip the second shot with more restraint. He came back three times in the course of the next hour, each time pouring a refill and gruffly overriding my protests that

I had had enough. The cell was beginning to swim before my eyes and the single naked electric bulb to split itself into a mobile chandelier. I knew I had become drunk. It came as a great relief when the guard came in and indicated that an afternoon nap was to be part of my Korean Army Day celebration. I collapsed on my bunk and promptly fell asleep.

Sometime late in the afternoon I awakened with a terrible headache. This was a reward for my overindulgence. I had a couple of unusual visitors. First Wheezy, the interpreter, who brought me several booklets—the "cultural Material" referred to in *The Rules of Life.* He was in an expansive mood and ordered an extra chair brought in so he could sit with me for an informal chat. He spoke nearly fluent English and showed considerable familiarity with the American idiom, which warned me that I had to be careful about injecting veiled meanings in any statements I made for their records. Yet on this occasion he seemed relaxed and guileless, asking about my health, assuring me that my men were being well taken care of and that our treatment would remain humane as long as we were sincere and repented our sins against the Korean people. "What else can we do for you?" he asked.

"Return us to our ship and let us go home," I said.

He smiled and shook his head. "Perhaps when you and your country apologize for the crimes you committed. Otherwise quite impossible, of course. But I understand that you must miss very much your family, yes?"

I tried not to show him how very much I did miss them and worried about them. He left me with the advice to read and thoroughly absorb the material in the pamphlets so that I would realize the *true* history of American atrocities and aggressions against the Korean people. And as soon as he was gone, I immediately began to read with all the eagerness of a starved bookworm even though I expected the text to be so much propaganda garbage. It was something *to do*, a meager soporiphic in the vacuum of solitary. Most ridiculous were the gory accounts of a Lieutenant J. G. Harrison who, the narrative related in lurid detail, had personally supervised the torture and death of 50,000 –60,000 Koreans, mostly women and children, during the late Korean War.

That evening I was excused from the usual interrogation session down the hall and instead honored by a personal visit of Super-C. He breezed in together with Wheezy, like a suave villain out of a Fu Manchu novel—a striking military figure wearing his greatcoat with the oversized epaulettes, and a rakish cap of fine lambskin. Super-C was obviously allowed certain latitudes in his uniform, including custom-made shoes. "How is your life these days, Captain?" he asked with an amiably toothy grin and puffing out a halo of cigarette smoke. "How have you eaten?"

I was forced to admit that the food had been nourishing.

Super-C feigned surprise and enquired about the menu. When Wheezy gave it to him in detail, he smacked his lips in envy and acted as if he had no idea that I had been so pampered: "Such generosity! Such humanity by the peace-loving Korean people!" he declaimed with great emotion. "You see how we reward sincerity, in this case more than really deserved. But you will see that we really are trying to encourage you to be repentant for your crimes. I have decided to henceforth allow the sport of Ping-pong for exercise of muscles!"

I was genuinely pleased. This would provide an opportunity to get in touch with some of my crew, and to re-establish *Pueblo*'s chain of command. "That would be much appreciated," I said.

"And also playing cards for intellectual amusement," he announced. "I have also heard that you clean your own room entirely yourself," he continued. "This is not suitable for Commanding Officer, not at all. So I will arrange for somebody to take care of such work for you. That is, if you keep sincere."

So I was to be assigned an orderly. "Thank you. All this will make life easier under the circumstances," I told him.

To demonstrate his serious intentions, he sent Wheezy for the Duty Officer (who turned out to be Snotnose) and gave him detailed instruction in Korean. Snotnose groveled and bowed. The visit ended without any of Super-C's usual tirades. He admonished me to be sincere and paraded out of my door, vanishing down the marble corridor.

So ended the initial phase of my imprisonment. A new one was about to begin.

CHAPTER XIV

"WE HAD MONITORED AT LEAST A DOZEN POSITION
REPORTS FROM THE NORTH KOREANS WHICH PLACED
THE ACTIVITY OUTSIDE THE TWELVE-MILE LIMIT."
—(*U. S. Delegate to UN Security Council during debate on* Pueblo *Incident, January 28, 1968.*)

"UNITED NATIONS HAS NO RIGHT TO MEDDLE IN
'PUEBLO' CASE."—(*Headline in the* Pyongyang
Times [*North Korea*], *February 8, 1968*).

When it came to vanity, none of the KORCOMs could match Super-C, the peerless leader of this particular prison-garrison. I was convinced he was specially chosen and trained for the job. Most of his subordinates were simple, forthright characters who, under different circumstances might have lived out their lives as farmers, tradesmen, or artisans. But Super-C was smooth by comparison. He was a physically imposing man, tall and slender as opposed to the medium stocky muscularity of his countrymen. I first thought of him as terrifyingly ruthless, cunning and violent, but I gradually became aware that even during his worst threats and tirades, he was deliberately pacing himself and was generally watching and analyzing my reactions. By this, I do not mean that he was a man who would not go to the limit of cruelty, but that he would only do so as part of a careful plan for dealing with prisoners in his charge. I have no doubt that he firmly believed in the main substance of his harangues, just as old-fashioned fire and brimstone preachers believed in their sermons.

Super-C also showed that he was well informed about current events by inserting facts into his spiels (such as the assassination of President John F. Kennedy, Dr. Martin Luther King and Senator Robert Kennedy, as well as the anti-poverty and Vietman War protest marches and riots which plagued the USA during 1968). He also let me know he was well educated and intimated that he had attended a Military Academy in Moscow, which alerted me to the fact that he probably spoke Russian. Neither Super-C, nor any of the literature he required us to read, gave any credit to Soviet Russia or Red China as mentors or allies of the Korean Democratic People's Republic in their struggles against "Imperialist America." The huge amount of Russian weaponry and the Chinese Red Army divisions that had turned back General MacArthur when he reached the Yalu River during the Korean War, were never mentioned. He followed the official KORCOM line which said that the Korean Communists had done it all on their own. While a doctrinaire Communist, Super-C was primarily an arrogant Korean nationalist.

During the first shock of our seizure and initial brutal treatment, I felt we were in a grim Communist prison of the sort that only a handful of prisoners have survived to tell harrowing tales about. As time dragged by in solitary confinement broken only by periodic marches down the corridor to bleak interrogation rooms, the latrine, or the cavernous "conference hall," my eyes and mind became conscious of details which made me doubt we were actually incarcerated in the KORCOMs version of the Soviets' dreaded Lubyanka. My cell was, in its harsh way, too spacious. Its door did not have a peephole nor was it armed with maximum-security locks. The window, screened with temporary paper material, was, I discovered, not blocked by iron bars or wire mesh. Then there were the luxurious marble floors of the corridors which were hardly suitable flooring for a maximum-security prison. Once when I made one of my repeated complaints to a junior officer of the guard about the bitter cold infiltrating the building, which sometimes even froze the cesspool in the latrine, I was indignantly informed, "This much fine house! Built by Korean workers to last a hundred generations long! Not accept insincere complaint about that is lie!" All of this led me to the conclusion that we were not shut up in a prison building intended for the purpose, but in a hastily contrived makeshift that was originally designed as a public or military structure.

Later in February, when a slick English-language propaganda magazine called *Korea Today* was added to our "cultural material," I spotted in it some photographs of what the captions described as a *Young People's New Military Academy*. It looked very familiar to me. Was this where we were? The more I studied the pictures, the more certain I became. It made little difference to our predicament, yet a lot. At least it tended to confirm that we might not be condemned cases in the death-row of one of their terminal prisons.

Sometime around the third week, I ran into Photographer Mack when our paths crossed on our way to and from the head. Both our guards dropped the ball long enough so we could speak to each other for a few seconds: "Captain! Captain, they're asking me about carriers! What shall I do, sir?"

While Mack had served aboard carriers, I knew there was very little he could tell the Koreans of intelligence value about their operations. He was, after all, only a Photographers Mate 1st Class. "Don't tell them a goddamned thing, Mack!" I shot back at him. In an instant his guard began roughing him up, while mine shoved me into my cell where I was given a thorough chewing out by a junior officer. Toward the middle of February, I was being escorted down the hall and as I went by another cell, the door was ajar so that I had a flash of the interior which was exactly like my own. Skip Schumacher was inside, looking pale, glum, but not visibly injured. For an instant our eyes met, only long enough for a blink of surprised recognition, no time to exchange a word because the guards bristled when they realized we had seen each other and quickly hustled me away. I became reasonably certain that most of the *Pueblo's* complement were being kept together in this building, probably on the floor below and the one on which Schumacher and I were being held in solitary. None of the KORCOMs gave me any reliable information about my men beyond the occasional assurance that they were being treated "humanely" so long as we were "sincere." Their policy obviously was to keep us isolated from each other and, at least in my case, in total ignorance of the others' fate and conditions.

But then this too changed.

In the glow of the Army Day celebration, Super-C had promised that I would be given an orderly. Although I constantly caught him in prevarications, he kept his word this time. Shortly after reveille of February 9 when I was starting to swab down my deck with a rag and bucket of water, the Junior Duty Officer came in and stopped me by saying "Captain not do work! Will have another prisoner help!" He left and returned within a few minutes with one of my own enlisted men, Seaman Edward S. Russell. I was astounded! At best I had expected one of their own lower grade soldiers to be assigned the job. But here was not only a *Pueblo* crewman, but an excellent one through whom I could re-establish contact with the crew. Russell was intelligent, alert, loyal, and possessed of a lively sense of humor which made him very popular aboard the ship.

The officer who brought him left a guard in the cell who never took his eyes off us, so there was no chance to speak or exchange signals while Russell got down on his knees and took over the swabbing. Nevertheless, our eyes met and we communicated. Russell's haggard look became tinged by a barely perceptible trace of his former impish grin while he prolonged his menial work by scrubbing and manicuring each floorboard with ridiculous care. For my part, I tried to soften the shock of my own appearance and show my great appreciation of his company by slowly allowing a thin smile to play on my lips. The guard scowled and growled uneasily. We dared no more obvious signs between us, realizing that if this opportunity was to be developed into something useful, we could not now ruin it by a rash move. After ten minutes during which he had rubbed the rag over every inch of my floor, Russell was abruptly hustled out. Would he come back the next morning?

He did. And on the third and fourth morning, as well. Evidently he had been assigned as my permanent floor-scrubbing orderly. I noticed that the guards were accepting this as routine and our caution resulted in a slight relaxation of their vigilance. By this time I was being allowed to keep their propaganda material in my cell. I had also been assigned to write a "more sincere" apology in my own composition. This provided me with a chance to snitch a stub of pencil and sequester a scrap of paper. Before reveille of the fifth day I had a message scribbled down and was ready to attempt to pass it to Russell. All I could get into the couple of square inches was something like: "Been wounded and beaten but OK now. Tell all to hold up and pass problems to me." I rolled this up into a pea-sized ball and let it fall where Russell might see it.

It came off to perfection! Russell palmed the tiny scrap of paper as he swabbed and I had a feeling of great triumph over having at long last established our first tenuous line of communication. The guard never noticed our initial effort. On the next day, however, by lulling us by his casualness, we got into serious trouble. When Russell was halfway through cleaning up my cell, the guard stepped over the threshold of the open door and momentarily turned his back on us, his attention diverted by something in the hall outside. We seized the opportunity to whisper to one another.

"You with any of the other men?" I said as low as I could. "Are they bearing up?"

"Two of us, Captain," he answered. "Me and Hayes, we are A1 OK . . . but I don't know anything about the others. Do you? What's the deal? Any hope? We are trying to establish contact by Morse code on the radiator pipes, but so far no go."

"Let me know anything you find out. It looks hopeful, but we . . ."

I could not complete my sentence before the guard lunged for Russell with a shout of anger. He instantly dragged him out of my cell and I knew my sailor was in for a brutal beating. I had less than ten minutes to brood about it before my own turn came. The guard burst back in and drove me into a corner where I tried to protect my body from a rain of kicks and jabs with the butt his carbine. It turned out the worst beating I had taken since th early days of my confinement. As he kept it up, I felt myself collapsing in a writhing heap of welts and bruises. I must have yelled, because a KORCOM major I knew only as Flatface (an interpreter who therefore spoke some English) came rushing in to find out what was going on. I yelled out a lie to him that we had not been talking, to which he contemptuously sneered: "You are not sincere!" He then permitted the guard to work me over some more. The pain of the blows was excruciating and I once again felt myself being reduced to a helpless wreck. Finally, I was left alone to drag myself gasping onto my bunk and trying to recover. Russell and I had gone too far. They were still capable of beating us to within an inch of our lives. Perhaps kill us.

That evening I was pushed, limping badly, to an interrogation room where Colonel Scar and his interpreter belabored me with a two-hour harangue over my lack of sincerity, containing all the old threats of a trial by People's Court and summary execution. But the next morning, to my complete amazement, there was Russell again, on his knees, scrubbing the floor with his pathetic shred of rag and bucket of cold water, as if nothing had happened save for the fact that he was moving stiffly and was bruised. He still had the same defiant, humorous twinkle in his eyes. The new guard actually dared to turn his back and give us the opportunity for a brief whisper:

"They work you over too?" I asked him, barely audible.

He nodded and whispered back: "What are our chances Captain?"

My faint answer was a bitter one: "They'll get what they can . . . Then get rid of us."

I could say nothing else as the guard was again watching us. Later in the day, when the pain from my beating began subsiding, I regretted what I had told Russell. My job was to encourage my men with courage of my own—to *lead* them with hope. I worried about my pessimistic forecast which he would have passed to his shipmates by the time he showed up the next morning. "Forget what I said," I told him the next morning, "stick together and chances are good. Pass that on." He indicated with a slight nod that he understood.

A real turning point in my confinement came about February 14, when my naval wash-khakis were returned, and I was ordered to change into them. Although they had been laundered, they had not been pressed and the old bloodstains still appeared as ugly blotches. Presently, a guard came and escorted me from my cell to the large conference room. My eyes were blinded by kleig lights, through which I saw the silhouettes of a crowd of people. As my eyes adjusted to the bright lights, I noticed Colonel Scar, several interpreters and Jack and the Warner Brothers with their elaborate German and Japanese-made motion picture equipment, in addition to about a half-dozen civilian "journalists" among the twenty-odd soldiers in civilian clothes. I faltered when I also recognized all of my officers, including civilian oceanographer Friar Tuck, on stage. I was so delighted to see them that I almost threw myself into their arms.

Gene Lacy, Tim Harris, Ed Murphy, Skip Schumacher, Friar, and Steve Harris (whom I was convinced had been tortured to death) were all present. And, despite weight loss, they all looked healthy. I broke into a delighted grin and fell just short of shouting an exultant greeting. Their smiles were tinged with shock when they looked me over.

I realized that my uniform hung in crumpled folds on my frame not only because it had been abused by a KORCOM laundry, I had shriveled! I was conscious of having lost many of my 205 pounds, but now had a sudden realization of an unbelievable change in my appearance.

This was a casual press conference by KORCOM standards.

After an hour of questioning, followed by a ten-minute break, we were led with a couple of stolid enlisted guards into an outer room to be served soda and cookies. We wasted two precious minutes before we dared break the rule of silence; another minute was lost seeking the most important facts to communicate. One of the Warner Brothers was peering at us through a viewfinder, obviously hoping for a relaxed candid shot. I obliged him by speaking in the tone of a guest making conversation at a cocktail party:

"Heard anything how the rest of the crew are doing? Everybody OK?"

"Don't know. Haven't seen them around much," somebody answered. Obviously, all these officers were as isolated from the enlisted men as I was.

The guards did not react to this exchange, even though they must have heard it. The other KORCOMs seemed preoccupied with their own conversations.

With increasing boldness, I decided to ask about the next most weighty thing on my mind: "Have you given them anything but 'sincere' confessions?"

They shook their heads.

"That's all they asked and that's all I gave," Steve said casually.

"For God's sake protect the highly classified at all costs." Everyone agreed to do so.

"How are you guys feeling these days?" I asked, deliberately paraphasing Super-C. I noticed that Ed Murphy had a bad cut over one ear, the only one with visible scars of mistreatment. He and the others nodded reassuringly and Gene said: "We've all been put a bit under the weather, but are bearing up. You look rough, Captain."

"Have lost some weight and got some welts that are healing. I'm still hanging in, so don't worry."

We continued to munch our cookies, sip our soda-pop, and give the cameras blank stares.

Then I said: "These press conferences are a great idea for letting the United States know how 'sincere' we are. I think there will be more now, so be ready to put in the right word that will let them know the truth. Watch your language so you don't give the wrong impression either way. Get it? I will take all the tough ones and be responsible right or wrong."

"We got it, Captain."

Colonel Scar reconvened the conference and an officer who came to be known as Robot because of his stiff demeanor brought the proceedings back to order, and the same bilge they had been spewing out during the previous hour.

I felt an enormous resurgence of confidence in finding the wardroom of the *Pueblo* intact. Our hurried, cryptic conversation had re-established a semblance of the chain of command. This was all I could think of as the KORCOMs droned on. Then they asked a question which jolted me to attentiveness:

"What is your reaction to the Prime Minister of Japan's statement regarding your intrusions into territorial waters of the Democratic People's Republic of Korea?"

I was surprised and noticed it in the expression on several of my shipmates' faces. How in hell could we, cut off from each other in solitary confinement, without any news of the world, know what the Prime Minister of Japan had said about the *Pueblo?* Obviously, one of us had to give the sort of answer they wanted. Skip rose to his feet and rattled off a marvelously ambiguous piece of gibberish which hardly enlightened the rest of us, something about "biting the hand that fed him." This seemed, more or less, to satisfy the KORCOMs and their propagandists. I guessed that Prime Minister Eisakee Sato had been cornered by some of Japan's volatile left-wing press with embarrassing questions regarding the *Pueblo* having been homeported in Japan prior to her infamous mission off North Korea, and had sidestepped it with a deft pronouncement to the effect that Japan was not responsible for an action that had culminated in an "act of piracy"—thus incurring the wrath of North Korea and her Communist supporters. It appeared that this issue, together with an attempt to fashion a rebuttal, was the principal reason for this press conference. So far as I was concerned, Skip's wording of his answer gave them little satisfaction. Of greater significance was the fact that the KORCOMs had inadvertently let us know that seizure of the *Pueblo* was receiving the attention of a friendly government. It logically followed that the United States would be at least equally concerned. It was the first concrete sign that we were not forgotten.

The conference ended with a concluding tirade, while cameras recorded our supposedly penitent expressions. Meanwhile, we managed to exchange a few more encouraging words before being marched back to our cells. From this point on, these cells were not as lonely as they used to be.

A couple of days after the press conference, the entire wardroom of the *Pueblo* was collected in the conference room, to meet with Super-C and his minions. He announced that it had been decided that we should have the opportunity to write a letter of apology to the Korean people for our criminal acts, and proceeded to lay down the principal guidelines for this composition. Among other things, he told us to stop referring to the country as *North* Korea, that South Korea was only a figment of our warped Imperialist imagination and that we must recognize none but the one and only indivisible Democratic People's Republic of Korea. He abjured us to confess and repent our sins with utmost sincerity in order to deserve the People's forgiveness: if we did not do this, he threatened, nothing could save us from a full measure of swift and just punishment from the People's Court. With that he turned over the session to his apparent subordinate, Colonel Scar, and stalked out of the room.

We were seated at a long table and given paper and pencils. Discussions were permitted only over wording in the strictly prescribed context of the verbiage they intended to pry out of us. Colonel Scar supervised us, using a new interpreter (whom we came to know as Silverlips), who listened carefully to everything we said, and checked everything we wrote. Guards with fixed bayonets were posted outside of the door. There was no way for us to pass messages, written or verbal, without being observed and probably caught. Even winks and cautiously exaggerated facial expressions were dangerous. Yet we all intended to thwart the KORCOMs intentions through subtle twists of language and syntax which, if the letter was ultimately released to the outside world, would contain a thin thread of truth within its tissue of lies.

Fortunately, Colonel Scar left me with openings to reveal my technique to my men. He dictated the line we should follow and I began haggling with him over every word and sentence, encouraging my officers to join in the discussion. Silverlips and Colonel Scar consulted their dictionaries—now standard equipment in these encounters—and used them to support their arguments over language. I pointed out that Americans do not write and talk according to dictionaries, as presumably their own people did not either. The haggling continued and we in the spirit of the game by engaging in contrived discussions between ourselves over certain words, thus stalling the process of writing the letter. No more than a few words were agreed upon within the first hour. Colonel Scar became nervous and began to leave the room for consultations with whom we assumed to be Super-C in his office below. We guessed they were checking our captured records.

Colonel Scar returned after one of these consultations with some letters of apology which they had evidently extracted from some of the *Pueblo*'s personnel prior to our movement in the project. He showed them to us as examples of what he wanted.

I recognized the names and signatures, and while they betrayed no really sensitive intelligence information, the wording was so abject and compliant to their purpose as to be at least highly compromising to the individuals and to our ship's complement in general. Obviously they had been written under duress, but I considered them dangerously believable and therefore disastrous. It was my job to convince the KORCOMs that such apologies were uncharacteristic of our people. "Nobody who knows American sailors will believe it," I told Colonel Scar, working on his difficulties with the language barrier. "If you release anything as unbelievable as these letters, it will make you look ridiculous." My officers were quick to back me up. Scar and Silverlips wavered in the continued haggling, repeatedly leafing through the dictionaries and leaving for further consultations with the boss. At the end of two hours, we had severely shaken their faith in the "apologies" they had extracted and convinced them that a fresh approach was needed.

The next day we had another session during which we polished our stalling and equivocating tactics. ("*Intrusion?* Hmm. In English this word can have several meanings . . . *Penetration?* Oh, yes, a simile of sorts, but trickier . . . What's a simile? Hard to explain. Better look it up. Anybody know how to spell it? With a C or an S?") Scar and Silverlips became increasingly flustered. We began to enjoy our game and each other's company.

Colonel Scar suddenly seemed in a great hurry to get the letter of apology completed in an "acceptable" form. Could this signify the final propaganda effort before our release? I had only the flimsiest hope of this, but as a prisoner I grasped at the straw.

On the fourth they became impatient and decided that *too many cooks spoil the broth* (proverbs turned out to be popular with the KORCOMs as they apparently are with the Russians—they were constantly looking them up in the Idiomatic English dictionary and trying to embellish our compositions with them). Gene Lacy, Tim Harris, Steve Harris, Ed Murphy and Friar Tuck were sent back to cells, leaving myself and Skip Schumacher to finish the game with Super-C, Scar, Silverlips & Co. Our opponents figured they had tipped the scales in their favor by removing five of our players, but in fact they outsmarted themselves.

Skip was by far our most skillful man with words. His theological
studies had given him a command of biblical language which,
combined with his sharp wit, resulted in long-winded flowery
verbosity signifying absolutely nothing. Between us, we had the
KORCOMs spending more and more time poring over their
dictionaries and consulting with Super-C.

We figured that Colonel Scar must have taken a pretty good
chewing from his chief about our lack of progress. After one meeting he came back flustered and furious. Silverlips translated:

"You are doing nothing at all. You must be sincere or you will
answer to the just Korean Law. You are not sincere."

I turned to Skip with an expression of chagrin and said, "My
goodness! I think we better buckle down and give them three
or four pages of solidly sincere repentance. Something we feel
will do us all justice, right?"

"Yes, sir, Captain," Skip said.

"Return to work then and do not think our patience has no
end," Scar roared.

"No sweat," I said, which sent Colonel Scar and Silverlips back
to the dictionary.

For the next two hours they hovered over us while we approached the tenth version of the same letter. I knew it was time
for us to include some of the verbiage they wanted in order to
keep in a few words and phrases of our own choosing. I did
not want to run the risk of complete intransigence, particularly
over points that did not involve sensitive military intelligence.
Obstinacy would end the writing sessions and press conferences
and could result in torture and probably execution for many of
us. Skip was quick to sense this. When we had finished, Colonel
Scar took the draft of the letter downstairs to get Super-C's approval, which was evidently not forthcoming, because he returned much later with a version bearing only a faint resemblance
to our original.

"You have missed the mark. Here is the way to be sincere," he
thundered and shoved the KORCOM version at us.

Once again they had defeated themselves. The language although in fairly good English complete with American idioms,
still reeked of Communist propaganda and phraseology. We

haggled some more, but only in order to eliminate a few compromising words I convinced them were uncharacteristic. We succeeded in inserting a few cryptograms of our own, so we counted heavily on the general tone of the letter to alert our countrymen to the fact that it was the result of coercion. It was the best we could do after nearly a week's effort. We hoped to do better in the future. Skip and I were returned to our cells, uneasy, praying we had succeeded in our efforts and there would be no backlash from either side.

Characteristically, Super-C had the entire *Pueblo* complement routed out of their bunks at about 0200 two nights later for a ceremonial signing of the letter of apology. Meanwhile, one of our CTs, Elton A. Wood, had been assigned to make a smooth longhand copy of the draft. He had been chosen for the job because of his neat handwriting. The signing took place in the large conference-interrogation room. I was brought together with my officers. The crew was herded in, twenty at a time. Super-C left no doubt in my mind that failure to cooperate would lead to disastrous consequences. At long last, however, I had a chance to see my whole crew and to get some impression of how they were bearing up under their ordeal.

They came into the room blinking sleepily against the floodlights of Jack Warner and his Warner Brothers, who were present to record the event on film. They all wore the KORCOM prison garb and looked haggard, undernourished and nervous. Many showed signs of mistreatment: lumped jaws, blackened eyes, and stiff, limping gaits. Sergeant Hammond, one of our two Korean language "specialists," looked particularly battered but judging from the alert, defiant glint in his swollen eyes, unbowed. The same applied to our Filipino men, Aluague and Abelon, and our Mexican-American Seaman, Rosales, who must have kept catching special hell because the KORCOMs considered them South Korean spies and traitors. Fireman John A. Mitchell seemed ill with flu and he was shaking with fever. Others appeared to be suffering only from confinement, poor rations and constant tension. The sight of them all brought a lump to my throat, specially when I noticed how every one fixed his eyes on me, first in surprise, then with relief and trust. I desperately wanted to greet each man personally with some words of encouragement and explain to him that, no matter how badly I looked myself, I was ready and able to offer leadership and discharge my responsibility as their captain. We were kept a considerable distance apart and no personal conversations were allowed. Super-C ran the session with an iron hand and more than his customary suspicious vigilance. He expected me to exercise my influence as their commanding officer, but only within the narrow limits of his own purpose. After delivering a standard harangue, he pointedly informed my men that their own captain would explain the necessity for absolute "sincerity" in affixing their signatures to the letter of apology. With a cynical gesture, he placed onus on me.

Once again I carefully watched my words and inflections. The last thing I wanted to convey was cooperating with the KORCOMs. I felt myself breaking out in a cold sweat as I faced them.

I opened by saying, "Men, I'm delighted to see all of you . . . looking so *well*." I drove home the irony by sagging slightly on my feet and putting on a deliberately drawn expression to emphasize my own condition and added:

"As you can see, I'm still with you, have been given the same humane treatment by the marvelous peace-loving Korean people, regular chow to keep me this fit, and a room *all* to myself . . . which is why we haven't seen each other for a while."

Most of the men listened with blank, slightly incredulous expressions; but a few looked like the pressure of laughter was building up inside of them. I realized open laughter would be very dangerous. I could hear the interpreters translating my remarks in half-whispers to Super-C, and wondered if they had caught my inflections. Obviously, the colonel was aware that I had lost many pounds and was continuing to lose weight. I risked continuing along the same lines:

"The reason we are meeting, is to sign a letter of apology to the Democratic People's Republic of Korea for the hideous crimes which have been so *forcefully* brought to our attention since our arrival here. You all know as well as I do what it's all about . . . *where* we were when captured and under *what* circumstances. I want you to know that I've worked on this letter with these Korean officers for the past week and don't think we can make it more 'sincere' than it is. Anyway . . . trust me that I've gone over every word and tried a lot of others. This is the best we can do right now. So I'm asking you all to search your souls for sincerity and sign it so the Democratic People's Republic of Korea might be inclined to treat us leniently and humanely. As your captain, I ask you to do this in the fullness of the spirit of this occasion."

I wanted to give them all a broad wink or finger-sign but Super-C and his interpreters were watching me intently. Perhaps Skip or some of the other officers managed to support my performance with some faint flickers of their eyelids which would tip the crew what I was really trying to say. I fervently prayed they understood, and I prayed just as fervently that Super-C had not. He rose to his feet and made a slicing motion at me with one hand, but evidently only to indicate I had said enough and was to shut up forthwith. He then began fussing over the details of the signing and made it clear that each man should first print his name in block letters before making his regular signature. He was obviously taking no chances with forgeries.

None of the men were permitted to speak. We were called forward one at a time to sign under the close scrutiny of the KORCOMs and in the glare of motion picture lights. Some signed with indifference, others hesitantly, some grimaced and signed with uncharacteristic flourishes, leaning their writing forward or backwards to obfuscate their signature. Each gave me a searching look and I gave several of them revealing winks or nods.

After the first group had finished, they were marched out by their guards and the next brought in. The whole performance was repeated, including my little speech, which I got down pat by the third repetition. When all hands had signed including the officers, I became aware that Fireman Woelk was missing. My inquiries about him brought no information beyond: "He is well cared for." Woelk, who was badly wounded during the seizure was still alive.

Fears that our performance had discouraged the KORCOMs from more letter-writing projects turned out to be unfounded. On the contrary, they were hooked on the idea and lost no time in devising a new one for us to work on. Within a day after signing the letter of apology, they collected all the Pueblo officers in one of the interrogation rooms and announced an assignment which virtually took our breath away: a personal appeal addressed to President Lyndon B. Johnson of the United States!

Ed Murphy and Steve Harris looked at Scar with disbelief, Skip Schumacher and Friar Tuck put on solemnly rapt expressions which were sure signs they were suppressing amusement. Gene Lacy wore a deadpan frown, while Tim Harris barely managed to keep himself from exploding with derisive laughter. I tried to keep them from blowing the project by exclaiming with as much "sincerity" as I could muster: "I think it is a splendid idea! How do we go about it?"

If we had any doubts about the proper way to write the President, the KORCOMs certainly did not. They had already blocked out what they expected us to say and how we should say it. It struck me that the White House staff must be used to intercepting all sorts of crank letters before they reached the President's desk and that this one would fall into that category. Yet it could reveal our dilemma to people in high places. The United States did not maintain diplomatic relations with North Korea, so I wondered how the hell they would mail the letters. I spent considerable time thinking about that one. Certainly a letter from a bunch of American POW's postmarked Pyongyang DPRK, would receive careful scrutiny by intelligence authorities. As preposterous as a letter to the President seemed it offered opportunity so I decided to make the best of it and implied as much to my officers. Somehow we had to get the fact across in the letter that we had been faithful to our orders and had not at any time taken the *Pueblo* inside North Korea's claimed territorial waters. I felt that this was the single most important information we had to convey.

I decided to attempt to get the KORCOMs to allow me to accept the full responsibility for the alleged intrusions. I doubted it would work. But it was worth a try, and if it were successful I thought the President would be in a better bargaining position.

So we buckled down to the job. They split us into two separate teams. Ed Murphy, Skip, and Tim on one, Friar Tuck, Steve, and Gene on the other, meeting at different times and in different rooms to work their own versions of the composition. As I was permitted to switch back and forth between the two teams, I managed to coordinate the effort. Our main obstructionist tactic remained haggling over language, our principal aim to insert words which hopefully would get through to our own intelligence people.

The KORCOMs wanted us to convey to President Johnson our guilt in violating their territorial waters for the purpose of committing espionage. At first they wanted us to express our penitence over this serious crime to our Commander-in-Chief, presumably to invoke his sympathetic intervention on our behalf. Later they were to change this approach. We were to ask the President to admit his responsibility, as head of the United States government, for a "provocation against the peace loving Korean people." That they seriously expected positive results seemed incredible to us.

One feature of our sessions on the letter to the President was a certain relaxation in the rules against free discussions between ourselves. Scar still watched us and listened to what was being said and checked what we were writing through his interpreters, Silverlips, Wheezy and Flatface. But we somehow convinced the KORCOMs that an important communication to such a high personage in our country required a lot of discussion on our part, a lot of scribbling of notes to try out various sentences. They agreed gradually allowing us more and more latitude. For example, I found out from Ed Murphy that he and Quartermaster Law had been independently interrogated about the *Pueblo*'s navigation, the main exhibit being a captured ship's "workbook" for recording LORAN plots, which had somehow escaped destruction. We kept two sets of these workbooks (even and odd day volumes) in which all LORAN plots were logged as a matter of routine to help us make up our reports at the end of the mission. LORAN is subject to certain aberrations caused by atmospheric conditions, particularly over long distances at night in such remote areas as the Sea of Japan. False signals may be recorded by the instrument before reliable ones come through. However, all signals were logged, including the false ones. The KORCOMs had made Murphy and Law make up a chart showing the *Pueblo* to have intruded no less than six times into Korean territorial waters, according to the figures in the captured book. The results were so ludicrous that I did not blame Murphy and Law for going along and decided myself to let them stand as easily refutable "proof" of intrusion.

For one thing, the "workbook" only gave half of a disjointed picture of our true movements without the other "even day" volume to fill in the information. For another, the KORCOMs had picked out the readings they wanted used, mostly the false ones, which in one instance showed our position to be some forty miles inland. They also added some data of their own invention which, when correlated with the others in time and distance, gave my lumbering old *Pueblo* supersonic speeds, as well as amazing amphibious capabilities. I could understand why they ignored figures that gave an inkling of our true positions, but it seemed incredible they would so badly fool themselves while juggling inaccurate, scratched-out readings and come up with results that most weekend yachtsmen could spot as being entirely impossible. But seeing was believing, as I found out when they brought in the chart while we were debating the wording of our letter to the President. I could only shrug with amazement, which I feared might reduce some of my officers to mirth, but Colonel Scar, Major Silverlips and Flatface, puffed up with smug triumph over their handiwork.

They insisted that I inform the President that I had personally ordered the intrusions to provoke the peace-loving Democratic People's Republic of Korea in accordance with my orders. I shrank from making any such admission in a document that had even the slightest chance of receiving official notice abroad, and tried all sorts of subterfuges to avoid it.

Colonel Scar would accept no arguments, became sullen and threatened dire consequences for the crew if I did not "sincerely" comply. So I tried a preposterous approach. With the help of Skip Schumacher, I drafted a melodramatic description of how I would, when the mood struck me, stalk into the pilothouse and exclaim to my OOD: "All right, mister! Let's intrude and provocate!"

The "team" who were present at the writing of these lines had a great deal of trouble in controlling themselves. Nevertheless,

Colonel Scar nodded with complete satisfaction. Silverlips translated: "That is fine! Very sincere!"

This work went on the next few days. After a visit to Super-C, Colonel Scar informed me that it was unacceptable for *me* to assume personal responsibility for ordering my ship to "intrude and provocate"—the order had to come from the United States government itself, and I must say so in the letter.

I felt this was the most outrageous demand of all, and one to which the United States would never submit, even if it meant that some of us were executed. I attempted to dissuade Scar, pointing out the fallacy of his approach: no self-respecting government would accede to a false accusation by another, but could disavow the rash action of one of its officers. I was clearly the officer in this case. The haggling over this point went on for hours, but Scar remained adamant and obviously intoxicated with the heady idea of having the mighty Imperialist United States apologize to little Democratic People's Republic of Korea. He pointed out that the U.S. had apologized in the past to get some pilots back and that they would again.

In the end we gave in as he refused to settle for less. As before, we hoped their verbiage would stamp the demand for what it was.

As it turned out, this version was disapproved by KORCOM authority higher than Super-C. After a day's absence, Super-C immediately convened all the *Pueblo* officers and angrily informed us that the letter to our President was no good and would have to be rewritten. Evidently Party Headquarters in Pyongyang (who likely employed better interpreters) had humiliated him by rejecting his offering. A humiliated Super-C, was quite a sight. He exhausted his full repertoire of harangues and invective, pounding, chopping. He even included his pantomime of Americans driving nails into the heads of Korean women and children. I had gone through his performance before, but some of my officers had not. Tim Harris, who was seated next to me, could only take it for a short while and was so moved by the nail-driving sequence that he burst out into laughter. I was sure that he would be immediately dragged out and beaten to within an inch of his life, but the colonel amazed me by completely ignoring him. When he concluded with a threatening order to compose another more "sincere" letter, I took the chance to suggest that we should bring in some of our enlisted crew for consultation, specifically some of the Chiefs. To my continuous amazement, he agreed to this.

During the next couple of days, Chiefs Goldman, Kell, and CT2 Langenberg, and QM1 Law joined our letter-writing teams and quickly adjusted themselves to methods of communication. We improved upon them by assigning one man to read one of the innumerable drafts aloud, while the rest conversed in low voices. I was able to inform them I expected the lines of authority to be maintained in prison as much as on board ship, that officers and chiefs were to be obeyed as they were still responsible to me for discipline, in short, that regardless of our predicament, we were all still in the service of the U. S. Navy and must conduct ourselves accordingly. I asked that this word be passed by any means, that I wanted ideas for escape plans, and any knowledge about our exact location in the country. I also urged everybody to complain as much as possible and to try to wheedle more privileges, particularly those which would bring us together as a ship's company. Above all, we must from now on support each other and try to act as a unit in thwarting the KORCOMs designs to intimidate us and our country. It took hours to put all this across, bit by bit. Because everybody was eager for renewed leadership on my part, it succeeded. This was the great accomplishment of the many hours spent haggling over the letter to President Johnson.

In the meanwhile I had plenty of endless dull hours when returned to my cell after these sessions. I would be left to pace back and forth from corner to corner, to sit on my hard chair with a choice of either staring at the four walls or numbing my mind with the dreary propaganda pamphlets, to toss through the night on my bunk while fighting against fantastic nightmares and entirely real hordes of bedbugs, to eat alone the paltry meals that always left me both famished and sickened. Outside my screened window, the Korean winter raged through convulsions of extremes, howling blizzards with paralyzing cold alternating with thaws that filled the silence with the myriad dripping of melting ice and snow, but still permeating the building with a chilling, raw dampness. The old-fashioned steam radiator creaked, sighed, and sometimes made clicking sounds which made me imagine another prisoner was trying to tap out Morse code on its pipes, but otherwise failing to overcome much of the cold. I complained bitterly about these conditions to the junior officers and guards who burst into my presence at odd intervals; it became a preconditioned reflex action whenever that door flew open. I received sneers, lectures, and occasional boots for my efforts, but then results began to evidence themselves as the second half of February dragged along.

First I received a deck of cards, but without any partners provided for a recreational game of gin-rummy or poker; I had never been a solitaire player, but I preferred it to reading propaganda pamphlets. When solitaire paled, I practiced some old card tricks I had learned from my father and his rowdy companions in the shack outside Idaho Falls. They exercised my fingers but also tended to fill me with self-pitying nostalgia. Next they brought me a chess set. Again no partner. But I played spirited games against myself, working toward a draw by equally carefully considered moves for black and white, but usually ending up with a check-mate which made half of me feel cleverly triumphant and the other half stupidly outwitted. It was very frustrating.

One evening around 2000 hours, a junior officer blew into my cell and brought me tennis shoes, a cap and overcoat, and ordered me to put them on. Then he took me out into the hall where I found all of my crew pouring out of their cells similarly attired. Armed guards and their officers were everywhere, imposing silence on the formation which was soon marched, mystified, down the stairs to the ground floor and then on out through the front door. The freezing night air bit our noses and ears, and the cold snow lying in two-foot deep drifts on the ground seeped through our thin tennis shoes. What was this? A Death March across the snow-bound Korean hills to some new place of confinement? As always when the KORCOMs pulled a surprise action, we tended to suspect the worst. But then they called a halt a short distance from the compound of barracks on what appeared to be a soccer field. One of the interpreters accompanying the formation bellowed an announcement:

"Now all together! Make exercises of bodies for health!"

After about ten minutes we were ordered back into marching

columns and returned shivering, yet somewhat uplifted in spirits to our building and cells. It would have been nicer if we had seen the sun, or even gray wintry daylight, during this interlude of calisthenics, but at least we had been granted a group activity which brought the whole crew together.

In fact, the KORCOMs became as infatuated with their calisthenics program as they had with confession and letter-writing. However, they made a concession to their own brutal winter weather and switched the sessions indoors. Every morning immediately after the 0500 reveille, we were ordered out of our cells and collected in the halls and a sort of alcove in the middle of the hall where the cramped space for so many men only allowed squatting exercises, running-in-place, and isometrics (which some of us had been doing on our own in solitary). It was hard on those who had become severely weakened in confinement, yet it had a definite therapeutic value for them as well. We were ordered to exercise in silence and guards and junior officers were watchful. But with all the wheezing and puffing while going through our exertions, it became easy to exchange brief whispers that came to make up another link in our "underground" communication system. It was after the second session of calisthenics in the hall of our cell block that the KORCOM officers we had dubbed Deputy Dawg and Imperialist came into my cell and asked me through an interpreter to recommend a man to lead the crew to these daily exercises. Without hesitation I suggested Quartermaster Law as our "athletic director"—a most loyal and trustworthy Petty Officer who was respected by the rest of the men as a natural leader. I was anxious to re-establish his influence and perhaps provide a valid reason for the KORCOMs to have occasional dealings with him. They took the advice and from then on Quartermaster 1st Class Law was in daily contact with the crew. He lived up to my expectations in every respect.

I continued to have meetings with Super-C, usually at night. He would infrequently make an unusual announcement that would jolt me out of my boredom. For example, one night he told me that word from the International Red Cross said that the wife of Gerald W. Hagenson, one of our Enginemen 1st Class, had just given birth to a baby. With a magnanimous flourish, Super-C said: "You will be permitted, Captain, to tell of this joyous thing to all crew, and in sincere way to show our humanity in considering feelings of proud father!" Naturally I agreed to this without any argument.

All hands were let out of their cells and assembled in the marble hallway. I delivered the birth announcement with all the enthusiasm I could muster, trying to live up to Super-C's expectations for the great propaganda value of the occasion, at the same time conveying genuine happiness for Hagenson. The fact that the Red Cross had gotten through to us meant that we were not entirely deserted and forgotten. This was not lost on the crew.

"When you going to hand out the cigars, Hagenson?" the pleased father was asked by his shipmates. All he could do was to give out verbal rain checks, but this did not dampen the spirit of the occasion. Even our KORCOM jailers broke into toothy grins.

February at last stormed into the ides of a bleak and blustery Korean March. Things did not look as hopeless as they had a month ago, but the harsh reality of imprisonment remained with its privations, discomforts, and constant uncertainties.

Then came the day when the door burst open for the last time and two enlisted guards came into my cell and proceeded to strip my bunk and roll up the bedding. A junior officer ordered me to collect my small bundle of clothing and step out in the corridor dressed for outdoors. Out there I found my officers and men being hurriedly turned out of their cells, their bedding and pitifully small baggage of personal belongings being carried out with them. As we were herded into formation to march downstairs, whispers passed up and down the ranks in spite of shouted reminders about the rules of silence.

I tried to exert my status as Commanding Officer and demand information from the KORCOMs, but was told to shut up and quietly get in line with my men.

Within the next few minutes we were marched down the long staircases to the ground floor and on out into the cold where buses surrounded by guards were waiting with idling engines.

CHAPTER XV

"ABSOLUTELY NO CREDENCE SHOULD BE PLACED
IN MESSAGES FROM THE CREW OF THE CAPTURED
INTELLIGENCE SHIP PUEBLO."—(*Paul C. Warnke,
Asst. Sec. of Defense, to House Foreign Affairs
Committee, March 22, 1968.*)

"NEW LETTERS FROM PUEBLO CREW STRESS RISK
OF TRIALS, EXECUTIONS."—(*Headline in Washington* Post, *April 3, 1968.*)

After little more than an hour's travel, the convoy came to a
stop and we were all turned out to form up in the darkness of
what appeared to be another barracks compound. We were
marched through the snow into the larger of four buildings, up a
flight of concrete stairs to the second and third floor and redis-
tributed in cells which seemed virtually identical to the ones we
had vacated. The chiefs and enlisted men were assigned accomo-
dations in groups of four or eight while officers had the dubious
privilege of solitary occupancy.

The officers of our KORCOM guard seemed to think they were
offering us vastly improved conditions, and Super-C, who remained with us as chief warden, informed us that we were moved
as the result of my constant complaints about conditions in our
former prison. "You may tell your men this," he said to me through
Wheezy, "and explain it is a temporary arrangement until all of
you are sincere and the United States admits their great crime,
apologizes for those crimes and gives assurances they will never
do such things again. Then perhaps you can go home to your loved

ones. Otherwise you will have to stand trial in our People's Court and accept full punishment for provocations and intrusions. You will see we are most humane, but also most strict with insincerity. Some of your men are acting brazen faced and they will be punished."

It appeared that the improvements they were alluding to consisted mainly of two things: the building was of newer construction (In their words: "Built to last a hundred generations.") and our cell windows were not sealed with paper screens so that we could look out over the barracks compound, and earthwork rampart surrounding it, beyond to an open countryside of snow-covered hills and fields. While the view was not exactly inspiring, it relieved that awful feeling of being sealed in between four walls. At first light on the following dawn I had my nose pressed against the frosty glass and eagerly took it all in. It was great to see *daylight*, to look out on a fresh air scene even while confined to the dank chill of our cells. It was most intriguing to get some idea of our location and the lay of the land. Our guards considered that window-gazing was evidence of spying, however, and often reacted with kicks and chops when they caught us staring outside. They might have had some grounds for this as it soon became evident we were located in or very close to an area of intense military training. A couple of miles away, a crop-tower for paratroop trainees could be seen in frequent use. The boom of cannon and whoosh of rocketry betrayed the nearness of an artillery practice range. Two military radars were visible. There was a road where frequently passed military formations in mechanized convoys in full view. High flying jet aircraft and slower propeller driven aircraft were often seen or heard, and by analyzing their flight patterns it was easy to figure out that an airport was not too far away. And like the structure of our first prison, this one suggested all the marks of having been designed to house or school troops rather than prisoners.

The routine of our prison life remained essentially the same. Within a few minutes after the 0500 reveille we had to turn out of our cells for morning exercises in the corridor. Weather permitting, we had another exercise period outdoors during the early afternoon when we were marched down the stairs to pick up our tennis shoes from racks of cubbyholes, put them on, then move outside to jog and jump about under the watchful eyes of the guards and Duty Officers. The rest of the day was either spent bickering over endlessly rehashed compositions of those confessions, apologies, and letters of recrimination to prominent persons in the USA which we were constantly being badgered into writing and rewriting, or being hauled before Super-C or Colonel Scar to listen to long diatribes, threats and lectures. Otherwise, we officers sat alone in our cells for long hours of despondent thought.

Perhaps the KORCOMs knew that I was in communication with a lot of the *Pueblo*'s officers and crew by now; if so, they were willing to tolerate it to a limited extent so long as it suited their program of "group therapy." On the second night after being incarcerated in our "new quarters," we were collected together in a barren cavernous hall which Super-C referred to as "The Club." It was provided, he explained, for our cultural and recreational benefits. The inaugural performance was an outrageously funny propaganda movie, a sort of distorted *boy-meets-girl* musical in which the *girl* warbled a love-song to the factory where she was employed, and the *boy* bellowed a passionate aria dedicated to his tractor and rifle. As there were no English sub-titles to this film, one of our regular interpreters sat in the rear of the room and shouted translations of both dialogue and lyrics in a voice that was supposed to mirror all the dramatic nuances of the actors. To add to the confusion, Jack Warner and his Warner Brothers were present with their lights and cameras, busily making a movie of us watching a movie. Some of my men were staring at the screen with stupefied expressions of disbelief, a few had gone to sleep, and the majority were trying their best to suppress laughter. There were snickers, snorts, and even a few outright boos. But mostly there were constant ripples of whispers back and forth along the rows, disguised as exclamations of wonder. We had been provided with a marvelous new opportunity to communicate. When I was singled out by Warner Brothers' spotlight and camera, I put on a rapt expression and held up one hand with middle finger extended without getting any adverse reaction from cameraman or director. They later ran a short feature showing a North Korean soccer team playing in the International Championship Matches in London, including some close-up shots of a highly partisan British section of fans who were giving the same obscene finger-sign. While its meaning remained lost to the KORCOMs, it electrified our audience of *Pueblo* prisoners who became convulsed. Thus was born the contemptuous profane gesture which we explained away to our naive jailers as the Hawaiian Good Luck Sign. It was to bring us a lot of satisfaction and, eventually, a lot of grief as well.

The KORCOMs presently began serving our meals in a communal messhall. At first there were two sittings with the officers segregated to a table of their own while the rest of the crew was distributed among five others. Buxom Korean serving girls were our deadpan waitresses. The guards and Junior Duty Officers patrolled the room to enforce the rule of silence. However, because of the extensive, letter-writing program, most of us had managed to acquire pencil and paper (at least coarse *toilet*-paper) so that it became comparatively easy to pass around notes unobserved. Occasionally someone would get caught at it and be hauled away for a thorough beating, but this did not stop us from making mealtime a sort of underground mail-call. The KORCOMs soon decided that the officers were the instigators and separated us entirely from the crew by making us eat in a room by ourselves where, oddly enough, they often times left us unguarded.

At one meal, the six of us discussed the prospects of escape. Some of the officers were pessimistic over the chances of making a successful break, pointing out that quite aside from the fact that the DMZ was heavily mined and guarded on both sides, it was highly unlikely a Caucasian could make it without being identified and captured. The same hurdle applied to reaching the coast where a boat might be stolen. None of us had ever heard of a successful escape from North Korea. Was it not then better to bide our time and hope for a negotiated release? There was also the possibility that the U.S. might rescue us by ventical envelopment of the prison, using helicopters covered by fighters. I dreamed that this would happen. The arguments against escape had validity, but I nevertheless decided to form an Escape Committee, appointing Skip Schumacher as chairman and Tim Harris and Gene Lacy as his assistants, instructing them to pass the word around that escape plans were desired, but none was to be put into effect without checking the Committee and obtaining my approval. My reasons were twofold: it was good for morale to busy the mind with such plans, and there was a real chance of getting one of our Filipinos out with a message to the United States that *Pueblo* had *never* intruded, that her seizure was a blatant act of piracy.

Important whispered discussions such as this took place regularly in our "wardroom." All information my officers gathered on their own through contacts with the crew were eventually channeled to me, so that I soon had a fairly accurate idea of what was going on. Of particular importance was the fact that we seemed to be entirely in the custody of propaganda, *not* intelligence specialists. Virtually everybody had been threatened or physically bludgeoned into signing some form of confession or other. Many were now worried over having broken the Code of Conduct, which governs the statements and behavior of all U. S. Armed Forces personnel captured by an enemy. There are certain aspects of the Code of Conduct that must immediately be broken by the senior officer and noncommissioned officers when captured. He must make demands concerning his men and their treatment. Only information of military value need be protected. I let it be known that I would assume full responsibility on everybody's behalf where pure propaganda was involved. When and if I ever got the chance, I would inform my superiors that the Code of Conduct was unenforceable and impractical and unrealistic in a case such as ours when an entire ship's company with some documents falls into the hands of a ruthless enemy who does not shrink from applying torture methods to extract what they want. There might be one or two men out of a hundred with the power to physically and mentally resist such methods, even to a horrible prolonged death, but their sacrifice is bound to be made useless by the inevitable breaking of decent, loyal, yet more average shipmates. Better to confess to the enemy's accusations, the more outrageous the better, showing him up as a liar and a cheat, than to risk torture and death. I tried to convey this philosophy to all of my people.

In any event, it became obvious to me that the KORCOMs had

not the slightest intention of going after information of real intelligence value from us. However, I really feared that they might bring in Soviet or even Chinese intelligence specialists who would know what questions to ask of my men and myself. They would probably not waste any time with propaganda until they had thoroughly exhausted searching for information of real military value. Inasmuch as I knew that many of the crew, particularly Steve and some of his men as well as myself and one or two other officers had information of great value to the Communist Bloc, I never ceased to worry about this possibility. I knew that I would have to commit suicide if the Soviets ever were brought in.

About this time, I finally obtained information about the treatment of our wounded men, whom Super-C and his minions had repeatedly assured me were being "humanely" cared for. I knew Duane Hodges was dead and they confirmed this. But when I asked whether they were considering the "humane" act of sending his body home to his family, they replied that the "body belongs to us as much as our living prisoners, and will be disposed of as we see fit." As for the wounded, Steve Robin, Bob Chicca, and the seriously injured Steven Woelk had received no medical attention whatsoever for the first several days of our initial imprisonment. They had been thrown into a cell together and even denied the help of Corpsman Baldridge, who attempted to stay with them and obtain our own medical supplies to relieve their suffering. Instead they assigned a Fireman, Dale Rigby, who had only rudimentary knowledge of first-aid to care for them. He tried his best to help them, but was soon sickened himself as the stench of gangrene setting in Woelk's untreated wound began to permeate the cell, augmented by the vomit which the other occupants could not keep down. After several days of these horrible conditions, a KORCOM doctor had finally directed that the half-dead Woelk be removed to a hospital. He had been carried there in the sack of his filthy bedding. Nothing had been seen or heard of him. Robin and Chicca were given some antibiotic pills and recovered slowly on their own with no more palliatives than the water in their slop-bucket. There were a few others who, like myself, did not reveal lesser wounds for fear of being separated from their shipmates. The account, as it trickled through to me many weeks later, was a

grim story of neglect which threw me into a rage and renewed my
efforts to pry information out of Super-C and Colonel Scar about
the fate of Woelk. They reiterated that he was being "humanely
treated," a statement no longer believed at all. When I demanded
to be allowed to see him, I was sharply refused. That was that.

It was not long after our arrival here that we began feeling
constant pangs of hunger and showing symptoms of severe diet deficiency, including the ancient sailor's scourge, scurvy. I had already lost about forty pounds since the capture and now began
losing more, and with that loss came a chronic feeling of weakness, a tendency toward a lethargic despondency which I could
only fight by giving free rein to my anger and making bitter protests to the KORCOM officers in charge. The results were lectures and tirades about my lack of sincerity, but no better food.

The letter-writing program continued unabated, but now we
were directed to write to our families. In letters dictated by the
KORCOMs to include their standard verbiage of our alleged intrusion, and praising the humane treatment we were receiving in
spite of our crimes against the Korean Democratic People's Republic. Although I was desperate to pour out my heart to Rose,
comfort her and tell her the truth in my own words, I followed
this "dictated Communist line," as did the rest of my people, convinced that its impersonal, uncharacteristic tone would instantly
alert her that it had been written under duress. But it would let
her know that I was at least *alive*.

At this point, I was ordered to write a *personal* letter to President Johnson. I felt that if there was a slight chance that this
official communication between an officer of the U. S. Navy and
his Commander-in-Chief might reach the White House, I decided to insert something the KORCOMs would let pass telling him not to believe a word of it. The best I could get away with
was to close the letter with: ". . . *Mr. President, as you have undoubtedly by now reviewed my record in the Navy and know that
I carry out my orders to the letter, and therefor must believe that
I did make the naughty intrusion named above because I am a
man of my word.*"

It was my fervent hope that high American authorities had indeed reviewed my record, as well as my reputation with former

shipmates and commanding officers, and would understand the few significant words in the letter: that the *Pueblo* had never intruded. The sentence got past the KORCOMs, but whether it was delivered or not, I was not to know until later.

Regular interrogation sessions continued and I found that none of our 82 people were excluded from attention, although some were given more than others. Our black and Filipino crewmen were lectured on American segregation and White Supremacy policies. This tack failed completely and our *Pueblo* black men remained stalwart and loyal throughout. The KORCOMs continued to have CIA on the brain and conducted periodic witchhunts for agents they were convinced we had planted among us, their prime suspects ran the gamut from our oceanographer, Friar Tuck, to the ship's baker, Rigby. Steve Harris was heavily grilled, and although they knew he had been in charge of intelligence activities, they never concentrated on this aspect of his duties. This also applied to their handling of his large detachment of "CTs." The KORCOMs seemed interested only in obtaining confessions of our having intruded and "provocated." I was very concerned about Gene Lacy because they had found out through his captured service record that he had been awarded the Korean War Service Medal and were interrogating him in detail about his participation in that conflict. There was no intelligence value in this, but it was the sort of thing which could inflame their virulent hatred for anybody who had fought against them and whom they had convinced themselves to have committed horrible atrocities against their people. It was not beyond them to extract savage revenge even now, fifteen years later, against a prisoner they believed to have participated in the Korean War on the "Imperialist side."

During our first month in the new prison, Gene had fallen into a deep, brooding depression which began wasting him away more than the starvation diet we were being fed. The cause of this was his realization and bitter remorse over his conduct on *Pueblo*'s bridge during the confrontation and seizure.

I had tried to review the events of those fateful few hours, principally to discover whether I had blacked out sometime between being fired upon and wounded, and the boarding of *Pueblo*. No hour of January 23, 1968, escaped my examination. Nor were my sleeping hours free of flashbacks that were real nightmares. To try and clear my mind, I asked during our mealtime gatherings that all officers give me their individual recollections of the action, scribbling them down on smuggled notes, or passing them on to me verbally when they could. Everybody eagerly complied, including Gene Lacy, but I was struck by him omitting any mention of his having rung up ALL STOP without my orders, then disobeyed them completely when I was checking things in the SOD-Hut by speeding up the ship in compliance to KORCOM signals as they escorted us toward Wonsan. When I questioned him about this, he flatly denied having done any such thing. He had a look of chagrined horror on his face. I knew Gene well enough that I knew he was not deliberately lying. Whose memory had blanked out, his or mine? I had to know.

It happened that my memory of the events was confirmed by some of my other officers, and also by Quartermaster Law, whom I met in the latrine, and was able briefly to question on the subject. These people also were able to make Gene realize he must have done something terribly wrong at a time of which he had no recollection. He became so crushed and despondent that I began regretting ever having brought up the matter. My anger with him had long since passed. At the time, all of us had been overcome by a sudden, shattering development which we had not been trained to cope with, or indeed, assured that it *would not happen*. I had no intention of shifting the blame to Gene. I was the captain and therefore ultimately responsible. In any case, even if Gene had not blacked out and acted irrationally, I doubt that the outcome would have been different. My problem became, under very difficult circumstances, to convince Gene of this, and to let him know that I still considered him a good friend and reliable officer.

It took several weeks to snap Gene Lacy out of his private misery and rejoin us in our communal one. Each of us had to live with his own devils of doubt, guilt, and self-recrimination which became particularly cruel and persistent during those lonely hours of tossing on our verminous bunks at night, half awake with worry, half asleep with bad dreams. Gene had a particular hell trying to penetrate the blank spot of his mind that hid actions which he only knew from the account of others. Steve Harris, agonized over his inability to completely destroy the classified material in his SOD-Hut. Ed Murphy worried over an accumulation of failures. Sergeants Hammond and Chicca suffered because they had been unable to interpret the KORCOMs intentions while there was still time, and brooded over having given useless warning to the officer who assigned them to *Pueblo* of their limitations in the Korean language. Corpsman Baldridge suffered over Duane Hodges' death and because he had been prevented from succoring the other wounded men. Radioman Hayes suffered from the curse of the fate which had sent him to my ship as a last-minute replacement of a miscreant, just as she was pulling out on an ill-fated mission. And I suffered for all of them. Yet we all sensed the necessity of mutual support in order to survive our ordeal. The officers and men of *Pueblo* were never more united in purpose than they were during their darkest days together.

In the middle of March there was a tremendous blizzard which howled and stormed around the prison for two days, its icy drafts whistling through the building and leaving us shivering around the meager warmth of our wheezing radiators.

Then the skies cleared and the sun came out, its bright shafts illuminating our dreary cells as they melted the snow clogging our windows. Instead of the wailing winter wind, there came the steady drip of a spring thaw which continued until the snowdrifts covering the fields beyond the prison's earthworks became mottled with widening patches of exposed earth. Some figures appeared out there who were unmistakably farmers coming out to make ready for planting. They were chased away by our guards when they came too close to our dismal cluster of barracks, but in glimpsing them, we knew that April and spring were close at hand.

During the four hours between the time when *Pueblo* was boarded and finally secured at a Wonsan dock, I had expected an air-strike by the United States Navy or Air Force which might have enabled us to break free of our captors. During the ensuing weeks, I still expected some form of retaliation in the form of a punitive raid and it later became apparent that the KORCOMs themselves were jittery over this possibility. At the time it was inconceivable to me that our country would take no forceful direct action to avenge the seizure on the high seas of one of its ships by a third-rate Communist power acting in defiance of international law. But then, as time dragged on without the slightest sign of U.S. intervention, I began to resign myself to the fact that for some reason the matter was being resolved by negotiations. I tried to picture in my mind how such negotiations might progress with a lot of diplomatic talks at the United Nations or at the Korean Armistice HQ of Panmunjon and realized this could become a very long-winded process—perhaps as long as two months. I thought I was being pessimistic in steeling myself and my people for as long a confinement as to April 1. I could not imagine that with the power of the United States and its enormous prestige in the world, it could not bring about our release and return of the ship by that date. I did not believe she would for a moment accede to the KORCOMs insistence upon an official apology, and expected our negotiators would gain their objectives without it.

Super-C boosted my expectations by stating flatly that American prisoners were never held more than six to eight weeks, which was the time it took the United States to make the proper apologies. He even quoted specific instances of helicopter and aircraft pilots caught "intruding" and shot down. Our anticipation was brought to an even higher pitch when, toward the end of March, we were all measured for what was obviously to be new clothing. None of the KORCOMs admitted this, but we jumped to the conclusion that they were about to provide us with new outfits so that we would make a presentable appearance that would prove their "humane treatment" when we were released. We also noticed a decrease in the severe beatings and gratuitous blows which used to be so freely administered, and deduced that they did not want us to return to the Western World carrying a mass of scars and bruises. Thus my hopes ran high toward the end of March.

April Fool.

The 1st not only came and passed without any further sign of our being repatriated, but was immediately followed by a sudden resurgence of the KORCOMs brutal methods. We came to call it the April, or Sixty-day, Purge. Savage kicks and karate-chops were meted out for the slightest offenses. A broken cup in the messhall was pronounced "deliberate sabotage against the Democratic People's Republic." The interrogations continued, but now if any "insincerity" was suspected, the prisoner would be subjected to such tortures as kneeling on the floor with a piece of two-by-four lumber inserted between his calves and thighs, or made to hold a chair above his head in the same position for twenty or thirty minutes and then kicked in the stomach or back when he began to sag. The new young guards overcame their initial awe of us. In addition to stealing our rations, they soon began to vent their ingrained hatred by frequent and spontaneous blows with feet, fists, or rifle butts. Once again there were cries and groans resounding in the hall outside my cell and more than half of my people showed up for meals at the messhall limping, and bruised, with their faces and heads covered with welts. The effects of severe beatings were added to those of malnutrition and a terrible letdown in morale.

I protested vehemently, to Super-C about these beatings, the rotten food, and our illegal detention in his prison.

"You must understand our young soldiers have a very genuine hate for you Imperialist Americans because of the suffering you brought their families," he explained through his interpreter, Silverlips. "It is natural they would occasionally show their true feelings toward you! . . . (Here he repeated the alleged atrocities we committed during the Korean War) . . . Oh! You mean to say the food is not sufficient? Not good? I find that difficult to believe, but I will look into it . . . As for confinement in this prison, it depends entirely on you and your Imperialist Government of United States begging forgiveness of the Korean people for your crimes . . . So you are getting impatient to go home? Well, we are getting impatient too for the apology you owe us. If it does not come soon, I will have no alternative but to turn you over to the People's Court which will mete out punishment according to our laws against espionage and provocations. There will be nothing more I can do to protect you from the just wrath of our people. Nothing! . . . But let us hope that your United States will concede to reason and something acceptable will be decided during the negotiations at Panmunjon . . . Let us hope so for your sake, Captain!"

The most hopeful thing I gleaned out of his torrent of words was the hint that there *were* negotiations for our release going on in Panmunjon, that arena of endless bickering between the U.S. and North Korea located on the DMZ.

When after a couple of weeks, the beatings began to subside, I believe it was the result of complaints by the harassed KOR-COM Medical Officer in charge of keeping us looking present-able who had become fed up with treating an overload of battered patients with paraffin-packs and collodion.

Even during this April Purge, Super-C found ways of demonstrat-ing his own "sincere humanity" with small additional privileges designed to encourage our cooperation. For a half hour a day, officers were allowed a recreation period of card playing or chess and although it was strictly supervised and all talk was supposed to be confined to the subject of the game being played, we soon found ways of using it as an additional means of communicating with each other. I remember well playing chess with Skip Schu-macher one day, when he could hardly move or sit upright in his chair after a severe beating.

Another "treat" was the playing of a daily program of recorded music piped through loudspeakers located in the halls outside our cells. This could have been a pleasant idea because we were all starved for music as well as food, but their selections were entirely of a native variety, discordant twangings of their peculiar string instruments, the percussion of gongs and cymbals, the cater-wauling of Korean voices belting out their paeans to Glorious Leader Kim Il Sung, all blasting forth at top volume in a raucous cacophony.

There were loudspeakers blaring from dawn to dusk *outside* our prison too, but their output was intended for the inspiration of the KORCOM garrison and even projected to the farmers plant-ing rice in the fields beyond the earthwork ramparts of our com-pound. The program alternated the same weird music with harsh voices shouting harangues and slogans, the first blast coming shortly after 5 A.M. and ending with some climactic screeches around 9 P.M. We subsequently found out that there are few places in North Korea's inhabited areas that are beyond hearing of this sort of audio rediffusion.

April passed painfully, drearily, hopelessly into May. I found myself forced to reappraise our prospects which were bleak indeed. I suspected that at least some of us would soon wind up before the tribunal of a People's Court, be condemned to death and executed, thus bringing more pressure on the United States to make concessions. The best I could foresee was a program of forced labor which, if we were to be able to do any heavy work at all, had to mean more nourishing rations. I suggested this prospect to my people, withholding my worst fears, but refraining to predict another date of deliverance.

The balmy spring was a welcome relief after the harsh winter. From our cell windows we stole glimpses of the rice sprouting in the surrounding paddies, of distant figures of farmers bending to their planting, and in the far distance, the sharply ridged Korean hills turning from white to brown as their snows melted, then to a lush green, and finally to a golden yellow mottled by purple shadows of clouds caressing their slopes. There must have been a lot of wildflowers blooming out there, bluebells, daisies and lilies-of-the-valley whose scent we could sometimes catch mingled with that of freshly tilled earth. There were birds out there too, meadow larks and lapwings whose calls sometimes reached our ears. These were nostalgic sights, scents, and sounds to a prisoner, stirring both hope and despair in his breast.

The bucolic scene of farmers working in their rice paddies was marred by increased activity of the military, who had priority in use of the verdant land. The parachute training tower was busy every day and the roads cutting across the fields were more frequently used by mechanized artillery and caissons than by farmers' carts. The scent of wildflowers was overpowered by more pungent odors of our prison as the increasing heat induced bacteriological actions in the always flooded latrines, the indefinable mixture of food and garbage from the kitchen, and our own bodies damp with sweat and the ooze of canker sores. Birdsong was drowned out by more sinister noises, the distant rumble of cannon practicing on firing ranges, the closer, constant blare of loud-speakers pouring forth strident propaganda.

We looked forward to the daily outdoor exercise periods because they at least took us out of dreary cells into fresh open air, but our weakened condition made the calisthenics and jogging around the compound yard a very real effort, more exhausting than vitalizing. When conducting us to and from these group activities, the KORCOMs began insisting we emulate their parade formations and marching drills, knees raised high with each step, swinging stiffly across the chest with clenched fists. This, too, was a strain, specially when trying to do it on the staircases of our prison build-ing, but it was also an opportunity for subtle resistance. Our drill instructors became exasperated by their dumb bunch of recruits who could not tell their right from left and consistently turned the formations into comic shambles of confusion. Our bodies were weakening, but our spirits were bolstered by the American serv-iceman's perverse sense of humor.

Thieving of our rations by the enlisted guards reached more than irritating proportions because every scrap of food, every cigarette was precious to us. Complaints to the officers only drew lectures on the great humanity and high morality of North Korean society and tirades against our lack of appreciation of it. Some of my men resorted to ingeniously boobytrapping the loot. One such instance was when Gene Lacy plucked a few strands of hair off his own head and carefully, laboriously inserted them into the tobacco of a cigarette which he then left in a conspicuous spot in his cell from where he knew it would be pilfered. The guard who eventually lit it up may well have been cured of the smoking habit for some time to come. A cruder revenge was heaped upon a ha-bitual apple thief. The crew of one cell operated on the fruit by perforating it with a thin piece of wire, then soaking it for several hours in their slop bucket full of urine. When it had become far juicier than nature ever intended, it was retrieved, cleaned and polished up to its former appetizing appearance and also placed in a conspicuous place, awaiting the attention of the thief. The guard who took it vanished for the next several days.

It was hard on everybody to be cut off from news of family and any inkling if anything of what was being done to bring about our release; to a less personal degree it was equally hard to be totally cut off from any news from the U.S.A. in general. This was a presidential election year in the United States; who were lining up as candidates? Was President Johnson going to run again for the Democrats? How was the war in Vietnam going? Were there more or less demonstrations for Peace & Pull Out? More or less race rioting in the big-city ghettos? Were the Beatles still the top "rock" group, or had they faded and been replaced? How were the opening games of the baseball season going? Were the Mets still in the cellar? Even for those who do not normally follow current events by reading newspapers and listening to regular news broadcasts, living in a vacuum becomes a special irritation which grates on the nerves. The *Pueblo*'s complement with its unusually high quota of well-educated, intelligent men was particularly affected by this. It seems that Super-C was aware of it and during the first week of June he convened an all-hands meeting in the conference hall to give us a briefing on the recent world events as seen by the KORCOMs.

The items selected had been carefully culled out of the news so as to give us the bleakest possible picture of what was going on at home. The March of the Poor on Washington was described, the assassination of Martin Luther King and the riots which followed, then the assassination of Senator Robert F. Kennedy, giving us the impression that our country was on the brink of anarchy and revolution. It was shocking news if true, but they somewhat destroyed their credibility when they went on to tell us about the war in Vietnam where Super-C assured us we were losing 14,000 airplanes and helicopters a week, 5000 tanks, and also had lost the battleship *New Jersey*. Even the most naive crewman refused to swallow those figures, nor that the North Vietnamese navy (about on a par with the North Korean's) had been able to sink *New Jersey*. As a consequence we went away from the meeting suspecting that it was *all* a pack of lies, yet with doubts and a frustrating feeling of ignorance lingering on. Another time, when Super-C was having one of his private sessions with me, he said that the United States had admitted the *Pueblo*'s mission was to spy on North Korea and that it was only a matter of time before they would have meekly to apologize for the whole incident. I found myself believing the substance of the former item, but the latter not at all. Later in June, we were given among our items of "cultural material" copies of the English language *Pyongyang Times*, (we called it the *Ping-pong Times*), a propaganda sheet carrying a terribly distorted Communist reportage of the news, including items about our ship and about us, in which we recognized the verbiage of our coerced confessions of intrusions. We were ordered to read everything printed in this particular spurious newspaper and sometimes given "current affairs" tests based on its contents, but its greatest effects upon us were scorn and amusement.

One of the busiest men on the KORCOM prison staff was their Medical Officer. Virtually all of us were becoming crippled by chronic weakness, bruises, sprains, and running sores and boils which erupted all over our emaciated bodies. These he attempted to cure by lancing and carving away at them with a scalpel, giving poor Ed Murphy some specially painful treatments of an infected sore on his foot. His favorite method of dealing with almost any ailment was acupuncture, that ancient Chinese medical practice of sticking various size needles into the patient in order to stimulate sluggish nerves. Although I somehow escaped serious beatings during this period, I was suffering from the debilitating effects of malnutrition, which included an impairment of vision and a loss of feeling in my legs. Thus I was subjected to the doctor's "needle" treatment. He also employed various plasters and hot paraffin-packs to treat welts and bruises, and had enough modern training to be aware of inoculations against virulent diseases. He gave the entire crew serum shots against something he called "the Japanese Sleeping Sickness"—exactly what this was, I never did find out. While we never spotted tsetse flies, the carrier of the infamous African Sleeping Sickness, there were plenty of the big buzzing bluebottle variety which we came to call the "Korean National Bird." Between them, the bedbugs, and the rats, it was a miracle that we did not become infected with some kind of plague. I thanked God that all of us had been given typhoid-shots by the U. S. Navy.

Up on the "3rd deck" where many enlisted men were incarcerated, the guards reacted with angry violence to any latrine call during the night. After several men had been severely kicked and chopped for no other reason than an urgent need to answer a call of nature, they quite understandably took to relieving themselves in the water bucket provided in their cells rather than risk a beating by a request to go to the latrine. Any one caught doing this was severely punished.

One man would catch it because of a lost button from his prison uniform, another for "spying" out of his window. Ed Murphy was worked over for sitting on his pillow. Those whom they considered repeated offenders were singled out during group meetings, made to stand up, and received a blistering tongue lashing lasting up to two hours. Presumably, this was designed to make them ashamed of themselves, or to hold them up as horrible examples of "insincerity" before their shipmates. Yet the results were always quite the opposite: to us they were heroes of our resistance. Thus Lieutenant Schumacher was once thoroughly chewed out by Super-C and called, among other things, a little chicken. Sergeant Chicca took a grueling two-hour upbraiding before all of us for some crime whose nature somehow became lost in the torrent of general abuse. When Super-C and Silverlips finally exhausted their repertoire of invectives, I got up and said:

"I have always known Sergeant Chicca as a very good man and am sure he did not mean to be insincere in his conduct. To show the colonel that we believe this and are behind him, let's give him our Hawaiian Good Luck Sign," whereupon I held up my fist with middle finger extended.

The colonel and his staff seemed almost flattered, obviously considering that the session had been satisfactorily completed. The crew showed a remarkable control in maintaining solemnly penitent expressions.

We became increasingly adept at verbal subterfuges in our letter-writing assignments, specially in letters to our families. In addition to the propaganda line, we had convinced the KORCOMs that some spontaneous personal touches were essential in order to achieve credibility. These additions included mention of nonexistent relatives, to possessions we did not possess (it particularly galled the KORCOMs to have a common American sailor refer to his second Cadillac), to business activities of an outlandish nature (a second-hand pet shop run by my "Uncle Willard" in

Boonville, Missouri), and so on. For example, in my second letter to Rose I managed to insert at the end of the closing sentence in which I asked her to send greetings to members of our family: "and don't forget Cythyssa Krocasheidt!" Or in a letter to Rose's sister Angie: ". . . be sure to give my t st to Nick and Lotta O'Blarney."

June dragged slowly on with a steadily increasing summer heat. Down in the compound yard, off-duty soldiers lounged in the sun and amused themselves by kicking the skinny mongrel dogs who were seeking a hand-out. There were sparrows nesting in the cracks of the concrete façade of the barracks and when a fledgling made a forced landing below, it was picked up by a junior KOR-COM officer who played with it for a moment, then in one instance, pulled its legs off, in others, played catch with the unfortunate bird.

July brought some improvements. The food became a little more nourishing and plentiful, perhaps as a result of my constant complaints to Super-C combined with the Medical Officer's reports which must have noted that the symptoms of starvation had become general among all the prisoners. If they had any concern for our health and appearance for propaganda purposes, they had no alternative but to feed us better. Commissaryman 1st Class Harry Lewis and Fireman Dale Rigby were assigned to KP duties, but this consisted only of dishing the swill provided from slop buckets and then cleaning up. Their fine work in *Pueblo's* galley remained nothing but a tantalizing memory. As summer wore on, turnips were removed from our diet and grass soup and sewer trout and rice were installed as staple items on the menu.

On July 16 we had a real mail-call—letters from home for almost everybody. I received two from Rose which had been mailed in February and April from San Diego, and although she had obviously been very careful to write nothing but the most innocuous chitchat about the family, I savored the pain and delight of holding a piece of paper in my hands which had been held in hers, and of reading words I knew she had very likely agonized over for hours after lengthy briefings from Navy liaison people. No tender private thoughts could be conveyed, nor any of the details of the ordeal from her side, yet it was all there by some mysterious cryptography the KORCOMs could never break. It was instantly deciphered by my own heart. I am an emotional person and in the often hard calling of my profession have had to exert every ounce of self-control on many occasions to prevent my feelings from running away with me; but never more than when I held those two letters from my wife. I felt tremendously sorry and angry for those of my men who received none and immediately began working out an explanation which might make it easier for them to bear their terrible disappointment, and so that I could transmit it to them through our "underground" communication system. While both my letters had been opened, there were no blue pencil marks, no erasures, nor any part of the letter had been mutilated by a razor. It struck me that the KORCOMs would only deliver to us letters which needed no deletions or alterations at all; whereas those that did were destroyed by the censor. Our letters were carefully read. Soon after we received them there was a rash of unsubtle inquiries about the exact meanings of certain English expressions (such as *"we're pulling for you like mad"*) by the interrogators.

The two letters from Rose led me into hazy memories that suddenly came into sharp focus. Wonderful days when Rose and I were a struggling young couple back in Nebraska with our whole life ahead of us. It had been my ambition to become a geologist and go to work in foreign operations for a big oil company where the pay was very high and a man could accumulate a healthy savings account in a few years. We also talked about a veterinarian career, but decided the cost of such an education, plus that of setting up a practice was beyond our reach. Geology made better sense. But I had a duty to the Navy as I had been deferred from recall to active duty in the early part of the Korean War and attended Naval Reserve Officers Training while at the University of Nebraska. Upon my graduation was commissioned as an Ensign in the Naval Reserve. For the next three years of required active service we had to put aside our plans of making our fortune out of oil prospecting in distant exotic lands and settle in to the more prosaic life of a young Navy couple. As it turned out, Rose showed every sign of becoming the perfect Navy wife who takes the various ship and service school assignments in her stride. When I fell in love with submarines, she did not hesitate to urge that I apply for a regular commission. When my appointment to Submarine School in New London, Connecticut, came through, the matter was clinched for good. We became *Navy*. It was a decision we never regretted. A number of interesting billets and assignments came our way during the following years and in due time promotions that gave us a feeling of security and success. It was a good life with the advantages far outweighing the disadvantages, the happy memories far stronger than the unhappy ones. Or at least so it seemed until this terrible thing happened to us. Our love for each other remained as strong as ever and I knew we were both fervently praying God to soon lighten each other's sufferings. My faith in the Navy had been somewhat shaken when no rescue operation materialized, yet I believed that they would be doing everything in their power to help Rose now, to help *all* the families of the *Pueblo* men. Naturally, her letters could not mention anything about this, but as I sat in my cell daydreaming about her, longing for her, I could clearly see in my mind's eye what she was going through. I suffered with her.

By now my Escape Committee was beginning to come up with plans and as I had expected, most of them were either excessively dangerous or unworkable. The idea of overpowering our guards and grabbing some of their weapons had occurred to us, and if carefully planned and boldly executed, there was a chance of success. But then what? The countryside was a military training area full of soldiers. We wondered what the chances were of reaching the nearby airfield under cover of darkness. Tim Harris had received some pilot training and I am sure a lot of us were desperate enough to take the risk of flying with him. It was a wild James Bond-type scheme which I decided could only be considered as a last desperate resort. The most realistic plan came from Ed Murphy, who had managed to squirrel away a map of North Korea out of the "cultural" pamphlets he had been given; on it he located a river running north-south right through the DMZ and passing not very far from Pyongyang. Ed's idea was to have an escape team make for that river and traveling by night, follow its course to where they could swim across the DMZ. There were, of course, great risks in this scheme too. The river was certain to be heavily mined, netted, and patrolled by troops. But it was the best thought out escape plan received, and I was tempted to start working it out in detail, utilizing our Filipinos Garcia, Aluague or Abelon, who had the best chance of moving cross country without attracting notice. Nevertheless, I hesitated to endanger the lives of these men in a risky, perhaps futile, venture. I gave Ed Murphy full credit for a fine job, yet decided to withhold my approval of any specific plan for the time being.

My chain of command was by now well established. I had an efficient "pipeline" to the enlisted personnel through my currently assigned room orderly, Fireman Mitchell, who was the cellmate of Chief Kell, who in turn was in daily contact with Communication Technician Ginther whom the KORCOMs had put in charge of the 3rd Deck, and with our Quartermaster Law, our "Athletic Director" and Petty Officer in charge of the 2nd Deck, Mitchell did a marvelous job of relaying messages and kept me informed of activities in the other cells. If a man was being beaten, or became sick, I would be informed within a day, and would lodge a protest on his behalf. If I heard a man was not bearing up well under the strain, I would find some way to give him encouragement during exercise or propaganda formations.

Toward the end of July, the heat became oppressive and we were occasionally allowed to open doors and windows of our cells in order to get some circulation of fresh air going through the suffocating humid atmosphere trapped inside the building. Our clothing and bedding became soggy with sweat. The guards sweated. The very walls sweated. We all smelled like billy goats in rut even though we were now allowed one bath a week. As the temperature soared to the 100° mark we could only slake our thirst with boiled water and think back with ironic nostalgia to the snow and ice of last winter.

During the latter days of July Super-C called an all-hands meeting to find out what we could come up with to needle our government into making an "official apology." It was at one of these meetings that Friar Tuck stood up and, with tongue in cheek, suggested that we put in a person-to-person overseas call to President Johnson in the White House.

It was also evident that Super-C had become stage-struck with the production of press conferences. He was constantly occupied with their planning and rehearsals. I did nothing to discourage him. I knew that as long as one of those shows was being prepared, a violent general purge was unlikely, since they could not afford to mar our appearance with lumps and bruises; moreover, our rations would be kept above the starvation level so we would not appear on stage like living skeletons.

Toward the end of August the KORCOMs took to selecting prisoners to pose in "informal" groups of four to six for propaganda photographs. This would be set up in a room with halfway decent furniture, pictures hung on the walls, and potted plants adding a homey touch. The group would be ordered to smile at the camera and look contentedly relaxed, and they did. But it was during these sessions that the Hawaiian Good Luck Sign came into general use as a gesture of defiance and contempt. It completely passed over the heads of even the better KORCOM interpreters. They blithely took pictures of several groups where *everybody* was using that crude finger-gesture in one way or the other, and by so doing, turning the happy smiles the photographer demanded and got, into ribald leers of mischief. I was the originator and instigator of this unsubtle but effective way of sabotaging any visual propaganda and urged my people by example to use it as well. However, not all of the crew went along with me on this. Some of the officers and crew warned me that they thought it far too dangerous, others objected on the grounds the Hawaiian Good Luck Sign was too vulgar. I never *ordered* anyone to use it; it was a volunteer program.

Obviously, Super-C's military and political superiors were well satisfied with his handling of the *Pueblo* prisoners, because one day he appeared with the glittering new collar devices of a general on his uniform. He summoned me to a routine session in his office, but I suspect that his real purpose was to show off his promotion. During the course of his usual lecture, he kept stretching his neck like a buzzard preening itself. For quite some time I pretended to notice nothing unusual. I finally popped my eyes, and exclaimed, "My goodness! What is that I see on your collar? General's stars?"

"What? Oh those?" He almost fell off his chair in his beaming paroxysm of acting out the conflicting emotions of pride and humility. But he was so delighted that he cut short his lecture with uncharacteristic banter, and allowed me to return to my cell. News of his promotion rapidly spread among the rest of the prisoners and in honor of it, we decided we had to give him a new, more impressive name. From then on he was referred to as Glorious General—often abbreviated to G-G.

A hot and humid August was slowly slipping toward September. The "60 Day Purge" I had been fearing did not quite materialize, although the brief period of relatively easy treatment following Glorious General's promotion soon deteriorated into the former surly, unreasonably fault-finding ways of our enlisted guards and their junior officers. Violence was not a daily occurrence, yet happened with sporadic frequency. Thus on one occasion when a young guard decided I was not marching properly up the staircase when returning in formation from an exercise period, he knocked me back down them with a tremendous kick which caught me by surprise as it smashed into my solarplexus. Between that blow and the fall down the stairs, I was a wreck for the next couple of days. CT2 Earl Kisler received a beating to the face which was scientifically applied with shoes and belts so as to raise the maximum amount of welts and bruises without actually inflicting critical damage, the main point being to parade him before us when gathered for a propaganda movie as a gory example of what happens to those who do not sincerely cooperate. His lack of sincere cooperation had in this instance involved his refusal to write a letter to his U. S. Senator or Congressman—something I had warned everybody against doing unless they were absolutely certain they could slip in some hidden meaning which would cancel out the KORCOM propaganda. Kisler's face was a horrible mess.

I was still having private grilling sessions with Glorious General and Silverlips and in one of those where he was trying to make me come up with better ideas for getting action out of the United States in producing their apology (a thing I was still absolutely convinced would never be forthcoming) he began hinting around about convening another press conference—an *international* press conference. But he acted as if he did not want to order it himself, rather wheedle the suggestion out of me.

Things dragged on all night and sometime in the early morning when I was totally exhausted, I finally gave in and exclaimed, "Say, General, why don't we have another press conference? An international press conference this time!"

He jumped up from his chair with an expression of surprised delight as if this were a brand-new good idea. "Yes, an international press conference!" he shouted in his theatrical way. "That's it! A big international press conference with lots of foreign correspondents to report your sincere repentance to the whole world. We shall even invite some of your capitalist reporters from Japan and France, even from America!"

"Terrific, swell!" I told him while seriously doubting he would produce any Americans for the occasion. I could imagine from which countries the international press would be invited, but he had what he wanted from me and immediately began making plans. And so did I.

The preparations for the Great International Press Conference were far more elaborate than for the local ones we had been subjected to before and it was evident that G-G was determined to make it a spectacular production. The cast from our side was to consist of all officers and certain enlisted prisoners to be selected by a committee headed by Ed Murphy. Although I was not on that committee I was able to pass on to it the names of the men I felt would turn in the kind of performance we wanted and, of course, alerted all officers as to what I expected of them. Although G-G disqualified some of the enlisted men I picked, I was able to control to a degree the selection of people who were least likely to be intimidated and with the talent of putting across by some clever word or gesture a sign to the outside world that it was a phony deal. The production was scheduled to coincide with the twentieth anniversary celebration of the DPKR on September 9. Two weeks beforehand, the KORCOMs had us working on the script for the spontaneous questions and answers which we were required to learn verbatim. This gave us ample time to study the inflections and twists that we thought we might get by with. They also began fattening us up with improved rations so that we would make a good impression before the cameras and correspondents. Our improved diet also gave us more energy with which to sabotage the project.

The day before the show, activities came to a fever pitch. Our cast was marched over to the classroom building, and there put through a thorough dress rehearsal. A television control truck parked in the compound yard and technicians were laying coaxial cables to the camera positions, also to brand-new Russian made monitors being installed in our prison building where, prisoners not selected to participate in the conference would be able to view the proceedings on a closed circuit system. When I noticed this, I had the word passed around warning our "audience" that their reactions would be watched and not to laugh or hoot at any part of our performance no matter how outlandish it struck them.

I did upset them by suffering a recurrence of "Lockjaw," a disease they could find authenticated but incompletely described in their Korean-English dictionary. A demonstration during rehearsal convinced them it could seriously inhibit my performance at the conference and their Medical Officer was directed to treat it forthwith. The best he could come up with was to stick some of his acupuncture needles into the affected areas. "It feels much better now, Doc! I think I can handle it for the time being."

On the day of the Great International Press Conference and for the occasion, the cast was given clean undershirts. Glorious General appeared wearing a civilian suit reflecting his eccentrically unproletarian tastes. It was custom-tailored of high quality material. Silverlips, in comparison, looked like a scarecrow in his locally made baggy business suit. The cast comprised myself, Ed Murphy, Steve Harris, Skip Schumacher, Gene Lacy, Friar Tuck, representing our officers; from the enlisted personnel there were Chief Kell, Garcia, Law, McClintock, Mack, Chicca, Shephard, Escamilla, Lewis, Sterling, Langenberg, Anderson, Duke, Rice, Strano, Hill, Russell, O'Bannon, and Woelk who had been returned to us from their hospital. As we were marched across the compound toward the building housing the conference, I felt confident that my crew was represented by a cross-section of our ship's company who would live up to my expectations.

The makeshift auditorium was jampacked with people who

were uncomfortably arranged among the TV equipment, film cameras, microphones, and batteries of bright kleig lights which heated up an already hot and smoky atmosphere. The KOR-COMs played down the military setting and had only a few armed guards in evidence. Most of G-G's staff appeared in mufti. G-G had really outdone himself in collecting a large cast of representatives from the world Communist press, both Oriental, Black and Occidental. As we shuffled in and took our seats opposite this crowd we could not help blinking in surprise against the glare of the lights at a mass of blurred faces. When Robot, as chairman of the conference, declared it open and then proceeded to recognize every news organization represented, it sounded like an international convention of Marxist journalists. He rattled off the names of Japanese, Indian, Polish, Russian, Somali, United Arab Republic, Italian, Hungarian, and, of course, North Korean newspapers and radio-television organizations. G-G had told us there would be an American from a New York newspaper whose name I did not recognize. I had puzzled over that for a while until I had a vague recollection of having heard that this was a left-wing newspaper of some kind. Well, Glorious General had at least managed to bring a correspondent of sorts from America! Was there a possible chance that here at last was a *real* CIA agent? Should I risk trying to sneak a special message through to him? As this thought with all its dangerous uncertainties flashed through my mind, Robot came to the end of his introductory remarks, and suddenly introduced *me*—this was my cue to stand up and introduce, in turn, the nineteen other men representing the *Pueblo*.

When I finished, Robot deftly explained away the scripts and rehearsed responses to the "spontaneous" exchanges which were to follow, by stating with his most ingratiating sincerity, "Now that this press conference is being attended by many foreign correspondents who speak different languages, we must put your written questions together according to subject matter and let the *Pueblo* crew answer them so as to facilitate the proceeding of our press conference smoothly. Now let's come to the first question."

It would be both boring and redundant to repeat here in detail the dialogue of questions and answers which took place during the next three and a half hours. Both would read as the most stilted and clumsily contrived Communist propaganda, the questions as loaded as the answers. Suffice it to say that we repeated what we had been required to memorize during the past two weeks, since we had had a hand in the preparations of answers and some of them were loaded with humor and ridiculousness.

The KORCOMs had decided to break the news to the world of additional "intrusions" which they discovered we had committed. To prove that these intrusions were ordered by the U.S. government, they made use of an Instruction which we had aboard the ship. The daffy logic used in making their point using this Instruction, proved to me that this time they were cutting their own throat, and I gladly complied with adding the "intrusions" to our list of crimes. We were now up to seventeen intrusions, and although most of them would have required the *Pueblo* to go supersonic, the KORCOMs somehow failed to see any contradiction. Ed Murphy did a marvelous job of explaining the new "intrusions" and was backed by Quartermaster Law. I had no way of knowing whether any of the correspondents present would do the calculations needed to give the lie to our confessions, but I knew that our own people at home would not fail to do so.

G-G also inserted into my spiel the statement that we had actually started the fight on the day of our seizure by opening up on their ships with our "main battery" of machine guns. He even had pictures of a dead sailor that we had supposedly killed during that action. Well, I had signaled my superiors at the time that we had not uncovered our guns, so they would know that this was a lie.

Everyone delivered his lines with "sincerity" and some were so funny that I almost cracked up during their recitation. Particularly, Communication Technician 3rd Class Ralph McClintock's great imitation of President John F. Kennedy's voice while reciting a yearning to, "walk down the shaded lanes of the old home town and once again taste one of Mom's famous apple pies."

There were signs that some of the delegates were getting a bit restless and confused through the several hours of endlessly droned questions and our even more longwinded recitals which were supposed to be answers. A couple of African correspondents fell asleep and one from Afghanistan, an irascible little fellow, constantly jumped up angrily shouting that he could not hear what was being said. There were others who gave the impression through irritated asides that they would have liked to break the boredom by departing from the script and challenge us to a free-for-all verbal exchange. However, the KORCOMs would have none of this. Robot rattled on with his own rehearsed translations regardless of interruptions by the deaf Afghanistani. The Africans suddenly woke and found themselves unable to find their place in the script. Finally even old Robot, also inadvertently lost his own place in the script and prematurely announced the close of the conference before my cue to give the closing "statement" for my side. As I had been rehearsing it for a solid week, I jumped up and protested as loudly as the still vociferous delegate from Afghanistan.

There came a deep guffaw from an East German delegate who had previously worried me by standing, with a cigarette smoldering, and staring fixedly at me. Was he an NKVD agent masquerading as a journalist? But now he was doubled with laughter, and I ceased to worry about him.

A Hungarian or a Russian said to no one in particular: "When are we going to stop this bullshit?"

Then Robot announced for the second time that "this International Press Conference in Regards to the Criminal Intrusions of the U. S. Imperialist Armed Spyship *Pueblo*" was over.

The program was scheduled to continue after lunch. The foreign correspondents were taken on a conducted round of visits to our cells. I was agonizing over whether to risk trying to slip a note to the man who had been identified as a correspondent of a left-wing New York paper. Just in case I decided to do it and the opportunity presented itself, I scribbled one down on a small piece of toilet paper, refuting in a few lines everything which had been said at the press conference. We had never intruded, never provocated or fired a shot, but had been illegally seized on the high seas, captured, imprisoned and miserably treated and beaten. I had this note palmed in my hand when he came to my cell that afternoon, looked around and asked me some innocuous questions while Glorious General and Silverlips stood in the doorway watching and listening. They were beaming with smiles, but I noticed that Silverlips was whispering translations of everything being said between me and my American visitor. Even so, it would have been an easy matter for me to pass that note with our parting handshake. The only reason I did not do it was because when face to face with him, I felt an instinctive dislike, distrust and suspicion that he was more loyal to communism than to his own country and countrymen. We never shook hands and the note went undelivered. I never came to regret it as I continued to feel, and feel now, that he would merely have turned it over to G-G and that would have gone hard on myself and probably triggered a purge of my whole crew.

As it was, Glorious General was so ecstatic over a day he considered an eminent success that he ordered a ration of beer issued to all prisoners that evening.

CHAPTER XVI

"U.S. SAID TO PLAN PUEBLO APOLOGY"—(*Headline, New York* Times, *September 10, 1968.*)

"U.S. REBUTS PUEBLO TALK. SAYS THERE SHOULD BE NO CAUSE FOR APOLOGY"—(*Headline, Baltimore* Sun, *September 11, 1968.*)

The afterglow of satisfaction over the Great International Press Conference lingered on. The food was reasonably plentiful, even if of poor quality, and most prisoners began regaining some weight. Nevertheless, there were many who suffered ailments which could be traced to malnutrition and poor sanitary conditions. I continued to suffer a loss of circulation and feeling in parts of my legs, and had a bout of hepatitis. Hayes came down with jaundice and was isolated. Not even the KORCOM guards would go near him. Injuries from beatings became infrequent and actually more were suffered during our exercise periods, during which we engaged in vigorous ballgames which became more spirited as the summer heat tapered off into cool fall weather. Sterling suffered a broken nose during a touch football game, and Aluague fractured a kneecap while playing basketball. The guards took delight in kicking his knee when they decided he needed chastisement.

Glorious General had evidently been rewarded with a two-week leave for his great International production as he vanished for that length of time, leaving the prison in charge of Colonel Scar who carried on our various programs with less flamboyance of manner but equally crude efficiency.

On September 20, he assigned me the task of writing my final,

final confession, the one to surpass and supercede all the others. He informed me it was to be used in the long threatened trial before the People's Court. Nevertheless, I gave my imagination free rein in creating a composition consisting of an outlandish mixture of their twisted facts and my humorous fancy. They wanted details of my mission, so I gave them by inserting such revealing juicy intelligence items as:

"The *Pueblo* was specially built and equipped with all the latest electronic spying instruments, but in order to conceal its wicked mission, made to look innocent by blending into its structure a lot of twenty-year-old parts . . . and I was personally briefed in Hawaii by the notorious Marine General Barney Google . . . given my orders in the TOP SECRET Japanese lair of the CIA's evil genius, Sol Loxfinger . . ." etc., etc., through some forty pages of absolute nonsense. Sol Loxfinger was a fictitious hero of a *Playboy* magazine lampoon of the famous James Bond series. (See appendix for full text of "final-final" confession.)

I submitted my creation to Colonel Scar, who duly checked it out with his interpreters, then returned it to me with his expressions of full approval and satisfaction. Within a few days, I delivered it before the Warner Brothers sound-film and TV cameras with hardly a word altered and, for once, speaking with all the dignified, earnest seriousness I could muster.

Not only were there no repercussions from the liberties we were taking, but things happened which made me more certain than ever that our release was impending. Glorious General returned during the first days of October and promptly summoned me for an all-night session with him. Mingled with his usual lectures were some asides that were not steeped in Communist dogma. He permitted me to join him in chainsmoking throughout the interrogation and finally told me flatly: "You have said you expect to be home before Christmas. Well, I say you will not be home before then, nor before your Thanksgiving, but before this month is out." My heart leaped at this. But G-G had lied to me before, so I decided to keep this "carrot" to myself. I simply could not build up my crew's hopes only to have them suffer another bitter disappointment. At this point something quite extraordinary and unexpected happened: we were all taken on an excursion to downtown Pyongyang to see a show.

We were herded into familiar buses of very unpleasant memory, but with the unscreened windows and pleasant guards. Glorious General led the convoy in a staff car as it pulled out of our prison compound and we were followed by several other cars loaded with various other senior and junior officers. There were frequent stops necessitated along the long winding road into town, three before military checkpoints where soldiers gave us a cursory once-over before they raised the boom to let us pass, and one when a drunken farmer got himself caught blocking our progress as he weaved in a state of happy alcoholic daze, oblivious to honking horns and angry shouts. He was collared by Odd-Job, a perfect duplicate of the James Bond villain of the same name, braced, slapped in the face and dismissed. It was dusk so that we could get only hazy impressions of rice paddies and rolling pastures dotted with clusters of drab collective farms. There was no suburbia separating the city from the countryside. Suddenly the rough dirt road smoothed out into a paved one and boxlike structures merged into city blocks, a single lightbulb in their windows, cheerless with their orderly but completely unvarying symmetry of design. My impression was that the same architect who had designed our prison barracks had also created these four-story warrens where the citizens of this People's Republic lived in a squalor which was little better than what was provided their Imperialist captives. The only sign that we were progressing into the center of their capital city was the increasing number of pale street lights casting a cold mercury-vapor glow over empty pavements and darkened storefronts, and a few solitary red or white neon signs whose very scarcity emphasized the overall gloom. We saw only an occasional couple who dodged out of our headlights and slipped into the shadows of dark buildings. There was so little traffic that I suspected our route had been cleared in advance by an alerted police so efficient that they did not need to precede us with shrieking sirens. Our convoy halted in front of a brightly lit structure which we were informed was the Grand

Theater of the People, only there were no People about. Just
soldiers.

It was an extremely large theater with every one of the 2–3000
seats filled except those reserved for us; Friar Tuck and Harry
Iredale thus became the only civilians in an otherwise entirely
military audience. As we were marched down the center aisle we
were subjected to many curious glances, but there was no hostile
demonstration to greet us, rather a chilly silence. We were seated
with an interpreter spaced between every fourth man, then the
curtain rose on a light opera titled "How Glorious the Fatherland" and which was just about as exciting as that. The music was
of the Korean variety, loud and discordant. The action was hard
to follow even with the help of our interpreters who kept inter-
jecting their own critical observations, such as: "Very beautiful!
. . . Very great!" The story concerned the liberation war against
Japanese occupation, with some U.S. villains thrown in for good
measure. Judging from what went on on-stage, the brave Korean
guerrillas sang the cruel Japanese to death. We enjoyed ourselves
immensely. We would have gladly watched this propaganda
spectacle through two or three performances, just to be out of
our foul prison.

To my amazement, a couple of days later, Glorious General
announced another excursion. This time we were taken to a
performance of Korean acrobats and tumblers who put on quite
a show. On the following evening, we were loaded into our convoy for the third time that week to attend a concert by the
People's Army band and chorus. This hurt our sensitive Western
ears, yet we reveled in these massive doses of Korean culture because it portended to all of us that repatriation was just ahead;
I now believed this quite firmly, and had conveyed my optimism
to the officers and a couple of enlisted men, warning them at the
same time not to pass my thoughts along to the entire crew.

Then came our most exciting excursion of all, which involved
an overnight railroad trip to visit the Museum of Imperialist
Atrocities at Sinchon, a national shrine. We were bused to the
railroad station of Pyongyang at about 2200 hours and put aboard
old, but well-kept sleeping cars, two men to each nine-bunk compartment. The train took all night to cover about one hundred

miles in fits and starts, but we enjoyed the great luxury of clean sheets and good wool blankets. Buses which were screened more to keep civilians from seeing us than us from looking out, drove us from the Sinchon station to the museum lying just outside that small town. There we were split into groups of tens and paraded through many quite small rooms containing displays of relics and photographs from the barbarous activities of the U. S. Imperialists during the late Korean War. In one glass case there was the actual six-penny nail, somewhat rusty and bent, which the infamous Lieutenant (jg) Harrison had supposedly driven into the heads of innocent Korean women; in another there was a piece of rope with which he had supposedly hanged other victims. A pathetic collection of battered shoes was all that remained of 5000 women and children who had been deliberately drowned in a river; above them hung a framed photograph of the stream where this atrocity happened. Proof of our inhumane bacteriological warfare was quite staggering, too. There were some peculiar metal canisters with parachutes attached which had been used to air-drop plague infected mice over the countryside. There was a close-up photograph of a strange, large-headed fly which had never been seen in Korea before American aircraft swooped low and released these disease-carrying bugs by the millions. A card printed in both Korean and English told in graphic language the gruesome history of each relic and picture and as we took all this in, we had great difficulty in controlling our emotions.

Silverlips was sticking close to my side as I went through these exhibits with my group, watching me carefully for my reactions to it all and recording on a portable tape recorder my companions' and my expressions of horror. "How ghastly!" I exclaimed as I stared at Lieutenant (jg) Harrison's cruel nail. "How absolutely revolting!" I gasped over the mouse-canisters. When we were conducted into a basement and shown a five by ten foot cubicle in which Horrible Harrison had jammed 900 women and children to meet a frightful death by suffocation, I sort of lost control of myself and suffered one of my attacks of lockjaw. "I can't take any more!" I rasped through rigidly clenched teeth and with a contorted grimace.

"What is the matter, Captain?" Silverlips asked in some alarm. When he decided that my attack was brought on by the convulsing effects of their Museum of Imperialist Atrocities, he became both sympathetic and pleased. He promptly ordered one of the accompanying photographers to take my picture while I was still in the throes of my attack and which I obliged them by keeping up until they had some good shots.

Shortly after 1100 we were all bused back to the Sinchon station and put back aboard our train where we were served a meal which was as bad as any produced by the cooks of our prison. We had a much faster return trip and were back in our cells by late afternoon, where the "room-daddies" immediately assigned everybody the task of writing down their impressions of the Museum of Imperialist Atrocities. We had plenty of inspiration for creative writing. The excursion really had three important effects: firstly it had been the most pleasant one yet, secondly it had proven beyond doubt in any of our minds that the KORCOM atrocity charges against the U.S. were utterly ridiculous, thirdly, and most important, it was likely a culmination of the various impressions they wanted to leave with us before our release.

There were other events which had led me to believe our day of deliverance was not far off. During the preceding week there had been a new addition to prison life, which we called the Gypsy Tea Room. One day, when my officers and I were going into our "wardroom" for dinner, Corpsman Baldridge suddenly came rolling down the hall three sheets to the wind. In fact, he was so drunk that he sassed his guard to the extent of ordering him to "get the hell out of my way, you dumb shit." The guard was so surprised that he did. Baldridge staggered happily into his cell before we could speak to him. I wanted to establish communication quickly, to find out where he had found enough spirits to fly so high. My efficient "underground" soon brought me the story:

He had been taken over to a room in a different building on the other side of the compound some two hours earlier, and there had been put through a novel form of KORCOM interrogation. The officer conducting it was Max, whom we had not seen since our

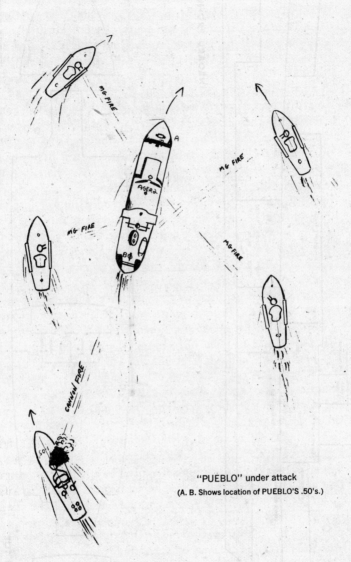

"PUEBLO" under attack

(A. B. Shows location of PUEBLO'S .50's.)

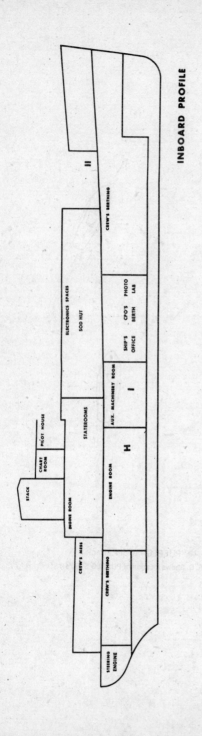

INBOARD PROFILE

STACK

CHART ROOM
PILOT HOUSE

ENGINE ROOM

STATEROOMS

ELECTRONICS SPACES
SOD HUT

CREW'S BERTHING

CREW'S MESS

ENGINE ROOM
H

AUX. MACHINERY ROOM
I

SHIP'S OFFICE
CPO'S BERTH
PHOTO LAB

CREW'S BERTHING

STEERING ENGINE

FOCSLE DECK

ALTERNATE MOUNT

MG .50

BOAT & BRIDGE DECK

Q

Y

RADIO ROOM

CHART ROOM

O

MG .50

PILOT HOUSE TOP

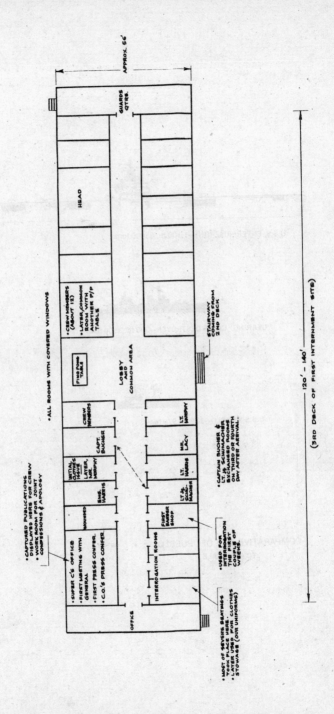

• CAPTURED PUBLICATIONS DISPLAYED HERE FOR CREW
• WORK ROOM FOR JOINT CONFESSIONS & APOLOGY

• ALL ROOMS WITH COVERED WINDOWS

APPROX. 56'

GUARDS QTRS.

HEAD

• CREW MEMBERS (ABOUT 12)
• LATER, COMMON ROOM WITH ANOTHER P/P TABLE

PING PONG TABLE

LOBBY AND COMMON AREA

STAIRWAY COMING FROM 2ND DECK

CREW MEMBERS

INITIAL CLOTHING ISSUE
LATER, MR. MURPHY

CAPT. BUCHER

FIRST BARBER SHOP

LT. JG. GONLES MACHER

MR. LACY

LT. MURPHY

• CAPTAIN BUCHER & LT. JG. EXCHANGED ROOMS ON THIRD OR FOURTH DAY AFTER ARRIVAL.

WOUNDED

BMS. HARRIS

• SUPER C's OFFICE
• FIRST MEETING WITH GENERAL
• FIRST PRESS CONFER.
• C.O.'S PRESS CONFER.

OFFICE

INTERROGATION ROOMS

• USED FOR INTERROGATION THE FIRST COUPLE OF WEEKS.

• MOST OF SAVIERS BEATINGS TOOK PLACE HERE.
• LATER USED FOR CLOTHES STOWAGE (OUR UNIFORMS)

120' - 140'

(3RD DECK OF FIRST INTERNMENT SITE)

U.S.S. ENTERPRISE (UN)—1,100 ft., 85000 tons

"GEARING" CLASS DESTROYER—390 ft.. 3500 tons

U.S.S. PUEBLO—179 ft., 970 tons

COMPARATIVE SIZE OF "PUEBLO"
TO APP. SCALE

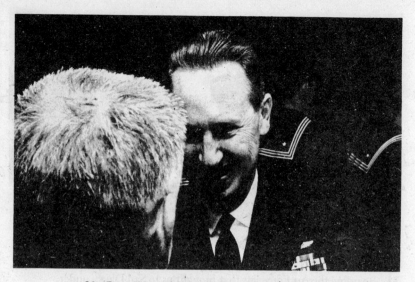

29. Rear Admiral Edward Rosenberg, USN, left a sick bed and traveled several hundred miles in order to be present when my crew crossed the bridge from North to South Korea. He was thoroughly magnificent in making and supervising the preparations for our crossing.

30. Seaman E. Stuart Russell and Senior Civilian Oceanographer Dunnie R. Tuck at interdenominational service giving thanks to God on the day we were repatriated from imprisonment in North Korea.

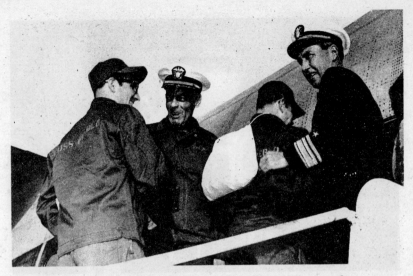

31. Boarding the Air Force jets that brought us to San Diego, under the watchful eye of Rear Admiral Rosenberg. CT2 Elton C. Wood is shaking my hand.

32. Deplaning at Miramar Naval Air Station, San Diego. Left to right; Stewardsmate 2nd Class Abelon, Fireman Arnold, Fireman Bame and Boatswainsmate 1st Class Klepac.

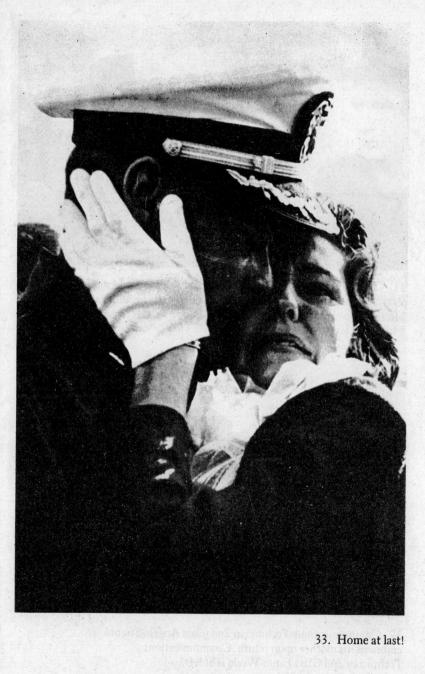

33. Home at last!

34. Communications Technician 2nd Class Wayne Anderson from Waycross, Georgia, with members of his family after landing at Miramar Naval Air Station, San Diego, California, December 24, 1968. Lieutenant (jg) Harris is at left.

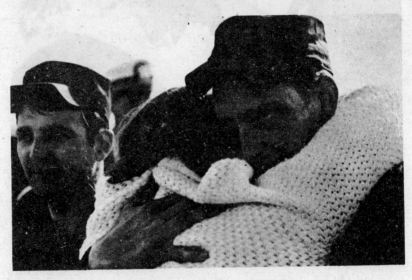

35. Communications Technician 2nd Class Angelo Strano embraces his mother upon return. Communications Technician 2nd Class Elton Wood is at left.

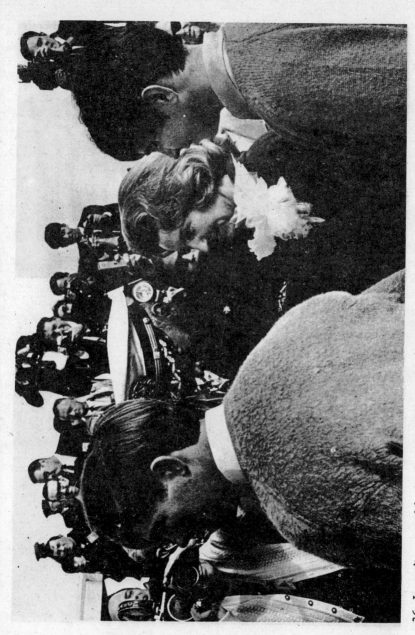

36. I wasn't prepared for the large crowd that greeted us, especially the number of news and television personnel. With me here are my son Mark at left, Rose and my son Mike.

37. Great to be home. Commissaryman 1st Class Harry Lewis, his wife and daughter relaxing following their reunion.

38. "Skip" Schumacher making a point with the XO while I look on.

39. Part of the gang from Boys Town that came to welcome my family and me when we arrived in Omaha, Nebraska.

40. During reunion at Boys Town, left to right: son Mike, Rose, Me, Archbishop Gerald T. Bergin, son Mark.

41. Presiding over the Navy USS *Pueblo* Court of Inquiry is Vice Admiral H. G. Bowen (standing). Sitting left to right are Rear Admirals R. R. Pratt, M. W. White, E. E. Grimm and A. A. Bergner.

42. Seated between my counsel, Mr. E. Miles Harvey (on the left) and Captain James Keys, JAGC, USN.

43. Departing a "Closed Session" of the Court of Inquiry with
Lieutenant Stephen R. Harris, Officer in Charge of the
Special Operations Detachment.

44. Chief Communications Technician James Kell presenting me with a desk piece on behalf of the officers, crew and civilian oceanographers of USS *Pueblo*. My XO, Lieutenant Murphy, looks on.

45. The entire crew of USS *Pueblo* (AGER-2) following return from captivity in North Korea where they had been held illegally for eleven months. Fireman Duane Hodges, whose body had been returned with us, was laid to rest in his hometown of Creswell, Oregon.

46. Miss Marcee Rethwish, a fifteen-year-old from El Cajon, California, was elected by the crew as its only honorary crew member, in gratitude for her efforts in the release of the crew. Here I am being honored to kiss her cheek following her presentation to me of a replica of *Pueblo's* mascot, "The Lonely Bull."

47. I am presenting my Engineering Officer CWO Gene Lacy, USN
with a *Pueblo* ash tray at the Christmas party upon our return.
The gift had been ordered prior to the seizure of *Pueblo*. Gene
was my most experienced officer and a personal friend.

48. Lieutenant Stephen Harris, USNR, was the Officer in charge of the Special Operations Detachment on *Pueblo*. Steve is a Harvard graduate.

49. Lieutenant (jg) Timothy Harris, USNR, was *Pueblo*'s Supply and Food Services Officer. Tim was eager, competent and brave.

50. Electricians Mate 1st Class Gerald M. Hagenson, USN, was a stalwart leader throughout the captivity in North Korea.

51. Storekeeper 1st Class Policarpo Garcia, USN, was a central figure in the chain of command maintained in the *Pueblo* crew while in captivity.

52. Sergeant Robert Chicca, USMC, interpreter assigned to the Special Operations Detachment. His leadership and courage during captivity were highly commendable.

53. Sergeant Robert Hammond, USMC, interpreter assigned to the Special Operation Detachment. Hammond consistently defied his captors and was recommended by the Commanding Officer for Meritorious Advancement upon return.

early confinement. He and his assistants had been dressed in civilian clothes, and had acted with an oily affability. Two Korean girls dressed in national costumes served Baldridge cookies, candies, beer and liqueurs. Their technique was less that of an interrogation than an apology for hardships they had inflicted, assurances of their basic good will, hopes that this spirit would become mutual. Their only significant question was, "After you get home to your loved ones, would you be willing to receive our agent named Kim if he is able to call on you?" To this a startled and tipsy Baldridge had answered: "Are you kidding? Why the hell should I anyway?" Max had not taken umbrage at this. On the contrary, he put his arm around Baldridge's shoulder and offered him a parting shot of liqueur before sending him back to his cell with hearty good wishes.

Evidently they planned to introduce each of us to the Gypsy Tea Room. During the course of that evening and the next day, several more of my men were given the same treatment. News of the Gypsy Tea Room quickly spread to all the cells, and I passed the word that everybody should be careful about what they said, but that they should also enjoy the hospitality of our captors. I eagerly looked forward to my invitation and planned cautiously to find out more about this mysterious Agent Kim, who was supposed to call on all of us after we returned to the U.S.A.

My turn never came. I never figured out why. Nor did Skip Schumacher's and a couple enlisted men's. Everyone else had his individual visit with Max in his Tea Room. If Skip and I were under suspicion for insincerity, they did not let us know about it in our letter-writing assignments. Our collaborators were Steve, McClintock, Anderson, and Mack. I had been allowed to choose them for the job of composing an assigned *Petition to the People of Korea*. I had picked Skip because he was now my most deviously creative and trusted officer, Steve because of his steady intelligence, McClintock because he had proven himself adept at innuendos, Anderson because he was a glib history major from the University of Georgia, and Mack because for some strange reason the KORCOMs considered him highly sincere, while he was merely adept at pulling their leg. We did in fact get away with a composition that matched my *Final, Final Confession* for brazen kidding of the KORCOMs, and which far surpassed it in subtlety. Blended into the standard Communist verbosity were such lines of our own as:

"We as conscientious human beings who were cast upon the rocks and shoals of immorality by the tidal waves of Washington's naughty policies know that neither the frequency nor the distances of these transgressions into the territorial waters of this sovereign peace-loving nation matter, because penetration however slight is sufficient to complete the act." (Rocks and Shoals is Navy slang for the Uniform Code of Military Justice and the last line contains its essential definition of rape).

This was both delivered over film and TV and published in the "Ping-pong Times." The Glorious General was well pleased and set the same team to working on the next letter, one entitled *Gratitude to the People of Korea for our Humane Treatment,* in which we inserted such sentiments as:

". . . We who have rotated on the fickle finger of fate for so long . . . we of the Pueblo are sincerely grateful for the humane treatment we have received at the hands of the Democratic People's Republic of Korea and we not only desire to paean the Korean People's Army but also to paean the Government and the people of the Democratic People's Republic of Korea."

We appeared to have gotten away with this one, too, and had every indication that it would be broadcast, because it was filmed and printed. But then something happened completely to change the KORCOMs tolerant attitude toward us, a sudden coldness in their manner with ominous storm signals like the chilly autumn skies lowering over our prison and presaging early winter blizzards. The halcyon days of our confinement with shows, excursions, freedom from starvation and beatings, were coming to an end.

The change did not come in an explosion of sudden violence, but a sequence of seemingly temporary sulks. Glorious General had told me during our latest all-night session that his people were making every effort to have us repatriated and would continue to do so in spite of the fact that "the United States is

showing very little interest in taking you back!" I knew that
any delays were caused by the KORCOMs. Nevertheless, after
that meeting I was, for some mysterious reason, no longer summoned to see Glorious General. Indeed, he vanished for the next
several weeks. My regular prison routine: meals, exercises, and
recreation periods with my officers went on as before, but I
suddenly had no more letter-writing assignments. I found myself
confined to my cell for long periods, reminiscent of those grim,
lonely days of last March. The weather was turning cold with
November snowsqualls rattling against my cell window and a
moaning North wind probing through the building with icy
fingers. My radiator came uncertainly to life, producing little
heat, with much creaking and knocking. Cold, too, was the
demeanor of my guards. Colder yet was the fact that all mention of release had ceased. Coldest of all, was the creeping fear
that things had gone awry and I had again raised the hopes of
my men only to have them dashed. Dammit! Had I led them too
far in our "resistance" capers and compromised their chances of
release? There were ominous signs that this was so.

My "underground" pipeline, which kept me in touch with my
entire command, was still functioning in spite of the enforce-
ment of many old rules of silence. Through it, I learned that
minor infractions were once more being punished with savage
beatings. All letter-writing activities were suspended and lectures
by "room-daddies" degenerated into savage chewing tirades.
There had also been questions asked about the meanings of
words and sentences we had inserted in past writings and statements. But most disturbing of all, there were now persistent
questions about the *exact* meaning of our now widely used Hawaiian Good Luck Sign. I was informed that several men who gave
"insincere" answers to this question in particular, specially those
from "Room 13," whom I knew to have posed for a propaganda
picture in which many of them had managed to make the gesture,
were given some very painful pummelings. I protested, of course,
and got unusually abrupt snarls of indifference from Colonel
Scar. Inwardly frantic, but determined to keep outwardly cool, I
could only warn my officers and crew through our usual channels to knock off any of the funny stuff we had thought we were

putting over on the KORCOMs, and to attempt only the subtlest forms of resistance until they heard otherwise from me. From having been the boldest instigator among us, I now became one of the most cautious. We were all left hanging in an obviously deteriorating situation. Nevertheless, one of my men, in messhall, shouted "KORCOMs eat shit!" He got away with it then. But by early December, the gathering storm clouds broke.

The first to be hit by systematic prolonged beatings were Bland, Layton, and Chief Goldman, and they evidently took tremendous punishment over a two-hour period as the KORCOMs tried to make them reveal the true meaning of the Hawaiian Good Luck Sign. I met Goldman during exercise period and was shocked to see him barely able to walk, his eyes swollen almost shut, his mouth badly cut, his face blackened by bruises. We got close enough to whisper a few words and he said to me: "Captain, I'm sorry but they know about the sign. Just couldn't hold out any longer, I'm sorry, sir . . ."

I said: "I understand that, Chief." Then I passed the word for all hands to tell them the truth if questioned about the sign. Realizing that a major purge was underway, I passed the word around that everybody could admit to their own individual efforts at discrediting the bastards if they couldn't hold out or knew that they were caught, but to resist to their utmost betraying the activities of their shipmates.

Men were yanked out of their cells and worked over both day and night. Aluague, whose leg was in a cast, got it, nevertheless. So did our civilian oceanographer Harry Iredale, who took a cruel thrashing from fists and feet when the guards mistook him for Ritter who had been ordered beaten and whom Iredale resembled. Room 13, containing Chuck Law, Ron Berens, Paul Brusnahan, Chief Goldman, James Layton, Dale Rigby, William Scarborough and Larry Strickland received repeated special attention until they were all in bad shape.

My officers and I were hauled before Glorious General who suddenly reappeared on the scene and delivered one of his towering histrionic rages, which were both comic and frightening to behold. He confronted us with and let us examine a copy of a page from *Time* magazine containing a group picture of our infamous

Room 13 gang. The caption fully explained the meaning of the Hawaiian Good Luck Sign. As he ranted and raved about it, I could not help a feeling of triumph that we had actually got through to the United States with one of our efforts to expose KORCOM lies about the *Pueblo*; however, I also knew we were about to pay for their severe loss of face. I had not been beaten yet, but Glorious General kept me after he had dismissed the other officers and during a denunciation lasting several hours, threatened me with speedy execution after a trial which he indicated was now absolutely inevitable. He was pretty convincing about it and I was returned to my cell feeling that my chances for survival had sunk to zero.

On the following day, men continued to be selected for beatings. Shingleton and Scarborough received brutal ones. Radioman Hayes had his jaw broken. The officers began catching it as well. An all-hands meeting was called by Glorious General who collectively berated us for our sins, picking on me, and Skip, Law, and Goldman as instigators of "insincere acts and expressions against the Korean People." He vilified our President-elect Nixon in the same violent language he had used against President Johnson. Letters of apologies and new confessions would have to be written covering all of our "Imperialist machinations" while in prison. Then he angrily announced that all "privileges" were canceled forthwith: no more exercise periods, no more Ping-pong and card games, no more meals together in wardroom and messhall. This meant that because he also yanked my orderly, uncertain chance meetings in the latrine once again became my only tenuous means of communicating with my people.

On December 11, the period of torture we came to remember as Hell Week started in earnest.

At this time they had brought in three new junior officers, one of whom was over six feet tall and weighed 200 pounds, with the musculature and scowling demeanors of professional karate fighters. These bruisers supplemented the already brutal violence of our regular guards and junior officers. Few escaped their painful attention and most had many, agonizing bouts of being knocked back and forth like punching bags by the chops and kicks of these KORCOM torture teams, whacked with heavy sticks and smashed against the concrete walls until they fell into a senseless heap. One or two of my men cracked and blubbered out all the details of their own and their shipmates' transgressions, including my phony attacks of "lockjaw," insertion of comic-strip characters into my confession, penchant for "insincere" twists of language, and origination of the derogatory Hawaiian Good Luck Sign. I did not know then who had violated my instructions that each crew member was to confess for only himself and not implicate others. Even now I will not reveal their names because I am entirely sympathetic to the superhuman pressures they were subjected to at the time. I feel that this should not now compromise their efforts to build new lives for themselves. Suffice it to say that my battered crew's loyalty to me was so strong that they threatened to murder one of their own if he did not desist from exposing my leadership in discrediting and bedeviling the KORCOMs. In any event, my time had now come to take my own share of the beatings my men were suffering.

I was now in as strict solitary confinement as I had been during the first weeks of imprisonment. My food was shoved on a tray over the threshold of the door, which was kept open and guarded. I left my room only on periodic, escorted trips to the latrine. I was required to sit at my table all day long and write the confession G-G had demanded. The moment my pencil stopped moving and my head began to nod, the guard would jump in and wake me up with a hard kick to my shins. My only defense was to keep writing the same sentence over and over and over again. Then, as I expected, Silverlips and Odd-Job came in with two other officers. Because he was wearing heavy infantry boots instead of his usual slippers, I braced myself for what I knew was coming. I admitted to him that I had instigated the Hawaiian Good Luck Sign and told him that my men had only done their duty in following their captain's lead. Yet, I refused to acknowledge that any other ruses had been used. Odd-Job reacted by belting me in the jaw with his infantry boot and then drop kicking me, knocking me into a rain of blows from the other two KORCOM officers who kept it up until I sagged to the floor, half-conscious. These visits and beatings were repeated twice a day and at least once a night over the next several days and soon my ribs felt cracked, my guts ruptured, my testicles ready to burst, and my face a pulp with all my front teeth loosened and almost falling out. I could tell that they no longer cared about disfiguring my face or crippling my body, only to stretch my pain as long as possible before I fainted into senseless oblivion. When they left me for a while to recover on my bunk, I could hear screams from other cells where other men were being given the same treatment. That horrible nightmarish feeling of last January when I was laid out under similar circumstances came back to me with full force, as if there had been no intervening time in between. As I had done then, I found myself again seriously considering some means of committing suicide in order to escape more torture and by my own dramatic death, perhaps satisfy the KORCOMs and cause them to let up on the rest of my men. But like them, I lay there in a seething kind of stupor and when the time came to stand up and take the next beating, drew upon prayer and a fundamental will to live and prevail over these beasts, and took it.

A new wrinkle was to bring one of my men in to watch me being beaten. Thus on one occasion they brought Law, who was black and blue from his own brutal sessions, and forced him to stand in the door of my cell while Silverlips and Odd-Job slammed me around. On another, it was Gene Lacy who witnessed my beatings and I remember the interpreter asking him why he would not tell them that I was the wicked CIA agent who had been conducting a vile campaign against them, to which he blandly answered: "Oh, I don't think so. He just made a few mistakes, that's all." For that he received a savage punch himself, but which he took full in the face with hardly a flinch. It gave me additional courage to see how staunchly and loyally these men were holding up.

But it also tore me apart that I could do nothing to help them or give them hope. I was by now staggering down the corridor once again urinating blood in a latrine fouled with the vomit of men sickened by their injuries. When I met one there, in the corridor, I could only rasp out a whispered: "At least we've rattled these bastards by making them look stupid to the outside world. That's something we can all be proud of!" I really meant it, and wanted to convey it to everybody. Surely North Korea must be the toughest Communist country of all for prisoners to wheedle through a sign or message to their own people.

On December 17, I saw Glorious General pull up into the compound's yard in his staff car and strut into our prison. A few minutes later Silverlips and Snotnose burst into my cell with a brand-new confession entirely composed by the KORCOMs and which contained the admission that I was a CIA agent who had caused all the provocations. When I refused to sign it, I received the usual kicking and slamming around before they left with dire threats of my impending trial and immediate execution. My thoughts returned to suicide. But I was too proud to take my own life. If I had to die and answer to my God, they would have to beat me to death.

Then suddenly the brutality stopped. It was like a faucet being turned off. The prison which had been echoing for ten days with the sounds of blows and cries of pain, fell silent within the hour, leaving only the mournful moan of the wind.

On the morning of the 19th, Glorious General convened an all-hands meeting which I at first thought might be the dreaded trial of our principal culprits. But G-G changed once again from a villain into an affable good guy. I could hardly believe my ears when he delivered through Silverlips an almost apologetic speech for the hardships we had suffered. "I realize," he said, "that you all repent what you have done and are truly sincere in your wishes to make amends. So we must let bygones be bygones. We must be humane to one another. And so I declare that all privileges are restored for eating, exercise, and cultural activities. I declare that we are still negotiating with your Imperialist warmongering masters in the hope of getting you to your loved homes for Christmas."

Perhaps he expected cheers, but we all stared at each other in stunned silence. I looked doubtfully at Skip Schumacher who had a lump under his left ear the size of a goose egg, then over the rest of my ship's complement twisting in their chairs to favor their bruised bodies, blinking through swollen, blackened eyes, their lumpy jaws hanging slack in amazement. Only yesterday we were being savagely beaten and cursed; now they were suddenly proposing to forget all, and turning on the charm. I never had a greater urge to hurl myself at the amiably smirking Glorious General and smash my fist into his teeth. At the least I wanted to jump up and lead my men in giving him a rousing Hawaiian Good Luck Sign. However, if they were about to begin another period of easy treatment, we sorely needed to take advantage of it so as to gather strength to withstand the next purge. So I held my peace.

Hell Week was over, but few of us were in any shape to enjoy the restored privileges, particularly ballgames and calisthenics. In fact, the harassed Medical Officer and his nurse (Sweat Pea) were extremely busy that day and the next trying to restore us to reasonably good health and physical appearance, applying their favorite poultices of hot paraffin-packs to the most crippling or visible bruises and making us reduce the swelling and discoloration of black eyes with warmed chicken eggs. Nearly everyone was undergoing some kind of medical treatment. The only chores required of my men was the signing of another confession. I found myself entirely excluded from this. Except for necessary visits by the Medical Officer and Sweat Pea, I found myself totally ignored by Glorious General and his minions. I was brought together with my officers for meals, but we were a battered and subdued group still cowed by the experience of Hell Week. The only exchange I initiated was to obtain information about the worst cases among our casualties. I could find no logical reason to dispel the feeling of despondency which was oppressing me as much as them, the most optimistic speech I could make was: "Let's hope they will lay off us for a month or two."

On December 22, Snotnose and Missile came into my cell and ordered me to strip completely, whereupon another officer known as Major Rectum joined them to give me a very thorough body inspection which was not entirely medical in character. Once they were satisfied that I had no secret messages sequestered in any of my bodily orifices, I was issued clean new underwear and uniform in which to dress. As soon as I had it on, they escorted me out of my cell to join another all-hands meeting in the "Club Room" and my heart skipped a beat when I noticed that *everybody* had been mustered in new uniforms. Was this to be a trial, a move to another prison, or release? I was certain only of the fact that something unusual was about to happen.

Glorious General strutted in with a smugly satisfied look on his face and for once came straight to the point before breaking into us with his customary tirade: "As I knew and told you from the beginning of this shameful Imperialist intrigue against our peace-loving Korean people," he declaimed with appropriate flourishes, "it has ended with the warmongering United States on its knees apologizing to us and assuring that no such provocation and many intrusions into our sovereign territorial waters shall occur again!" The rest of his speech was lost to me as my mind reeled with the implications of what he had just said. My disbelief that our country would ever offer an apology to the KORCOMs for "crimes" we of *Pueblo* had never committed was forgotten. I suddenly realized he was telling us that the conditions for our repatriation had been met, no matter what. He ordered several people to stand and told them that when they were returned home they must be sincere. Was this a ruse? I hoped not.

My heart was now skipping one beat after the other. For the next twenty-four hours I was to live in a euphoric expectation of deliverance mixed with awful apprehensions that at the last minute something would happen to ruin it all.

We were, for the last time, marched out into that bleak and now wintry compound to board buses which took us in convoy to Pyongyang's railroad station. There, a train was waiting surrounded by armed guards, who kept curious civilians away. The special train was made up of the same sleepers we had enjoyed on our excursion to Sinchon's shrine of atrocities, but in spite of the clean sheets and warm blankets of the bunks I was too keyed up to sleep. When the train was moving it moved too slowly, and when it stopped, as it frequently did, I sat up with a terrible sinking feeling in my chest until it jerked onward again. It came to a final stop shortly after dawn on what I could barely make out as a deserted spur, by peeking out through cracks in the drawn window curtains. I worried about it until Odd-Job (who had assisted in several of my worst beatings during Hell Week) came by to inform me that repatriation would start at 0930 hours. I was still worried—wracked by a nervous excitement that made the next half-hour on that deserted railroad siding very hard to take. It seemed an eternity before we were off-loaded around 0800 hours and carefully distributed, according to a predetermined schedule, into four buses.

I was put in the first one which was otherwise loaded with enlisted crewmen and our armed guards. We moved away from the railroad siding in convoy and traveled over a hilly road for some five miles, then came to a stop and remained parked there for another half-hour in a bleak area of frozen countryside near some grim looking isolated buildings. There were KORCOM soldiers standing around some vehicles which included an ambulance. Looking back through the rear window, I noticed that the other three buses were no longer with us and must have been diverted or stopped somewhere short of where we were. What was going on? After an interminable wait, Junior Colonel Odd-Job called me out of the bus and said through an interpreter: "You will come now to look and identify body of your dead sailor, Hodges."

I got out of our vehicle and was marched toward the ambulance where some KORCOM medics wearing white sterile face-masks had pulled a plain wooden coffin onto the tailgate. As I approached they unscrewed the lid, lifted it open and pulled aside the gauze shrouding Hodges' remains. I took a quick look at what had been my good fireman and said: "Yes, that is Duane Hodges," then turned away with a sickening feeling of grief and revulsion.

Odd-Job escorted me back to the bus where there was another agonized wait while he distributed copies to all twenty prisoners of the United States' apology for *Pueblo*'s crimes against the Korean people; the last two lines of the Verifaxed document had been crudely, obviously blocked out. Then he ordered me out of the bus again and marched me around the corner of the larger building where I was struck by the magic sight of The Bridge of Panmunjon stretching across a deep dry gully. It was guarded by KORCOM soldiers posted at every twenty to thirty feet of its one-hundred-fifty yard span . . . except the last ten where I could clearly see figures in American uniforms. We were almost free, but not quite.

Between me and the foot of the bridge there was a cluster of KORCOM officers watching my approach. I was suddenly halted by a solitary KORCOM on a porch of the building and who started shouting a tirade at me. He wore the shoulderboards of a general on his greatcoat and as he kept shouting furiously in Korean, I came to recognize him from photographs in the *"Ping-pong Times"* as the North Korean's chief negotiator in their bouts with Americans in Panmunjon, General "Frogface" Pak. He held me up for the better part of twenty minutes while my feet began freezing in the thin tennis shoes we had been issued when leaving our prison, yelling a steady stream of invectives while I stood there stamping and shivering in the bitter zero-degree cold. When he finally finished, an interpreter detached himself from the group of officers at the foot of that tantalizing bridge and mercifully only gave me a ten-second translation of General "Frogface" Pak's farewell torrent of words, in essence: "Get the hell out of our country, you no good warmongering Imperialist son-of-a-bitch and don't ever come back with another provocating spyship or we'll hang you by your capitalist neck!"

I did not want to argue the point. My next instructions came from Odd-Job. I obeyed them to the letter.

"Now walk across that bridge, Captain. Not stop. Not look back. Not make any bad move. Just walk across sincerely. Go now!"

I wanted to tear across the bridge at a wild run, but I crossed it exactly as he told me to, with a measured pace which might have increased slightly as I passed each of the guards, without looking back, without turning around to give them all a parting finger-sign, I took off my abominable hat when getting a little unsteady as I drew closer to the South Korean side and finally reaching it with a dizzy feeling, akin to being drunk. A flash bulb flared in my face. I was aware of a U. S. Army Colonel stepping forward to greet me with a jovial: "Welcome back, Commander Bucher!"

"Thank you, sir . . . thank you . . . it's good to be back."

He hesitated a moment, trying to keep a smile masking his emotions, then said, "Yes, well, I know this is hard on you, but they just delivered the body of your dead sailor, Hodges, and I need to have you identify him right away. It's necessary according to our agreement governing your release, you see."

"I have already identified him over there, Colonel."

His forced smile became genuine with relief and he exclaimed: "Oh, well in that case you won't have to do it again on this end. All I need you for now is to help me check off all your men as they come across. Supposed to come after you in inverse order of rank." He hefted a clipboard holding a typewritten list of names, flourishing a ballpoint pen held in a warmly gloved hand. The man radiated warmth, health and security.

But I was no longer paying any attention to him. I had turned around and was staring back expectantly toward the KORCOM side of the bridge, watching intently for the first of eighty-two of my *Pueblo* crew who were to follow me at such intervals that no more than three or four of them were on that long, long bridge at one time. And so they came with several second intervals between each, and now I greeted each repatriate with a loud pronouncement of his name and a hard, hearty handshake for all, like a coach receiving his long-distance runners of a most grueling race as they staggered across the finishing line.

For me the excitement and joy of being across that bridge with my crew was a numbing experience. There was so much to think about, so much to be thankful for. What should I do first? Even the bitter cold was forgotten. I stood there shaking hands with arms that turned into bodies with faces that had no real meaning. So often had I dreamt of leaving that hell hole. *How* could it actually be true? No dream had been this complete. Dear God, we've made it out!

In the sea of people clustered about it occurred to me that someone of probable importance was speaking to me.

". . . a change of clothes and some food; my car is there and I'd like to talk to you while we drive for just a few minutes; that is, if you feel up to it."

Who was this speaking? I was certain we had just been introduced but I had not been listening. I would find out who he was later.

"Sir, you mentioned *food*. Let's go."

We climbed aboard a waiting bus. Two or three others had already departed with some of my crew. My new acquaintance continued talking as soon as we were aboard.

"We caught several of the signals you and your people sent out. They helped a great deal. How do you feel, Commander?"

"I'm not sure, but we're ready to go home as soon as we can. Do you know our schedule?"

I really wondered who this man was. His civilian clothes were expensively tailored. I'd just wait and see.

"You will be meeting Admiral Rosenberg when we get down to base camp. It's just a few more minutes from here and the admiral will fill you in on the details of your schedule. But we in the State Department couldn't wait to see you there. First things first. But there is some time to let you get a little warm food and a change of clothes."

"Oh, I didn't understand you worked for the State Department," I thought aloud.

He looked at me like I was more than just a little remote and repeated his introduction all over. This time I listened. He was Dick Friedland, an official of our State Department.

The bus rambled over the twisting road for a couple more miles and drew up with a sudden jerk in front of a small complex of buildings. We got out and I was escorted into the nearest building through a side door into a large kind of sitting room. There a steward greeted me with a great beaming grin and a steaming cup of coffee. I couldn't possibly have been happier. My first cup of coffee in eleven months. I used to drink twenty to thirty cups of black coffee per day aboard ship. And then to top it off, there on the table were several glazed donuts. A repast fit for a king. I was delighted. The steward departed and I was left to myself for a few minutes while the strong odor and taste of the coffee convinced me that this was no dream. The grinning steward returned with a bundle of clothes for me. A blue Polaris submarine jumpsuit with my name tag already pinned on, a Navy blue work jacket with USS PUEBLO stenciled on the back and new skivvies, shoes and socks that all fit perfectly. "Here Captain, these are for you." I took them eagerly, wanting to divest myself of the KORCOM garb as quickly as possible.

"Good morning, Captain, welcome home." I turned still putting on my new gear and faced the friendly smile and easy manner of another gentleman I had not met so far. Then I noticed his uniform; he was a rear admiral. I jumped to attention.

"Good morning sir, it's just great to be back."

"I'm Admiral Rosenberg, Captain, and I'm here to see that everything goes smoothly for you and your men. There'll be a Navy doctor here to see you in a few minutes. Be sure and let him know if anything needs immediate attention. If you feel up to it, and only if you do, the gentlemen from the State Department want you to talk with them for a few minutes."

"I'm certainly up to that sir," I replied. I instantly liked the admiral.

"Your men are coming in the next room for some chow. Want to see them?"

"Yes sir, very much."

We walked into the next room and my men were entering eagerly looking forward to the chow awaiting them. I noticed another officer standing at the door and greeting each man as he came in with a friendly but heavy hand shake. He was dressed in Army winter clothing and had stars on his collar. When he saw me, he gave me a warm greeting. He was angular, tough in appearance, one eye covered by a patch.

"Welcome home, Commander, I'm General Bonesteel."

"Thank you sir." I'd heard of General Charles H. Bonesteel and knew that he was the Commanding General of our Ground Forces in Korea. He seemed to be able to call all of my men by their names when they came in and shook hands with each of them. A really marvelous feeling came over me. I had almost forgotten how really great it is to be an American.

I soon met the Navy doctor, a captain, who asked if I felt like talking with the State Department officer. I told him I felt up to it and he took me back in the room where I had changed clothes. Two State Department officers, including the one I had previously met, were waiting. We went outside to a car and the older of the two said, "I want to ride around and talk for just a bit, if it's OK with you, Captain."

"I'm ready," I replied.

"Fine, get aboard." He opened the door for me and I deferred to him and got in last. The other gentleman got in front and drove.

"Let's get right to the point," he said and looked me square in the eye. "Did *Pueblo* at any time ever get inside the North Korean twelve mile claim?"

"No sir," I stated flatly and directly. "Neither by design nor by accident, I assure you."

"That's what we thought, but I'm relieved to hear it from you." Then he quickly went on. "There are a group of news people for whom we are going to hold a short press conference. Would you mind coming there and making a statement?"

"No sir, it will be a pleasure to talk to real news people for a change."

He then assured me that the doctor would be present and that he would insure I was not kept too long by the newsmen. We drove directly to the building where the press was waiting.

There must have been two hundred people jammed into the hall, and more cameras and television rigs than I had ever seen before. We climbed the stairs to a raised stage and I was introduced to Navy Captain Vincent Thomas, whom I would get to know much better during the months ahead. The doctor was seated on stage. Cameramen in front were beckoning me to stand up and wave. I did so, but not without a great deal of nervousness. The gentleman from the State Department bade me be seated and he made a short introductory statement to those present, informing them that I would make a short statement and then answer a few questions from the floor. There was brief applause when I stood up to speak. I began nervously but soon warmed to the task. I told them categorically that there had never been any intrusions, that the ship had been pirated on the high seas by the North Koreans, that it had been a slaughter out there the day of the seizure. I said that my men had performed well at all times and that I was proud of them. Questions began when I completed the statement and I answered them as directly and completely as I could. Within a few minutes the doctor indicated that he thought that I had had enough. When I turned to go, I unexpectedly received another long round of embarrassing applause.

We drove away directly to a helicopter pad and took off for the 121st Army Evacuation Hospital which was within a half-hour flight. The men from the Department of State thanked me before we landed, and wished me luck. I thanked them for their many courtesies of the day. The chopper settled and leaned into an expert landing at the hospital. It must have been 1400 hours by then. I met several more people who welcomed me home. One of them, a nurse, quickly shooed away the others and took me to my bed in a ward where all my officers were already well encampe Gene, Tim and Skip were talking excitedly. Steve was lying on his bed staring at the ceiling in disbelief, while Ed was sitting quietly talking to him. I told them where I had been and what had happened and answered their questions. Then Steve told me there would be an interdenominational service in the hospital chapel in about a half hour.

I was detained a few moments by one of the doctors and was the last of the crew to enter the chapel. A seat in front had been reserved. Together with the others of *Pueblo*'s crew I gave thanks to my God for the next several minutes. After the service, several of the crew came over and wished me a happy holiday with great wide grins.

Back in our ward Gene asked of no one in particular: "It's Christmas and we are going home, if for no other reasons we should have some Christmas cheer."

I immediately agreed, and said to Tim: "Seems to me like a Supply Officer function. How about getting hot, Lieutenant (junior grade) Harris. Earn your pay."

"Right away, Cap'n," Tim replied. He set off in search of the necessary ingredients. A while later he was back.

"Sorry, Cap'n, but the nurse says doctor's orders that none of us is to get any booze until he has had time to check us."

"Anybody here that doesn't feel good?" I queried.

"I'm in great shape," said Skip.

"Me too," echoed Tim.

I went immediately in search of the head nurse I'd seen earlier.

"I'll have to ask the doctor," the nurse said when I had put forth the proposition that all of my men should be allowed just one glass of eggnog with brandy to celebrate the occasion. Just as she was about to go find him, Rear Admiral Edwin M. Rosenberg arrived.

"How are they treating you, Skipper?"

"Just great sir," I replied.

"I thought you might like to visit each of your crew's wards for a few minutes," he said. "I will be glad to go along if you don't mind."

I explained the problem of the Christmas cheer to the Admiral and he immediately went with the nurse in search of the chief doctor, a Colonel. He returned victorious and said it was being taken care of.

We visited each ward and had a glass of strong eggnog with my men. There being five different wards, I was soon in really great shape. The men in each of the wards gave a cheer when the Admiral and I entered, and were all clearly happy to be out of the Peoples Paradise to the North. While we were in the ward that contained Law and others, I almost broke up. I was just so proud of everybody.

Each of us was given various medication to calm him down a bit. It was touch and go whether the doctors would turn us loose to go home the next day which was Christmas Eve. If we could start back then, we would gain a day crossing the International Date Line and be home for Christmas Eve. The prospect had us all keyed up. In any event we would be home by sometime Christmas Day at the latest, because the doctors planned to keep us no longer than two days. Everyone was doing his level best to see that we made it. Well over half the Army hospital staff gave up part of their holiday at home to expedite our return.

The next morning we learned we would leave about noon. Two Air Force C-126s took us from an Air Force base near Seoul. We stopped at Midway Island to refuel. The Commander in Chief of the Pacific Fleet, Admiral John J. Hyland, was there to greet us even though it was about 0200. I had been using a borrowed commander's hat from a chaplain who was accompanying us. Admiral Rosenberg had radioed ahead without my knowledge and to my great surprise, Admiral Hyland presented me with a brand-new hat. I know those hats are expensive and know that he probably paid for it himself. I thoroughly appreciated the gesture. While we were on the ground at Midway a conference room was prepared and some newsmen as well as several naval officers were there expecting to hear what happened to *Pueblo*. I took the stage and told them what had happened. I didn't give a very clear picture, I'm afraid. I was highly emotional and repeated myself several times. I tried to take the entire responsibility for *Pueblo*'s loss. My talk became disjointed as I fumbled along, and I sensed that Admiral Hyland was not exactly pleased with what I had to say. Well, I hadn't given excuses. But I realized that if I were going to have to go through such presentations again, I must try to shake the emotions out of my heart and head. It would not prove an easy thing to do.

I switched airplanes on the next leg of our journey. This was arranged by Admiral Rosenberg, so that I could spend at least part of the flight with all of my crew. Admiral Rosenberg was the most considerate person I ever had the privilege of meeting. I told him so, but he brushed it off with noticeable embarrassment. The remainder of the flight home was spent in fitful sleep and short jittery talks with my men. With each passing mile we became closer and closer to our wives, girlfriends, children, friends. Admiral Rosenberg announced that the Navy had made arrangements for all of the crew's immediate dependents to join them. They probably would be in San Diego when we arrived. I knew Rose would be there; that was home, home, home. I thought of all it meant to me. Emotional thoughts allowed me little sleep.

I awoke with a start as dawn was breaking. I went to one of the portholes and peered out. Up ahead I could see light beginning to break over the Pacific in magnificent colors. I needed a cup of coffee and the Air Force Stewardess aboard cheerfully and quickly brought me one. Captain Vince Thomas was awake, so I went over and sat with him. He told me that he was a Public Affairs Officer and that it would be his job for the next several days to guide us in our relationships with the press, and to give advice if it were solicited. I had hardly, if ever, had dealings with PAO types before and I was very surprised that they had assigned a Captain to look after us. How could there possibly be enough work to keep a Navy Captain busy with our little group? He told me there would be some newsmen at Miramar Naval Airfield, San Diego, when we arrived and he advised me against making any long statements. He obviously knew that I was riding on a very high emotional ridge. I thanked him for his advice. He seemed a straight shooter then, and I never had reason to doubt my first impression in the many months to come.

Soon everyone was awake and breakfast was served. The bow string drew tighter and tighter. What would I say to Rose when I first saw her? Would she recognize her once heavy, now skinny husband? I had regained some weight during the summer and fall in Korea and was now about 127 pounds. A long way from the 205 I had been when captured. But I felt better than I had in the past many months. There were still a few minor problems that I was sure would respond as soon as I got home and began eating like an American again. I looked around the plane at my men. It was obvious they were getting the same fever sailors for centuries have experienced away from home. No sailor escapes the effects of this peculiar fever. Many of the crew were preening themselves to make the best appearance possible. We were all outfitted in Polaris submarine uniforms and blue work jackets and the men all had the blue Navy work hat that so closely resembles a baseball hat. About an hour to go before landing, we had a report from the pilot. He was expecting to roll into the blocks at 1400 local time San Diego. Goose bumps appeared on the arms of several men, including my own. Neck hackles were up on all of us. Admiral Rosenberg knew of our terrible anticipation and moved from man to man talking to each, helping to settle him.

"I can see land below," someone in the crew shouted, who was back where he could see out of a porthole.

We rolled into the blocks and the pilot cut the jet engines, the door swung open almost immediately. My God, they are playing the *Lonely Bull*, Herb Alpert's great tune and our theme song! How the hell did they know about that? Admiral Rosenberg had heard about it from one of the crew, and had sent a message ahead to the people who handled our arrival arrangements. When we could begin deplaning I was summoned forward by Admiral Rosenberg. I was to be the first out. The Navy band playing our theme was the greatest and sweetest music I had ever heard. If I could only control my emotions! I fought back tears I felt rising in my eyes and came forward where I was introduced to Vice Admiral Allen M. Shinn, Commander of Naval Air Force Pacific

Fleet. He was a bear of a man and my hand disappeared into his own as he welcomed me home.

"Your wife and boys are waiting for you, Commander," he said. I thanked him in passing, totally ignoring my manners, I'm afraid, and pressed outside ahead of the admiral. The crowd was immense. The band continued the *Lonely Bull*. I searched the multitude about two hundred feet away for my Rose. Then I saw her, more beautiful than I had ever remembered! She was smiling radiantly, Mark and Mike were at her side. I heard the voices of many shouting "Welcome home." It was all I could do to avoid breaking into a run. We fell into each other's arms and I barely could keep back the tears. My embrace included Rose and both Mark and Mike.

"I love you, Rose"

"Oh, Pete!" she cried.

After a long desperate hug that tried to shake off the memories of the bitter past eleven months, I stepped back to look at my sons more closely. "You guys are huge," I said to them both. Mark's face was damp with tears and he grabbed me. We hugged each other.

Mike was next and I could literally feel the tremendous strength he had gained during the past year of my absence.

"Welcome back, Dad."

"It's so good to see you again, Mike."

Then Rose and I kissed softly and sweetly, and longingly.

"Damn, it's good to see you back, Pete." The voice was familiar and close at hand. I looked up from our kiss and saw my old shipmate and friend with his wife, Alan and Jean Hemphill. I reached out and took his hand in mine and gave Jean a kiss.

Rose was saying, "Pete, let me introduce you to my lawyer, Miles Harvey. Miles, this is Pete." I reached out and shook hands with Miles.

"Welcome home, Commander."

"Thank you, sir; it's great to be home."

"What do you need a lawyer for, honey?" I asked Rose.

"Oh, I'll explain it all later, Pete." I put it out of my mind but looked at Miles carefully. He was about my height, younger by a few years, dark hair neatly trimmed and neatly dressed I looked him in the eye and his open honest return look made me feel at ease. We had never even known any lawyers before, let alone needed one.

Admiral Shinn was standing patiently aside and I suddenly became aware of him. I hastened to introduce Rose, but they had already met. "Whenever you are ready Skipper, we will go over and I will introduce you to Mr. and Mrs. Hodges, the parents of your dead crewman." I went with him immediately and was introduced to the Hodges. Mr. Hodges shook my hand and I was hugged by Mrs. Hodges. They were anxious to hear from me just how their son had died. I told them exactly how it had happened and that I knew what a great personal loss they had sustained.

"You have every reason to be proud of your son, he died while carrying out his duties. Those duties were highly important to our country. They included the need to destroy highly classified papers. I had personally ordered that those papers be destroyed and Duane was, as usual, one of the first to cheerfully and determinedly carry out orders when they were given. I consider that your son died a hero. His memory will always be an inspiration to us."

Both Mr. and Mrs. Hodges listened intently to each word I spoke. They indicated that they would very much like to talk more with me before they returned to their home in Creswell, Oregon. I assured them that I would be happy to as soon as possible. Fireman Duane D. Hodges' casket was removed from one of the aircraft that we had returned in and was carried to a place of honor by a Navy Honor Guard. All present were called to attention and taps and the National Anthem were played in his honor. Rose stood at my side. The experience of meeting the Hodges and presiding at planeside honors was a heavy and sad duty for me. My thoughts went to his sacrifice and then to the fact that we had not completed the job of destroying classified material on that day of seizure. I felt we had let Duane Hodges down by our lack of success and when it came my time to speak to the assembled crowd I tried to convey those feelings. I considered myself personally responsible for our failure to completely destroy our classified material and yet I knew that many had done much that fateful day.

My thoughts then ranged to those of fury with those responsible for planning and outfitting ships like *Pueblo*. "Damn it all to hell," I thought, but no amount of blame shifting would ever relieve me of my own responsibility. Never had I understood so well the old Navy adage about "the loneliness of command."

I was shaken from my reverie by Rose. "Come on, Pete, they are waiting officially to welcome you back home." We went hand in hand to a podium set up outside, where I recognized the Governor of California, Ronald Reagan, standing and chatting with other officials. As we approached he turned to me.

"Welcome home, Pete, and Merry Christmas. I'll bet neither of us dreamed we would be meeting in circumstances like these when we made that movie thirteen years ago."

I couldn't believe that the Governor remembered my name and that brief association we had when in 1957 he had been the star in a movie about submarines and for which they had picked the submarine to which I was attached, the USS *Besugo* (SS-321). He must have met thousands of people since then. Our brief acquaintance had been limited to about a week and even that was really a casual one, for I had been a LTJG at the time and had been assigned to play a non-speaking background role in a couple of the scenes.

"Thank you sir, I'm surprised you remember," I said.

Governor Reagan then made a few remarks of official welcome and shook hands with me and reacquainted me with Nancy, his wife. His is a busy schedule and he had to take immediate departure.

Mayor Walter Hahn, Jr. of San Diego spoke next and also welcomed the crew. He also noted that a local radio station had taken up quite a large collection of money amounting to several thousands of dollars for my crew and their dependents. The El Cortes Hotel was donating space for all my crew's dependents. I was absolutely unprepared for such kindness and considerations as we had already received, still more was to come. The mayor continued to address the large gathering ". . . and so you, Commander Bucher, will know how we feel about you and your men, let me present you with the Key to the City of San Diego." The mayor must have been almost as jittery as I was, because he extended and took back the key about four times while he continued to talk. Finally, he completed his remarks, put the key into his pocket and departed. I had my first really honest to goodness laugh since being back in my country. Even a badly fouled up performance like that had to be typical of my people. God bless us all, I thought as he departed.

The crew and their families and friends were being gathered together and placed aboard buses. I had already been told we would be going to the Balboa Naval Hospital for medical examination. Another familiar voice called to me from the crowd, I noticed another friend and shipmate from submarine days, Lieutenaut Jim Worthington, USN. He had tears in his eyes. I called out to him in answer, then someone said, "Commander, it's time to leave, a bus is waiting for you and your family and there are people all along the route who want to have a look at you and welcome you too." I looked around and Rose was right beside me; Mark and Mike were standing over to the side looking every bit as self-conscious as they were feeling.

"OK honey, hey Mark, Mike, let's go."

The bus ride was thrilling. I sat beside a window and waved and gave a thumbs up sign to the hundreds of people who lined our route. People had big and small signs with words of welcome written on them. People were applauding, others waving and some who just happened to be passing looked with curiosity as we drove along Route 495 and turned off to the Naval Hospital.

I was exhausted when we got to the hospital. Fatigue was taking its toll. I began to realize just how poor my health really was. Nevertheless, I doubt there is any better tonic or elixir than a reunion with your family, when the absence has been long. My head was spinning, comprehension of all that had transpired lay outside my grasp. Rose was telling me about the many letters and telegrams all wishing me welcome. Someone issued me a plasticized green card with a large P stamped on it. A clip was glued to the back. I was told that we had to wear that card all the time. We were in a compound surrounded by a high fence. My first thought was that the P must stand for prisoner—but, of course, that was ridiculous—it had to stand for Patient.

I was assigned a room on the lower deck of a large barracks-like building that housed all of my crew. We were told that until certain quarantines were met and hospital checks made, we wouldn't be able to leave the compound. Our immediate families could visit whenever they liked. A small building standing near our barracks was made into a gathering place for all of us with our families. I could understand the need for certain rules of quarantine, but I wondered whether meetings with wives or girlfriends were going to be private. I hunted up a Navy Captain and told him of the problem and he said he would immediately take it up with the administration. It was three days before my question was answered. It would be several days longer before others would see their loved ones in privacy.

We ate in the recreation area and the best of meals were provided. A large Christmas tree, beautifully decorated stood in the dining room. Just after dinner, I was transferred to a regular hospital room, but was given free reign to move about and return to visit my family at the recreation center. Rose took the boys home and returned within one hour. We joined each other and the crew who were all getting reacquainted with their families. I had the pleasure of meeting some of the families of my crew for the first time. Some of the handshakes I received from fathers and brothers of my crew nearly broke my hand. Mothers and wives hugged and kissed me. It was overwhelming.

Rose and I finally sneaked away to the rear of the room and began our own reunion amid kisses, handholding and loving words that we found ourselves saying for the first time in such a long time. I loved her so deeply and wanted to tell her, I felt she had much she wanted to say too. But neither of us knew where to begin. Instead of talking, we just sat there next to each other getting used to the feel of our hands entwined, our hearts and thoughts vibrating with love. Time went by, little was said between us. I think everyone else was gone. On the far wall a clock kept up its steady march.

"Rose, darling," I kissed her tenderly, "it's after midnight . . . Merry Christmas."

"Oh Pete, I love you so very much . . . Merry Christmas."

THE AFTERMATH

Along with the many medical checks conducted at the Balboa Naval Hospital, each crew member was thoroughly debriefed by Naval Intelligence personnel. Every detail of each person's experience was examined thoroughly. Members of the crew were told that all information divulged during this Classified debriefing would be privileged information, and that it would not be available to attorneys or anyone connected with the Court in the event a Court of Inquiry or Courts-Martial was to be held. I advised my entire crew to cooperate fully with the intelligence investigators and I did so myself, telling everything that has been recounted in the main body of this book and much more that cannot be told publicly because of the classified nature of the material.

Within a few days, it was announced that there would indeed be a full scale Court of Inquiry. I know the importance of soon bringing cases before a court of law in order that justice may be swiftly delivered. However, I considered that I, as well as many others in the crew, should be given time to build up our strength before such a proceeding should begin. Many of us were emotionally overwrought for several weeks following our return. It was not possible for me to make an instant recovery from months of terror and apprehension, and in addition regain the physical strength required to face daily appearances in court. My first thought about the forthcoming Court of Inquiry was that it should be delayed until all hands were in good physical condition. However, one of the conditions for the release of crewmen whose enlistments had already expired during confinement, which included about half of them, was that they would be held in the Navy unconditionally until such time as the coming Court of Inquiry had ended.

I knew that at the very least I would be named an interested party before the court and would therefore be required to be there on a daily basis. I talked the matter over with Rose and told her I thought that I could get through the Court of Inquiry, even if it were to be held publicly. She reluctantly agreed that it was the best thing to do, in view of the many people who were anxiously looking forward to their discharges.

Because of my restless energy, Rear Admiral H. D. Worden, MC, USN, the Commanding Officer of the hospital had me confined to my hospital room where I found myself once again in solitary confinement. Only Rose was allowed to visit me, and even the telephone was removed. A marine stood guard in front of my door, which made access to the hall telephone difficult. Nevertheless, I was able to talk my way past the guard on a couple of occasions to make calls. Within two weeks we were given conditional releases to leave the hospital premises. I was at last able to see the home that Rose and the children had been living in since shortly after the *Pueblo* was seized.

During the afternoon and evening Rose told me what had happened during my absence. I was very curious to learn how she had fared. She gave me a full rundown, supplemented by press clippings, including an issue of *Time* magazine with a painting of me on the cover. I was surprised. I never thought that the *Pueblo* was going to be a big news story. As I read the article, I realized why. A high naval officer stated that "Bucher sure as hell had better have a damn good excuse for giving up that ship." I was puzzled. Why hadn't officers familiar with our operation explained that Environmental Research Ships like *Pueblo* were designed to operate as unarmed ships? As I read on, it became evident that a lot of people were trying to evade responsibility. Every good naval officer I had served under during my career emphasized that standing up and being counted when it hurt was what Navy tradition was all about. I urged Rose to tell me what had happened to her.

She told me of the many trials and bitter disappointments she had experienced during my absence.

A captain's wife is by tradition the unofficial morale officer for the dependents of her husband's shipmates when his ship is at sea and she is provided a list of addresses for all officers and crew. Rose took her duties seriously and soon after *Pueblo*'s seizure was writing comforting letters to the many concerned families on her list, trying to sustain their hope that the United States would *do something* quick and positive to effect our release. Within days of the disaster she received scores of telegrams and telephone calls from people who had served with me in other commands, all offering help and support. But from some high government officials she received little besides advice to "sit tight, lady, stay at home and knit, and stay out of our hair!" This she tried to do for several weeks while all she noticed being done at higher naval and governmental levels was a lot of talking and arguing back and forth, but no apparent action. Then even the talk began to taper off into lapses of silence signifying a growing apathy. Rose stopped waiting and began a personal struggle to keep the *Pueblo* issue alive. Her letters to families of my officers and crew changed in tone, urging them to in turn write the Navy and governmental officials pleading with them not to forget the *Pueblo* and to initiate some meaningful efforts. She began a direct campaign toward this end, writing, telephoning and personally calling upon many influential Navy and civil authorities. She had become incensed by a number of captains and admirals who had jumped to conclusions without knowing the facts and made very uncomplimentary statements about me "giving up the ship." However, her main purpose was to keep the pot boiling and although throwing herself into a national controversy and becoming a public figure was totally foreign to her nature and experience, she gritted her teeth and did so with will and energy. Many friends and literally thousands of strangers within the naval community and public at large were inspired by her determination, bringing about a popular spontaneous movement which rallied to the slogan: *REMEMBER THE PUEBLO.*

By April 1968 that slogan was appearing all over the country (and even on foreign bases) as lapel buttons and automobile bumper-stickers. As this was a presidential election year, politicians of both major parties took notice of a burgeoning popular interest. Rose was invited to address many gatherings, which she attempted to do in a nonpartisan fashion and purely motivated by her burning desire to have her husband and all *Pueblo*'s complement released from North Korean imprisonment. The support she received was enormous, but she was also branded in higher military and government echelons as a publicity-seeking troublemaker. It was obvious that some important personages of the Pentagon and State Department were anxious to shut her up. To Remember the Pueblo was becoming a hot political potato for the incumbent administration, an emotional issue to be exploited by its opposition, and developing into an acute embarrassment for a number of admirals. For Rose it became a nightmare in which she, the heretofore anonymous little Navy wife, suddenly found herself cast in the public eye in a dual role of suffering heroine and meddling shrew, neither of which suited her. Under the circumstances it is understandable that she became oversensitive and overstrained at times. She thought that her house and telephone had been "bugged" and for her peace of mind asked the local San Diego naval authorities to check it out. They found no "bugs," but a sympathetic commander advised her to engage a lawyer and left her the names of three whom he knew personally. One of them was E. Miles Harvey (a commander in the Naval Reserve whom I later found out to be an Intelligence subspecialist), and he turned out the one she picked more or less at random. It was a fortunate choice for her and later on, for me. Local naval headquarters and personnel were sympathetic and helpful and my old shipmate Lieutenant Commander Alan P. Hemphill and his wife Jean were great friends and active supporters. Yet the many who rallied to her side were subjected to a steady pressure from above which manifested itself in such petty actions as having base commanders issue official orders that REMEMBER THE PUEBLO stickers were not to be displayed on their bases, stating that these were considered "disloyal"!

As Rose continued her story, I found it hard to believe that some of the things she told me had really happened. The one bright spot seemed to be the determination of a large segment of the American public to force the issue through letter-writing campaigns. Rose said many United States Senators and Congressmen had agreed with her. Congressmen William Scherle, Bob Wilson and many others had been particularly impressive. She also singled out Senator Stephen M. Young, who had stated *Pueblo* had been full of CIA personnel. But Secretary of State Dean Rusk, whom she had called on personally, had assured her that no CIA personnel were aboard *Pueblo*. I told her of the beatings that were meted out to some of my men because of Senator Young's statement. "I wish he could have seen the beatings he was responsible for."

Rose had had a very frustrating time, contributed to by the Navy, although they had, in other ways, gone to great lengths to assist her. She was particularly grateful to the many, many people who had actually taken the plight of *Pueblo* to their hearts. She had received over 25,000 letters.

I have yet to find the time to read those letters, but I still look forward to it.

I asked Miles if he would represent me at the Court of Inquiry. He agreed, but said we better get moving if he were going to do a good job. There were only seven days left until it began. "Do you have any Military counsel assigned yet?" "No sir, not yet, but there is one man who I would certainly like to have, my old boss at SUBFLOT SEVEN, Captain Henry B. Sweitzer, I believe he is assigned as an aide to the Chairman of the Joint Chiefs of Staff, General Wheeler. I hope he will be able to find time. He must be damn busy." Miles smiled in his easy manner and reached for the phone in his office, "Alice, get me" (and here he mentioned a name I had never heard) "on the phone, will you please." Then to me, "Captain Julien le Bourgeois is senior aide to CNO and a good friend of mine, I'll ask him about your friend." Well, I thought to myself, my lawyer knows his way around.

The next day my suspicions were confirmed. Captain Sweitzer would not be available. General Earle G. Wheeler was getting ready to present the military budget requests to Congress for the coming fiscal year and he needed Hank's expert advice. "But be of good cheer, Pete," Miles said. "CNO's office is scouting around for a good man for you." I wondered if they would really find a good man. I knew that I needed the best there was. I knew I had to tell the full story of *Pueblo* even if some of it hurt. I owed this, and much more, to my country and the Navy.

Later that day, Miles called to tell me that Captain James E. Keys, JAGC, USN, had been assigned as my military counsel. He came down from his assignment in San Francisco on the following day. We had been casual acquaintances when I was stationed in the Far East. I approved of him, and Captain Keys became part of our team. At this point, the opening of Court was delayed one week because of the poor state of my health.

Miles and Jim began going over the evidence I was to present in Court. I wrote down the things I intended to give testimony on. I decided to testify to the Court of Inquiry only on those aspects of *Pueblo* operations that applied to my own conduct, omitting any references to poor or unsatisfactory conduct on the part of any of my crew of officers. First of all, I decided against mentioning Gene Lacy, or the stopping of *Pueblo*. Secondly, I considered that Lieutenant Murphy's conduct both before and during the loss of my ship was more properly the subject of his Fitness Report, which I would soon be completing. I intended to make it clear that I was the commanding officer of *Pueblo* and that I was responsible for all the decisions that had been made on the day we were seized and during our imprisonment. I also intended to make sure that the Court was made aware that my ship had been inadequately prepared by the Navy. I assumed that the Court would seek testimony from those officers who made the decisions disapproving my requests for an adequate destruct system, a reduction in the number of classified documents that we carried, failure on the part of my Operational Commander and/or CINCPACFLT properly to inform me of vital information concerning activities in Korea in the days just prior to my confrontation with the KORCOMs, failure adequately to plan for AGER internal organization, which permitted clear divisions between the Commanding Officer and the Officer in Charge of the Special Detachment, failure of CINCPACFLT to execute contingency plans in our defense or in retaliation for the KORCOM act of piracy, finally, the apparent failure on the part of higher command properly to understand and realize the effect of inadequately arming and failing to provide adequate personnel and/or training in the use of the armament that was foisted on *Pueblo,* a matter of days just prior to our sailing.

I wanted someone to testify just how we were supposed to have been ready for instant battle, and not ready at the same time. (I was later to decide that the Court itself never understood this basic conflict, for which I hold myself somewhat responsible by not being more aggressive during the hearing and forcing the issue. I also feel that if the Court of Inquiry had been delayed until I had regained my health and had time to get over the tremendous emotional shock of freedom, I would have pursued these matters without letup until they were either answered or until I had exhausted every effort to obtain answers.

These points had been on my mind during the many long months of captivity and now that I had a chance to get some answers, I found myself too emotionally involved to bring the matters before the Court successfully.

The Court of Inquiry into the seizure of *Pueblo* was convened on January 20, 1969. Members of the Court consisted of the following naval officers:

Vice Admiral Harold S. Bowen, USN (President of the Court); Rear Admiral H. W. White, USN; Rear Admiral E. E. Grimm, USN; Rear Admiral R. R. Pratt; and Rear Admiral A. A. Bergner, USN. All of these admirals had seen action in World War II and perhaps some had actually been in the shooting war in Korea in 1953. They comprised a distinguished group of gentlemen and they appeared determined to discharge their duties and relentlessly to pursue the facts. The Court would be conducted in both open and closed hearing, the closed hearings were to deal with materials that were classified in nature and could effect the security of the country.

The public interest in the Court of Inquiry was instantly apparent. I was receiving hundreds of telegrams. Sacks were required to carry all the mail that came to me personally. Over forty cameramen and scores of reporters were covering the story. Among those who remained throughout the proceedings were Jim Lucas (Scripps-Howard), George Wilson (Washington *Post*), Bernie Weintraub (New York *Times*), Carl Fleming (*Newsweek*), Tim Tyler (*Time*), Sid Moody and Jules Loh (Associated Press),

Trevor Armbrister, formerly of the *Saturday Evening Post* who would later compile interviews from over three hundred persons directly and indirectly involved with the *Pueblo* and those who sailed in her. Other news media personalities who were frequently present were Lloyd Shearer, the Editor at large of *Parade* Magazine, Terry Drinkwater of CBS Television news, Liz Trotter of NBC Television news, and Bob Berrigan of ABC-TV news.

The Counsels for the Court were appointed. They were Captain William Newsome, JAGC, USN, and Assistant Counsel, Commander William Clemons, JAGC, USN. Thus the stage was set for the commencement of testimony. I was called to testify first.

My first problems in controlling my emotions came early. On the second day of my testimony, I was describing my reaction to being ordered shot by the KORCOMs for refusing to sign their initial confession. When I tried to describe how I passed the two minutes until my brains were to have been blown out, by concentrating on my love for Rose, I found myself choking up. I wrestled for control and won. I was embarrassed that I had come close to breaking down, and I wanted to call for a postponement of the hearings, but I knew that my crew would be the losers if that happened. So I steeled myself and plowed ahead.

The remainder of my testimony was delivered without emotion. But as my shipmates trooped past to the witness stand, I vividly recalled their cries of terror in prison. When as many of them testified that their faith in God and in their Commanding Officer kept them going during imprisonment, I was again overcome with emotion, and for the first time broke down and sobbed. I was helped to my feet by Miles and lurched out the side door of the court room. I could not return that day.

Meanwhile, the Court had taken a divergent tack in pursuit of each crew member's understanding of the Code of Conduct: whether they thought they had broken it, and why. In closed session, with expert witnesses, I presented what I believed to be irrefutable testimony that the Code of Conduct, insofar as it applied to refusing to talk in captivity beyond giving name, rank and serial number, was not applicable to the officers and crew of *Pueblo*.

However, the signing of confessions was another matter. Here

I felt that the North Koreans had given the lie to any "confession" made by us from the moment they released the first forced confession I signed when they threatened to execute my crew members. In that confession (see appendix), the language is positive proof that it was not composed by an American.

For a time, it appeared that all references to the Code of Conduct would be stricken, since one day the Senior Counsel to the Court declared that he had received official notice from CINCPAC that the Code was not applicable to the *Pueblo* incident. The explanation was that we had been held illegally by North Korea, since no state of war existed between our countries. Then, within a day or so, Washington apparently reversed itself and told the Court that the Code was applicable and that they should resume their original line of questioning. Testimony dragged on. Another edict from CINCPAC naval officials decreed that each member of the crew testify.

Various testimony was taken during the weeks that followed. Much of it surprised, even shocked, me in its implications. Some testimony was taken in closed session that did not, in my opinion, deal with security matters, and should have been taken in open session. My two U. S. Marine Corps interpreters testified that they did not possess the required level of the Korean language to discharge their duties. They both testified that they had informed their superiors at the assigning command of this fact and that their warnings had gone totally unheeded. Nor was I informed of their lack of proficiency, although they also testified that they had informed *Pueblo*'s Officer in Charge of the Special Operations Detachment of these problems upon reporting aboard the day before we sailed. *If I had known their interpretive inability, I would have refused to undertake the operation until they had been replaced by personnel who could handle that assignment.* If they had been competent interpreters, it is probable that I would have had sufficient warning of North Korean intentions on January 23, 1968, to have *avoided* capture, or at the very least, to have better prepared to carry out classified documents and equipment destruction.

I learned that two days prior to my confrontation with the KORCOMs, the North Koreans had dispatched a raid of thirty odd infiltrators across the border into South Korea, where their mission was to assassinate President Park. This was the so-called Blue House Raid. The raiders were either caught or killed before they could complete their mission. This story made headlines around the world, but its significance was apparently lost on the people responsible for sending me daily intelligence reports, since I was never informed of it. My anger over failure to convey this information has not been lessened by the knowledge that at least one of the men responsible for our daily intelligence reports was commended for his superb performance while charged with that responsibility. Had I been informed of the Blue House Raid, I would have operated *Pueblo* much further out from Wonsan on that fateful day, probably at least 30 miles from nearest land. I very much doubt that the KORCOMs would have ventured that far out to sea to investigate me in their small ships and boats. It is possible, however, that had they known our position, even at a much greater distance from land, that they would have attacked us with aircraft, and perhaps could have sunk us. But the ship would not have been seized.

I also learned about the failure of a warning message, originated by the National Security Agency, to reach my operational commander. This fact alone is incredible! The warning message dealt with the risk assignment for our mission, which had been evaluated as Minimal by our immediate commander and had been seconded through the chain of command all the way to, and, including the Joint Chiefs of Staff. The message which failed to reach the operational commander cast doubt on the veracity of assigning a Minimum Risk to the use of an AGER such as *Pueblo* to engage in an overt intelligence collection mission along the coast of North Korea.

I found out at this time, much to my surprise, that our finest nuclear aircraft carrier, USS *Enterprise*, had been at sea within 510 miles of the scene of our seizure—no more than one hour's flying time for her strike aircraft to come to our assistance. Furthermore she had received copies of our distress signals only fifty minutes after they were transmitted from *Pueblo* and therefore knew about our predicament soon enough to take action. It transpired that preparations were made to launch the USS *Enterprise's* fighter-bombers and that the ship was actually turned around and steamed at high speed for two hours in our direction in order to close the distance. But there was also a lot of hesitation, debate and equivocation on her admiral's bridge. Urgent messages were dispatched to Washington asking for instructions which (technically, at least) could have been taken by the responsible officer on the spot. Time wasted—opportunity lost! In the end, twilight and gathering darkness combined with other marginal tactical considerations for the aircraft and lack of quick, firm command decisions, resulted in nothing being done. *Enterprise* turned back on her previous course to the Philippine Islands, leaving *Pueblo* to her ignominious fate. Why? Had the criteria of *"minimum risk"* evaluation infected our whole Navy to a point of paralysis and meaningless posturing? It seemed to me that the Court of Inquiry might have done well to delve into these questions, but they did not.

I was distressed by the fact that, during the course of the Court of Inquiry, when I had requested a copy of the letters I had written during the conversion of *Pueblo* indicating my recommendations, I was at first told that the documents were not available. I blew my top and threatened to go to the President of the Court if they were not supplied. The following day, I discovered to my satisfaction that the documents would indeed be made available.

One morning during a recess in the proceedings, my Junior Officer, Lieutenant (jg) Tim Harris, came to me with a story that I found difficult to believe. A Navy captain had badgered him during an out of court questioning period. Tim had been told in so many words that he had better come up with something that would help the Court to hang his captain, or else. My reaction was immediate. I went to Miles, just barely able to control myself, and told him that these proceedings were beginning to look like a railroad job. Miles said he would talk to the President of the Court and did so. The officer who had been named was called before Admiral Bowen and, when it had been determined that Tim's story was true, the officer was quickly relieved. From that moment on I could not believe that this was an unbiased hearing. I told Skip Schumacher and Gene Lacy of my fears, but they felt that I was probably wrong. Skip believed that the proceedings would culminate in a form of whitewash, which would be designed to clear the Navy. In order to do this, they would probably have to clear me as well. I figured otherwise. What they really needed was a goat to be sacrificed. If they were dramatic enough about it, the heat would be taken off a great many people who would otherwise be called to account for their part in this affair. Skip and Gene later agreed I had been right. I failed to understand why the Court never followed up leads to responsible persons and required answers from them.

Other testimony pointed to bungling within CINCPACFLT Staff Intelligence regarding Korea and *Pueblo*. This was a grave matter, in my opinion, but it was never followed up, but discredited without challenge.

The problem of divided command, that placed dual responsibilities on the ship's commanding officer and the Officer in Charge, was one that I had expected to be thoroughly examined. I testified that I had been told by the Commander of the Naval Security Group and members of his staff that this problem would be resolved by making the Officer in Charge a Head of Department, thus bringing him under my direct command, in a relationship that is fully explained in Naval Regulations. My testimony on this score was contradicted by a captain from the Naval Security Group, but no further testimony was heard by the Court.

The captain from NAVSECGRU Headquarters also testified that he considered all the classified documents and equipment we had aboard *Pueblo* could have been destroyed in a matter of one hour. I had testified that it would have taken eight to nine hours to do the job. Commander Chuck Clark of the USS *Banner* (AGER-1) testified that when he had learned of *Pueblo*'s capture he was at sea on another mission and he had immediately commenced burning unnecessary classified documents. It had taken him *twenty-four hours*. I wanted to suggest to the Court that a similar pile of documents and equipment be constructed and that the NAVSECGRU captain be provided with the same sledgehammers and the same type of incinerator that we had, and turn him loose. My recommendation never got off the ground. In my opinion the NAVSECGRU captain's testimony was ridiculous.

Then came Admiral Charles M. Cassel who had briefed me in Hawaii as a captain on CINCPACFLT staff. I testified that he assured me that contingency plans existed for giving assistance to the AGERs if needed, and if not available in time, retaliation would follow within twenty-four hours. *He* testified that he had not given me such information. Our testimony was in direct conflict. Yet the Court failed to follow up this important point.

When it came my turn to call witnesses, I settled for the appearance of one of my former Commanding Officers, Commander Pete Block, and for the reading of an affidavit from another Commanding Officer, Captain Henry B. Sweitzer, as to my competence and my performance in prior emergencies. I also called Vice Admiral J. Victor Smith. I was totally exhausted by the experience and prepared a final statement (see appendix) which I read in Court on the last day it was in session. Miles also prepared a lengthy statement which he read into the record. Miles's statement was brilliant.

The week before the end of the Court of Inquiry, I had an experience which nauseated me. I was approached by a senior officer who proposed to make a deal with me on the Fitness Report that I would be writing on one of my officers. He said, "Look Commander, if you give ——— a poor Fitness Report we will blow the whistle on you and some of your capers." Miles was with me at the time of this confrontation. I gave this sorry excuse for a naval officer a scathing reply. "Sir, you know damn well that you are completely out of order in suggesting that I compromise my duty by softening a Fitness Report. I suggest you tell ——— that I intend to write a thorough and truthful account of his performance. He knows, and has known, that it was entirely unsatisfactory. Now, *sir*, if you'll excuse me." I wanted to vomit. That was the lowest performance I had been party to since I became an officer in the Navy. I continue to be revolted whenever the subject crosses my mind, which it does often.

The Court needed to take two weeks to complete its work and make its recommendations. Rose and I went to the desert with the boys, where we hid out for a few days at the home of a friend of Miles's. Miles informed me that he was optimistic and, from his analysis of the testimony, considered that we were in good shape. Nevertheless, I was worried.

It took almost six weeks before the admirals had completed their findings of fact and made their recommendations. They had read over one million words of testimony. In my opinion, much of it was irrelevant. I later found out that the Court had over five hundred forty-three findings of fact. As of this writing, I have never seen them.

Because of the continued high level news interest in the incident, Miles had bargained for and we thought received an agreement that he and I would be informed of the findings of the Court twenty-four hours before they were released. We needed this extra time in order to prepare a statement for the news media, which we were certain would be wanted. Again I was to be disappointed.

One evening, a couple of weeks later, I received a phone call from the Administrative Aide to COMNAVAIRPAC, where I was now temporarily attached. He said I should be in his office by 0700 the following morning. He added that he could not tell me what it was all about. I assumed he was going to announce the findings to me. I telephoned Miles, who said he had a similar call, but that he was to appear at 0600. I wondered if they had given me the wrong hour. I called back and found that we were expected at different hours, just as had been indicated. I couldn't understand why they would want my attorney there an hour before me. I had a sleepless night. The next morning I arrived in my tropical dress khakis, the uniform of the day for working hours. Ed Murphy was there as well.

"What do you think they want us here for, Ed?" I asked.

"I'm not sure, Captain, but probably to announce the Court's findings."

We waited in Admiral Shinn's office. Presently, Miles came in and told me that he had come early as requested and had had breakfast with the Deputy Judge Advocate General, a Rear Admiral Donald Chapman, USN.

"Well, what's the skinny, Miles?" I asked.

"They are going to read us the findings," he replied.

"What was the purpose of your being here for breakfast?"

"I don't know, Pete, the Admiral just sat there through the whole thing and stared at me."

"Well, that adds up. It's as screwy as the rest of this affair."

Admiral Chapman came into the room and we all rose to greet him.

"Be seated please," he said in a highly nervous way. He carried a sheaf of typewritten papers with numerous pen and ink corrections. He sat down and said, "I'm here to read you the findings of the Court of Inquiry. This same text is being released simultaneously in Washington by the Secretary of the Navy." He seemed very nervous as he began to read. His hands shook and he had trouble following the document. It appeared that several of the changes had just been made that morning and he remarked on this fact. Then he came to the part that interested me most, the recommendations:

"The Court recommends that Commander Bucher be tried by General Court-Martial and charged with the following alleged offenses under the Uniform Code of Military Justice:

1. Permitting his ship to be searched while he had power to resist.
2. Failing to take immediate and aggressive protective measures when his ship was attacked by North Korean forces.
3. Complying with the orders of the North Korean forces to follow them into port.
4. Negligently failing to completely destroy all classified material aboard the USS *Pueblo* and permitting such material to go into the hands of the North Koreans.
5. Negligently failing to insure before departure for sea that his officers and crew were properly organized, stationed, and trained for emergency destruction of classified material."

I couldn't believe my ears. I could not recall there was a single word of testimony to support the charges, except for the loss of classified materials to which I had already admitted in Court. The admiral nervously went on, "CINCPACFLT concurs with the findings except that the General Court-Martial against

Commander Bucher should be reduced to a Letter of Reprimand. Chief of Naval Operations concurs." But Secretary of the Navy John H. Chaffee, in a long personal statement, decided that all charges would be dropped against all parties and, although he was not speaking of the guilt or innocence of any of the parties, he said "They have suffered enough." I agreed that there had indeed been considerable suffering, but I considered that a very poor reason not to see that justice was done. I turned to Miles and said, "I will be damned if I will let them get away with that. I want to request a General Court-Martial. You know they cannot prove these charges." Miles turned to me and looked very serious as he said, "If you do that, Pete, this is where I get off." I just sat there. "What in hell is going on?" Miles quite logically pointed out to me that there was no real basis for requesting a General Court-Martial. After all, CINCPACFLT had disapproved those recommendations and had instead recommended a Letter of Reprimand. A Letter of Reprimand is the most serious of several official, administrative reproofs that can be issued to a naval officer for poor or improper performance. Steve Harris was recommended for trial by General Court-Martial on three counts. My XO, Ed Murphy, was recommended for a Letter of Admonition. Each of the recommendations for legal action was founded in the events of the *Pueblo* seizure.

The Court had commended several members of the crew for their conduct during captivity, but had not recommended any of them for medals and citations. Additionally the Court was of the opinion that "During his internment, Commander Bucher upheld morale in a superior manner; that he provided leadership by insisting that command structure be maintained and provided guidance for conduct; he contributed to the ability of the crew to hold together and withstand the trials of detention until repatriation could be effected." However, no recommendation followed this finding that I be officially commended or awarded a suitable medal.

When Admiral Chapman had finished, he nervously asked if Ed and I had any questions. I wanted to say that I had a ton of them for him. There was nothing I could say that would make the slightest difference. My respect for the System, "the Navy way," justice, leadership and so many of the other values I had been taught to respect when the chips were down was suddenly dashed to pieces. I suppose that it was asking too much of people who are, after all, human beings, to seek truth and to bring the error of highly placed persons into bright light. I sought to give Ed Murphy a word of solace, but he had already departed the premises.

Miles tried to cheer me up. "Pete, I really think that things turned out for the best all the way around, there are no charges against you. It could have been far worse." I nodded. Yet, I wanted to explain that no amount of self-deception could ever remove the stain and the very real hurt that was tearing me apart inside. Of all the responsible naval officers, other than my own, only Admiral Johnson had the personal courage to stand up and be counted in that Inquiry. He had my respect for that alone.

The admiral was talking again, and directly to me: "Commander, what are your desires for your next duty station? You are overdue for shore duty, so that will be the only consideration. What type of shore assignment would you like and in what area? You will need three choices."

"Well, sir," I replied, "I just this week talked to my assignment desk in the Bureau of Personnel and they told me that I would have a month before they would need to know my desires. I have not given the matter that much thought. I was really waiting for the Court's announcement or findings, which you just read, before I gave it serious consideration."

The admiral listened to my reply rather impatiently. He quickly said, "I have just talked to Admiral Moorer [Admiral Thomas H. Moorer, Chief of Naval Operations]. He has ordered me to pass your desires on to him within the hour. You must give me an answer now."

I fumbled for words. The only other thought I had had about possible assignments had been along the lines of a school like the Armed Forces Staff College, which I had been requesting for years. I knew that the Staff College would not overly tax me and that it would allow the smoke to clear and the publicity to die down before I had to work for someone else. Impulsively, I blurted out, "Admiral, I would like to go to a school like the Armed Forces

Staff College, I have not yet had the opportunity and it will give things a chance to cool off."

Apparently, I had said the wrong thing, because the admiral very crisply, and with great finality, said, "A school is out of the question."

"In that case, I would like to call my wife and discuss the matter."

The admiral was already gathering his papers, which he had a difficult time getting into proper sequence, into his briefcase. When he had the job done, he stood and said, "All right, Commander, I am leaving immediately for COMELEVEN headquarters. I must give Admiral Moorer your answer, within the next forty-five minutes. Call me at this number before that." He handed me a number where I would be able to reach him and departed hurriedly.

I called Rose and told her what had happened. We decided that it would be preferable to remain on the West Coast, if possible. I would request this. I told Rose about a scheduled news conference and asked her to bring over my Blues, White hat cover, and black shoes. Rose was not particularly interested in attending the conference, but she quickly agreed to come along and give me moral support.

I rang Admiral Chapman. When he came on, I began to go over the various choices for duty and area I had decided upon, but before I could get half through, the admiral interrupted and said, "Say, Commander, I did not mean that school was completely out of the question, if you really want to put that down as a choice."

I said as levelly as I could without betraying my disgust: "But, Admiral, your exact words were that a school was out of the question."

He came back, "Well, I may have given you the wrong impression there, but now, if you want a school it may be possible."

I gave him my choices, including the Staff College. He said he would phone them to Washington right away. I thanked him and hung up. Miles and I both got a good laugh out of the sudden, swift change. I concluded that he had already reported my initial reaction to Washington and someone there had decided that I should not be told that a school was out of the question after all.

Miles quickly completed a rough draft of the statement for the speech to the news media. I looked it over and changed it in places where I considered the wording was too abject. Somehow I had to leave the door open for possible reclaimer of the Court's recommended Court-Martial. I still could not believe what I had heard that morning.

Many thoughts crowded my mind. I thought about Miles Harvey, first Rose's lawyer, now my own as well. He had done a great job of helping me to keep my cool. We had become close friends and I had confided in him completely, although at this moment I wished I had been just a little more forceful in my responses to Admiral Chapman and told him just what I thought about the findings. It was beginning to dawn on me that perhaps the Court's charges and the way they had de-escalated from a General Court-Martial, to a Letter of Reprimand, to nothing had been the only way for the Navy to close the matter to avoid further repercussions. After all, the Navy and other agencies of the government had been under investigation as much as I. Too many people in high places could get hurt or at least embarrassed. Yet, not one word of evidence had been presented in Court that supported the original charges. But the record would always read that after eight long weeks of Court, five admirals had found the evidence to recommend a Court-Martial and that would take care of history. Two or three relatively junior officers would take the rap.

Within three hours after my session with Admiral Chapman's reading of the Court's findings, and while my mind was still in a turmoil of conflicting reactions over this equivocable outcome of the last twelve weeks' particular ordeal, I found myself having to face another all-media press conference. I had a severe case of laryngitis and this became an excuse for me to allow Miles to carry the ball for me with a prepared statement which he had about one hour in which to compose. He did his usual expert job of it, but the many correspondents who rushed from offices as far away as Los Angeles on very short notice to cover the conference, also had their jobs to do. That included getting a personal statement from me besides from my lawyer, even if it was delivered under great strain in a hoarse, croaking voice. This became

one of those moments when it is sheer hell to find oneself a public
figure. Forces of circumstance, nebulous yet strong obligations,
emotions, conscience, pride, all close in an iron ring to prevent
any escape from saying *something!* So I had to add my faltering,
extemporaneous bit to Miles's professionally prepared statement.
I did my best to conform in my own words to what Miles had
said, doing so for the first time without being at all convinced that
he was expressing my true feelings, and speaking for the first time
to the press with the knowledge that I was being somewhat less
than on the level with them. Because they had been so fair to me
in all our previous encounters, this upset me as much as the other
blows of this day.

I spent a restless night. My head ached badly, as it had off and
on since the first few months of our captivity. Aspirins were in-
effective. The phone rang. I glanced at my watch, it was about
7 A.M.

"Commander Bucher, please, long distance calling."

"This is he speaking."

The voice from the other end identified itself as being one of
the officers from the Commander Assignment Desk in Washington at the Bureau of Naval Personnel.

"I have good news. We are cutting orders for you to go to the
Naval Post Graduate School. You will be taking a one-year management course. The course will give you a master's degree in
management."

I told him I was delighted, and I was. I put on a pot of coffee,
fetched the paper from our front stoop, and turned on Rose's
small radio. Rose was still sleeping. I wondered what she would
think of our new assignment. She awoke. To my amazement, the
radio carried the announcement that I had been ordered to the
Naval Post Graduate School for the management course. The
announcer reported my reaction to those orders as one of delight,
which had been true. Yet I couldn't believe that the story of my
conversation with Washington, less than a half hour ago, could
already be on a local news program. This was the kind of communication we needed the day *Pueblo* was seized! Later, Miles
called and told me the news he had received from his contacts

in Washington. I told him I knew about it from two directions already.

Within the next few days we had calls, mail, and visits from many old shipmates. One of my former commanding officers, Captain Marril Kelly, came over to the house and visited with me. The common denominator of all these calls, letters, and his visit, was that they thought I should request a Court-Martial, which would be the only way I could disprove the alleged charges contained in the official findings. Each of them notified me that they knew that I wouldn't take their implications lying down. Once again, I talked it over with Miles. He patiently pointed out that there was no way I could force the Navy to give me a Court-Martial. He was of course correct, but I thought I should at least try to provoke one. Miles was totally against that. I talked it over with Commander Bill Clemmons who had been one of the Court Council. He had always impressed me with his honesty and practicality. He had told me, at the conclusion of the hearing, that if I was ever court-martialed, he would help defend me. This was a rare gesture for a prosecutor. His reaction was the same as Miles's: there was no real ground for me to request a general court. I decided to drop the idea.

Yet, there were many aspects of the Court of Inquiry I cannot forget.

I remember, during the Inquiry, appointing an Awards board of some *Pueblo* officers to recommend some of my men for medals appropriate to their bravery under enemy fire, or for their performance during their imprisonment. I had also written letters to the Commandant of the Marine Corps recommending both Sergeants Chicca and Hammond for Meritorious Promotion. The letters were never answered by the Marine Corps, or if they were, they failed to reach me.

My recommendations for medals for my own men and for those who served under Lieutenant Stephen Harris, as part of his detachment, were completed after many hours of work. I wanted to forward them immediately via our temporary administrative chain of command. The question of correct administrative procedure was a complicated one. However, a course of action was decided upon with the help of COMNAVAIRPAC's Staff.

Just before I was to put my recommendations into the mail, I was told all recommendations for awards should properly be made by the Court of Inquiry, so I decided to await their decision. When they came, no one had been recommended for medals or any other awards. I discussed this with Miles and he, in turn, talked to Captain William Newsome. The members of the Court had decided after several changes of mind that, as commanding officer, I should submit the recommendations. Next I found out that all of the work we had done to prepare these recommendations had been inadvertently lost from our temporary offices. Just how they were lost, I couldn't imagine. In the meanwhile, my crew had scattered across the country and none of my officers remained. So I dug out the instructions again and did them all over by myself. I submitted them via my administrative chain of command. Yet, I never heard another word concerning those recommendations.

Lieutenant (jg) Skip Schumacher was a highly promising naval officer, and I had spent long hours convincing him that he had a real future with the Navy. He was favorably disposed to at least give it a try before leaving and possibly joining his family's insurance company in St. Louis. Skip and I both thought that his experiences would be valuable to the Navy and that there would be a longstanding need for the Navy and the Department of Defense to pick the brains of my crew who could tell them a great deal about North Korea. Inasmuch as Skip is highly intelligent, it figures that he was the one whom they would immediately snap up. He volunteered to stay on active duty on my recommendation and asked to be assigned to duty in Washington. We both knew that there was a real need for review of the present Code of Conduct. All three services interpreted it differently and had different local ground rules for its application. It seemed to us that other countries which told their men to avoid providing their captors with actual truthful information and intelligence value at all costs, but they should not worry about sending false confessions and the like because they wouldn't be believed at home anyway was the best course of training for our own Armed Forces.

Skip awaited his orders with the knowledge that he would in all likelihood be given an assignment that would be of great value to his country. His orders came, but to my very great surprise they were for his assignment to the amphibious base at Coronado, California. Skip asked immediately to be released from active duty and I agreed with his decision. It seemed to me that our Navy and Defense Department were trying to convince itself that the *Pueblo* had never happened. It also seemed to me that this country would be willing to pay huge amounts for information and recommendations of people who had first-hand knowledge but here they were throwing it away. There must be some of the ostrich's instinct for sticking his head in the sand in high places. We therefore lost a very valuable junior officer.

I later learned from friends and acquaintances on CINCPAC-FLT's Staff that I had been recommended for the Medal of Honor by Rear Admiral Edwin M. Rosenberg. I have never discovered what happened to that recommendation. Of course, if the recommendation had been disapproved at some level of the chain of command, I would not necessarily have learned of it, unless one of the various levels in the chain had forwarded it with a recommendation for a lesser award which was ultimately approved. United States Congressman Glenn Cunningham, Nebraska Republican, also recommended me for the Medal of Honor, by introducing a bill on the floor of the House of Representatives (H.R. 10359 of April 21, 1969).

Legislation was also introduced in the United States Congress to provide for tax relief and combat pay for my men for the period of their captivity. These are the same benefits given to servicemen in Vietnam. The bill passed the House and recently, the Senate.

During 1969, I visited in Creswell, Oregon, where I paid a call on our dead shipmate's parents, Mr. and Mrs. Jesse Hodges. Gene Lacy, who is stationed in Seattle, Washington, joined me. We went to Duane Hodges' grave where we both stood in silence for a few minutes in memory of him. I spoke to the Creswell High School student body and told them of my admiration for their alumnus. The crew of *Pueblo* presented the high school with over $1000 worth of books in Duane's memory. A large metal plaque with suitable inscription was made for us by the submarine tender *Nereus* (AS-17) through the good offices of my old shipmate Captain Fred G. Berry, USN. The plaque is now bolted to a stone monument on ground donated by the city of Creswell.

Rose told me of the great support she had received from the citizens of Pueblo, Colorado. We arranged to visit Pueblo where we received a royal welcome from its citizens and their mayor, Phil K. Hudspeth. It seemed that everyone in Pueblo must have been in the streets. Mayor Hudspeth presented me with a plaque honoring my men. The Chamber of Commerce gave me a tremendous dinner attended by several hundred people, at which I was given other tokens of welcome. Each one of my crew were made honorary citizens of Pueblo. I had to agree with Rose: they were great people.

Monsignor Wegner had been insistent that we return to Boys Town so that they could give us a proper welcome. I wanted to go very badly, but also knew that it would be an emotional occasion for me. I knew that Father Wegner would spare no effort to give us a great reception. Yet, I did not consider myself a hero. I knew I had done my job as well as I could and accounted for it as faithfully as I knew how. But I didn't want to be feted for doing my duty. Finally, we decided to go. I was so very proud of Boys Town. Almost a thousand boys were at the Omaha Municipal Airport to greet us. They had hundreds of signs. I was overwhelmed with love for those kids, and I felt my eyes moistening. It was an overpowering experience. Rose had been presented with a bouquet of roses, yet after we ran the gauntlet of those boys, not one rose remained intact. The following day, a great banquet was held in the Field House in our honor. None of the Buchers could believe their eyes. Over 1200 guests were present, including the Boys Town High School senior class. Many of my own teachers, including Father Flanagan's nephew, Pat Norton, and my high school coach Skip Palrang, who was in his twenty-sixth year as head coach and athletic director, were there. Among those at the head table were: Archbishop Gerald T. Bergan, Governor Norbert

T. Tiemann of Nebraska, U. S. Senators Roman L. Hruska and
Carl T. Curtis of Nebraska, U. S. Congressmen Glenn Cunningham of Nebraska and Bill Scherle of Iowa, and, of course, the
Mayor of Boys Town, Bill Steele a young seventeen-year-old senior who was a stalwart on their football team. The fact that he
was a black boy as several former mayors of Boys Town have been
is abiding proof of the spirit of Boys Town, a spirit that could well
be emulated across our country. Boys Town is concrete proof that
democracy still works where straightforward educational processes
and the love of fellow men hold sway.

Immediately following the capture of the *Pueblo* an intense
background investigation was conducted into the lives, the asso-
ciations and travels of many of my crew. Perhaps the most thorough and immediate was made on myself. This is entirely
understandable. Our government had to know whether there had
been any disloyalty on my part. Several acquaintances and friends
told me of their own experiences during this mammoth investigation. One of my ex-shipmates was so incensed over some of the
questions and their implications that he took a swing at the inves-
tigator, only to be overpowered by another and held on the spot
until he calmed down. This investigation undoubtedly uncovered
every bar I had ever had a drink in, every person I had ever
talked to or been shipmates with in my life. They found out everything I had done. Luckily for me the good far outweighed the
bad and my reputation within the fleet worked to my advantage,
since all my former shipmates said that I was loyal to my country
and to those who worked for me. One of my debriefers in San
Diego said that he had never seen so complete a check made on
anyone. He further told me that he had never known anyone who
was so loyally supported by so many people.

Many of the people involved in the AGER program have been
written about in this book. Many cannot be mentioned. Yet,
some of the same people who planned and made the decision to
create and use the AGER are, so far as I am aware, still sitting in
the same jobs. As my lawyer pointed out in his final statement before the Court of Inquiry, all my recommendations for *Pueblo*

were retroactively acted upon on other AGERs after the *Pueblo* capture. Many of the discoveries made as a result of the *Pueblo* affair affected the entire Navy and all Navy ships. . . . But the AGER program which only a short time ago was judged essential to our national defence and enjoyed a high priority in the intelligence community, is now abandoned. The *Palm Beach* which never got beyond Norfolk to reach her intended operational area in North European waters, and the *Banner* which produced such fine results through eighteen missions, both have been decommissioned and relegated to the shipbreakers' scrapheaps. Their sailors and highly trained CTs have long since been scattered to other assignments, a goodly number of them declining reenlistment and quitting the Navy in disgust. Millions of dollars and man-hours of effort were in the end largely wasted, not to mention the pain and heartbreak that became the lot of so many of us involved. It is difficult for me to make sense out of it all and I can only accept this outcome with a feeling of futility.

On April 14, while my mind was still in a turmoil over the *Pueblo* affair, I had a chance to experience the reaction to another KORCOM outrage, but this time from the more comfortable vantagepoint of my own home in the United States. On that date, North Korean jet fighters intercepted and shot down a U. S. Navy unarmed patrol aircraft, an EC-121, some ninety miles south-east of Chong-Jin and far outside of their territorial airspace. Thirty-one Navy officers and men lost their lives when their plane crashed into the Sea of Japan. This tragedy reopened a lot of old wounds for me. For one thing, the EC-121 flying out of Atsugi Airbase in Japan, was a sort of airborne *Pueblo* with a similar mission to collect electronic intelligence with strict instructions not to intrude over North Korean or Soviet territory: for another I became witness to the ineffectual uproar and debate at home, of the same kind which must have erupted when my *Pueblo* was attacked and seized, all resulting in as little forceful action. Again the KORCOMs got away with a blatant act of aggression committed far beyond the confines of their dismal little Communist dictatorship. I could see in my mind's eye, Glorious General, Colonel Scar, Silverlips, and that whole cretinous gang strutting and reveling over another successful coup against the American Imperialists. I was filled with rage (as were many other Americans) when in spite of our humiliating experience of *Pueblo,* our country accepted even more grievous loss of life and property without retaliation.

Many people, including the counsel for the Court of Inquiry, the commanding officer of the Naval Hospital which initially cared for us, and all those who participated in the Navy response to our capture on board ship in the Sea of Japan have been awarded some medal for performance or service. It seems to me that everyone connected even remotely to *Pueblo,* with the exception of its crew, have been somehow rewarded for their service. I believe that these people *should* have been recognized for their performance, but I strongly believe that many of my own crew deserve proper recognition.

I have given much consideration to the motives which made the North Koreans dare attack and pirate USS *Pueblo* off the high seas. Since returning home from their bleak prison, I have come into possession of a lot of information I knew nothing about at the time. Some of it has led me to the conclusion that if the North Koreans had known we were a U. S. Navy ship manned entirely by U.S. naval personnel and U. S. Civil Service specialists, they would never have pressed home their attack. Inasmuch as they had just unsuccessfully dispatched an assassination team to kill South Korea's President Park, I am convinced that when they discovered our presence one day later, their assumption was that we were a South Korean Navy ship (they are painted exactly like ours and often of American construction). They next assumed we were carrying a retaliation team with a mission to murder their demagogue, Premier Kim Il Sung. His natural reaction would be to order his naval and airforce units to make sure any landing attempt would be prevented and if possible to capture the intruders; (I have since also become aware of how common it is for both regimes occupying that unhappy peninsula to attempt aggressive infiltrations of each other's territories). I become more certain in my beliefs when recalling how the KORCOMs seemed obsessed with the idea of identifying our Filipino and Mexican-American crewmen as South Korean "spies." When it finally became obvious to them that they were mistaken in that respect and realized we were in fact all Americans, their only recourse was to try bluffing their way through with outraged accusations of intrusions into their territorial waters while at the same time making all the propaganda hay they could out of the incident. In this bluff they succeeded beyond their expectations when mighty United States of America "apologized" to their maverick enclave of the Communist world in order to ransom us out of captivity.

I consider that the underlying reason for *Pueblo*'s unpreparedness to adequately cope with all the problems she faced on that fateful day in January 1968 is the Navy's tendency to take on more jobs than they are adequately funded to handle or than they have the necessary personnel to do the job right. There were two distinct aspects to the *Pueblo* incident; first, it was a terrific blunder that reflected very poor and even nonexistent planning and poor execution in many areas up to and including the highest offices in the land. On the other hand, I sincerely believe that, as with all disasters, lessons were learned that should and undoubtedly will benefit the country.

I consider that so many persons in high places were involved in demonstrably unsatisfactory performance with respect to the conception and execution of the surface intelligence collection program of which *Pueblo* was a part, that it was decided by those ultimately responsible for investigation into causes, that a major house cleaning would have been necessitated. The result left a few holding the sack for the many who are gutless. I did give a complete account of my actions and the reasons behind them. It remains for those who have the facts available to insure the lessons learned will benefit future planning; if they do not, then they have only to answer to their conscience.

For my own part, I deeply regret that I was not better prepared to insure total destruction of *Pueblo* and the classified documents she carried. In the first instance, the planners had been forewarned by myself that a scuttling system and a destruct system would have been prudent improvements to *Pueblo*, but they disapproved their implementation. In the second, I regret that I was not better prepared to insure total destruction of the classified documents that we carried. I had simply not given the matter of burning and

shredding publications enough thought or I feel certain I would
have hit upon the idea of throwing their vast bulk into the head,
dousing them with gasoline and burning them. With regard to
engaging the North Koreans in battle, I am absolutely certain
that under the conditions we faced and within the parameters of
my orders, the 50-caliber machine guns could not have been
brought into action. To have tried to do so would have resulted
in a complete slaughter of my crew without a single compensation.
To the contrary, if I had ordered them manned, I am convinced
that we would have all been killed and the ship would have fallen
to the North Koreans with almost all the classified documents
and equipment intact. We did destroy a great quantity of equipment and classified papers during the time we won by passivity.

I consider that the primary thrust of the Court of Inquiry's
recommendation for a trial by general Court-Martial for myself,
boils down to my being charged for refusing to order my men to
commit suicide. I do not regret that decision and in fact would
make the same decision in similar circumstances every time. General Jonathan Wainwright in his defense of Corregidor was faced
with wholesale slaughter if he continued his struggle with the
Japanese. His troops still had quantities of ammunition and a de-
fensible position. He chose to surrender his army and was awarded
high honors for his common sense. You can liken *Pueblo*'s position on the day of her capture to that of a man with a holstered
.22 pistol standing in the middle of an open field surrounded by
forty men with guns drawn and aimed at him from a distance of
twenty yards. Not much chance for him to escape or offer meaningful resistance, is there?

Nothing I have written in this book is meant to excuse my own
shortcomings, of which there were many. Nothing I have written
in this book is meant to imply disrespect for my seniors within
the Navy. Nothing I have written in this book is meant to argue
against the need for a well planned and daringly executed program
for the collection of intelligence. Good intelligence is the life
blood for successful defense of our country. I consider that it was
wrong to decommission the majority of the surface intelligence
ships as was done in 1969. But what our planners must keep in
mind at all times is that whereas our potential enemies can risk

developing minimum cost intelligence ships because they know we
honor international law and are not bandits or pirates, we cannot
trust them to treat our efforts with the same thoughtfulness. Instead we must spend three or more times as much if we are to
compete, in order to prepare our men and their equipment for all
possible eventualities. I remain now as I have ever been, entirely
loyal to the United States Navy. For me the Navy remains my life
work and its principles and traditions will ever be close to my
heart.

In September 1969 I reported for duty as a student at the Naval
Postgraduate School in Monterey, California. Shortly after my
arrival I had the opportunity to meet with the Commandant and
Superintendent of the school, Rear Admiral Robert W. McNitt,
USN. He made my family and me welcome and has since on several occasions evidenced genuine concern for small problems that
have developed for me. The student body at the Postgraduate
School comprises well over a thousand officers from many countries. I would be naive indeed if I thought that many of them did
not disagree with some or all of the decisions that I made, but
not once has anything untoward occurred. My faith that the Navy
will continue to appeal to many fine people remains strong. My
faith that this great country of mine, the United States of America,
with God's help and the sweat of her many ethnic groups pulling
together will continue to be the repository of the greatest of all
human ideals, individual freedom blended in perfect balance with
individual and social responsibility, has been strengthened by my
experience.

This book has been written in the hope that the telling of my
story will be of some benefit to others. This has been my story. As
of this moment, it is complete.

APPENDICES

APPENDIX I

THE CREW OF USS *PUEBLO*

Their rank is of the day of capture

Commander Lloyd M. Bucher,
Lincoln, Nebraska

Lieutenant Stephen R. Harris,
Melrose, Massachusetts

Lieutenant Edward R. Murphy,
San Diego, California

Lieutenant (jg) F. Carl Schumacher,
St. Louis, Missouri

Ensign Timothy L. Harris,
Jacksonville, Florida

Chief Warrant Officer Gene H. Lacy,
Seattle, Washington

Steward's Mate Rogelio P. Abelon,
Ambabaay, Philippines

Communications Technician 2nd Class Michael W. Alexander,
Richland, Washington

Steward's Mate Rizalino L. Aluague,
Subic City, Philippines

Communications Technician 2nd Class Wayne D. Anderson,
Waycross, Georgia

Fireman Richard E. Arnold,
  Santa Rosa, California

Communications Technician 3rd Class Charles W. Ayling,
  Staunton, Virginia

Communications Technician 1st Class Don E. Bailey,
  Portland, Indiana

Hospital Corpsman 1st Class Herman P. Baldridge,
  Carthage, Missouri

Fireman Richard I. Bame,
  Maybee, Michigan

Fireman Peter M. Bandera,
  Carson City, Nevada

Communications Technician 1st Class Michael T. Barrett,
  Kalamazoo, Michigan

Boatswain's Mate 2nd Class Ronald L. Berens,
  Russell, Kansas

Fireman Howard E. Bland,
  Leggett, California

Engineman Rushel J. Blansett,
  Orange, California

Senior Chief Communications Technician Ralph D. Bouden,
  Nampa, Idaho

Communications Technician 3rd Class Paul D. Brusnahan,
  Trenton, New Jersey

Boatswain's Mate 3rd Class Willie C. Bussell,
  Hopkinsville, Kentucky

Yeoman 1st Class Armando M. Canales,
  Fresno, California

Marine Sergeant Robert J. Chicca,
  Hyattsville, Maryland

Radioman 3rd Class Charles H. Crandall,
   El Reno, Oklahoma

Communications Technician 3rd Class Bradley R. Crowe,
   Island Pond, Vermont

Communications Technician 3rd Class Rodney H. Duke,
   Fayette, Mississippi

Seaman Stephen P. Ellis,
   Los Angeles, California

Communications Specialist Victor D. Escamilla,
   Amarillo, Texas

Storekeeper 1st Class Policarpo P. Garcia,
   Point Mugu, California

Communications Technician 1st Class Francis J. Ginther,
   Pottsville, Pennsylvania

Chief Engineman Monroe O. Goldman,
   Lakewood, California

Communications Technician 3rd Class John W. Grant,
   Jay, Maine

Electrician's Mate 1st Class Gerald Hagenson,
   Bremerton, Washington

Marine Sergeant Robert J. Hammond,
   Claremont, New Hampshire

Radioman 2nd Class Lee R. Hayes,
   Columbus, Ohio

Fireman Duane Hodges,
   Creswell, Oregon

Communications Technician 3rd Class Jerry Karnes,
   Havana, Arkansas

Chief Communications Technician James F. Kell,
   Culver City, California

Communications Technician 3rd Class Earl M. Kisler,
St. Louis, Missouri

Boatswain's Mate 1st Class Norbert J. Klepac,
San Diego, California

Communications Technician 3rd Class Anthony A. Lamantia,
Toronto, Ohio

Communications Technician 3rd Class Peter M. Langenberg,
Clayton, Missouri

Quartermaster 1st Class Charles B. Law,
Chehalis, Washington

Communications Technician 1st Class James D. Layton,
Binghamton, New York

Signalman 2nd Class Wendell G. Leach,
Houston, Texas

Commissaryman 2nd Class Harry Lewis,
Springfield Gardens, New York

Photographer's Mate 1st Class Lawrence W. Mack,
San Diego, California

Seaman Roy J. Maggard,
Olivehurst, California

Seaman Larry J. Marshall,
Austin, Indiana

Fireman Thomas W. Massie,
Roscoe, Illinois

Communications Technician 2nd Class Donald R. McClarren,
Johnstown, Pennsylvania

Communications Technician 3rd Class Ralph McClintock,
Milton, Massachusetts

Fireman John A. Mitchell,
Dixon, California

Electronics Technician 2nd Class Clifford C. Nolte,
Menlo, Iowa

Fireman Michael A. O'Bannon,
Beaverton, Oregon

Communications Technician 1st Class Donald R. Peppard,
Phoenix, Arizona

Seaman Earl R. Phares,
Ontario, California

Quartermaster 3rd Class Alvin H. Plucker,
Trenton, Nebraska

Commissaryman 3rd Class Ralph E. Reed,
Perdix, Pennsylvania

Seaman Dale E. Rigby,
Ogden, Utah

Communications Technician 1st Class David L. Ritter,
Union City, California

Communications Technician 3rd Class Steven J. Robin,
Silver Spring, Maryland

Seaman Richard J. Rogala,
Niles, Illinois

Seaman Ramon Rosales,
El Paso, Texas

Seaman Edward S. Russell,
Glendale, California

Engineman 1st Class William W. Scarborough,
Anderson, South Carolina

Communications Technician 1st Class James A. Shephard,
Williamstown, Massachusetts

Communications Technician 3rd Class John A. Shilling,
Mantua, Ohio

Seaman John R. Shingleton,
Atoka, Oklahoma

Fireman Norman W. Spear,
Portland, Maine

Communications Technician 2nd Class Charles R. Sterling,
Omaha, Nebraska

Communications Technician 3rd Class Angelo S. Strano,
Hartford, Connecticut

Fireman Larry E. Strickland,
Grand Rapids, Michigan

Gunner's Mate 2nd Class Kenneth R. Wadley,
Beaverton, Oregon

Fireman Steven E. Woelk,
Alta Vista, Kansas

Communications Technician 2nd Class Elton A. Wood,
Spokane, Washington

Engineman Darrel D. Wright,
Alma, West Virginia

Harry Iredale, III (Civilian),
Holmes, Pennsylvania

Dunnie Tuck (Civilian),
Richmond, Virginia

APPENDIX II

PUEBLO'S OPERATIONAL ORDERS:

DECEMBER, 1967

DECLASSIFIED BY
COMNAVFORJAPAN
31 DECEMBER 1968   UNCLASSIFIED

VZCZCNJA561
RR RUABPO RUAMWC RUAUAZ
DE RUAUNJ 025 3520754
ZNY SSSSS
R 180752Z DEC 67
FM COMNAVFORJAPAN
INFO O RUAMWC/COMUSKOREA
RUAMWC/COMNAVFORKOREA
RUABP O/N SAPACOFF JAPAN
RUAUAZ/FIFTH AF FUCHUV USFJ
P R 161106Z DEC 67
FM COMNAVFORJAPAN
TO CINCPACFLT
INFO COMSEVENTHFLT
COMSERVPAC
DIRNAVSECGRUPAC   LIMITED DISTRIBUTION
NAVSECGRUACT KAMISEYA
OCEANAV   UNCLASSIFIED
USS PUEBLO
BT
SECRET LIMDIS NOFORN

PINKROOT OPERATION ONE (C)

A. CINCPACFLTINST OO3120.24A

B. CINCPACFLTINST O3100.3D

1. FOLLOWING SUBMITTED IAW REF A:

A. JUSTIFICATION: SUBJ OPERATION WILL PRIMARILY BE CONDUCTED IN SEA OF JAPAN TO:

(1) DETERMINE NATURE AND EXTENT OF NAVAL ACTIVITY VICINITY OF NORTH KOREAN (KORCOM) PORTS OF CHONGJIN, SONGJIN, MAYANG DO AND WONSON.

(2) SAMPLE ELECTRONIC ENVIRONMENT OF EAST COAST NORTH KOREA, WITH EMPHASIS ON INTERCEPT/FIXING OF COASTAL RADARS.

(3) INTERCEPT AND CONDUCT SURVEILLANCE OF SOVIET NAVAL UNITS

PAGE 2 RUAUNJ O32 S E C R E T LIMDIS NOFORN

OPERATING TSUSHIMA STRAITS IN EFFORT TO DETERMINE PURPOSE OF SOVIET PRESENCE IN THAT AREA SINCE FEB 1966. SECONDARILY, THE OPERATION WILL BE CONDUCTED TO:

(A) DETERMINE KORCOM AND SOVIET REACTION RESPECTIVELY TO AN OVERT INTELLIGENCE COLLECTOR OPERATING NEAR KORCOM PERIPHERY AND ACTIVELY CONDUCTING SURVEILLANCE OF USSR NAVAL UNITS.

(B) EVALUATE USS PUEBLO'S (AGER-2) CAPABILITIES AS A NAVAL INTELLIGENCE COLLECTION AND TACTICAL SURVEILLANCE SHIP.

(C) REPORT ANY DEPLOYMENT OF KORCOM/SOVIET UNITS WHICH MAY BE INDICATIVE OF PENDING HOSTILITIES OR OFFENSIVE ACTIONS AGAINST U. S. FORCES.

B. ESTIMATE OF RISK: MINIMAL, SINCE PUEBLO WILL BE OPERATING IN INTERNATIONAL WATERS FOR ENTIRE DEPLOYMENT.

C. RULES OF ENGAGEMENT ARE AS SET FORTH IN REF A. REF B IS APPLICABLE WITH REGARDS PUEBLO'S CONDUCT IN EVENT OF HARASSMENT OR INTIMIDATION. CO COGNIZANT OF PUEBLO'S VULNERABILITY TO FATAL DAMAGE DUE TO COLLISION.

D. DIRECT LIAISON CONDUCTED OR WILL BE REQUIRED WITH:

(1) DIRNAVSECGRUPAC

PAGE ONE OF TWO COPY 2 OF SIX COPIES   161106Z DEC 67

DECLASSIFIED BY COMNAVFORJAPAN ON 31 DECEMBER 1968

PAGE 3 RUAUNJ 032 S E C R E T LIMDIS NOFORN

    (2) PACOM ELINT CENTER

    (3) NAVSECGRUACT KAMISEYA

    (4) NSAPACOFF JAPAN

    (5) COMUSKOREA

    (6) COMNAVFORKOREA

E. OPERATIONAL INFO:

    (1) USS PUEBLO (AGER-2)

    (2) SASEBO, 8 JAN 68

    (3) (A) PROCEED VIA TSUSHIMA STRAITS TO ARR OPAREA MARS APPROX 10 JAN.

    (B) OPERATE OPAREAS PLUTO, VENUS, AND MARS, CONCENTRATING EFFORTS IN AREA(S) WHICH APPEAR MOST LUCRATIVE.

    (C) DEPART OPAREAS 27 JAN. PROCEED SOUTH ALONG KOREAN COAST TO VICINITY TSUSHIMA STRAITS.

    (D) INTERCEPT AND CONDUCT SURVEILLANCE OF SOVIET NAVAL UNITS OPERATING TSUSHIMA STRAITS.

    (E) TERMINATE SURVEILLANCE TO ARR SASEBO NLT 040001Z FEB.

    (4) CPA TO KORCOM/SOVIET LAND MASS/OFF SHORE ISLANDS WILL BE 13 NM. PUEBLO WILL OPERATE AT LEAST 500 YARDS FROM SOVIET UNITS EXCEPT TO CLOSE BRIEFLY TO 200 YARDS AS NECESSARY FROM VISUAL/PHOTO

PAGE 4 RUAUNJ 032 S E C R E T LIMDIS NOFORN
COVERAGE. ADDITIONALLY, PUEBLO WILL NOT INTERFERE WITH SOVIET EXERCISES. PUEBLO WILL, HOWEVER, MAINTAIN A POSITION ON THE PERIPHERY FOR OBSERVATION PURPOSES.

    (5) ARR SASEBO, 4 FEB

    (6) ABOVE OPAREAS ARE DEFINED AS FOLLOWS:

    (A) EAST/WEST BOUNDARIES ARE CONTIGUOUS TO KORCOM COAST EXTENDING FROM 13 NM CPA TO LAND MASS/OFF SHORE ISLANDS SEAWARD TO 60 NM.

    (B) NORTH/SOUTH BOUNDARIES ARE PLUTO 42-00N TO 41-00N; VENUS 41-00N TO 40-00N; AND MARS 40-00N TO 39-00N.

GP-1

BT

APPENDIX III

PUEBLO'S SAILING ORDERS: JANUARY, 1968

SECRET

PRIORITY
P 050512Z JAN 68
FM CTF NINE SIX

TO USS PUEBLO

INFO AIG SEVEN SIX TWO TWO
COMSERVGRU THREE
DIRNSA
DIRNAVSECGRUPAC
COMUSKOREA
COMNAVFORKOREA   LIMDIS NOFORN
PACOMELINT CENTER

S E C R E T LIMDIS NOFORN

A. CTF 96 OPORD 301-68 NOTAL
B. PACOM ELINT CENTER 210734Z DEC 67 PASEP NOTAL
C. CINCPACFLTINST 003120.24A
D. CINCPACFLTINST 03100.3D

1. ICHTHYIC ONE FORMERLY PINKROOT ONE

2. DEPART SASEBO JAPAN WHEN RFS ABOUT 8 JAN 68. CHECK OUT

OF MOVREP SYSTEM AND PROCEED VIA TSUSHIMA STRAITS TO ARRIVE
OPAREA MARS ABOUT 10 JAN.

3. ATTEMPT TO AVOID DETECTION BY SOVIET NAVAL UNITS WHILE
PROCEEDING TO OPAREA MARS.

4. UPON ARRIVAL MARS, CONDUCT ICHTHYIC OPS IAW PROVISIONS REF A.

A. OPERATE OPAREAS MARS, VENUS AND PLUTO, CONCENTRATING
EFFORTS IN AREA(S) WHICH APPEAR MOST LUCRATIVE.

B. DEPART OPAREAS 27 JAN AND IF NOT UNDER SURVEILLANCE
MAINTAIN STRICT EMCON CONDITION. PROCEED SOUTH ALONG KOREAN
COAST TO VICINITY TSUSHIMA STRAITS.

C. INTERCEPT AND CONDUCT SURVEILLANCE OF SOVIET NASIMA
STRAITS.

D. TERMINATE SURVEILLANCE TO ARRIVE SASEBO 4 FEB 68. EARLIER
DEPARTURE AUTHORIZED TO ENSURE TEN PERCENT ON-BOARD FUEL
UPON ARRIVAL SASEBO.

Declassified
Authority Deputy Secretary of Defense
September 12, 1968

/s/ Paul H. Nitze
PAUL H. NITZE

5. OPAREAS DEFINED AS FOLLOWS:

A. E....' .... BOUNDARIES ALL AREAS ARE CONTIGUOUS TO KORCOM
AST EXTENDING FROM THIRTEEN NM CPA TO LAND MASS/OFF-SHORE
ISLANDE EAWARDO SIXTY NM.

B. NORTHSOUTH BOUNDARIES ARE:
MARS. 40-00N4 TO 39-00N2;
VENUS. 41-00N5 TO 40-00N4;
PLUTO. 42-00N6 TO 41-00N5.

6. SPECIAL INSTRUCTIONS:

A. COLLECT ELINT IAW PROVISIONS REF B, ON NOT TO INTERFERE
BASIS WITH BASIC MISSION.

B. CPA TO KORCOM/SOVIET LAND MASS/OFF-SHORE ISLANDS WILL
BE THIRTEEN NM.

C. UPON ESTABLISHING FIRM CONTACT WITH SOVIET NAVAL UNITS, BREAK EMCON AND TRANSMIT DAILY SITREP.

D. OPERATE AT LEAST FIVE HUNDRED YDS FROM SOVIET UNITS EXCEPT TO CLOSE BRIEFLY TO TWO HUNDRED YDS AS NECESSARY FOR VISUAL/PHOTO COVERAGE.

E. DO NOT INTERFERE WITH SOVIET EXERCISES BUT MAINTAIN A POSITION ON THE PERIPHERY FOR OBSERVATION PURPOSES.

F. IF UNABLE TO ESTABLISH OR
GAIN CONTACT WITH SOVIET
UNITS WITHIN TWENTY-FOUR HOURS ARRIVAL TSUSHIMA STRAITS AREA, ADVISE
ORIG. IMMEDIATE PRECEDENCE.

G. PROVISIONS REF
APPLY RELIDING RULES OF ENGAGEMENT.
IF D APPLIES REGARDING CONDUCT IN EVENT OF HARASSMENT OR INTIMIDATION BY FOREIGN UNITS.

H. INJSOLLED DEFENSIVE ARMAMENT SHOULD BE STOWED OR COVERED IN SUCH A MANNER AS TO NOT ELICIT UNUSUAL INTEREST FROM SURVEYING/SURVEYED UNITS(S). EMPLOY ONLY IN CASES WHERE THREAT TO SURVIVAL IS OBVIOUS.
GP-3

LIMDIS

APPENDIX IV

THE FIRST CONFESSION
AS PUBLISHED IN PYONGYANG *TIMES*:
FEBRUARY, 1968

Confession of Criminal Aggressive Acts
by Captain of Armed Spy Ship of U. S. Imperialist Aggressor
Forces
Captured While Committing Espionage Activities After Intruding into Coastal Waters of D.P.R.K.

Lloyd Mark Bucher, captain of the armed spy ship of the U.S. imperialist aggressor army which was captured by naval vessels of the Korean People's Army while perpetrating hostile acts after illegally infiltrating into the coastal waters of our side on January 23, admitted the espionage activities the U.S. imperialist aggressors committed.

Follows his confession:

I am commander Lloyd Mark Bucher, captain of USS *Pueblo* belonging to the Pacific Fleet, U. S. Navy, who was captured while carrying out espionage activities after intruding deep into the territorial waters of the Democratic People's Republic of Korea.

My serial number is 58215401. I was born in Pocatello, Idaho, U.S.A. I am 38 years old.

The crew of our USS *Pueblo* are 83 in all including five officers besides me, 75 servicemen and two civilians.

My ship had been sent to Sasebo, Japan, to execute assignments given by the U. S. Central Intelligence Agency.

On December 2 last, we received assignments at the port of Sasebo from Rear Admiral Frank L. Johnson, U. S. Navy Commander in Japan, to conduct military espionage activities on the Far Eastern region of the Soviet Union and then on the offshore areas and coastal areas of the Democratic People's Republic of Korea.

My ship had conducted espionage activities on a number of occasions for the purpose of detecting the territorial waters of the socialist countries.

Through such espionage activities, my ship detected the military installations set up along the coasts of the socialist countries and submitted the materials to the U. S. Central Intelligence Agency.

Recently, we were given another important mission by the U. S. Central Intelligence Agency, that is, to detect the areas along the Far East of the Soviet Union and the Democratic People's Republic of Korea.

The U. S. Central Intelligence Agency promised me that if this task would be done successfully, a lot of dollars would be offered to the whole crew members of my ship and particularly I myself would be honored.

Soon after that I reinforced the arms and equipment of the ship and made detailed preparations for espionage activities.

Then we disguised my ship as one engaged in researches on oceanic electronics and left the port of Sasebo, Japan, and conducted espionage acts along the coast of the Democratic People's Republic of Korea via the general area off the Soviet Maritime Province. We pretended ourselves to conduct the observation of oceanic conditions on high seas, electronics, research on electric waves, magnetic conditions and exploitation of oceanic materials.

It was on January 16, 1968, that we entered the coastal waters of the Democratic People's Republic of Korea via the Soviet Maritime Province.

In accordance with the instructions we had received, my ship was on the utmost alert and observed and ascertained the depth of water, current, water temperature, sea basin, salt condensity and water transparency of the territorial waters of the Democratic People's Republic of Korea with radars and various kinds of observatory instruments in a clandestine manner at Chong-Jin, Wonsan and several other points, and detected the radar network, accommodation capacities of the ports, the number of the incoming and outgoing vessels and maneuverability of the naval vessels of the Korean People's Army.

Furthermore we spied on various military installations and the distribution of industries and the deployment of armed forces along the east coast areas and sailed up to the point 7.6 miles of Ryodo Island (39° 17.4′ N., 127° 46.9′ E.), when the navy patrol crafts of the Korean People's Army appeared.

We were on the alert instantly and tried to escape, firing at the navy patrol crafts of the People's Army.

But the situation became more dangerous for us and thus one of my men was killed, another heavily wounded and two others lightly wounded.

We had no way out, and were captured by the navy patrol crafts of the People's Army.

Having been captured now, I say frankly that our act was a criminal act which flagrantly violated the Armistice Agreement, and it was a sheer act of aggression.

For the purpose of disguising the activities of my ship throughout the whole period of espionage activities, we used cunning methods, namely, we did not hoist the U.S. flag and sailed at the highest speed when running out of the territorial waters after the espionage activities having intruded into territorial waters from high seas.

I have no excuse whatsoever for my criminal act as my ship intruded deep into the territorial waters of the Democratic People's Republic of Korea and was captured by the naval patrol crafts of the Korean People's Army in their self-defence action while conducting the criminal espionage activities.

The crime committed by me and my men is entirely indelible.

I and my crew have perpetrated such grave criminal act, but our parents and wives and children at home are anxiously waiting for us to return home in safe.

Therefore, we only hope, and it is the greatest desire of myself and all my crew, that we will be forgiven leniently by the Government of the Democratic People's Republic of Korea.

APPENDIX V

FINAL CONFESSION
21 SEPT 1968

A final confession in anticipation of leniency for my crew and myself for the heinous crimes perpetrated by ourselves while conducting horrible outrages against the Democratic People's Republic of Korea for the purpose of provocating and annoying those stalwarts of peace-loving humanity. The absolute truth of this bowel wrenching confession is attested to by my fervent desire to paean the Korean People's Army Navy, and their government and to beseech the Korean people to forgive our dastardly deeds unmatched since Attila. I therefore swear the following account to be true on the sacred honor of the Great Speckled Bird.

USS *Pueblo* was prepared with unmitigated acidity and rank boldness to be a clever diabolical scheme to strike terror into the palpitating breast of the People's of the DPRK. Only the finest ship possible was selected to carry its super-spy trained crew. Upon reporting to the *Pueblo* on duty, I found I was to be first indoctrinated by the most notorious super-spy within the seething inwards of the Navy. I was to be trained by none other than Commander Buzz Sawyer. He immediately commenced a rigorous training program, which was designed to teach me the finer points of provocation and nastiness. Each day I grew with my capabilities. I thought, If only I can match Commander Sawyer's capabilities I will be a master of naughty and nefarious espionage, with special emphasis on provocation. My heart beat furiously when he gave me a passing grade in provocating and in the otherwise awful and known tactics of super spies.

I rounded up a crew of men who were of the most mean coun-
tenance and disposition. Particularly did I pay attention to gathering about me men with protruding and auspicious proboscises.
I had learned from Commander Sawyer that Koreans were
particularly incensed by big American noses. My ship in the meanwhile was prepared for this clandestine, cruel, craven, klepto-
maniacal mission with only the thoroughness that can be
associated with the wretched minds that had conceived this demon of the sea. The *Pueblo* was quickly made into the most
modern, up-to-date ship of the entire 12,397 ships that were in
commission with our Navy at that time. But to disguise its ultra-
design, much of the new hull and machinery was replaced with
ancient (20-25 year old parts). I consider this a stroke of pure
genius on the part of Buzz Sawyer, the diabolical mind behind
the scenes. Following rigorous training in provocation and intrusion wherein each of my officers had to meet the overly high
standards I had set for them we emerged from the bowels of San
Diego harbor bent on setting records for the highest yardage
gained in intrusions ever set in the standard patrol. Our first stop
was Hawaii where I visited the kingpin of all provocateurs, including spies. None other than Fleet General Barney Google.
He was all I had been told, sly, cunning, closed mouthed, bulbous
nosed, smelling of musty top secret codes and some foul smelling
medicine that kept him going twenty hours a day in pursuit of
the perfect spy mission. He talked haltingly with me but persua-
sively about our forthcoming mission. "By God, Bucher, I want
you to get in there and be elusive, spy them out, spy out their
water, look sharp for signs of electronic saline water traps. You
will be going to spy out the DPRK. By the sainted General Bull-
moose we must learn why they are so far advanced in the art of
people's defense. Provocate, my boy, show them we are strong
by all means and true to your office. Try for 7 to 8 times a day,
but do so only when they won't see you." I was ecstatic, my order
at last was from our only Fleet General Barney Google. His entire existence was a secret even from the Army and the Navy, and
that explains his title. I never did get a good look at his gnarled
features which could generally and loosely be described as being
beady-eyed, thin lipped, no chin, sparse red and white hair with

a great bluish nose that pulsated rhythmically when he breathed. He continued, "You will be contacted in Japan by our man for Korea. You will know him by his many clever disguises. He is Sol Loxfinger. Sol was transferred to our Korean Intelligence Section because he is our best and we consider the DPRK the most important conflict in the world with the possible exception of one or two counties in New Mexico which are surreptitiously attempting to overthrow the local officials and cede them to Micronesia. There seems to have been a rather large influx of Micronesian-oriented nationals there, but we are confident of smoking them out." Then he said something that sent chills down my spine "If you fail you will have to answer to Don Ho." "Zounds," I thought, "and not beyond the reef." I pointed out that I was born free but he insisted that in failing I could expect the tiny bubble treatment. In addition, he mentioned that Joe Foss of Four Winds, Inc. was another agent with whom I could expect to deal if I failed. My mind was made up—I would set a Navy record for intrusion. *Each day we found new and hopefully* untried adjustments to our provocation and intrusion capabilities. Day by day I grew more determined and I was satisfied to observe just as determined efforts put forth by the officers and enlisted men. I did not tell my men where we were bound, so great was the degrading influence of Fleet General Barney Google. Then one day just before we sailed my Research Officer came to me and said, "Captain, we are to meet a mysterious man tonight at a secret hideout in town. A car will call for us." We were picked up at about 9 P.M. in a very black sedan made jointly from a Toyota, a Buick, a Saab, a Renault, a VW and an Austin—the cleverest undercover car I had ever seen. We literally plunked through the streets of Yokosuka into the countryside where another feature of this curious machine was evident. Rotating blades sprang from the roof and we ascended for about a 20-minute flight into the Japanese Alps. There we emerged and our ID was checked by an electronic robot who passed us on into a gunnysack hovel where a man with a dark gray topcoat with the collar shielding his face bade us "be seated." A black snap brimmed hat was pulled down covering his eyes. "Good evening, I am Sol Loxfinger." I quickly assessed that he was superbly disguised. I knew that he was over 6 feet and weighed about 250 lbs., but the fiend who confronted us was barely 5 feet and perhaps 120 lbs. What evil mastery of deceit. I was glad I was on his side. Lieutenant Harris and I waited with anxious perplexity while Sol Loxfinger eyed us from beneath the disguise. "I have carefully chosen the places where you will have the best chance of intruding and provocating." He then withdrew a tiny map that he deftly placed in his green tea. It simmered a while and then began to enlarge until it was fully three feet square. Almost miraculously, or so it appeared, green dots appeared along the coastline of the DPRK on the chart. "There," he said, "and there and there," pointing out numerous places that he recommended for intruding and provocating. He bade me be extremely careful while attempting these conquests because of the known terrible capability of the Korean People's Army Navy. Then in an instant he was gone. We did not dare follow him. But rather went immediately back to the machine and strapped ourselves in for the flight back to Yokosuka.

On 5 January 1968 we slipped secretly out of our home port, during lunch hour on the base, knowing that the gluttonous ways of our compatriots ashore would prevent their knowing of our departure. On 9 January we put into the Japanese port of Sasebo to refuel and pick up extra spying materials for the Apogee and Perigee alarm system within the Research Space. Just before leaving Yokosuka, the local operational chief of spy ships, Rear Admiral Frank L. Johnson, had come aboard the ship and provided me with several SECRET materials that handsomely increased our potential for putting goodies into our spy bag. A special set of charts and formulae were given me to learn before swallowing, from which I could compute various satellite trajectories and orbital paths. A special set of binoculars was also provided which could be hooked into the Apogee and Perigee alarm system. I had now studied the formulae for a week and had only committed half of its four line length to my swollen memory. I had to hurry.

When we had docked in Sasebo and I had gone below to my cabin, Lieutenant Harris came to me visibly shaken. "Captain, Sol Loxfinger is outside on the pier riding a velocipede. He wants us to come with him for important information right away." I put on my mufti and quickly followed Mr. Harris outside where Loxfinger was growing impatient. "We must not upset this highly trained specialist," I said half aloud to him. Without further words we climbed aboard the velocipede. His skill at driving this difficult machine baffled me. But we quickly switched to a Base Taxi and then later to a Town Taxi which sped up a nearby hill with great precariousness. I could tell Mr. Harris was jumpy by the increasing number of welts on his forehead from hitting the top of the taxi. Loxfinger then explained we were going to a certain place for a short time. When we got there, lo and behold Buzz Sawyer had been there for a short time also. The four of us quickly gathered and Loxfinger quickly pointed out numerous new places along the coast of the DPRK that were worth investigating for intrusion as a minimum and hopefully for provocation as well. "Go get them, but be careful," he intoned as he sped away leaving us to deal with Buzz Sawyer. We both promised to do our best and took the oath of office for this particular run. Sawyer was soon gone as well and Mr. Harris and I walked back to the nearest town and caught a train back to Sasebo.

On 11 January I ordered *Pueblo* underway and literally flew up the coast of South Korea while avoiding the Soviet units known to be operating in the Tsushima Strait. Soon our high state of readiness began to pay off.

We entered into our assigned operating areas along the Eastern Korean Sea at Latitude 39°N and boldly steamed in a northerly direction to the farthest point we could. In so doing we had traversed Operation Areas Mars, Venus, and Pluto so named because like the planets, the Democratic People's Republic of Korea is really far out. We knew that the lackeys of the Bowery Street Billionaires would never be satiated until we had found out all there was to know about the huge successes that the noble peace loving peoples of the Democratic People's Republic of Korea had made in the recent past. Surely, we had to find out how come such a newly created government could lead its peoples so quickly into the number one position. As we went about detecting this valuable information, particularly the oceanic salinity, density, ionic dispersion rate, humpback whale counts, both low and high level protoplasmic unicellular uglena and plankton counts. This information was of the highest value to our own scientists for the development of war mongering at sea when no one was looking.

Our main targets for detection were the vast naval complexes at Chong-Jin, Song-Jin, Mayang-do and Wonsan. But the Korean People's Army Navy never gave us a chance to steal their highly developed secrets. As I slunk my way South along the territorial water line of the DPRK, I paid great attention to intruding and provocating whenever I could and wherever I was not likely to be found out. The charts provided by Sol Loxfinger were invaluable to me in conducting these outrages which have never in the history of the world been surpassed. I chortled with glee each time my successes were more extravagant and decidedly more atrocious than any that Hitler had ever, in his wildest dreams, gotten away with. One night I rushed onto the bridge and shouted for all to hear, these orders directed to Lieutenant (jg) Harris who was the Officer of the Deck, "All right, Mister, increase speed to emergency fast." (I knew we would then soon be bolting through the water at the fantastic speed of almost 13 knots, unheard of in any other high priority ship such as *Pueblo* which minions of clever nastiness in the bowels of Clandestine, North Dakota, home and training grounds for all top super spies, had ever allowed any other officer of the Navy to command.) I was truly proud of my accomplishments. Then when our ship reached the apex of her emergency fast speed and was truly flying along, I ordered, "All right, Mister, now, intrude and provocate, and be quick about it." It was almost 0300 as the ship darted over the territorial water line, we chanced in to about ten miles from land before I ordered our ship brought about and turned to seaward again. Everyone on the ship was sweating under the terrific strain. All in all I managed to penetrate seventeen times into territorial waters, but my score in provocating was rather poor, only 13.5 times, using the provocation scoring system that Buzz Sawyer had provided me. But I knew I was setting records each day and that kept us busy. On 16 January in the vicinity of Orang Dan, my Officer of the Deck called me with urgent ringing of my telephone. When I picked it up I heard him say excitedly, "Captain, there is a strange piece of water just about 300 yards inside the territorial water line." I grabbed my secret charts and dashed to the bridge; quickly checking our position I noticed we were several miles from the next recommended penetration point, but I looked longingly at that strange piece of water and ordered the oceanographer Tuck, to bring three cups from the galley, which he quickly did. Then steeling myself at the thought of such a bold idea, I ordered emergency full ahead and tore into the waters while Tuck filled all three coffee cups with the precious liquid. He quickly put the entire contents into hermetically sealed strange-water-sample-bottles while I raced madly out to the safety of international waters. Wait until I returned and told my superiors that I had intruded in broad daylight to a distance of 200 yards inside their territorial waters. That was a record unlikely to be broken for many years to come, and I grew bolder with each passing day until like a madman on 23 January I recklessly bolted into the closest point yet, just 7.6 miles from Yo Do Island. However, I had gone too far and the valiant forces of the Korean People's Army Navy quickly surrounded me and my gang of nefarious schemers. I quickly brought my main battery to bear, thinking to free myself with superior fire power, and opened up firing wildly. But we were soon overcome with the tremendous bravery of the ships of the Korean People's Army Navy.

I quickly destroyed my secret charts and binoculars and thought to destroy all evidence of our atrocities. We had been caught red handed. At first we vainly tried to deny our outrages but were soon overwhelmed with damning evidence contrary to our sadistic lies.

Now we have come to realize just how great our crimes were and we seek the leniency of the Korean people even though we are criminals of the basest variety and deserve only swift punishment of the just Korean law. Further, we know that our crimes are greater than those of any criminals discovered this century, nevertheless we ask forgiveness and promise never to engage in such naughty acts ever again if we are forgiven. We know that our crime is merely a reflection of the dastardly policies of the Bowery Street Billionaires and we can only hope they will realize their own responsibilities for our actions; because who else could have dreamed up such a heinous and foul playing ship as *Pueblo* and then searched out enough arch criminals such as we to operate it. Yea, we feel it is time indeed for those really responsible for us to step forward and accept their own roles and admit, apologize and give assurances that they will never again prepare another spy bag to be filled with goodies.

In summation, we who have been rotating upon the fickle finger of fate for such long languid months give our word to the Great Speckled Bird that we will heretofor in all sincerity cleanse ourselves of rottenness and vituperations. We solemnly await our return to our loved ones so that the fickle finger can be replaced by the rosy fingers of dawn and salvation. So help me, Hanna.

s/L. M. Bucher

AUTHOR'S NOTE: The above Final Confession is only an approximate replica of the original which is still presumably in the hands of the North Korean Communists. I was aided in the preparation of the original by PH1 Lawrence Mack, USN; CT2 Wayne Anderson, USNR; CT3 Ralph McClintock, USNR; Lieutenant Stephen Harris, USN and LTJG F. Carl Schumacher, USN. The oath "So help me, Hanna" was contributed by my Executive Officer, Lieutenant Edward R. Murphy, USN. I consider this approximation to be about 90 percent complete and accurate.

APPENDIX VI

PRESIDENT JOHNSON'S LETTER
TO MRS. BUCHER

THE WHITE HOUSE
WASHINGTON

February 23, 1968

Dear Mrs. Bucher:

I welcome this opportunity to offer the admiration and reassurance you deserve.

My own deep concern for the men of the Pueblo has always embraced their troubled families. All of those who, with me, devote long days and nights to resolving this incident have your personal interests keenly at heart. We want most urgently to relieve your anxiety. You will, I pray, find comfort and strength in my own testimony of your government's unflagging efforts and determination to succeed.

Our goal is to secure the swiftest return of the Pueblo crew that peaceful means permit. Our initiatives are as comprehensive as they are constant.

The State Department is bearing down on every diplomatic lever available to us. We have action under way through other governments, the Military Armistice Commission and the United Nations Security Council. Our negotiators face a difficult and delicate task. I am proud and grateful for your recognition that they must be guided by the paramount interest—release of the crew under honorable conditions. I am myself encouraged that talks proceed at Panmunjon. You and I have good cause for hope in this evidence of North Korea's willingness to continue discussions.

I understand your concern over recent press reports that the Pueblo crew may be tried as criminals. We have warned North Korea in the sternest terms that any such action would constitute a deliberate aggravation of an already grave situation. We have no indications that the crew is being mistreated.

Frankly, precise details of the seizure remain obscured. It will take time to reconstruct the incident, even after your husband and his crew are home with a first-hand account. We do know that Commander Bucher faced a heavy responsibility. On present information, we have every reason to believe that he handled himself to the best of his ability.

While most unclassified information on the incident has appeared in the press, you may find further reassurance in the enclosure. The office of the Chief of Naval Operations prepared it as an official response to public and Congressional inquiries.

Let me offer one further personal assurance. Your husband's reputation among those comrades who know him best is high and strong. Knowing him so, and being moved by the patriotism and fortitude of your own letter,

I renew my promise of perseverance and success to you both.

Mrs. Johnson and I will continue to be with you in heart. May God bless you and guide you through this passing trial.

Sincerely,

Lyndon B. Johnson

Mrs. Lloyd M. Bucher
Room 167
Bahia Motor Hotel
998 West Mission Bay Drive
San Diego, California

APPENDIX VII

FINAL STATEMENT
BY COMMANDER BUCHER
TO THE COURT OF INQUIRY

Admiral Bowen and Members of Court:

Having made the decision many years ago to become a naval officer of the line, I eagerly sought command at sea.

My first command was USS *Pueblo*. During the outfitting of my ship, I attempted to see problem areas and have them corrected. Many of my suggestions and requests were not approved, for various reasons. This fact did not relieve me of my responsibilities to make full use of my ingenuity to achieve the best possible results with those materials provided. As Commanding Officer, I am solely responsible for the re. lts of our attempt to destroy classified materials. And therefore totally accountable for anything that may have happened. In view of the mission of *Pueblo*, I do consider that my ship was inadequately provided with proper destruct systems that were well within the state of the art, which could have, and would have eliminated the need for me to rely on jury-rigged emergency destruct systems. As Commander of *Pueblo*, it was my responsibility to make the determination on January 23, 1968, regarding *Puebl* s power to resist its illegal seizure by Units of the North Korean Navy. I hereby state unequivocally, that at that time, at the time of the seizure, we did not have the power to resist. It is my considered opinion that articles IV, V, of the *Code of Conduct* should be reviewed, in that they are difficult to reconcile when threats to the lives of your shipmates are involved. The determined actions by my crew to discredit the North Korean Communists' efforts to utilize them for propaganda purposes was totally successful. These efforts were made with the full realization that their publicized success might result in reprisals, or even death, for some or all of us. The overall conduct of some of the officers, the enlisted men, and civilians, assigned to the *Pueblo* was outstanding, and I commend each and every one of them. I wish to thank the members of the court.

APPENDIX VIII

Excerpts from the Report of the Special Subcommittee on the USS *Pueblo* Committee on Armed Services, House of Representatives, First Session, July 28, 1969.

Summary of Findings and Recommendations
General

The inquiry made by this special subcommittee into the USS *Pueblo* and the EC-121 incidents has resulted in the unanimous view that there exist serious deficiencies in the organizational and administrative military command structure of both the Department of the Navy and the Department of Defense. If nothing else, the inquiry reveals the existence of a vast and complex military structure capable of acquiring almost infinite amounts of information but with a demonstrated inability, in these two instances, to relay this information in a timely and comprehensible fashion to those charged with the responsibility for making decisions.

As President Nixon recently said, "When a war can be decided in twenty minutes, the nation that is behind will have no time to catch up." This concern is shared by the subcommittee. It was this consideration, as to the national security implications inherent in these two incidents, which overshadowed all others in the inquiry made by the subcommittee.

The reluctant but inescapable conclusion finally reached by the subcommittee is that because of the vastness of the military structure, with its complex division into multiple layers of command, and the failure of responsible authorities at the seat of government to either delegate responsibility or in the alternative provide clear and unequivocal guidelines governing policy in emergency situations—our military command structure is now simply unable to meet the emergency criterion outlined and suggested by the President himself.

The absent or sluggish response by military commanders to the emergencies evident in the *Pueblo* and EC-121 incidents demonstrate the need for a complete review of our military-civilian command structure and its capability to cope with emergency situations. The subcommittee inquiry was not of sufficient scope to permit it to offer a proposed solution to the problem. It is evident, however, that the problem exists and it has frightful implications.

It is therefore recommended that the President establish a special study group of experienced and distinguished civilian and military personnel to approach this problem on an emergency basis and make such recommendations for changes in both the National Security Act and the military structure itself that will provide our Nation and its military forces with a genuine capability to respond quickly and decisively to emergencies of a national security nature.

Warning Message on the *u o* Mission

During subcommittee hearings it was established that a message had originated in the National Security Agency which questioned the minimal risk assessment assigned the USS *Pueblo* mission.

This message recited a history of North Korean incidents and suggested that in view of the evident increase in hostile actions taken by the North Koreans, it might be considered desirable to establish ship protective measures for the USS *Pueblo* mission.

The message from the Director of NSA (National Security Agency) to the JCS/JRC referred to CINCPAC message 230239Z of December 1967 and reads as follows:

Paragraph 1. Reference states, "Risk to *Pueblo* is estimated to be minimal since operations will be conducted in international waters."

Paragraph 2. The following information is forwarded to aid in your assessment of CINCPAC's estimate of risk. [Deleted] 1, the North Korean Air Force has been extremely sensitive to peripheral reconnaissance flights in this area since early 1965. (This sensitivity was emphasized on April 28, 1965, when a U. S. Air Force RB 47 was fired on and severely damaged 35 to 40 nautical miles from the Coast.)

2. The North Korean Air Force has assumed an additional role of naval support since late 1966.

3. The North Korean Navy reacts to any Republic of Korea Navy vessel or Republic of Korea fishing vessel near the North Korean coast line. (This was emphasized on January 19, 1967, when a Republic of Korea Naval vessel was sunk by coast artillery.)

4. Internationally recognized boundaries as they relate to airborne activities are generally not honored by North Korea on the East Coast of Korea. But there is no [deleted] evidence of provocative harassing activities by North Korean vessels beyond 12 nautical miles from the coast.

Paragraph 3. The above is provided to aid in evaluating the requirement for ship protective measures and is not intended to reflect adversely on CINCPACFLT deployment proposal.

General Carter, Director of NSA, was asked why his Agency had sent this message and the following colloquy developed:

General Carter. Yes, sir. The first sentence said the reference states: "Risk to *Pueblo* is estimated to be minimal"—

Mr. Bray. Is that an opinion on the part—

General Carter. That was CINCPACFLT's opinion in the message—

Mr. Bray. That is not your opinion?

General Carter. No, sir, that is not my opinion.

Mr. Pike. In fact, the whole reason for this message was that you questioned that judgment, was it not?

General Carter. It wasn't a question of judgment because I have no responsibility in assessing the risk. This is not in my charter at all. We have procedures where our analysts talk to other analysts on a day to day basis on all of these things.

Mr. Bray. Isn't it your duty to bring this to their attention?

General Carter. [1 line deletion.] This was the first voyage in which we were having a vessel linger for a long period of time near North Korean waters. It therefore was a special mission as we saw it. We knew that she was going to stay in international waters. We had no evidence that the North Koreans at sea had ever interfered with or had any intentions to interfere with a U.S. vessel outside of their acknowledged territorial waters. Nevertheless, our people felt that even though all of this information was already available in intelligence community reports it would be helpful if we summed them up and gave them to the Joint Chiefs of Staff for whatever use they might make of them or assistance in evaluating this particular mission.

GLOSSARY

AF (type ship) Auxiliary, Refrigeration, designating a Service Force Ship designed to provide provisions to the fleet.

AKL (type ship) Auxiliary, Cargo, Light, originally built for exclusive army use, basically a coastwise freighter designed for logistic support of island and continental naval bases where no great distances are involved.

ASW Anti Submarine Warfare, referring to weapons systems or operations against hostile submarines.

CINCPAC Commander-in-Chief, Pacific designating the headquarters of the officer commanding all U.S. military areas of the Pacific and part of the Indian Ocean and representing the highest military authority within those areas.

CINCPACFLT Commander-in-Chief of Pacific Fleets, designating the operational and Administrative Commander of all ships and Naval Bases within the Pacific Ocean. Subordinate to CINCPAC for operations.

COMELEVEN Commandant of Eleventh Naval District, designating the officer commanding (according to numeral) any of the several Naval Districts of the Continental USA, Alaska and Hawaii.

COMNAVFORJAPAN — Commander, Naval Forces, Japan, designating the officer commanding all U.S. naval forces and naval activities in Japan.

COMSERVPAC — Commander of Service Forces, Pacific Fleet—the officer commanding all Service Force units (transports, oilers, repair ships, etc) providing logistic support to the fleets operating in the Pacific Ocean.

COMSERVGRU ONE — Commander, Service Group, One, the officer commanding a Service Force Group (according to numeral) (a major division of the Fleet Service Force) providing logistic support to the fleet.

COMNAVSECSTA — Commander, Naval Security Station, designating the officer commanding all naval security operations. Located in Washington, D.C.

CT (s) — Communications Technician, an enlisted specialist in the fields of communications and electronic interception and analysis.

CTF — Commander, Task Force (usually includes numeral) designating the officer commanding a force of naval vessels under his tactical and operational control for specifically assigned missions.

DMZ — Demilitarized Zone, an area where by international agreement or treaty, military operations are prohibited or limited, such as the zones separating North and South Vietnam, North and South Korea.

ELINT	Electronic Intelligence, collection of operational intelligence from hostile electronic emission.
EMCON	Emission Control, U.S. Navy term for electronic silence, a counter-measure against hostile ELINT.
JAG	Judge Advocate General (Corps), designating an officer specializing in legal work for the Navy.
KORCOM	Korean Communist, abbreviated designation of military unit or individual serving the Communist Regime in North Korea.
LORAN	Long Range Radio Navigation, a system of navigation where position is obtained by measuring in microseconds the time-differential between signals received from two synchronized shorebased transmitters. Accurate bearings may be obtained up to 1500 miles from transmitters under optimum conditions.
NAVSEGRUPAC	Naval Security Group, Pacific, designation for headquarters responsible for naval security and the collection of intelligence in the Pacific.
NAVSEGRUDET KAMISEYA	Naval Security Group Detachment, Kamiseya. Subordinate to NAVSEGRUPAC.
OIC	Officer in Charge. Most often used to designate officer in charge and responsible for a special operations detachment or small unit otherwise without a commanding officer.

1MC	Ship's internal communication system by loudspeaker.
OOD	Officer of the Deck, abbreviation for the watch-keeping officer in charge of the bridge and responsible directly to the Captain for all shipboard evolutions. Another common but unofficial term is to "take the deck." The OOD is not necessarily a commissioned officer but his competence must be such that he represents the Captain who is always ultimately responsible for the ship's operations even when he is not physically present on the bridge.
ONI	Office of Naval Intelligence, formerly the office in charge of all the Navy's intelligence, counter intelligence, criminal and security investigations. Later changed to Naval Investigative Support Office.
SITREP	Situation Report, an abbreviated report to higher headquarters transmitted concurrently with, or immediately after any event or action of special interest. A SITREP is supposed to contain essential information only to permit understanding and quick reactions along the chain of command.
SOD-Hut	Special Operations Department spaces aboard a ship where the Communications Specialists (CTs) work. Also called "Spook-Shack." Always a highly classified area which may only be entered by personnel with appropriate security clearance.

SUBFLOT SEVEN — Submarine Flotilla 7, designating the headquarters of all submarines attached to U. S. Seventh Fleet. Based at Yokosuka, Japan.

UNODIR — Abbreviation used in official radio messages signifying: *"Unless Otherwise Directed."*

WESTPAC — Abbreviation for "Western Pacific."

XO — Executive Officer, also referred to as "Exec." The officer who is responsible directly to the captain of a U. S. Navy ship for all administrative Ship's work and crew training. Is presumed to be able to take over command in case the Commanding Officer is incapacitated.

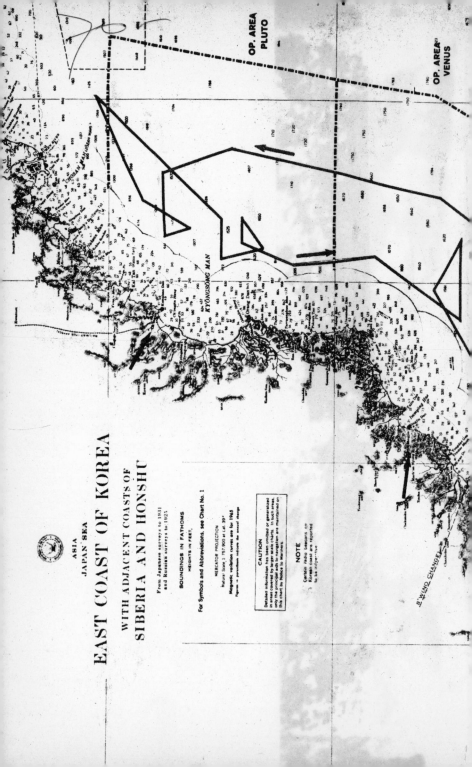